This is the fourth volume.
I'll have to part with these characters until
the next time I continue this story. I'd
like to thank everyone who bought all the
volumes, including this one, and everyone
who stuck with me 'til now.
Okay then, see you later!

-Tite Kubo, 2000

Tite Kubo is best known as the creator
of the smash hit *Bleach*, which began
serialization in *Weekly Shonen Jump* in
2001. *ZOMBIEPOWDER.*, his debut
series, began serialization in 1999.

ZOMBIEPOWDER. VOL. 4
The SHONEN JUMP Manga Edition

STORY AND ART BY
TITE KUBO

Translation/Akira Watanabe
Touch-up Art & Lettering/Stephen Dutro
Design/Sean Lee
Editor/Jason Thompson

Managing Editor/Frances E. Wall
Editorial Director/Elizabeth Kawasaki
Editor in Chief, Books/Alvin Lu
Editor in Chief, Magazines/Marc Weidenbaum
Sr. Director of Acquisitions/Rika Inouye
Sr. VP of Marketing/Liza Coppola
Exec. VP of Sales & Marketing/John Easum
Publisher/Hyoe Narita

Printed in the U.S.A.

Published by VIZ Media, LLC
P.O. Box 77010
San Francisco, CA 94107

SHONEN JUMP Manga Edition
10 9 8 7 6 5 4 3 2 1
First printing, June 2007

THE WORLD'S
MOST POPULAR MANGA

www.viz.com

www.shonenjump.com

ZOMBIEPOWDER.

Vol. 4
WALK LIKE A ZOMBIE

Story & Art by
Tite Kubo

Under the clawlike air
Spread out to the point of creaking

Each time I gaze up at the sky
I realize that I am trapped within this world

If only that sky would come crashing down
Then I could fly far away.

CHARAC
TERS

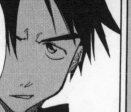

IT'S NOT SO SERIOUS THAT TWO ADULTS HAVE TO BEAT UP ONE LITTLE KID, IS IT?

Elwood
エルウッド

Akutabi Gamma
芥火(あくたび)ガンマ

R Y

But the rings are alive...and hungry. Arriving in a small town, the Powder Hunters discover that a Ring has burrowed inside the head of Emilio, the younger brother of Wolfina, a muckraking journalist. Balmunk the Mystic, the ringmaster of a deadly circus troupe, steals Emilio's comatose body and fuses it to the engine of a train. While Gamma fights Balmunk, Wolfina climbs the speeding train to rescue her brother... only to face Balmunk's deadly servant...

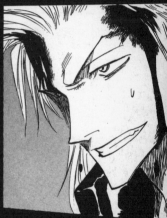

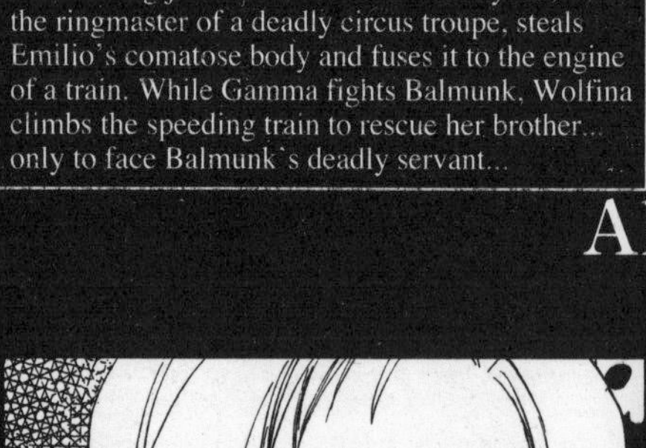

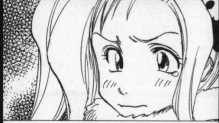

Angelle
エンジェル

CHARACTERS

Wolfina
ウルフィーナ

C.T.Smith
C.T.スミス

S T O

The Rings of the Dead: the world's only source of "Zombie Powder," a substance said to be able to raise the dead and give the living eternal life. In the badlands of blood and smoke, no one is more feared than the "Powder Hunters"…reckless souls such as Gamma, C.T. Smith and Elwood, who are willing to risk their own lives in pursuit of the dream.

Nazna
ナズナ

ZOMBIEPOWDER.

Vol. 4

WALK LIKE A ZOMBIE

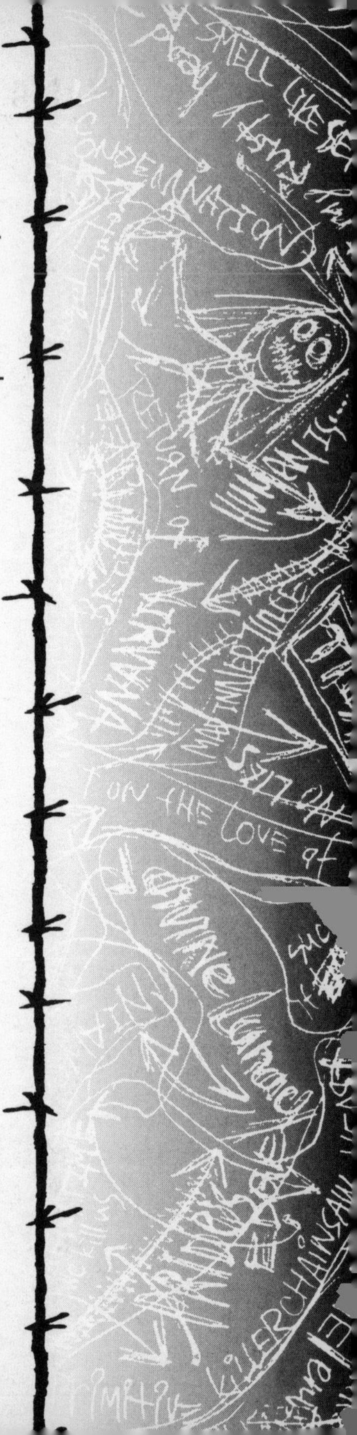
CONDEMNATION
ON THE LOVE OF

CONTENTS

Track 22: Lay Your Heart on Me

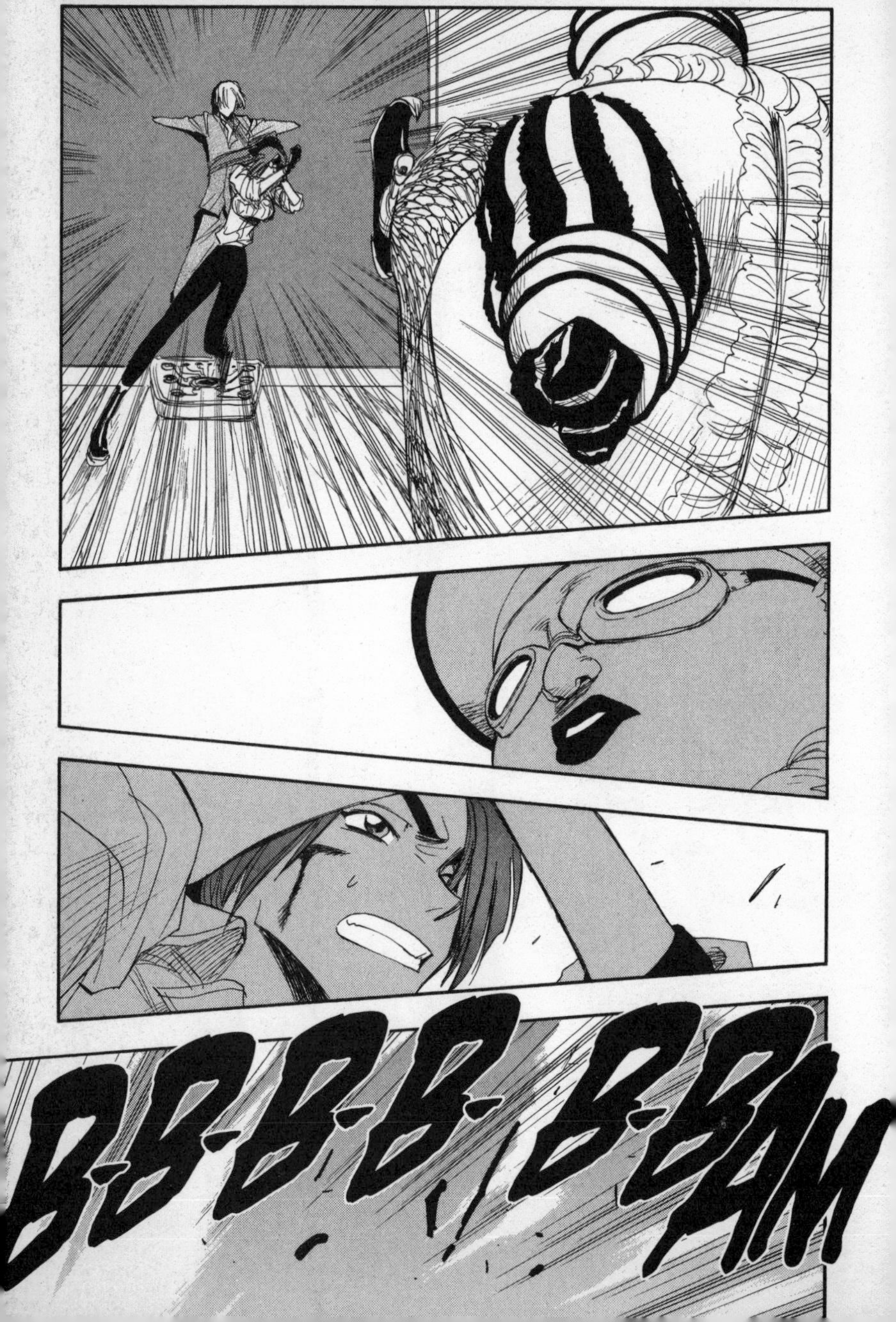
B-B-B-B-B-BAM

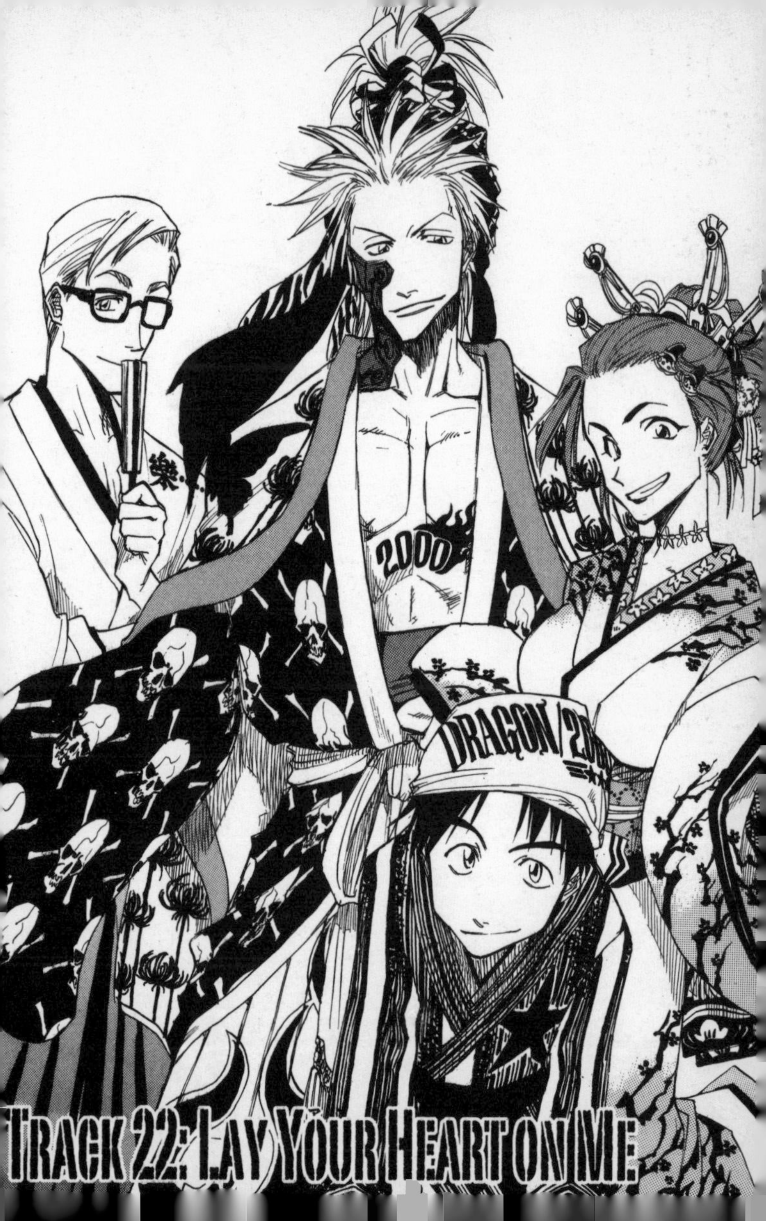
2000
DRAGON

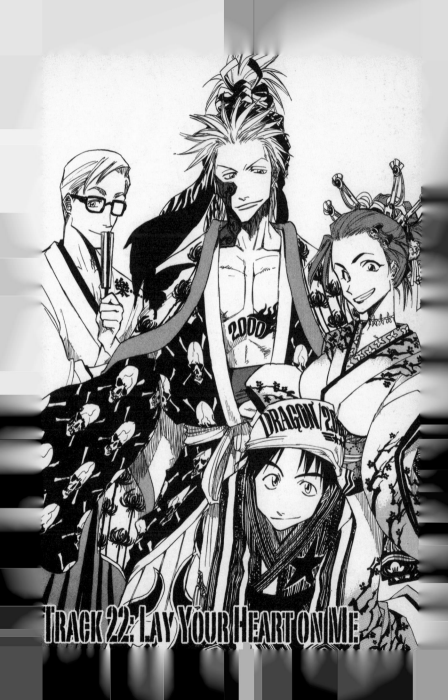

Track 22: Lay Your Heart on Me

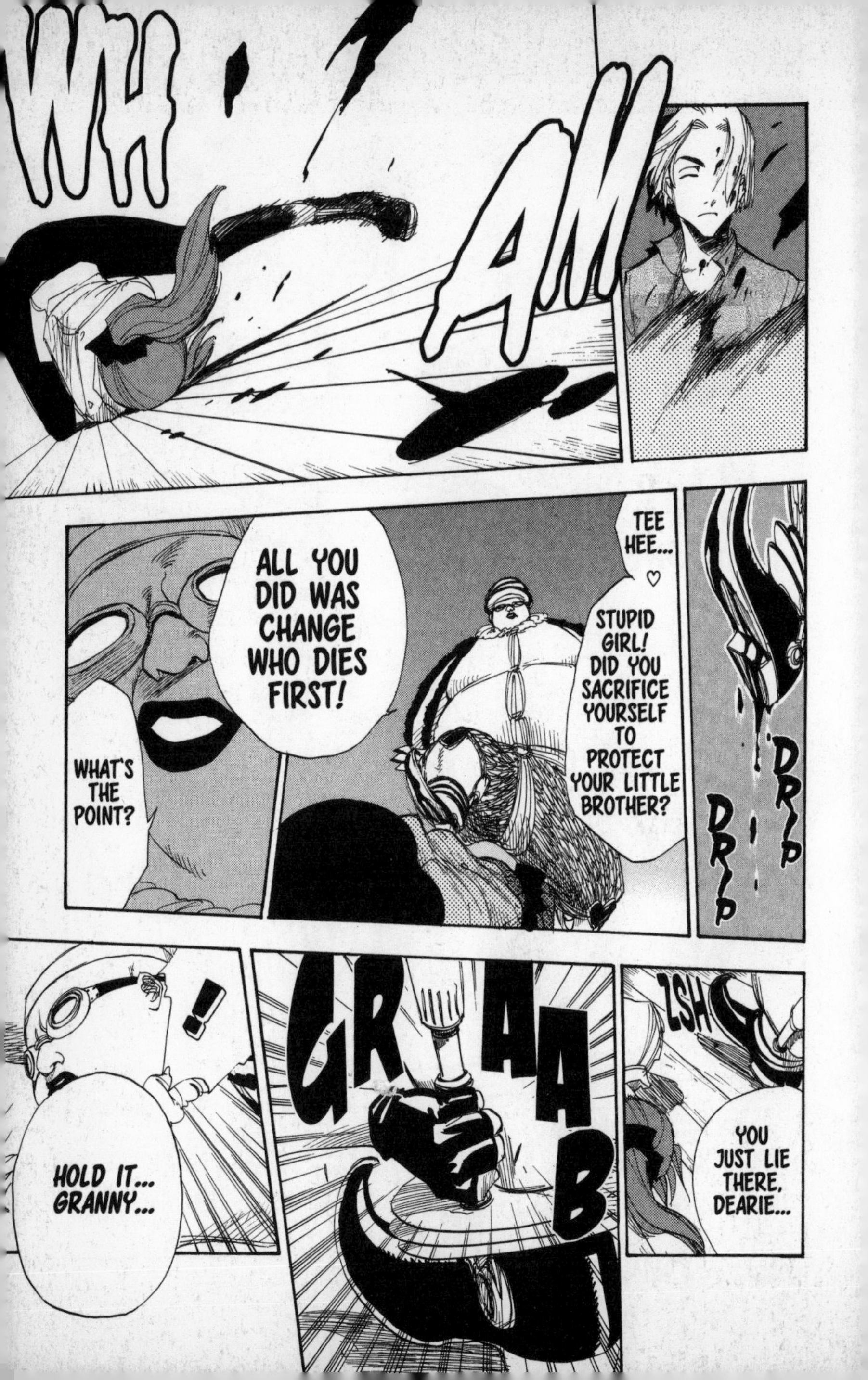
WHAM
DRIP DRIP
TEE HEE... ♡
STUPID GIRL! DID YOU SACRIFICE YOURSELF TO PROTECT YOUR LITTLE BROTHER?
ALL YOU DID WAS CHANGE WHO DIES FIRST!
WHAT'S THE POINT?
ZSH
YOU JUST LIE THERE, DEARIE...
GRAAB
!
HOLD IT... GRANNY...

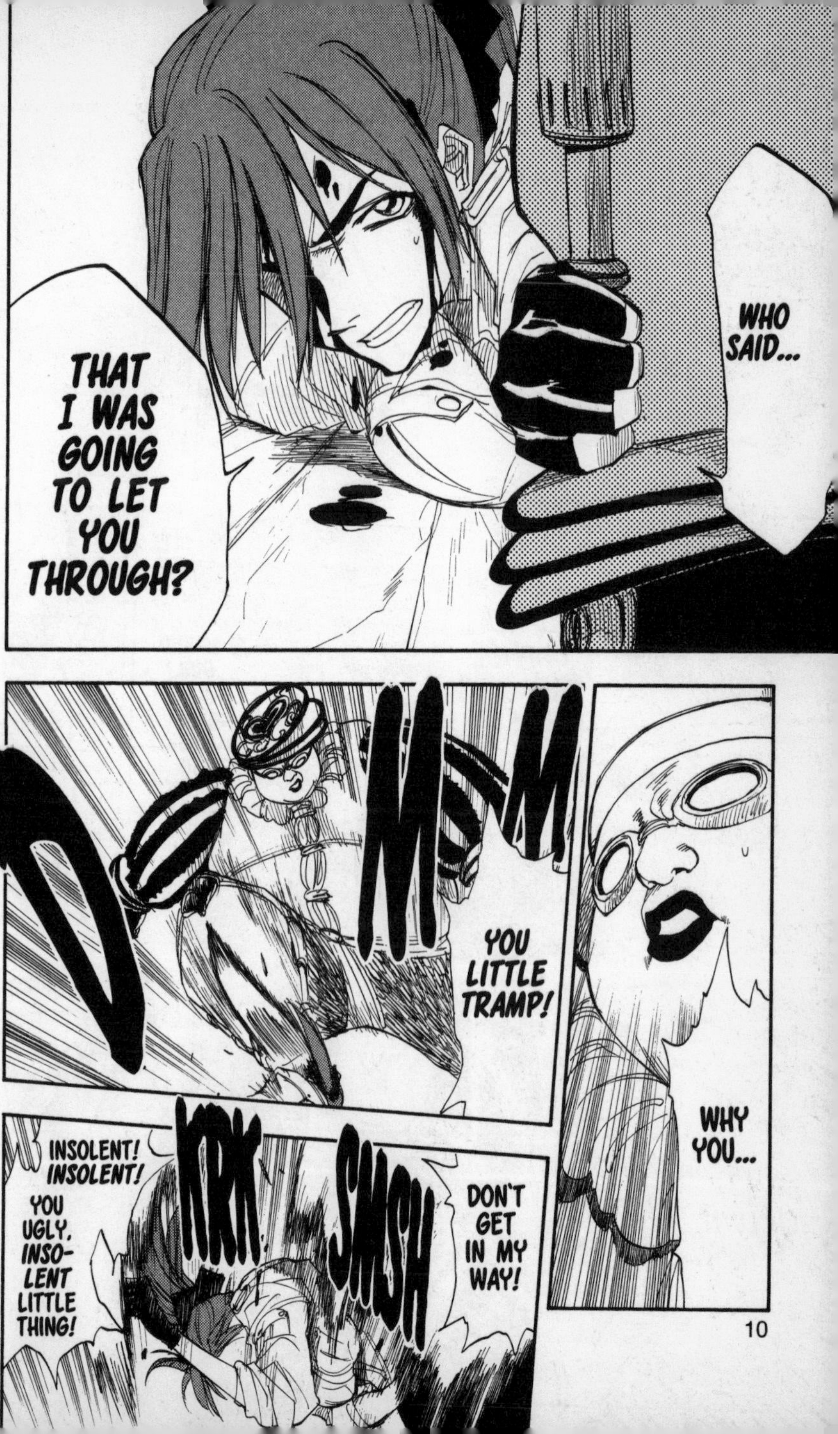
WHO SAID...
THAT I WAS GOING TO LET YOU THROUGH?
WHY YOU...
DMM
YOU LITTLE TRAMP!
DON'T GET IN MY WAY!
SMSH
KRK
INSOLENT! INSOLENT!
YOU UGLY, INSO-LENT LITTLE THING!

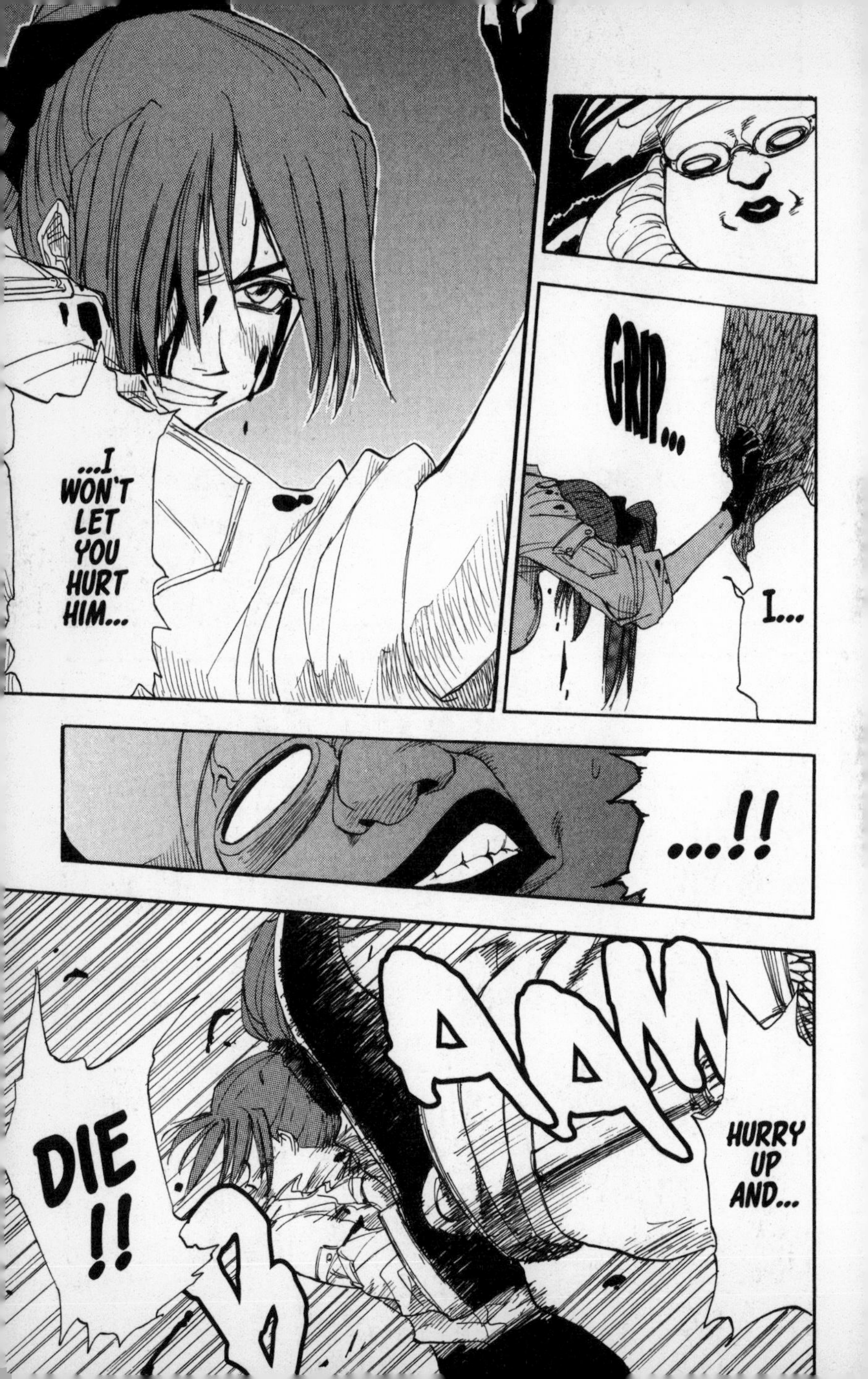
GRIP...
I...
...I WON'T LET YOU HURT HIM...
...!!
HURRY UP AND...
AAM
DIE!!

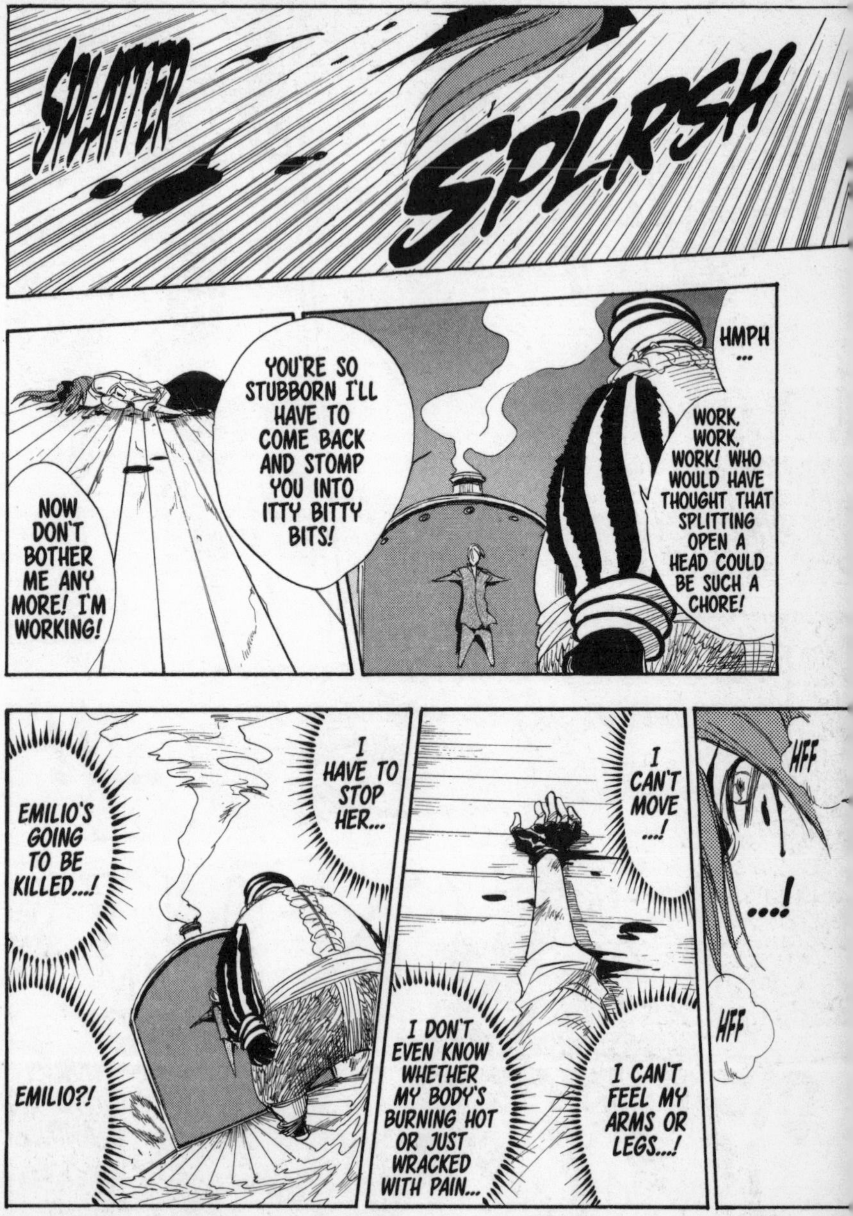
SPLATTER
SPLASH
HMPH...
WORK, WORK, WORK! WHO WOULD HAVE THOUGHT THAT SPLITTING OPEN A HEAD COULD BE SUCH A CHORE!
YOU'RE SO STUBBORN I'LL HAVE TO COME BACK AND STOMP YOU INTO ITTY BITTY BITS!
NOW DON'T BOTHER ME ANY MORE! I'M WORKING!
HFF
...!
HFF
I CAN'T MOVE ...!
I CAN'T FEEL MY ARMS OR LEGS...!
I DON'T EVEN KNOW WHETHER MY BODY'S BURNING HOT OR JUST WRACKED WITH PAIN...
I HAVE TO STOP HER...
EMILIO'S GOING TO BE KILLED...!
EMILIO?!

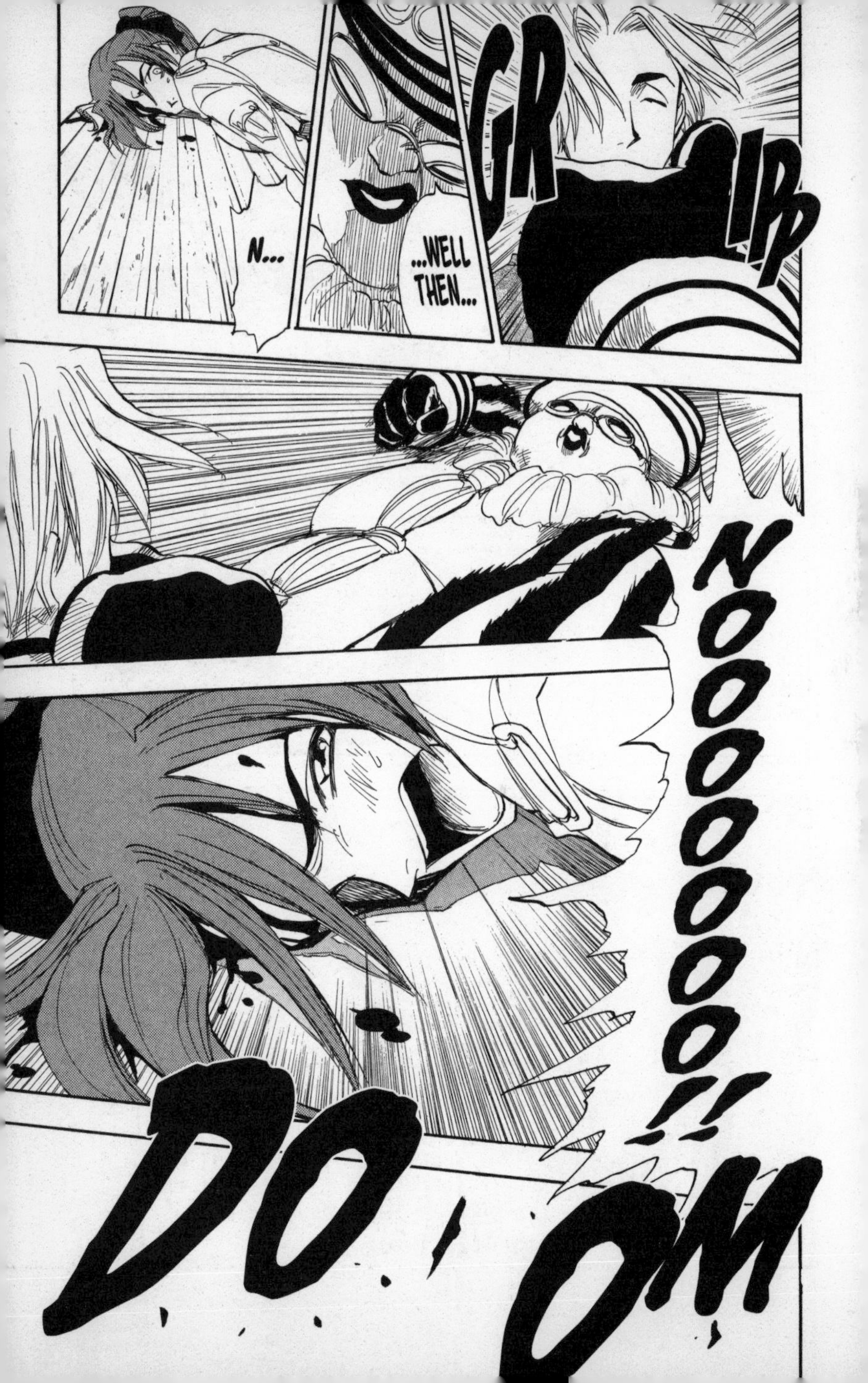
GRIPP
...WELL THEN...
N...
NOOOOOOO!!
DO OM

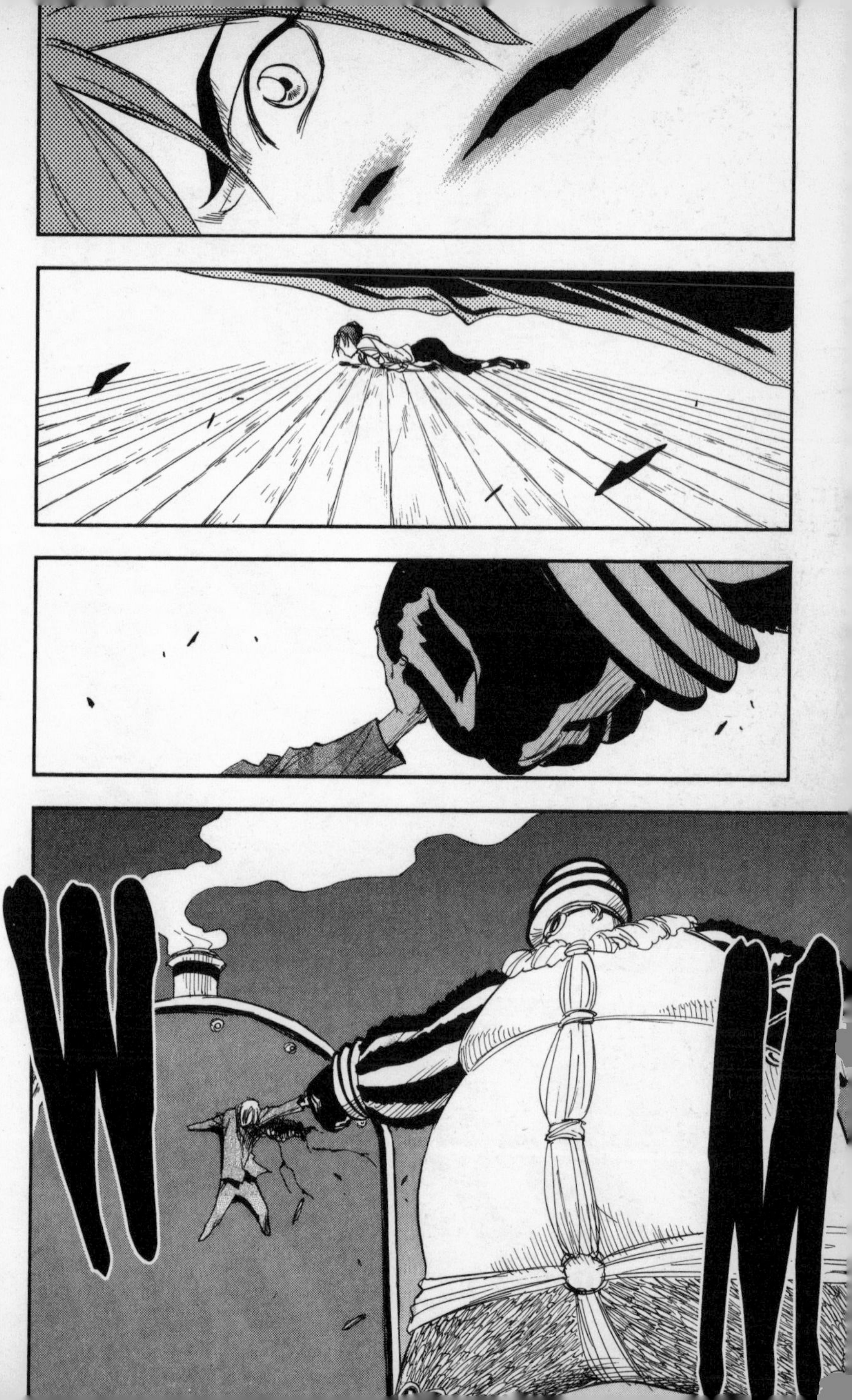
W
M

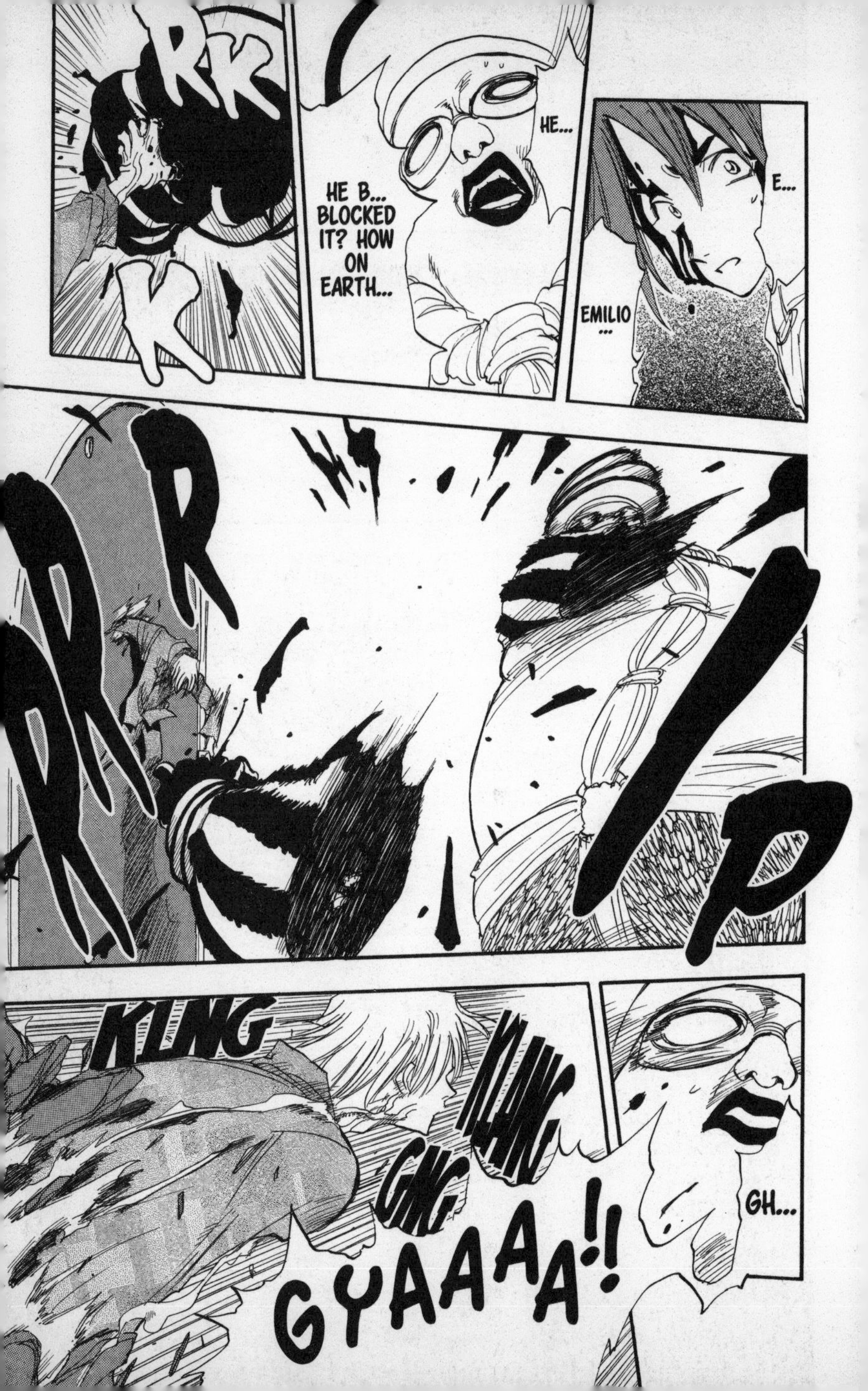

E...
EMILIO...
HE...
HE B... BLOCKED IT? HOW ON EARTH...
RKK
RRRIP
GH...
KLANG
GING
KLING
GYAAAAA!!

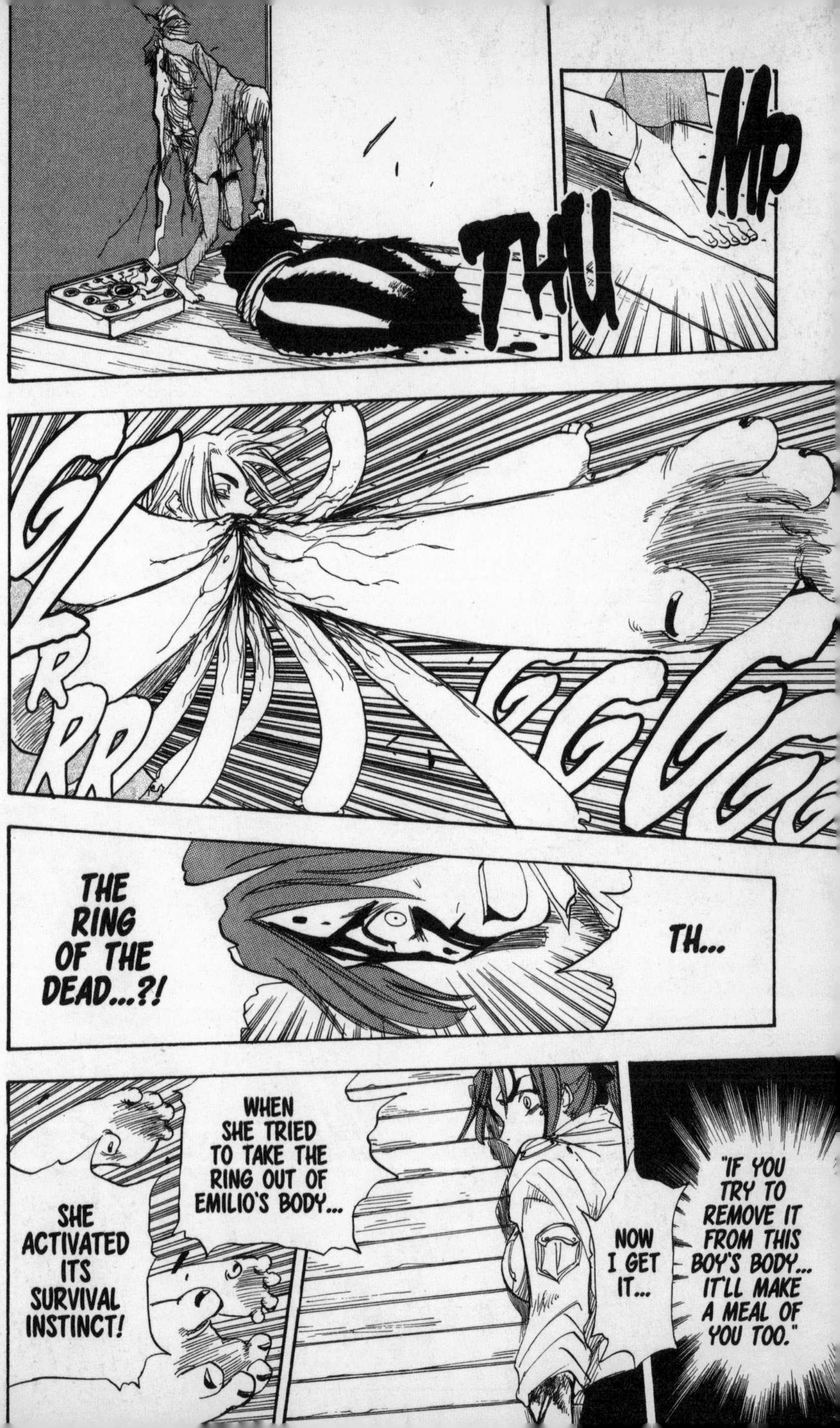
THUMP
TH...
THE RING OF THE DEAD...?!
"IF YOU TRY TO REMOVE IT FROM THIS BOY'S BODY... IT'LL MAKE A MEAL OF YOU TOO."
NOW I GET IT...
WHEN SHE TRIED TO TAKE THE RING OUT OF EMILIO'S BODY...
SHE ACTIVATED ITS SURVIVAL INSTINCT!

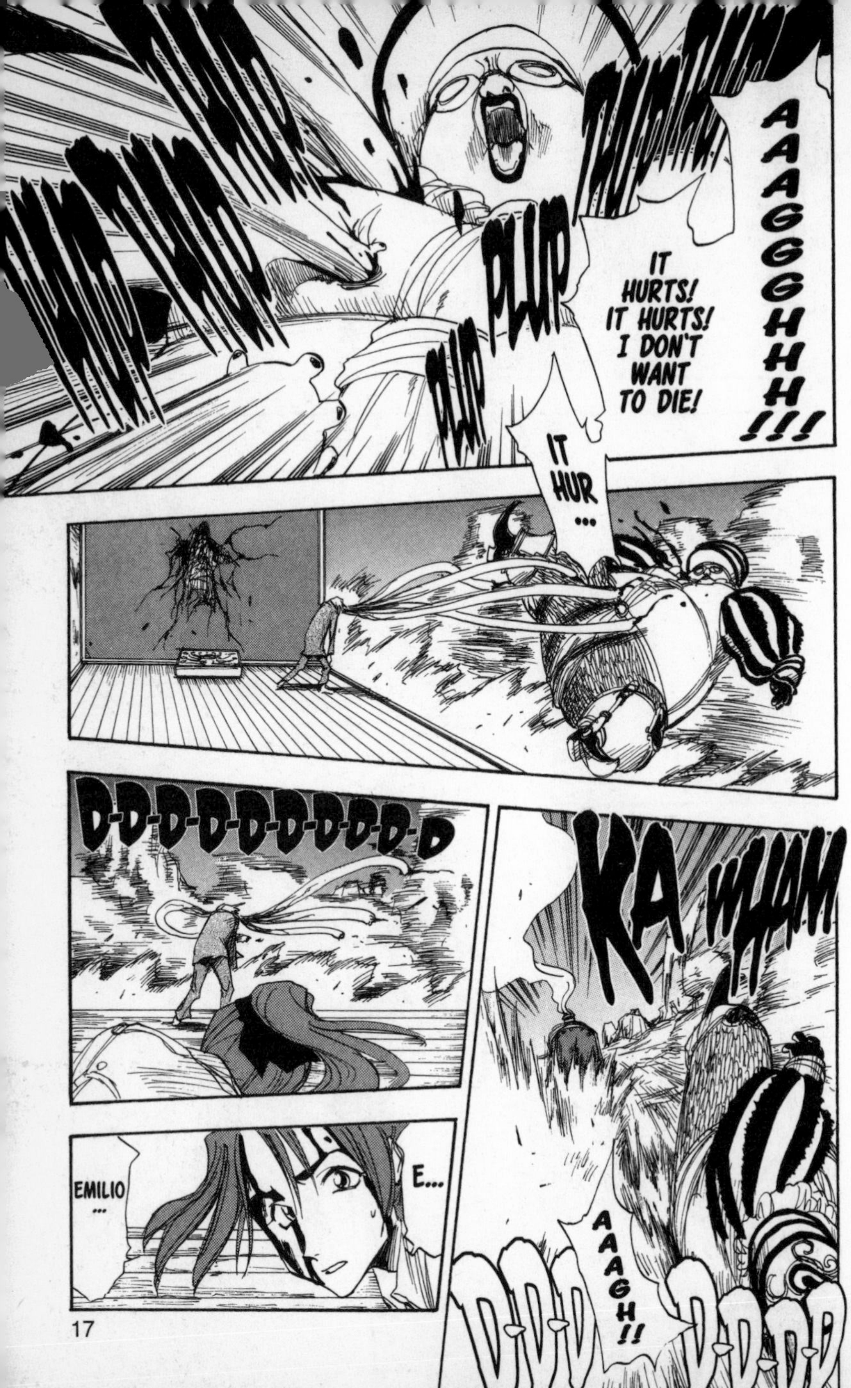
AAAAGGGHHHH!!!
IT HURTS! IT HURTS! I DON'T WANT TO DIE!
PLUP
PLUP
IT HUR...
KA WHAM
AAAGH!!
D-D-D
D-D-D-D
D-D-D-D-D-D-D-D-D-D-D
E...
EMILIO...

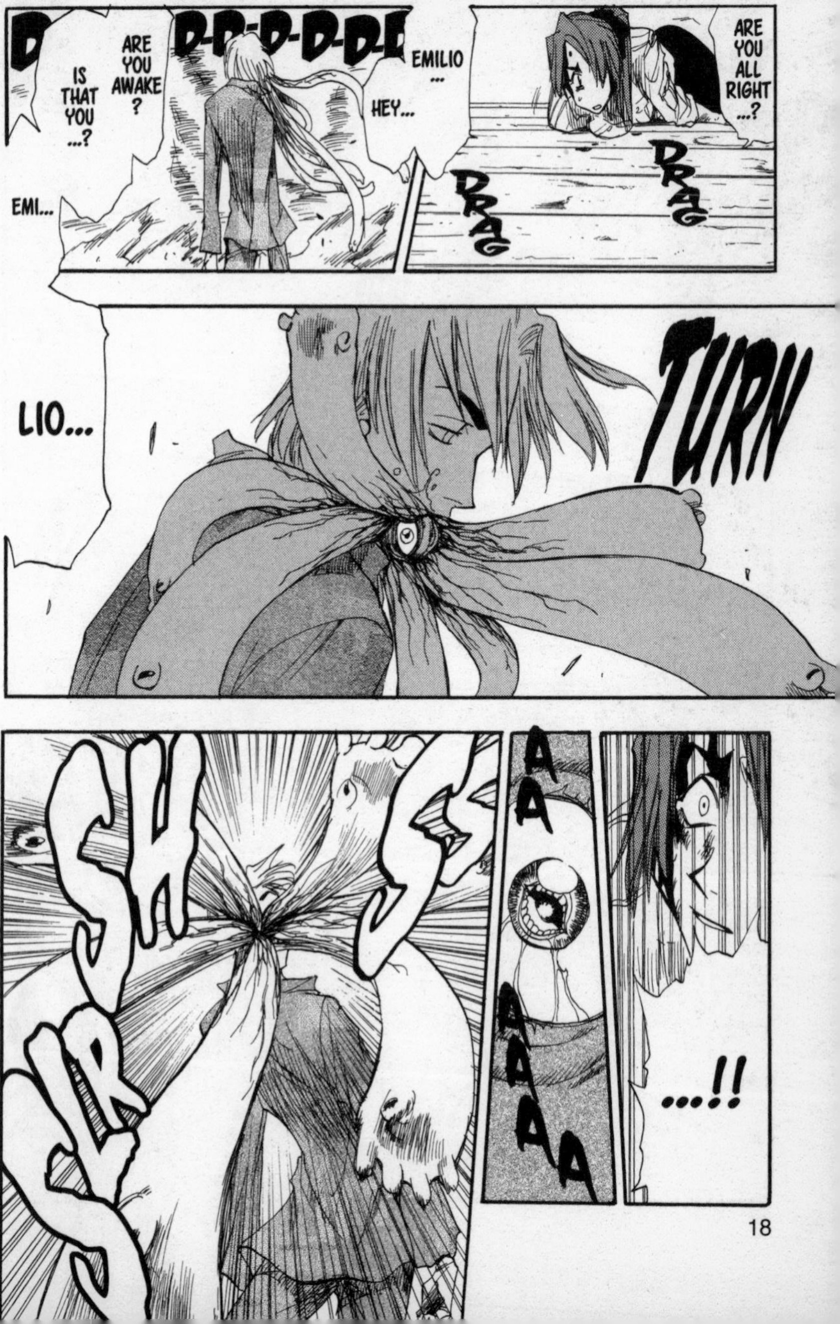

ARE YOU ALL RIGHT ...?
DRAG
DRAG
EMILIO ...
HEY...
D-D-D-D-D-DE
ARE YOU AWAKE ?
IS THAT YOU ...?
D
EMI...
TURN
LIO...
...!!
AAAAAAA

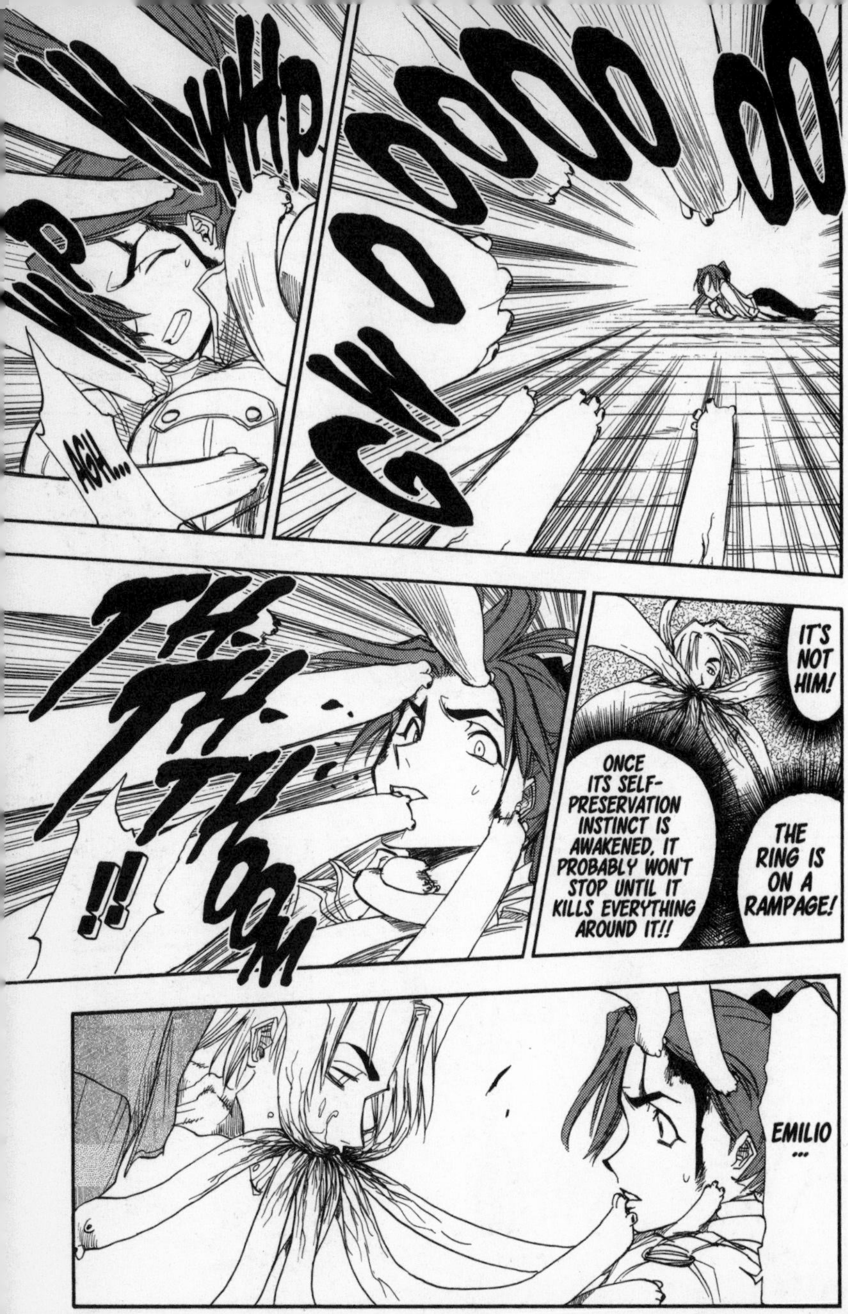
GWOOOOOOO
WHIP
AGH...
IT'S NOT HIM!
THE RING IS ON A RAMPAGE!
ONCE ITS SELF-PRESERVATION INSTINCT IS AWAKENED, IT PROBABLY WON'T STOP UNTIL IT KILLS EVERYTHING AROUND IT!!
TH-TH-THOOM!!
EMILIO...

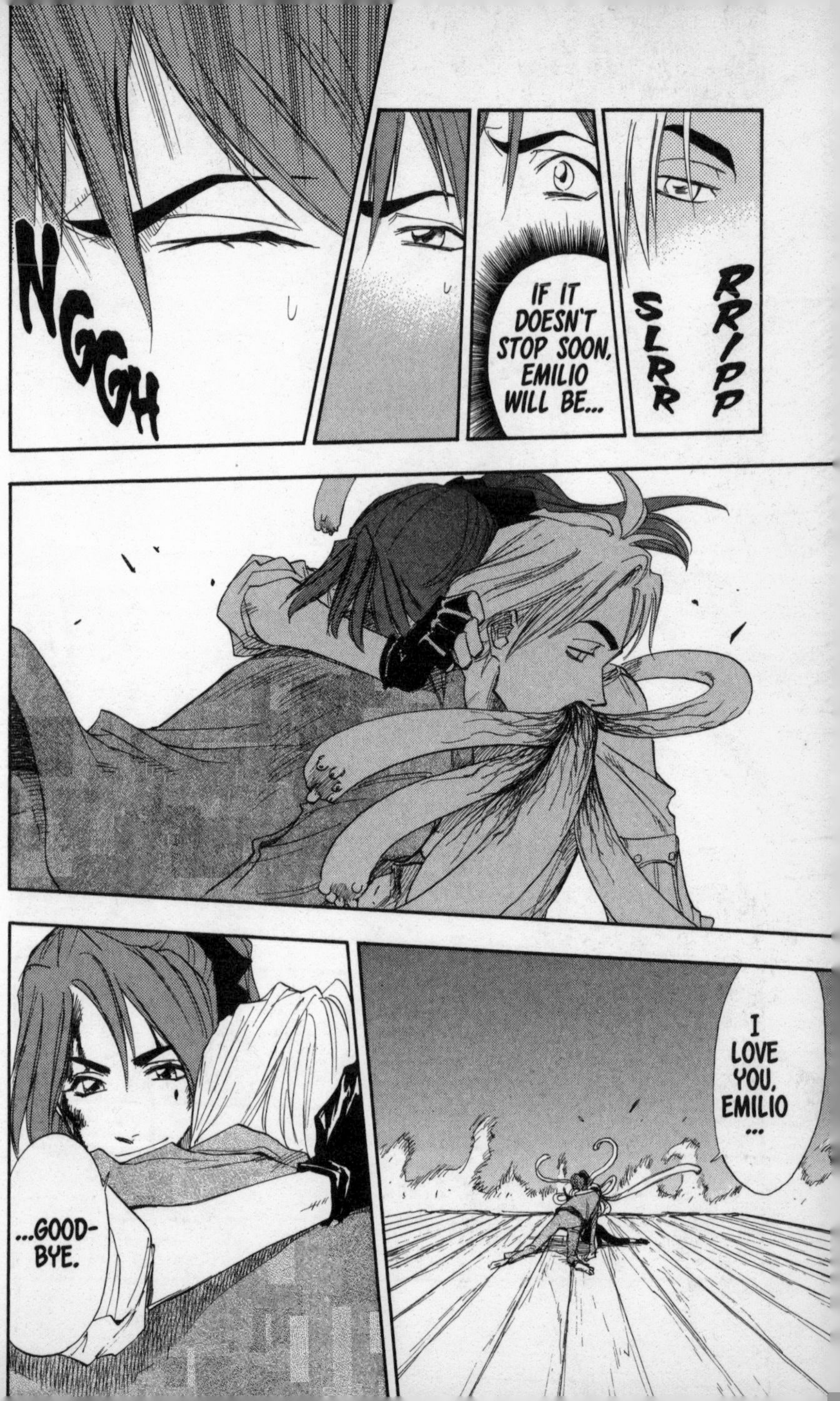
RRIPP
SLRR
IF IT DOESN'T STOP SOON, EMILIO WILL BE...
NGGGH
I LOVE YOU, EMILIO ...
...GOOD-BYE.

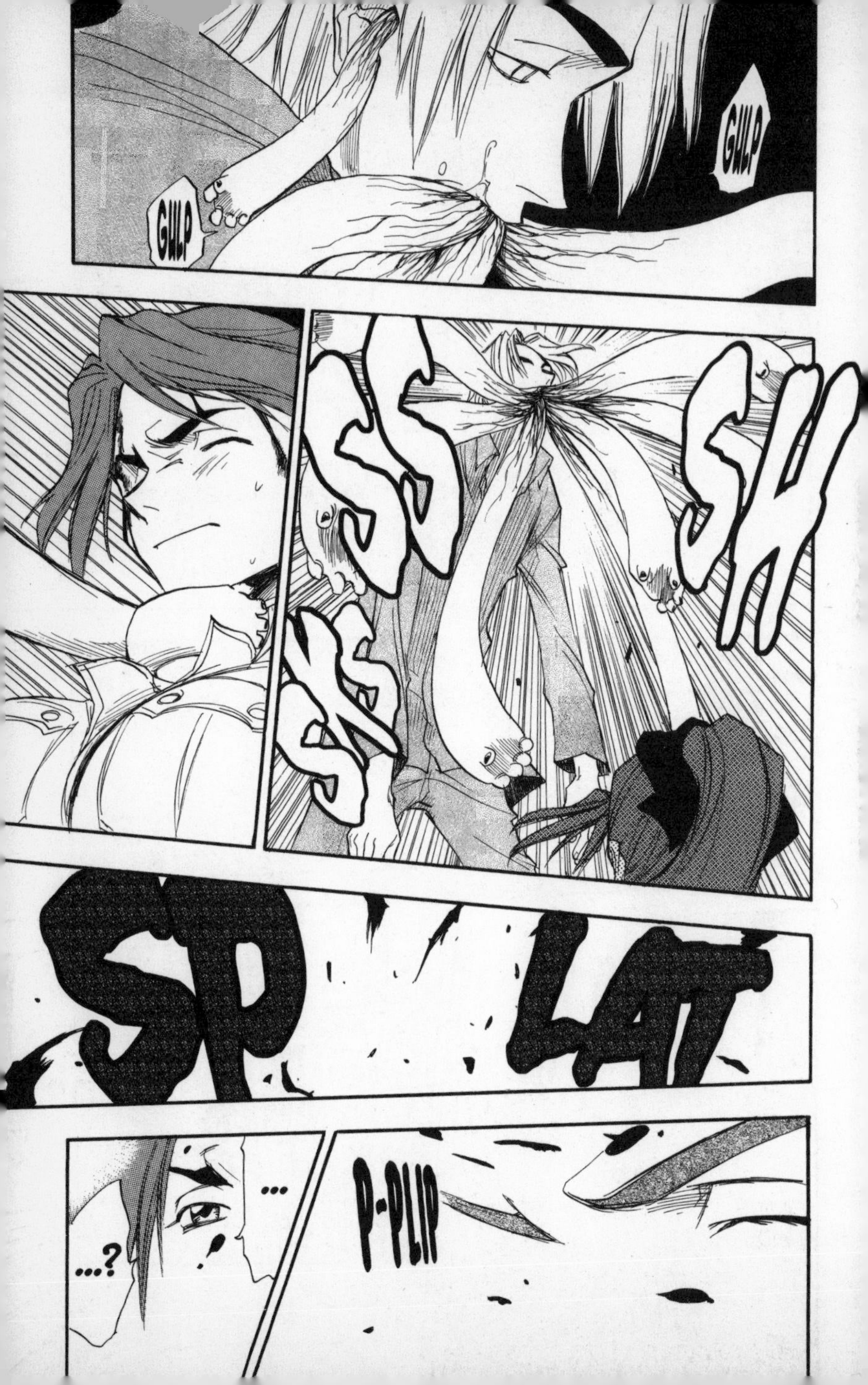
GULP
GULP
SH
SS
SS
SPLAT
P-PLIP
...
...?

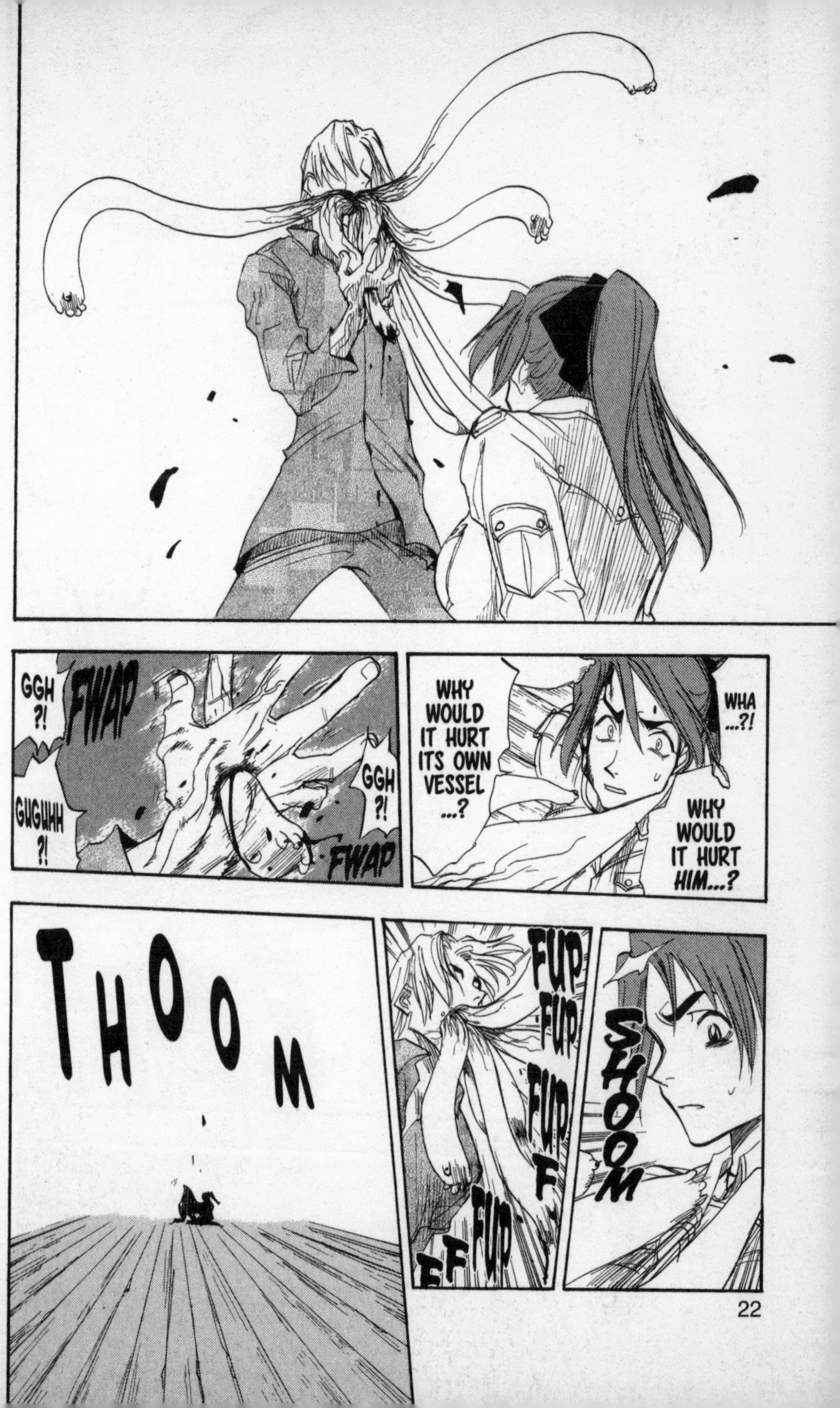
WHA...?!
WHY WOULD IT HURT HIM...?
WHY WOULD IT HURT ITS OWN VESSEL...?
GGH ?!
FWAP
GGH ?!
FWAP
GUGUHH ?!
SHOOM
FUP FUP FUP F FUP FF F
THOOM

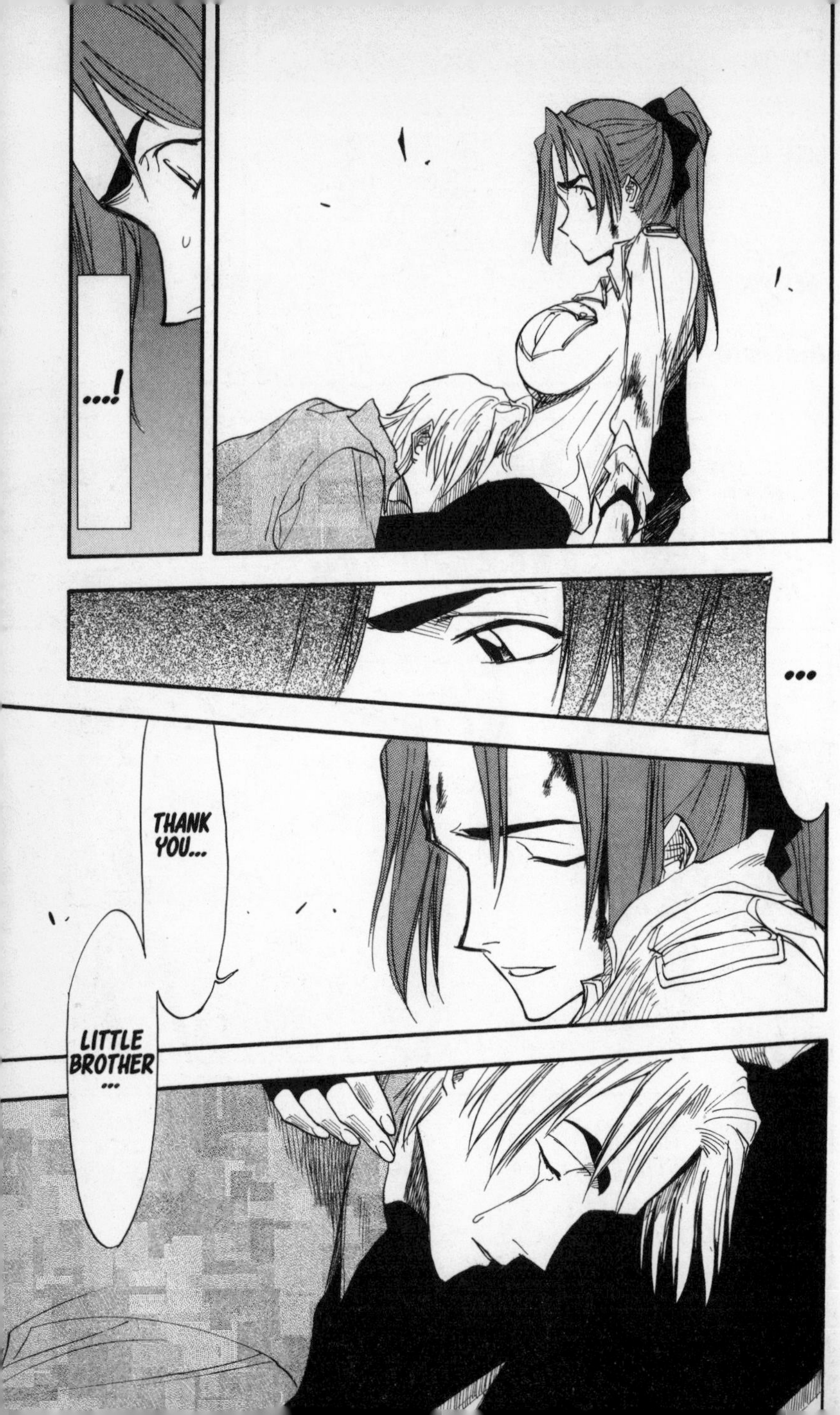
...!
...
THANK YOU...
LITTLE BROTHER ...

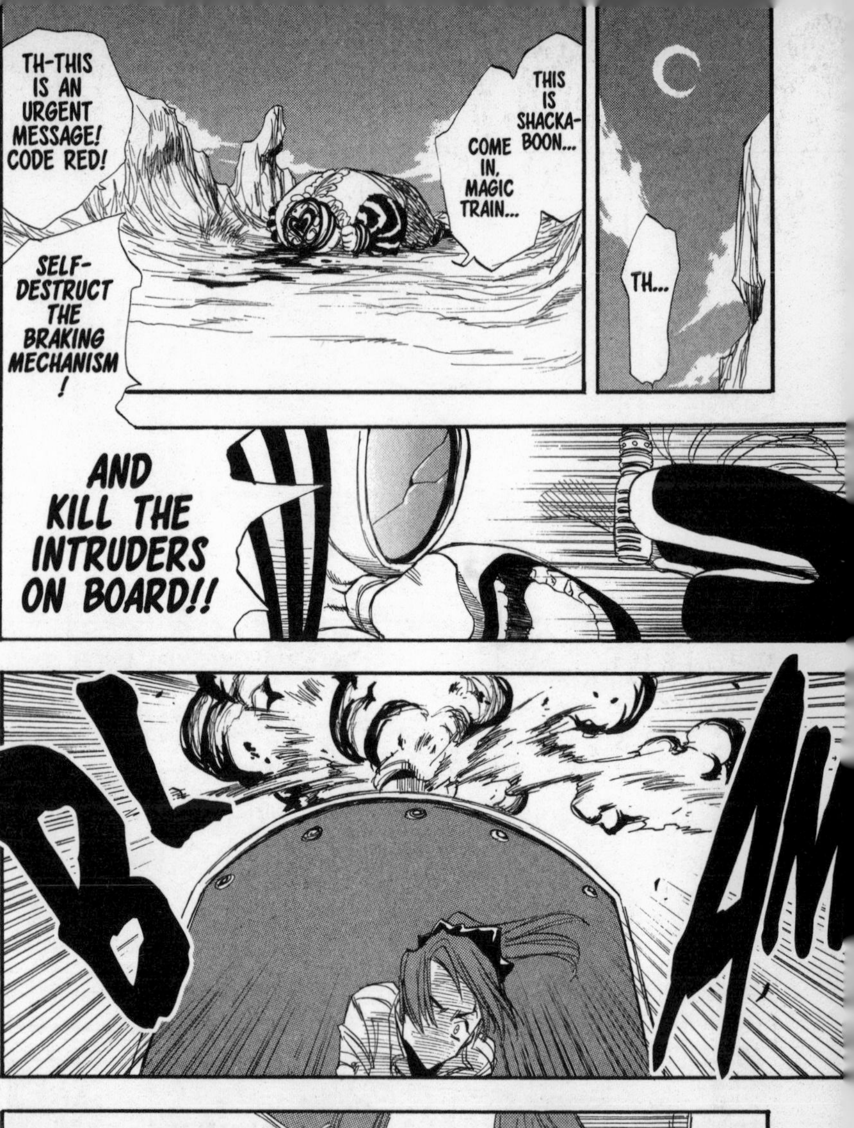
TH...
THIS IS SHACKA-BOON...
COME IN, MAGIC TRAIN...
TH-THIS IS AN URGENT MESSAGE! CODE RED!
SELF-DESTRUCT THE BRAKING MECHANISM!
AND KILL THE INTRUDERS ON BOARD!!
BLAM
BRAKES DE-STROYED!
BRAKES DE-STROYED!
CLIMBING TO FULL SPEED. REVERSING COURSE. OUR NEXT STOP IS ALCANTARA!

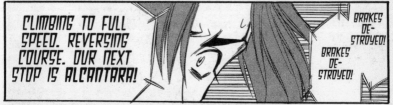

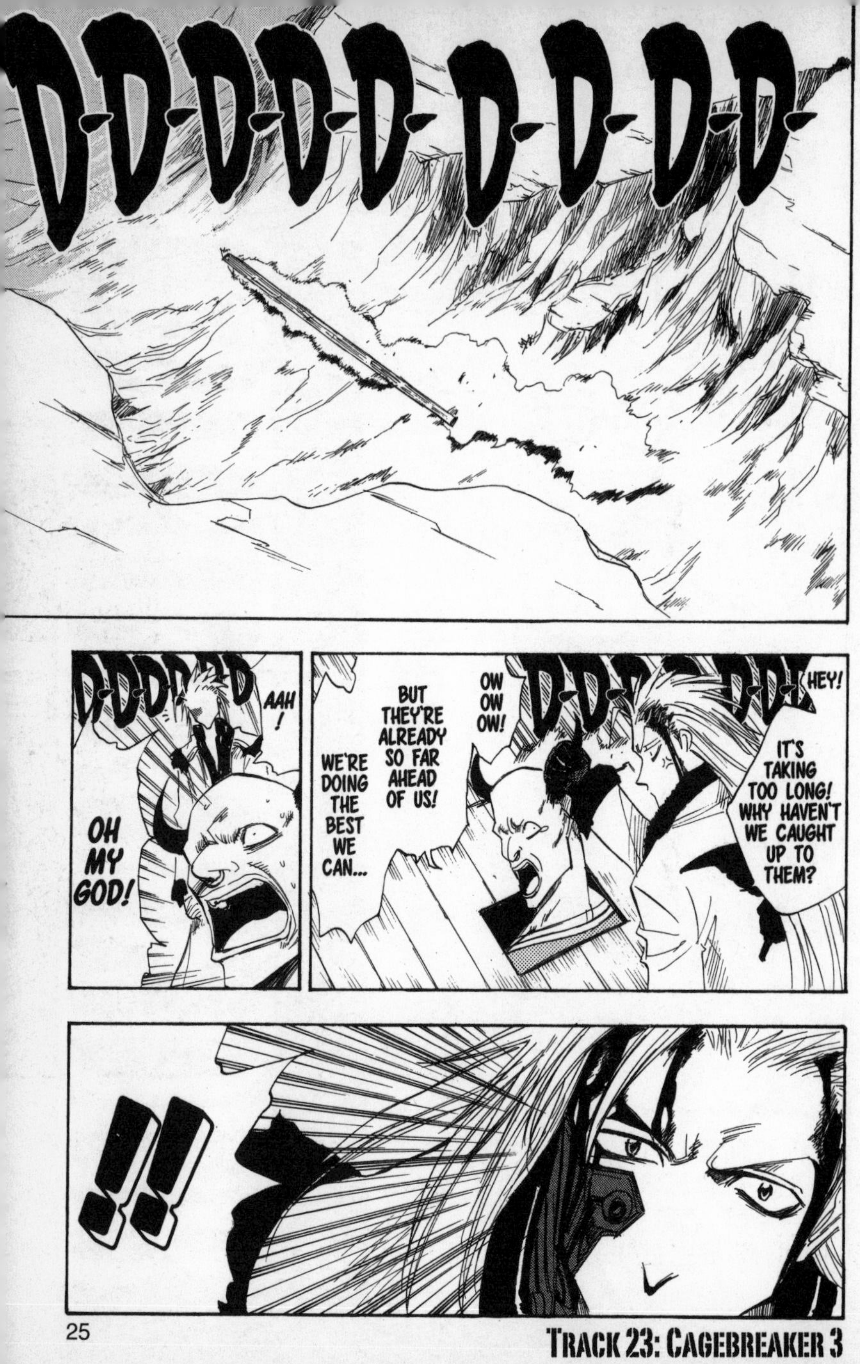
D-D-D-D-D-D-D-D-D-D
HEY!
IT'S TAKING TOO LONG! WHY HAVEN'T WE CAUGHT UP TO THEM?
OW OW OW!
BUT THEY'RE ALREADY SO FAR AHEAD OF US!
WE'RE DOING THE BEST WE CAN...
AAH!
OH MY GOD!
!!

TRACK 23: CAGEBREAKER 3

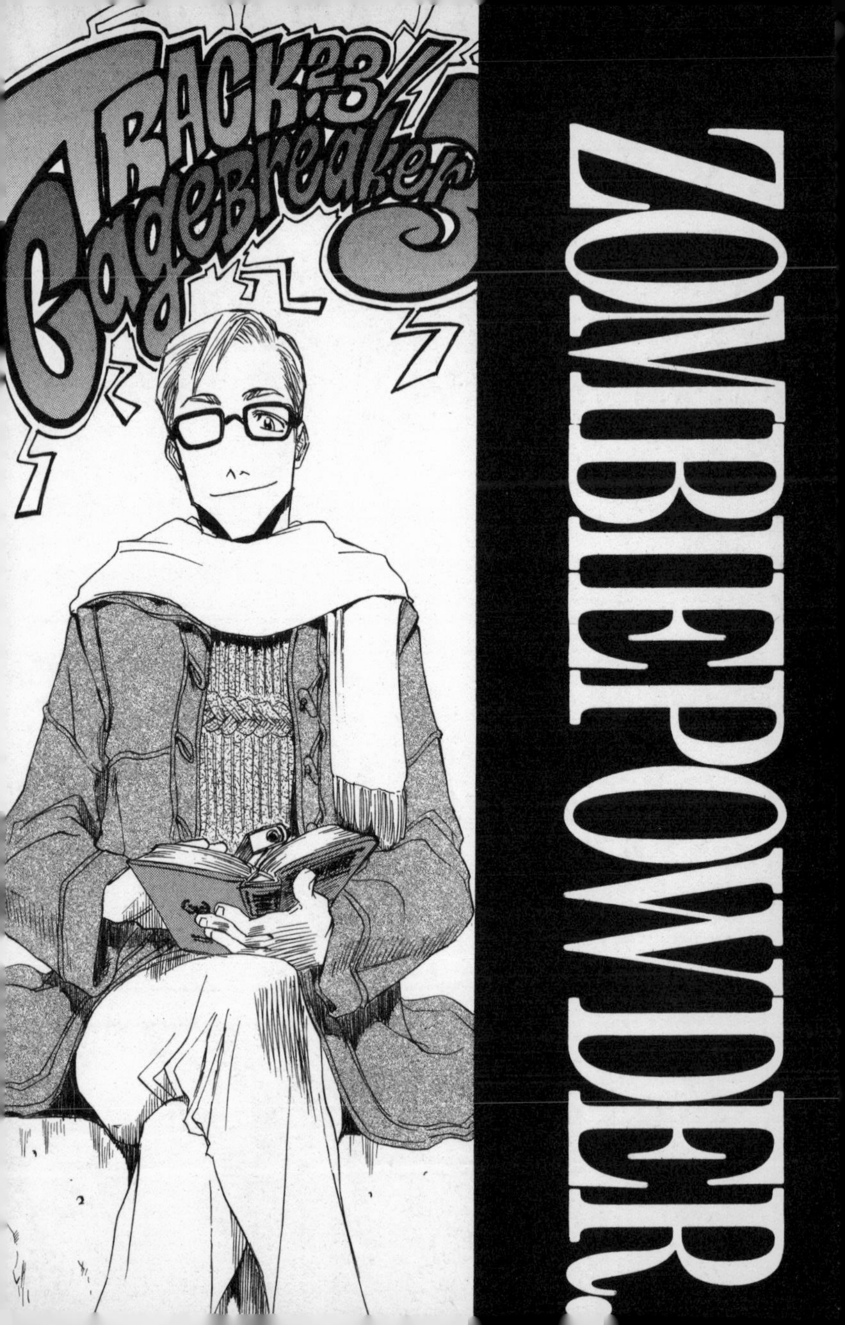
TRACK.23/
Cagebreaker
ZOMBIEPOWDER.

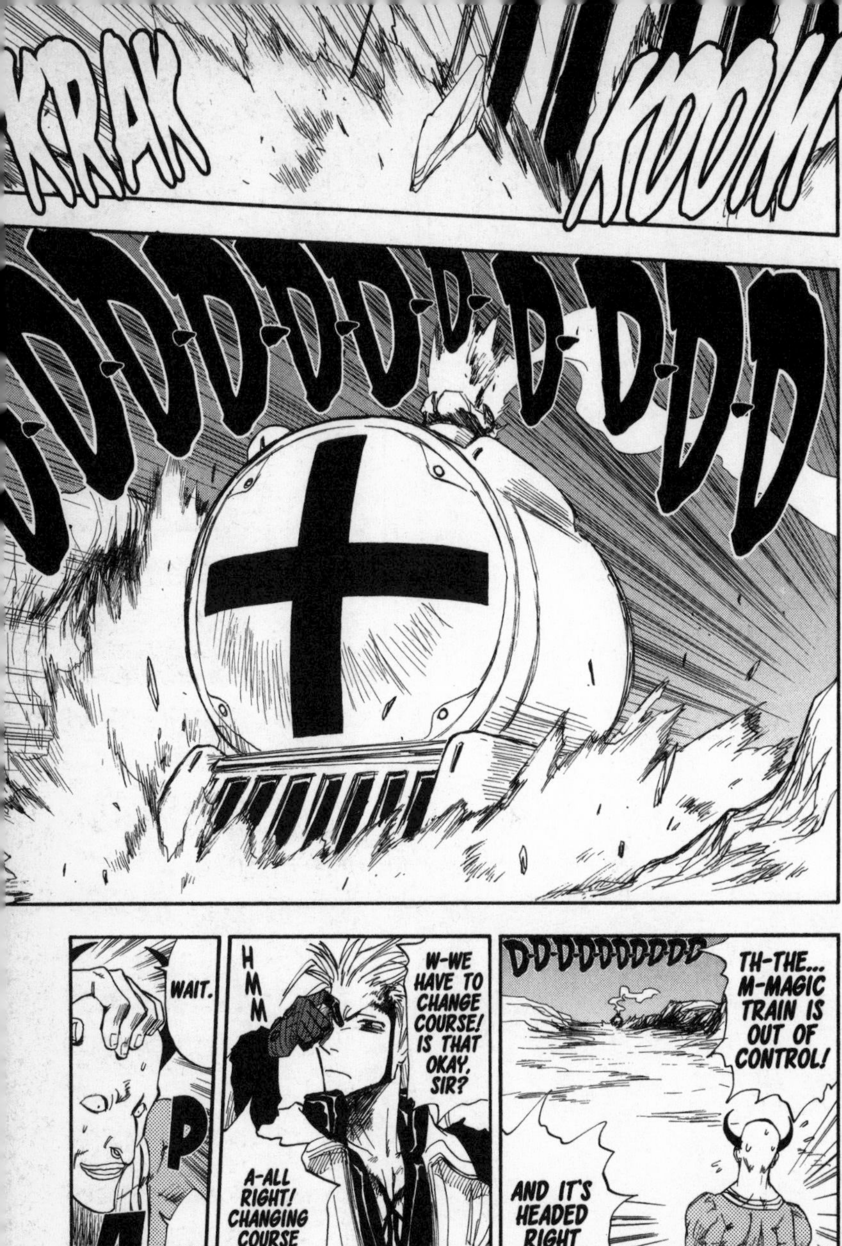
KRAK
D-D-D-D-D-D-D-D-D-D
TH-THE... M-MAGIC TRAIN IS OUT OF CONTROL!
AND IT'S HEADED RIGHT FOR US!
W-WE HAVE TO CHANGE COURSE! IS THAT OKAY, SIR?
HMM
A-ALL RIGHT! CHANGING COURSE RIGHT AWAY!
WAIT.
PAT
...HUH?

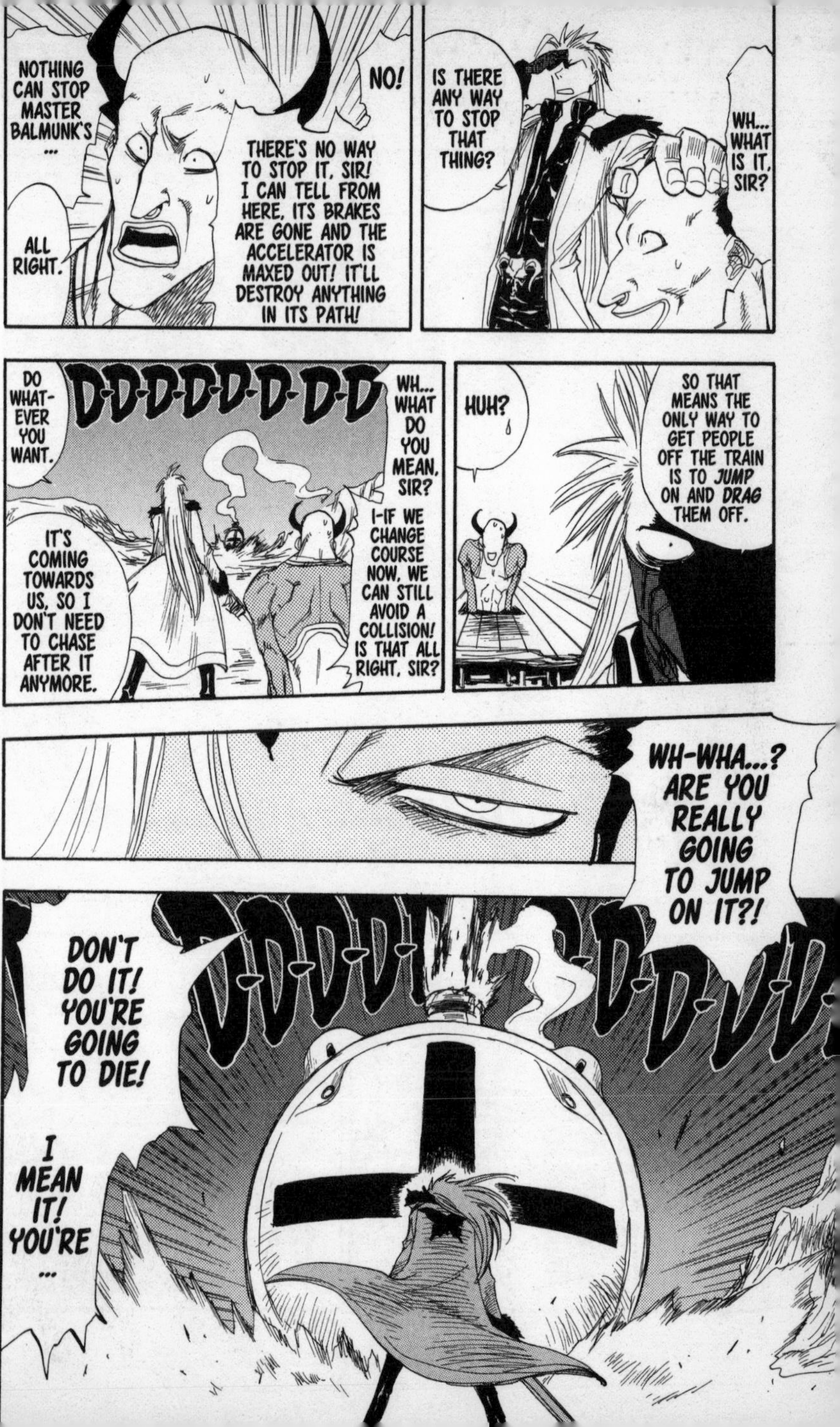
WH... WHAT IS IT, SIR?
IS THERE ANY WAY TO STOP THAT THING?
NO!
THERE'S NO WAY TO STOP IT, SIR! I CAN TELL FROM HERE, ITS BRAKES ARE GONE AND THE ACCELERATOR IS MAXED OUT! IT'LL DESTROY ANYTHING IN ITS PATH!
NOTHING CAN STOP MASTER BALMUNK'S ...
ALL RIGHT.
SO THAT MEANS THE ONLY WAY TO GET PEOPLE OFF THE TRAIN IS TO *JUMP* ON AND *DRAG* THEM OFF.
HUH?
WH... WHAT DO YOU MEAN, SIR?
D-D-D-D-D-D-D-D
DO WHATEVER YOU WANT.
I-IF WE CHANGE COURSE NOW, WE CAN STILL AVOID A COLLISION! IS THAT ALL RIGHT, SIR?
IT'S COMING TOWARDS US, SO I DON'T NEED TO CHASE AFTER IT ANYMORE.
WH-WHA...? ARE YOU REALLY GOING TO JUMP ON IT?!
DON'T DO IT! YOU'RE GOING TO DIE!
I MEAN IT! YOU'RE ...

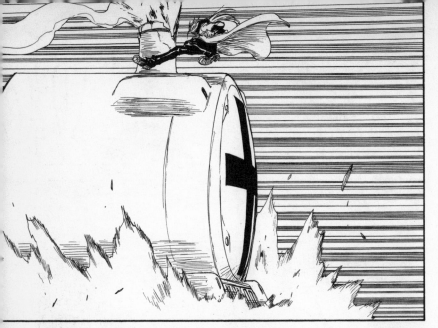

CH OOM

WAAGH?!

LE AP

D-D-D- H....

THAT GUY'S CRAZY ...

HE REALLY JUMPED ONTO THE TRAIN...

D-D-D-D-D-D-D-D-D-D

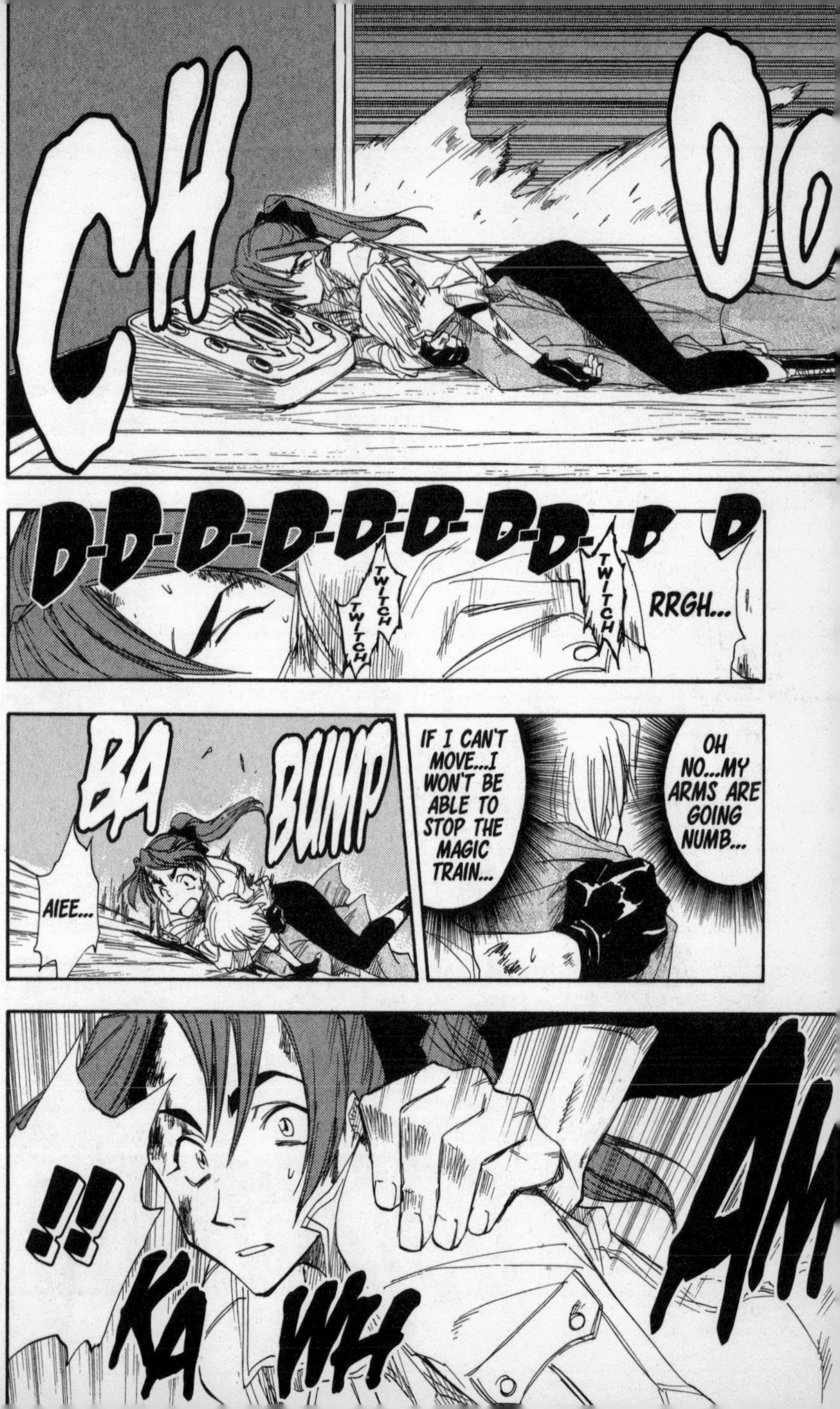

CH
O
D-D-D-D-D-D-D-D-D-D-D-D
RRGH...
TWITCH
TWITCH TWITCH
OH NO...MY ARMS ARE GOING NUMB...
IF I CAN'T MOVE...I WON'T BE ABLE TO STOP THE MAGIC TRAIN...
BA BUMP
AIEE...
!!
KA WH AM

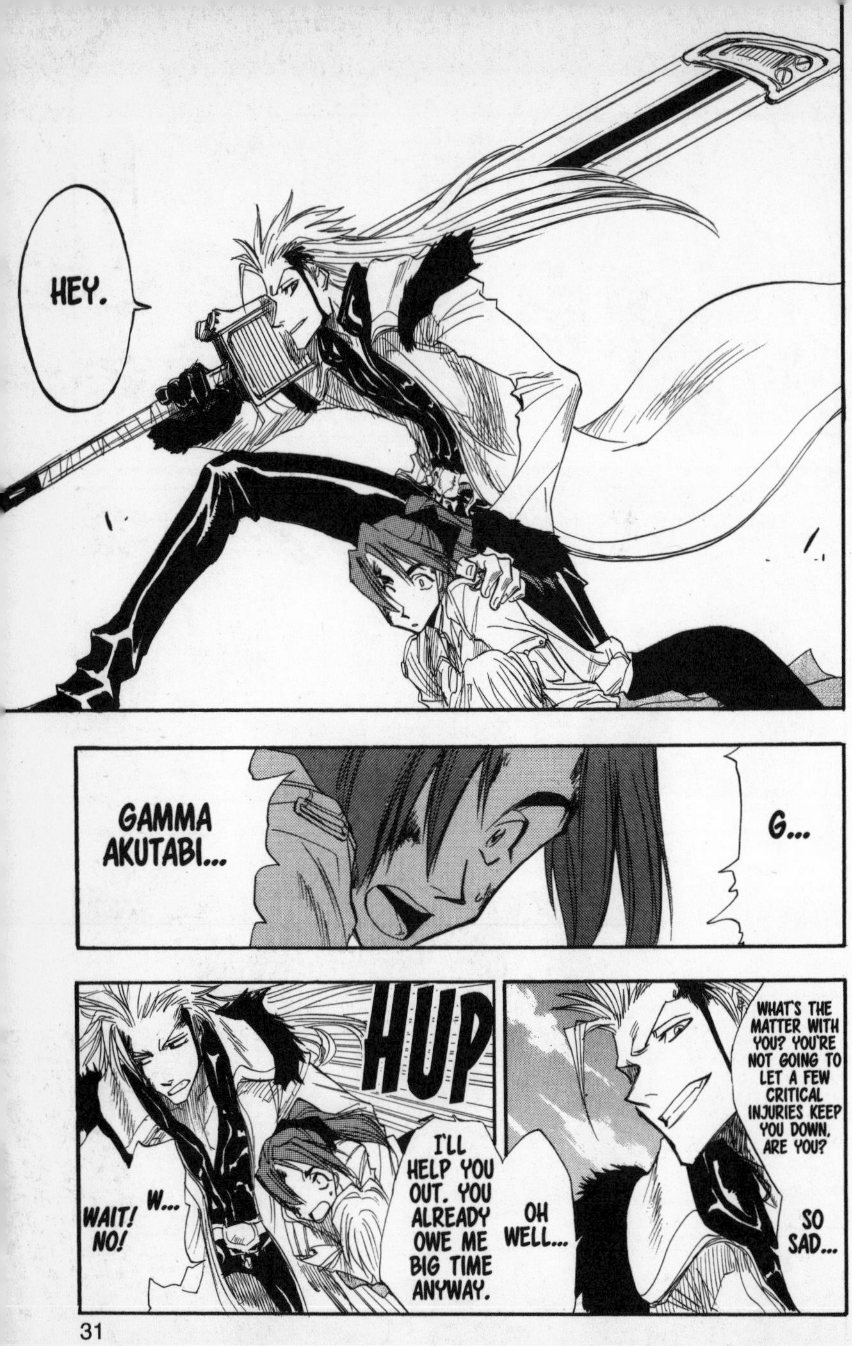
HEY.
G...
GAMMA AKUTABI...
WHAT'S THE MATTER WITH YOU? YOU'RE NOT GOING TO LET A FEW CRITICAL INJURIES KEEP YOU DOWN, ARE YOU?
SO SAD...
OH WELL...
HUP
I'LL HELP YOU OUT. YOU ALREADY OWE ME BIG TIME ANYWAY.
W...
WAIT! NO!

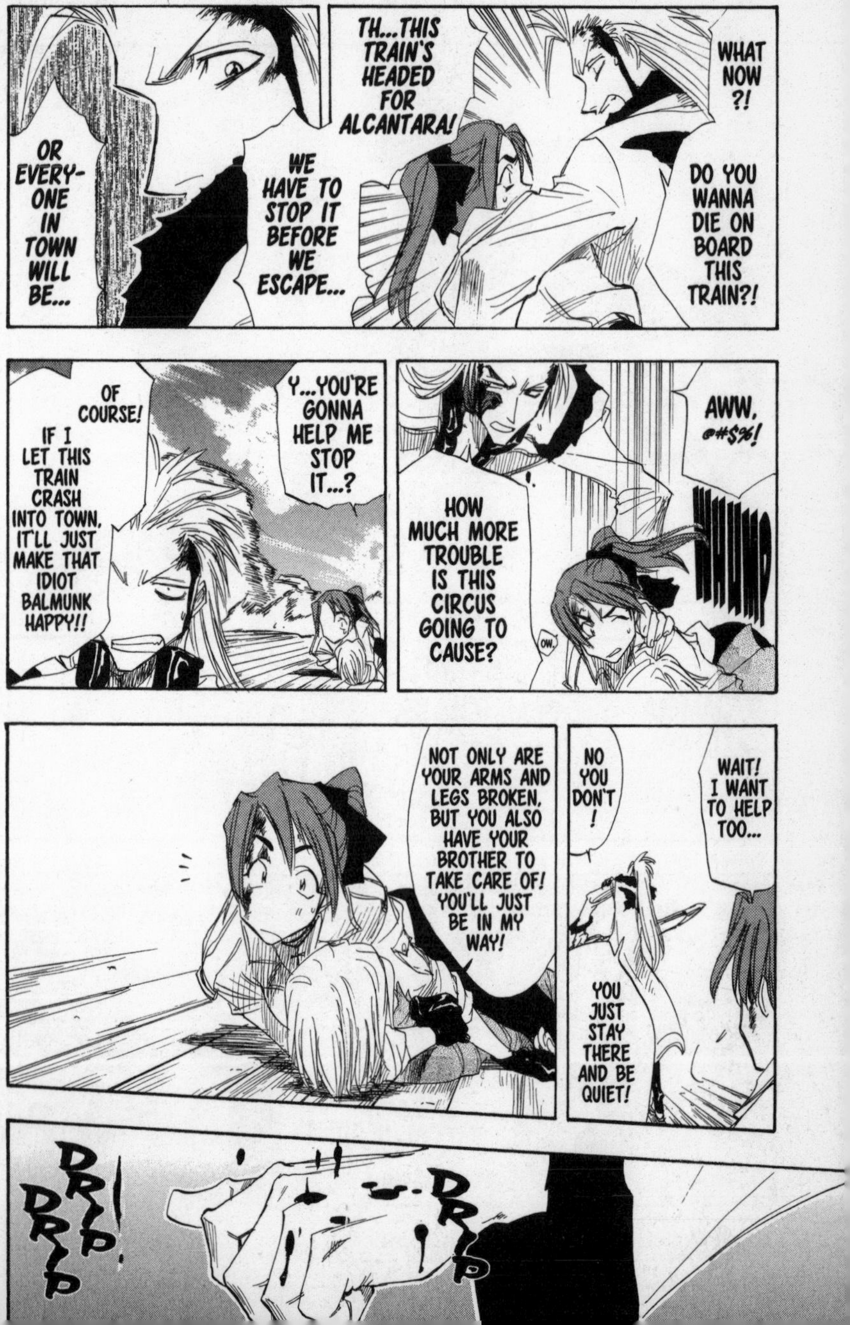
WHAT NOW?!
TH...THIS TRAIN'S HEADED FOR ALCANTARA!
DO YOU WANNA DIE ON BOARD THIS TRAIN?!
WE HAVE TO STOP IT BEFORE WE ESCAPE...
OR EVERY-ONE IN TOWN WILL BE...
AWW, @#$%!
WHUMP
HOW MUCH MORE TROUBLE IS THIS CIRCUS GOING TO CAUSE?
OW.
Y...YOU'RE GONNA HELP ME STOP IT...?
OF COURSE! IF I LET THIS TRAIN CRASH INTO TOWN, IT'LL JUST MAKE THAT IDIOT BALMUNK HAPPY!!
WAIT! I WANT TO HELP TOO...
NO YOU DON'T!
YOU JUST STAY THERE AND BE QUIET!
NOT ONLY ARE YOUR ARMS AND LEGS BROKEN, BUT YOU ALSO HAVE YOUR BROTHER TO TAKE CARE OF! YOU'LL JUST BE IN MY WAY!
DRIP
DRIP DRIP DRIP

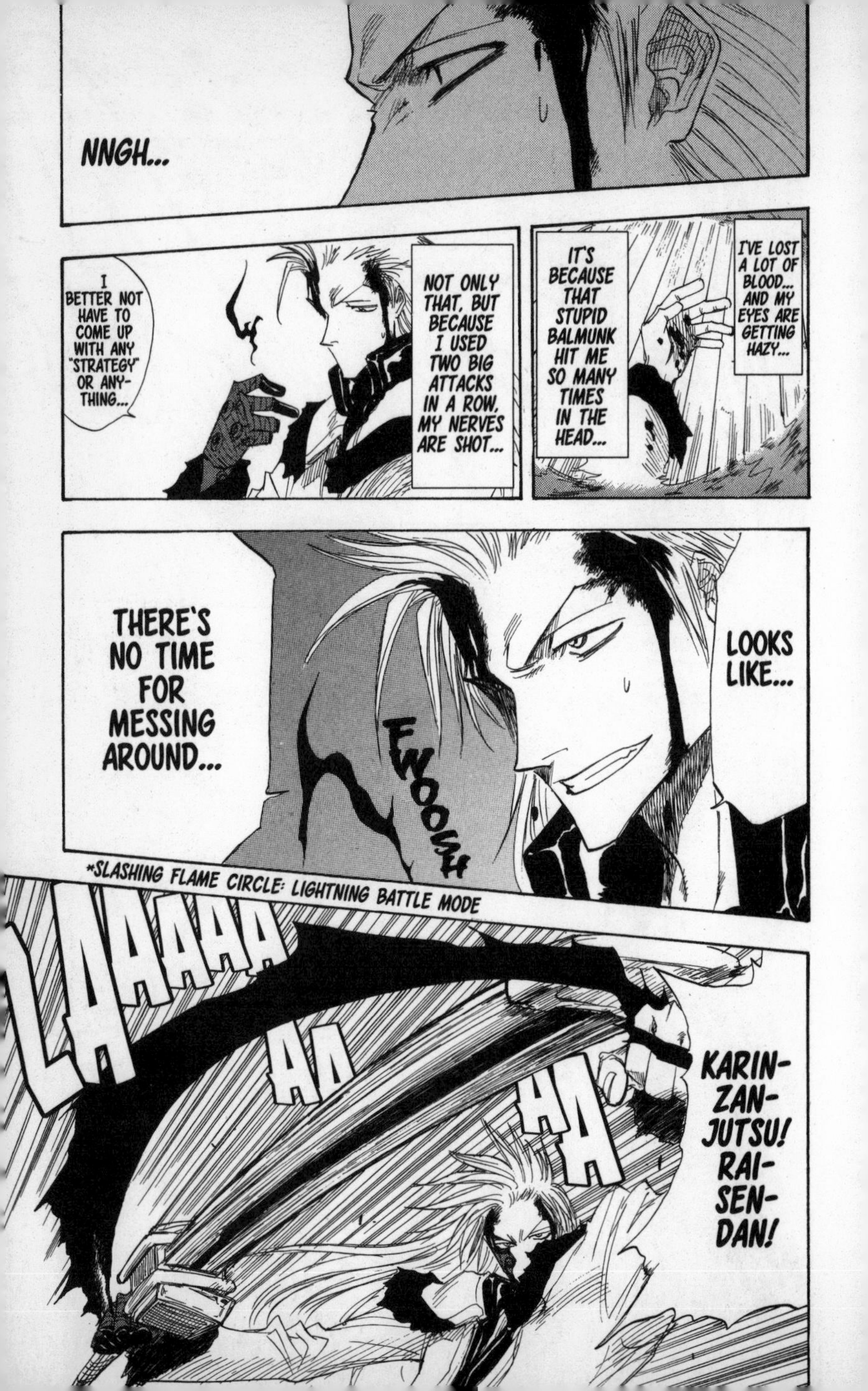
NNGH...
I'VE LOST A LOT OF BLOOD... AND MY EYES ARE GETTING HAZY...
IT'S BECAUSE THAT STUPID BALMUNK HIT ME SO MANY TIMES IN THE HEAD...
NOT ONLY THAT, BUT BECAUSE I USED TWO BIG ATTACKS IN A ROW, MY NERVES ARE SHOT...
I BETTER NOT HAVE TO COME UP WITH ANY "STRATEGY" OR ANYTHING...
LOOKS LIKE...
FWOOSH
THERE'S NO TIME FOR MESSING AROUND...
KARIN-ZAN-JUTSU! RAI-SEN-DAN!
LAAAAAAAAAA
*SLASHING FLAME CIRCLE: LIGHTNING BATTLE MODE

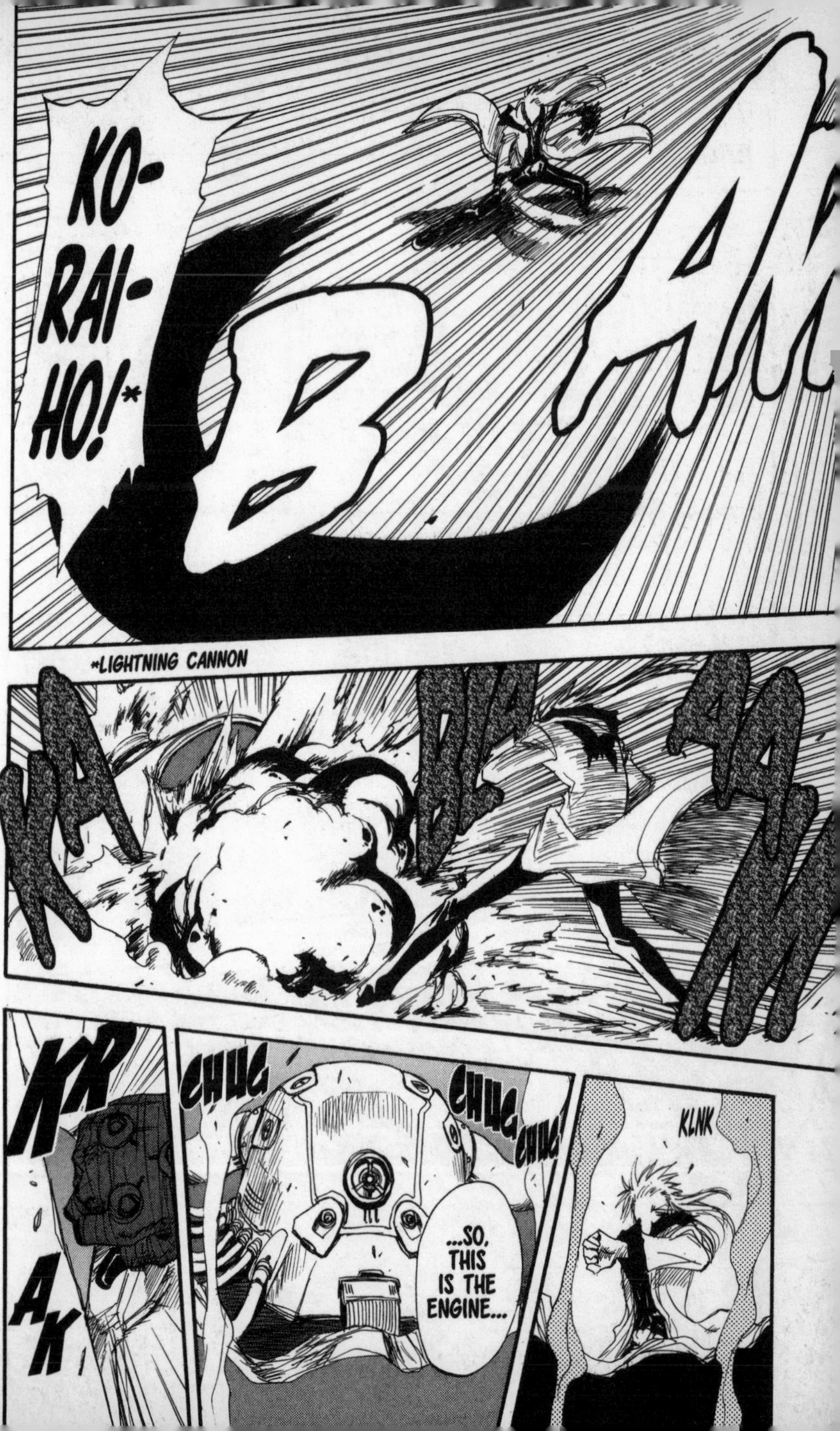
KO-RAI-HO!*
BAM
*LIGHTNING CANNON
BAAM
KA-BLA
KLNK
CHUG
CHUG CHUG
CHUG
...SO, THIS IS THE ENGINE...
KRAK

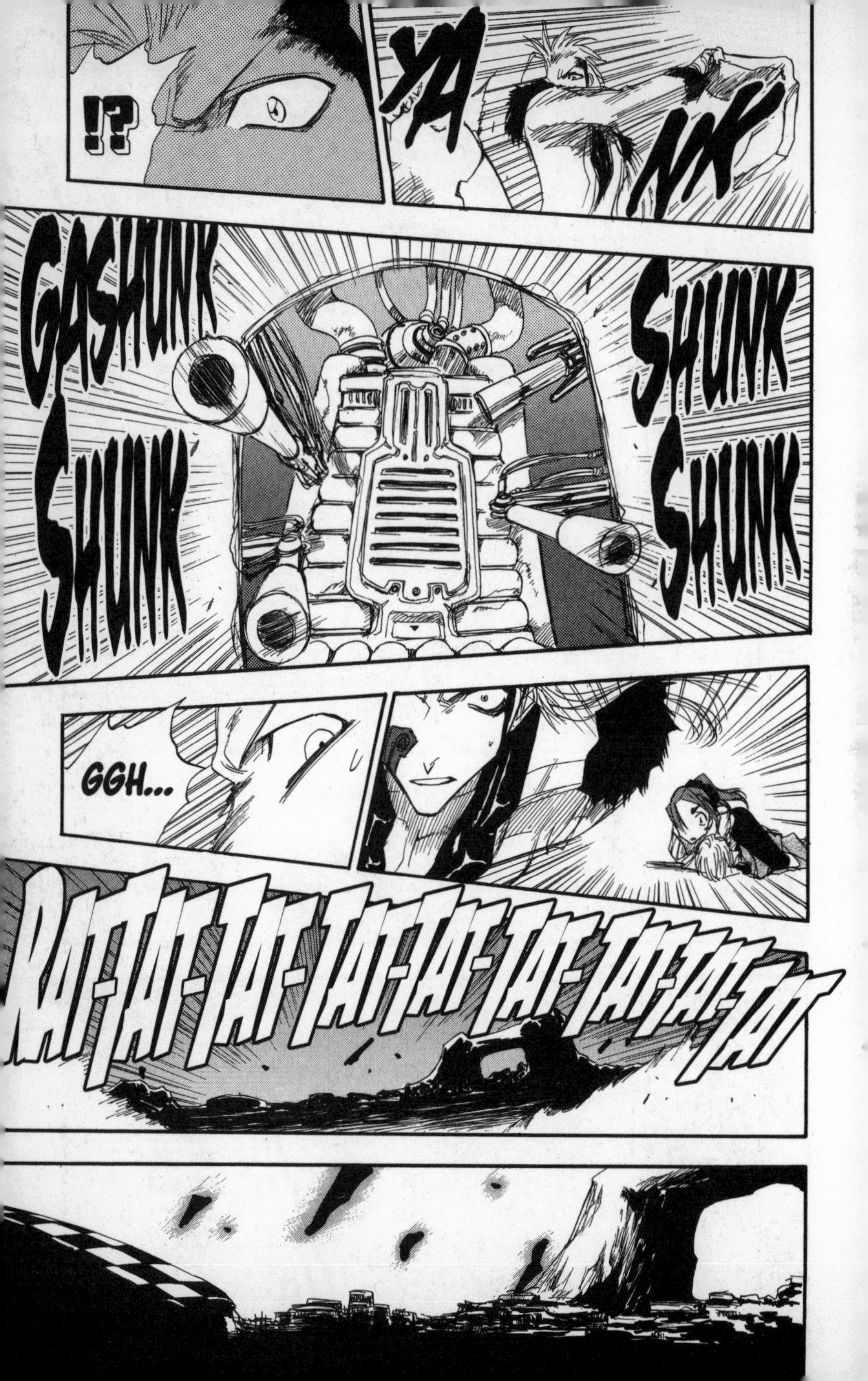
YANK
!?
SHUNK
SHUNK
SHUNK
GASHUNK
SHUNK
GGH...
RAT-TAT-TAT-TAT-TAT-TAT-TAT-TA-TA-TAT

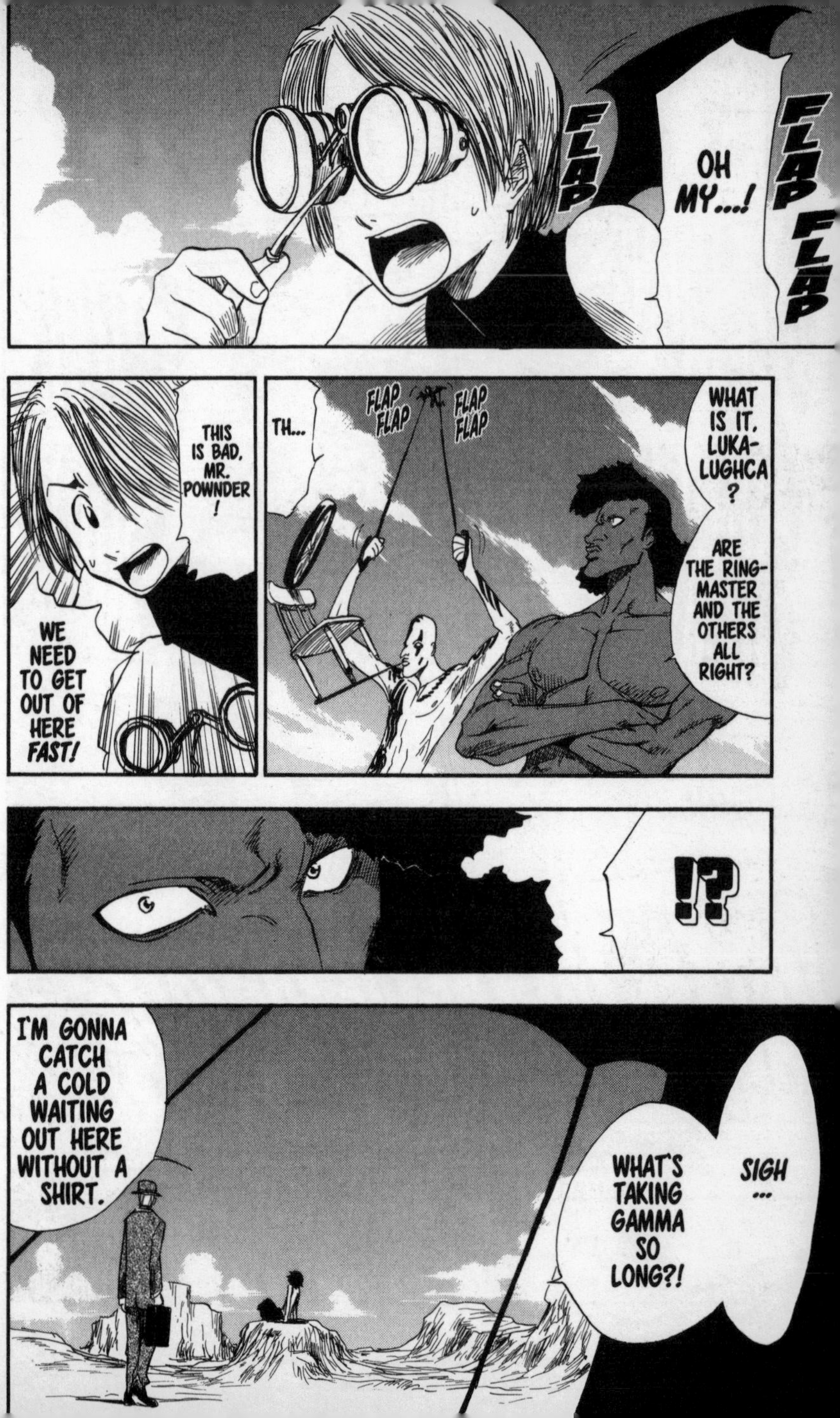
FLAP FLAP
FLAP FLAP
OH MY...!
FLAP
WHAT IS IT, LUKA-LUGHCA?
ARE THE RING-MASTER AND THE OTHERS ALL RIGHT?
FLAP FLAP
FLAP FLAP
TH...
THIS IS BAD, MR. POWNDER!
WE NEED TO GET OUT OF HERE FAST!
!?
SIGH...
WHAT'S TAKING GAMMA SO LONG?!
I'M GONNA CATCH A COLD WAITING OUT HERE WITHOUT A SHIRT.

READ THIS WAY

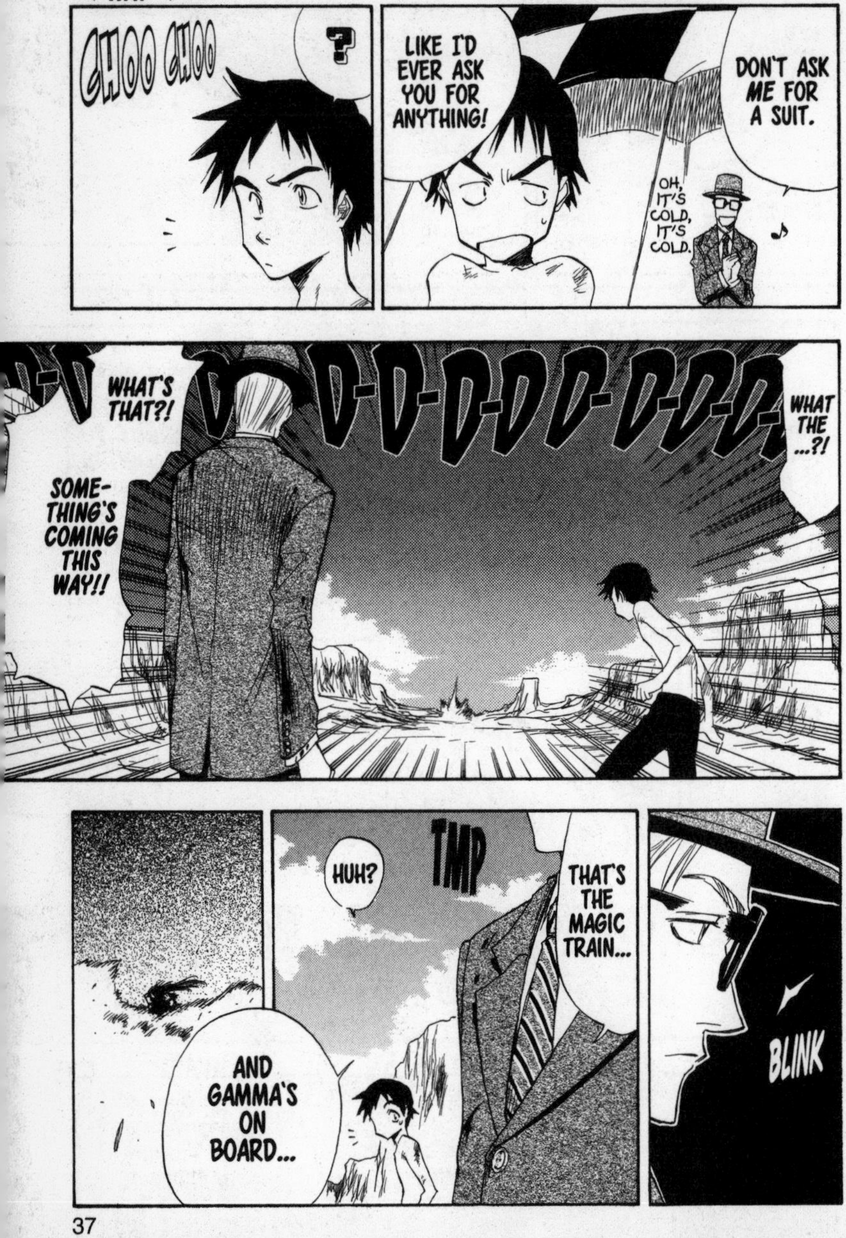
DON'T ASK ME FOR A SUIT.
OH, IT'S COLD, IT'S COLD.
LIKE I'D EVER ASK YOU FOR ANYTHING!
?
CHOO CHOO
D-D-D-D-D-D-D-D-D-D-D-D
WHAT THE ...?!
WHAT'S THAT?!
SOMETHING'S COMING THIS WAY!!
BLINK
THAT'S THE MAGIC TRAIN...
TMP
HUH?
AND GAMMA'S ON BOARD...

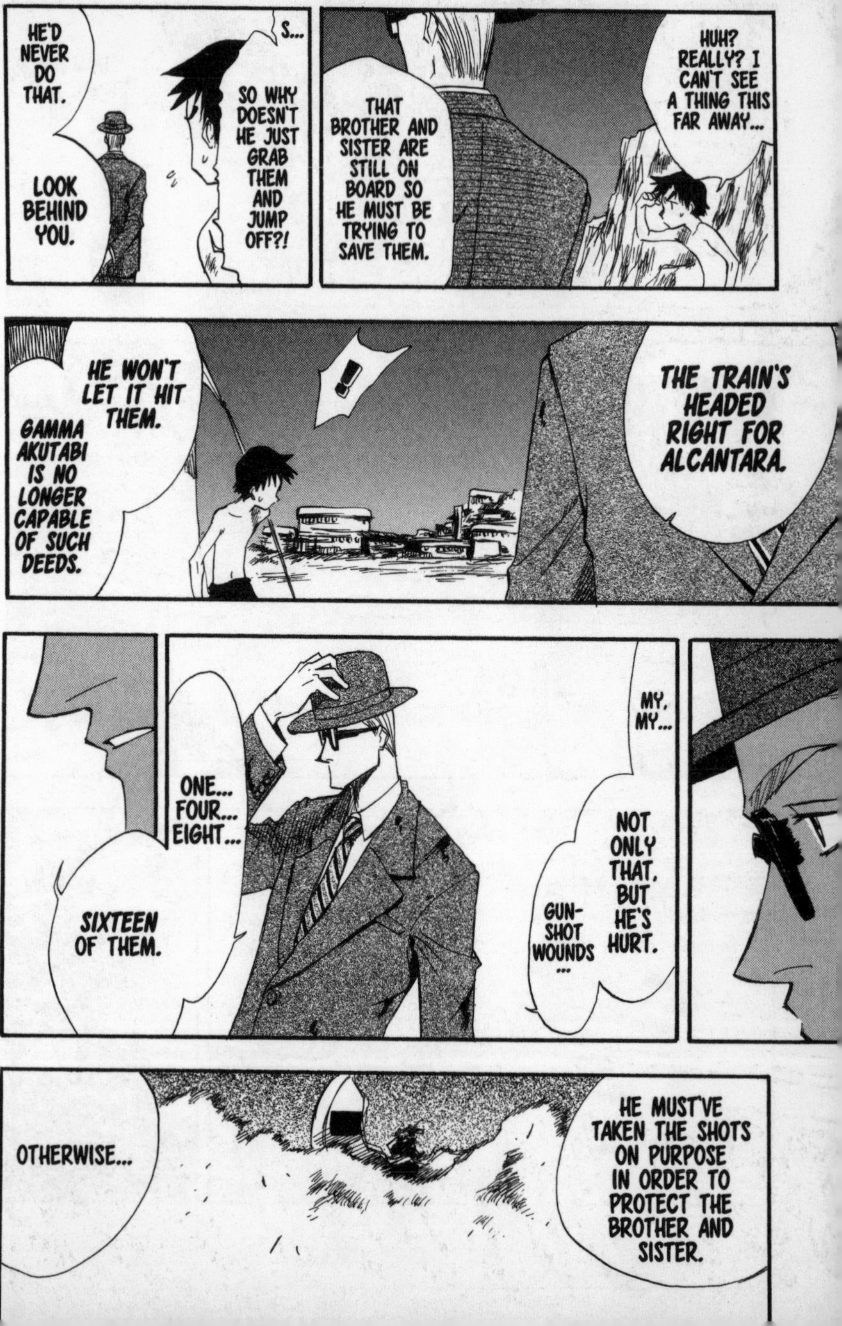
HUH? REALLY? I CAN'T SEE A THING THIS FAR AWAY...
THAT BROTHER AND SISTER ARE STILL ON BOARD SO HE MUST BE TRYING TO SAVE THEM.
S...
SO WHY DOESN'T HE JUST GRAB THEM AND JUMP OFF?!
HE'D NEVER DO THAT.
LOOK BEHIND YOU.
THE TRAIN'S HEADED RIGHT FOR ALCANTARA.
!
HE WON'T LET IT HIT THEM.
GAMMA AKUTABI IS NO LONGER CAPABLE OF SUCH DEEDS.
MY, MY...
NOT ONLY THAT, BUT HE'S HURT.
GUN-SHOT WOUNDS...
ONE... FOUR... EIGHT...
SIXTEEN OF THEM.
HE MUST'VE TAKEN THE SHOTS ON PURPOSE IN ORDER TO PROTECT THE BROTHER AND SISTER.
OTHERWISE...

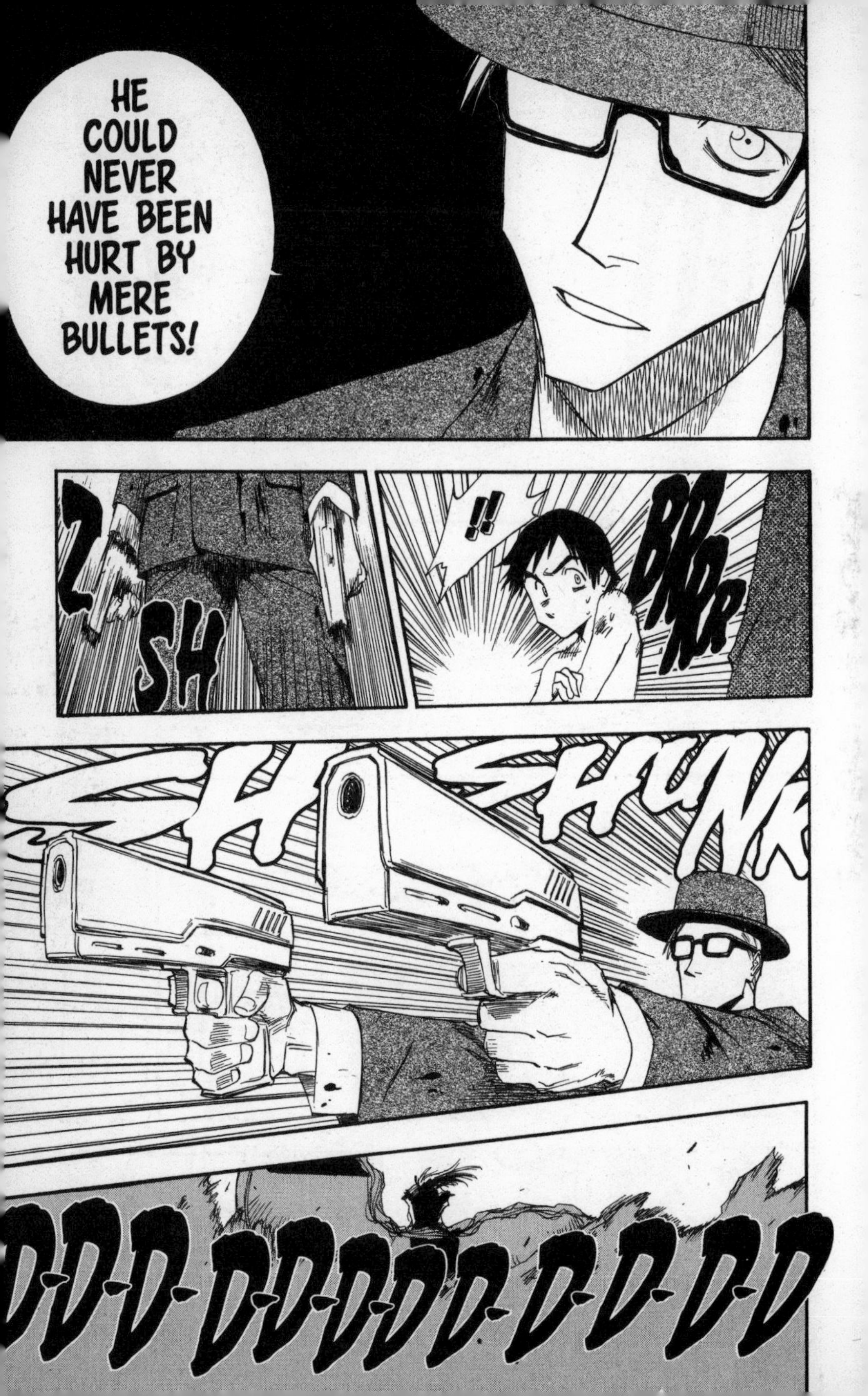
HE COULD NEVER HAVE BEEN HURT BY MERE BULLETS!
!!

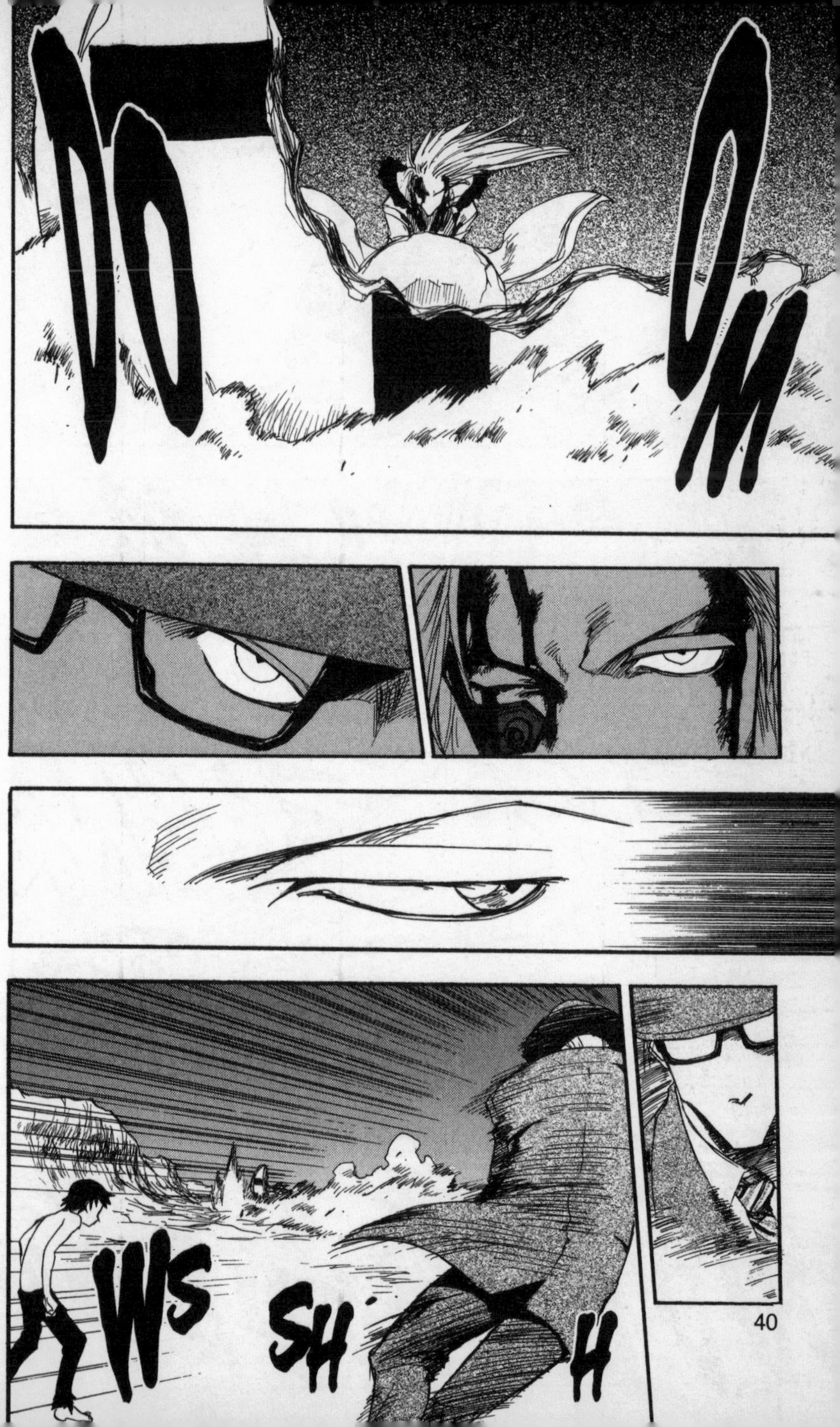
DOOM
WSSHH

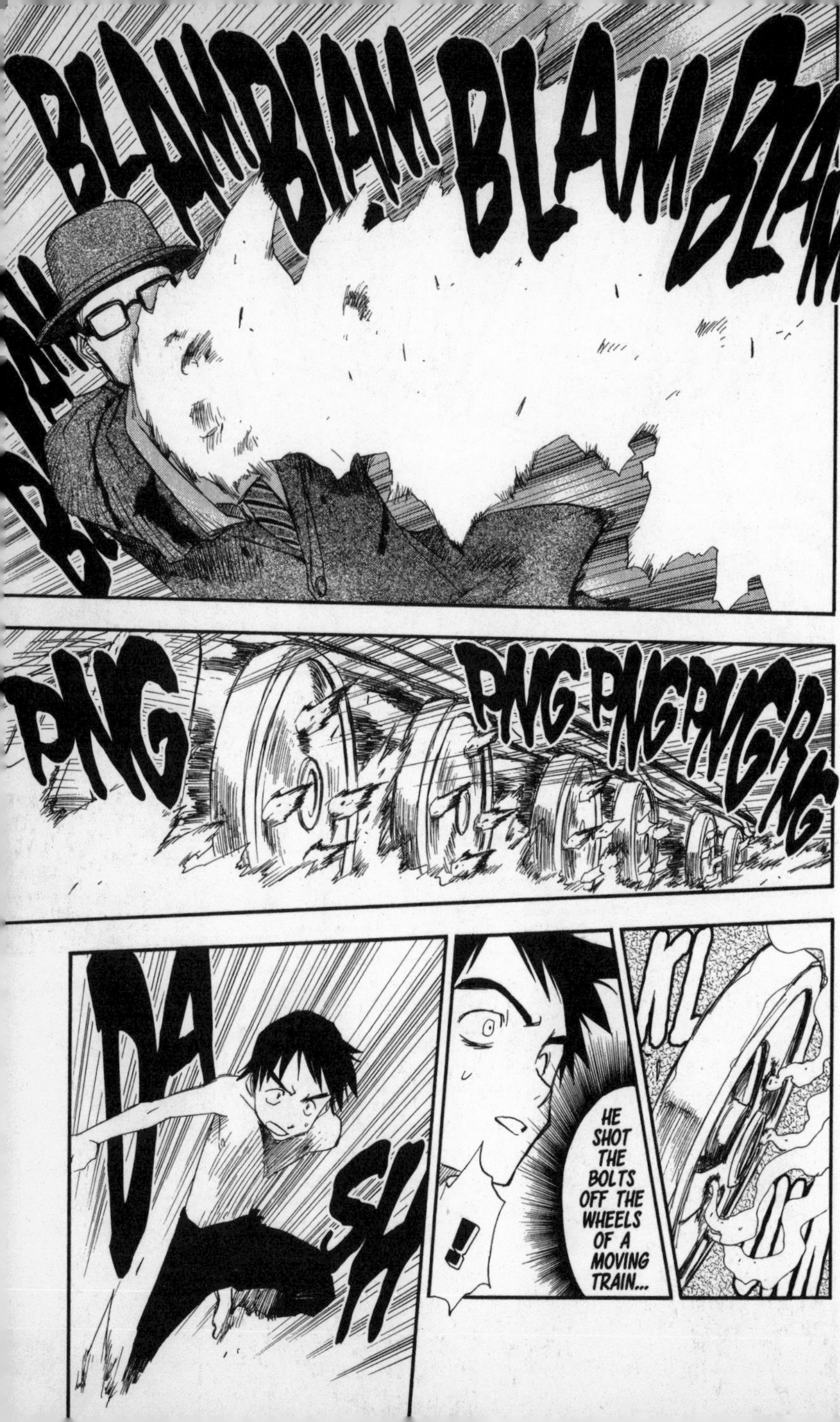
BLAM BLAM BLAM BLAM
BLAM
PING PING PING PING
PING
HE SHOT THE BOLTS OFF THE WHEELS OF A MOVING TRAIN...
!
DASH

YOU DID IT!
THE TRAIN'S TURNING! IT'S NOT GOING TO HIT ALCANTARA!
KLANNG
G
G
G
EEYAA...
OH CRAP...

READ THIS WAY

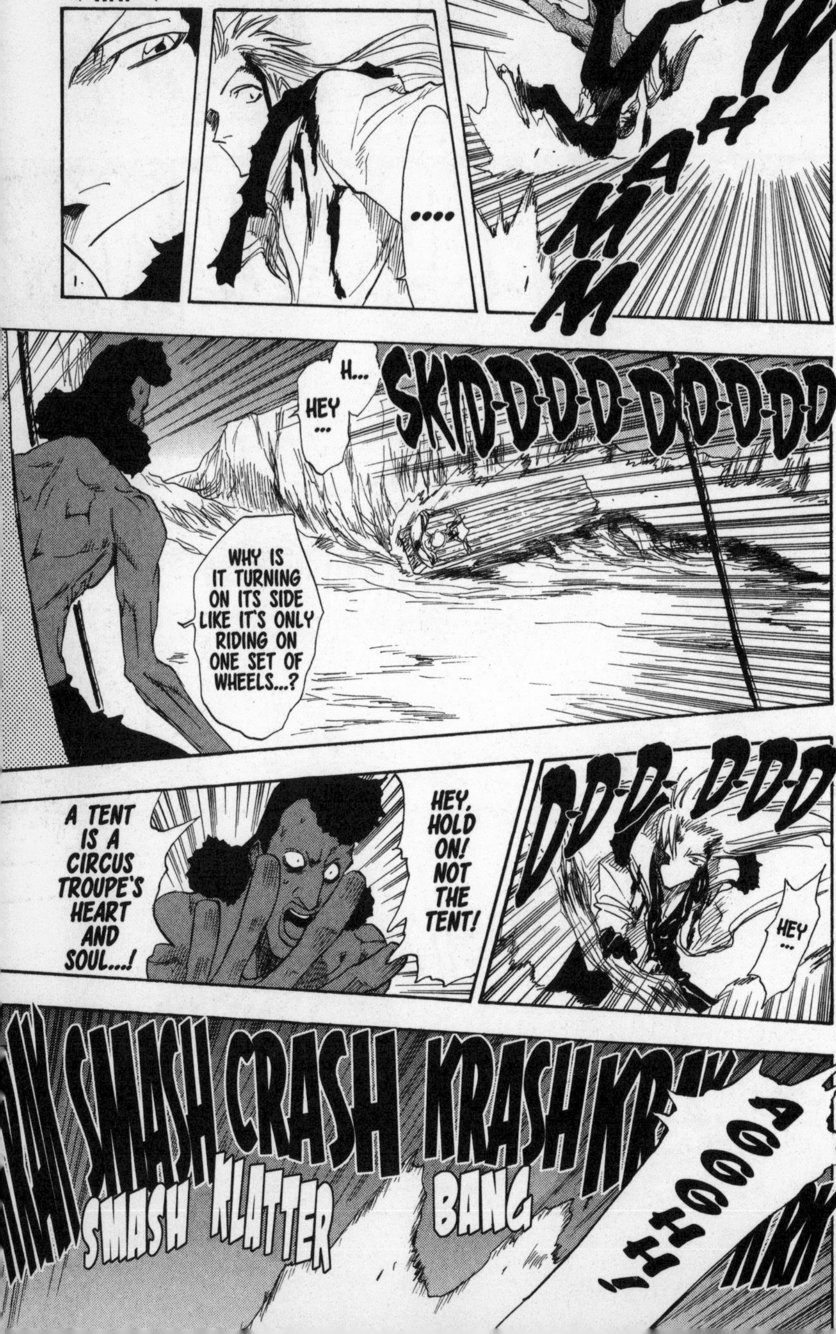
WHAMMM
....
SKID-D-D-D D-D-D-D-D
H... HEY ...
WHY IS IT TURNING ON ITS SIDE LIKE IT'S ONLY RIDING ON ONE SET OF WHEELS...?
D-D-D-D-D-D-D
HEY ...
HEY, HOLD ON! NOT THE TENT!
A TENT IS A CIRCUS TROUPE'S HEART AND SOUL...!
AGGGH!
KRASH
BANG
CRASH
KLATTER
SMASH
SMASH

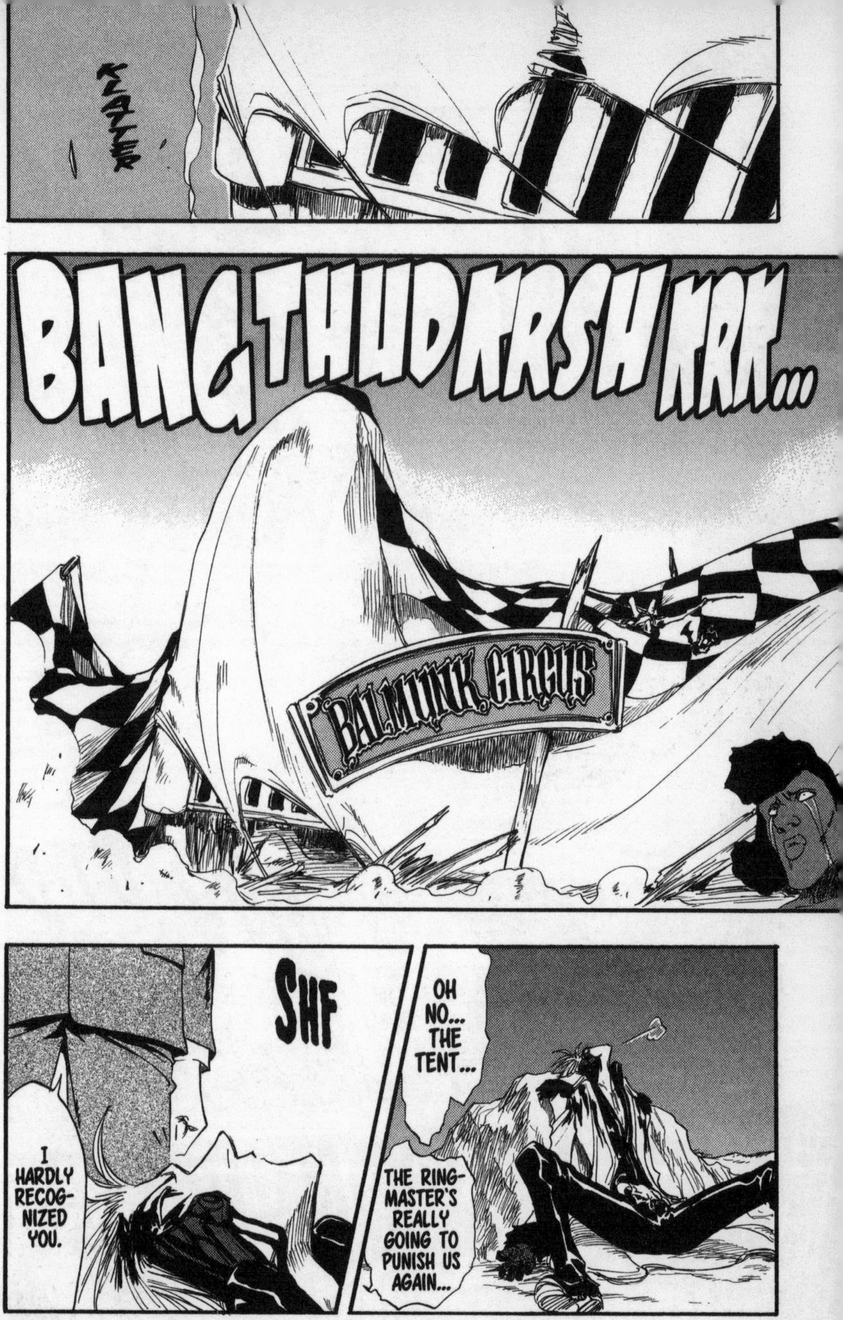
KLATTER
BANG THUD KRSH KRK...
BALMUNK CIRCUS
OH NO... THE TENT...
THE RING-MASTER'S REALLY GOING TO PUNISH US AGAIN...
SHF
I HARDLY RECOG-NIZED YOU.

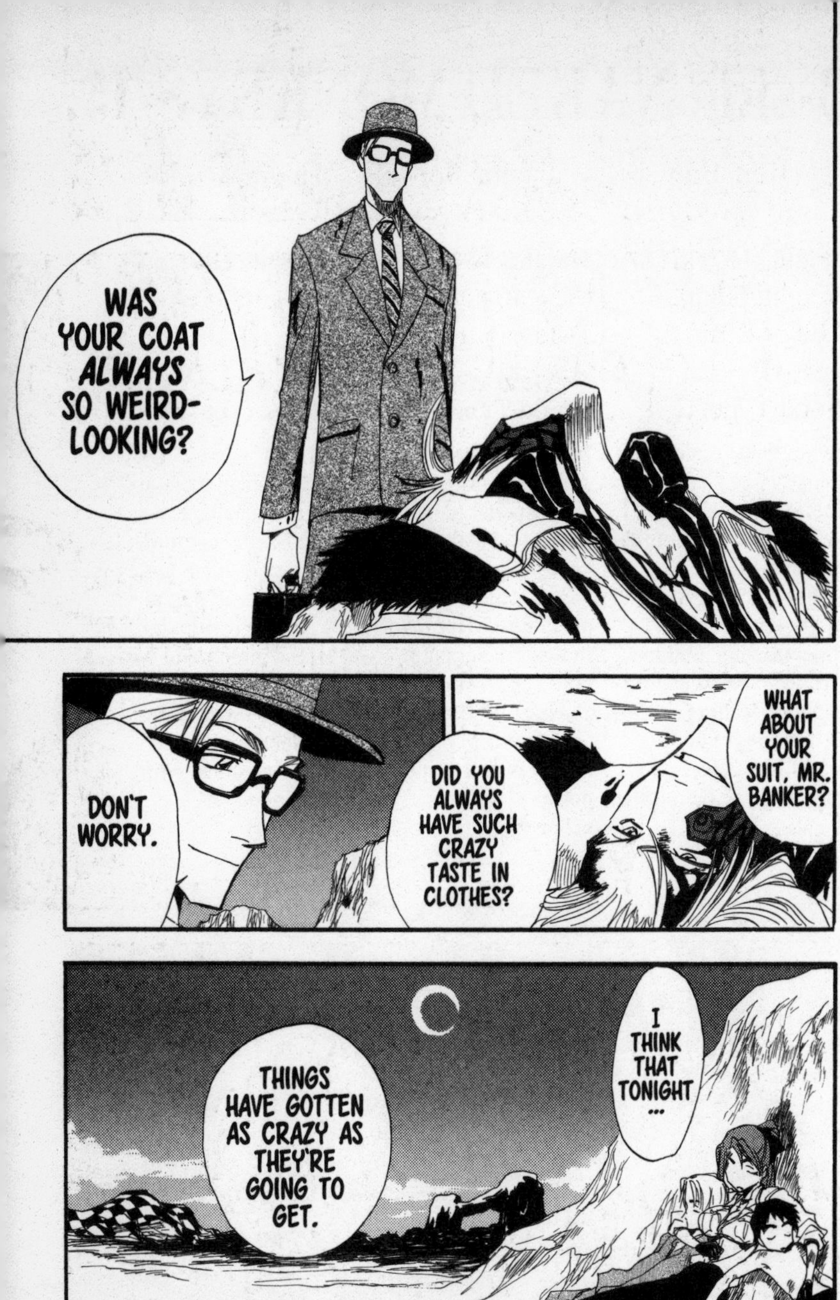
WAS YOUR COAT *ALWAYS* SO WEIRD-LOOKING?
WHAT ABOUT YOUR SUIT, MR. BANKER?
DID YOU ALWAYS HAVE SUCH CRAZY TASTE IN CLOTHES?
DON'T WORRY.
I THINK THAT TONIGHT...
THINGS HAVE GOTTEN AS CRAZY AS THEY'RE GOING TO GET.

B-side NAKED MONKEYS 15.

Jiān Bǎo
チェン・バオ
蒭宝

Height: 167cm
Weight: 50kg
Date of Birth: 5/7
Age: 17
Blood Type: O

The youngest maid in the history of Gemini Laboratory, she is in charge of the accounting, cleaning, and cooking. She has red hair. She is serious, studious, temperamental, and has a strong sense of justice. Her favorite things are blue clothing. She doesn't like celery, slugs, rock music, or Geraldine.

Tasha Forkel
タシャ・フォーケル

Height: 154cm
Weight: 42kg
Date of Birth: 10/16
Age: 22
Blood Type: BO

Her full name is Anastasia Forkel, and she's in charge of biological sciences at Gemini Laboraory. She has chestnut hair and black eyes. Her favorite things are eggplant, crab cakes, snakes, and earrings. She's a hardcore masochist and her hobby is collecting porno magazines. Jian is her roommate.

Lippy(Lisa PinkDiamond)
リッピー(リサ・ピンクダイアモンド)

Height: 199cm
Weight: 116kg
Date of Birth: 7/5
Age: 26
Blood type: BO

His real name is Daniel Sebastian Vadek, and he is a mechanical engineer at Gemini Laboratory. He has a shaved head but he wears colorful wigs. He's a giant maid with dark brown skin. His hobbies are making confectionaries and doing pushups with his fingers.

TRACK 24: BUT STILL LIVIN' UNDER THE SKY

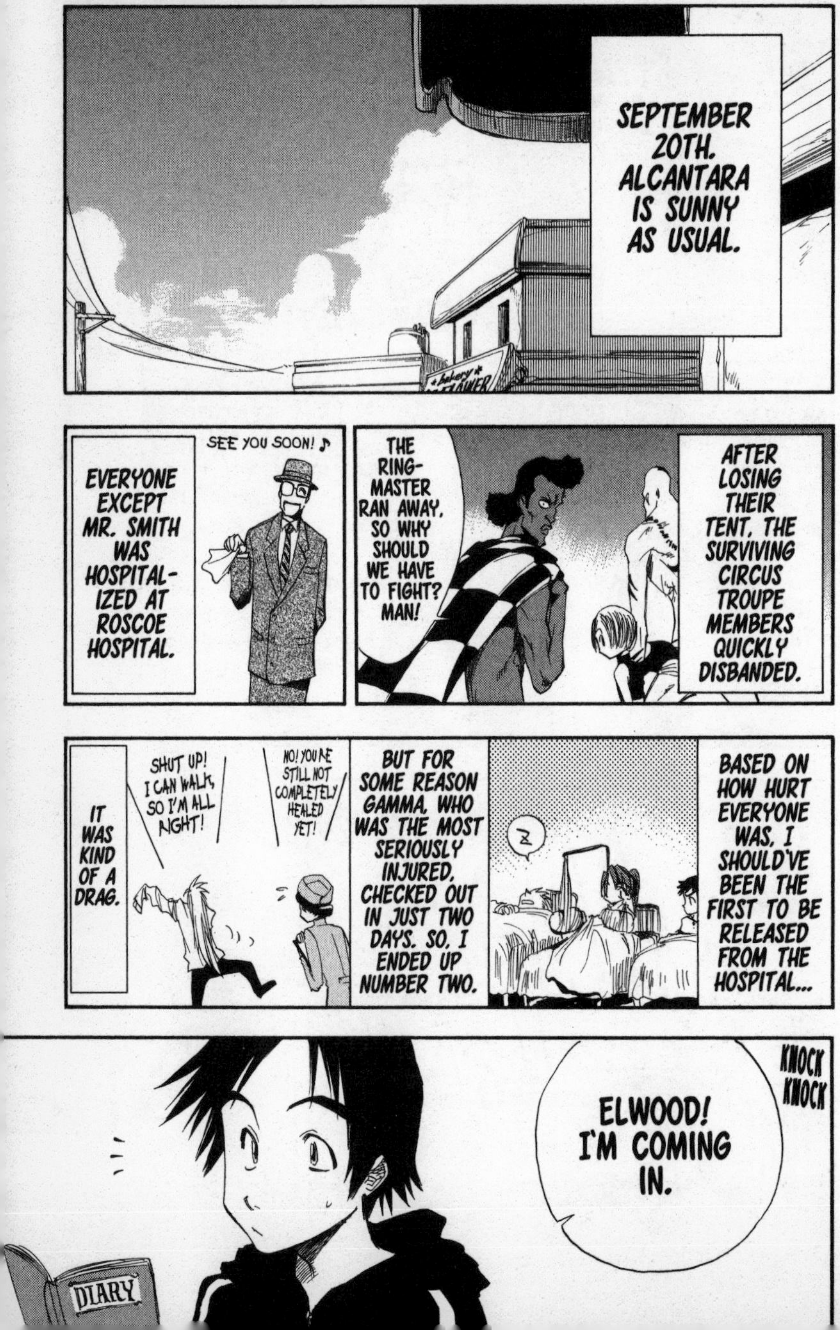

SEPTEMBER 20TH. ALCANTARA IS SUNNY AS USUAL.
AFTER LOSING THEIR TENT, THE SURVIVING CIRCUS TROUPE MEMBERS QUICKLY DISBANDED.
THE RINGMASTER RAN AWAY, SO WHY SHOULD WE HAVE TO FIGHT? MAN!
SEE YOU SOON! ♪
EVERYONE EXCEPT MR. SMITH WAS HOSPITALIZED AT ROSCOE HOSPITAL.
BASED ON HOW HURT EVERYONE WAS, I SHOULD'VE BEEN THE FIRST TO BE RELEASED FROM THE HOSPITAL...
BUT FOR SOME REASON GAMMA, WHO WAS THE MOST SERIOUSLY INJURED, CHECKED OUT IN JUST TWO DAYS. SO, I ENDED UP NUMBER TWO.
NO! YOU'RE STILL NOT COMPLETELY HEALED YET!
SHUT UP! I CAN WALK, SO I'M ALL RIGHT!
IT WAS KIND OF A DRAG.
KNOCK KNOCK
ELWOOD! I'M COMING IN.
DIARY

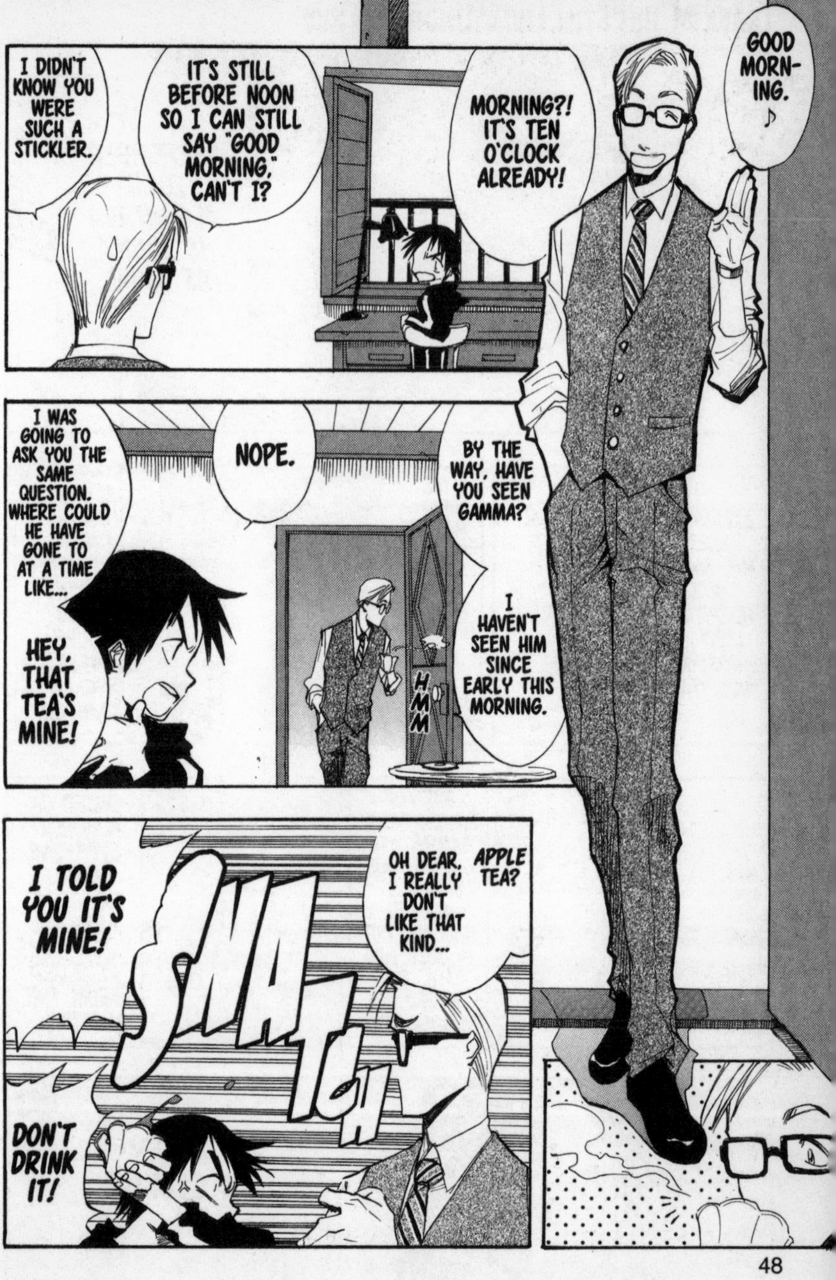
GOOD MORNING. ♪
MORNING?! IT'S TEN O'CLOCK ALREADY!
IT'S STILL BEFORE NOON SO I CAN STILL SAY "GOOD MORNING," CAN'T I?
I DIDN'T KNOW YOU WERE SUCH A STICKLER.
BY THE WAY, HAVE YOU SEEN GAMMA?
I HAVEN'T SEEN HIM SINCE EARLY THIS MORNING.
HMM
NOPE.
I WAS GOING TO ASK YOU THE SAME QUESTION. WHERE COULD HE HAVE GONE TO AT A TIME LIKE...
HEY, THAT TEA'S MINE!
APPLE TEA?
OH DEAR, I REALLY DON'T LIKE THAT KIND...
SNATCH
I TOLD YOU IT'S MINE!
DON'T DRINK IT!

READ THIS WAY

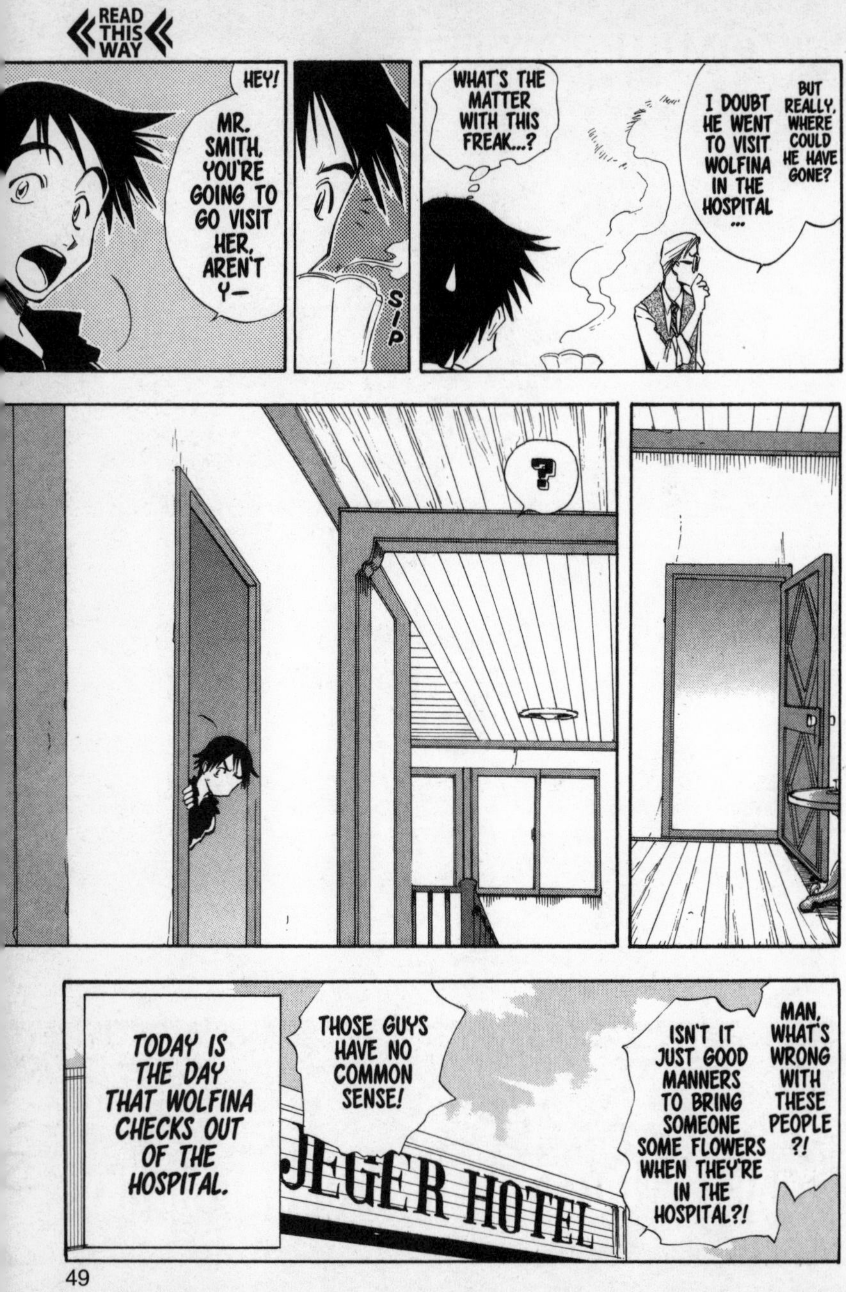
BUT REALLY, WHERE COULD HE HAVE GONE?
I DOUBT HE WENT TO VISIT WOLFINA IN THE HOSPITAL...
WHAT'S THE MATTER WITH THIS FREAK...?
SIP
HEY!
MR. SMITH, YOU'RE GOING TO GO VISIT HER, AREN'T Y—
?
MAN, WHAT'S WRONG WITH THESE PEOPLE?!
ISN'T IT JUST GOOD MANNERS TO BRING SOMEONE SOME FLOWERS WHEN THEY'RE IN THE HOSPITAL?!
THOSE GUYS HAVE NO COMMON SENSE!
JEGER HOTEL
TODAY IS THE DAY THAT WOLFINA CHECKS OUT OF THE HOSPITAL.

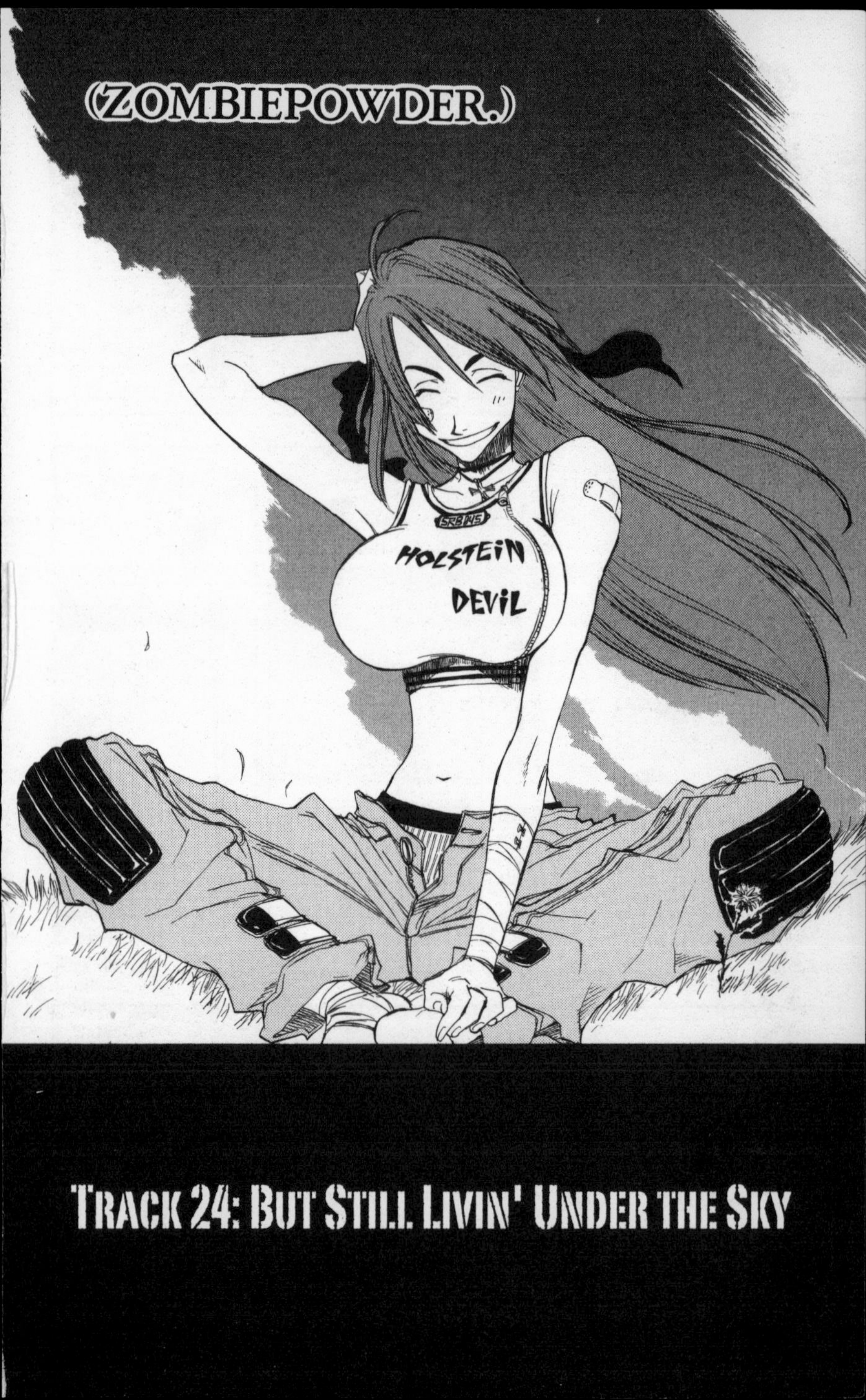
(ZOMBIEPOWDER.)
HOLSTEIN
DEVIL

TRACK 24: BUT STILL LIVIN' UNDER THE SKY

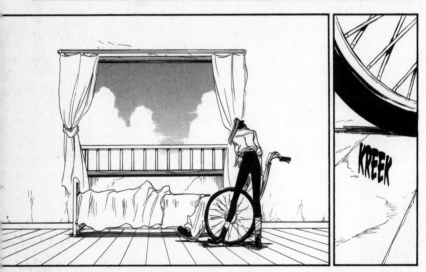

KREEK

HOW'S YOUR NEW CHAIR, EMILIO?

DO YOU LIKE IT?

DOCTOR ...

...ARE YOU LEAVING ALREADY?

CONSIDER IT MY PARTING GIFT. I'M SORRY IT'S NOT MORE.

...

OF COURSE. TAKE IT.

UM...THANK YOU SO MUCH FOR THE WHEEL-CHAIR!

ARE YOU REALLY SURE WE CAN HAVE THIS...?

BUT FOR EMILIO, IT WAS A VERY LONG TIME...

IT WENT BY FAST FOR ME...

IT'S BEEN TWO YEARS SINCE YOU CAME TO THIS TOWN.

SEEMS LIKE JUST YESTER-DAY...

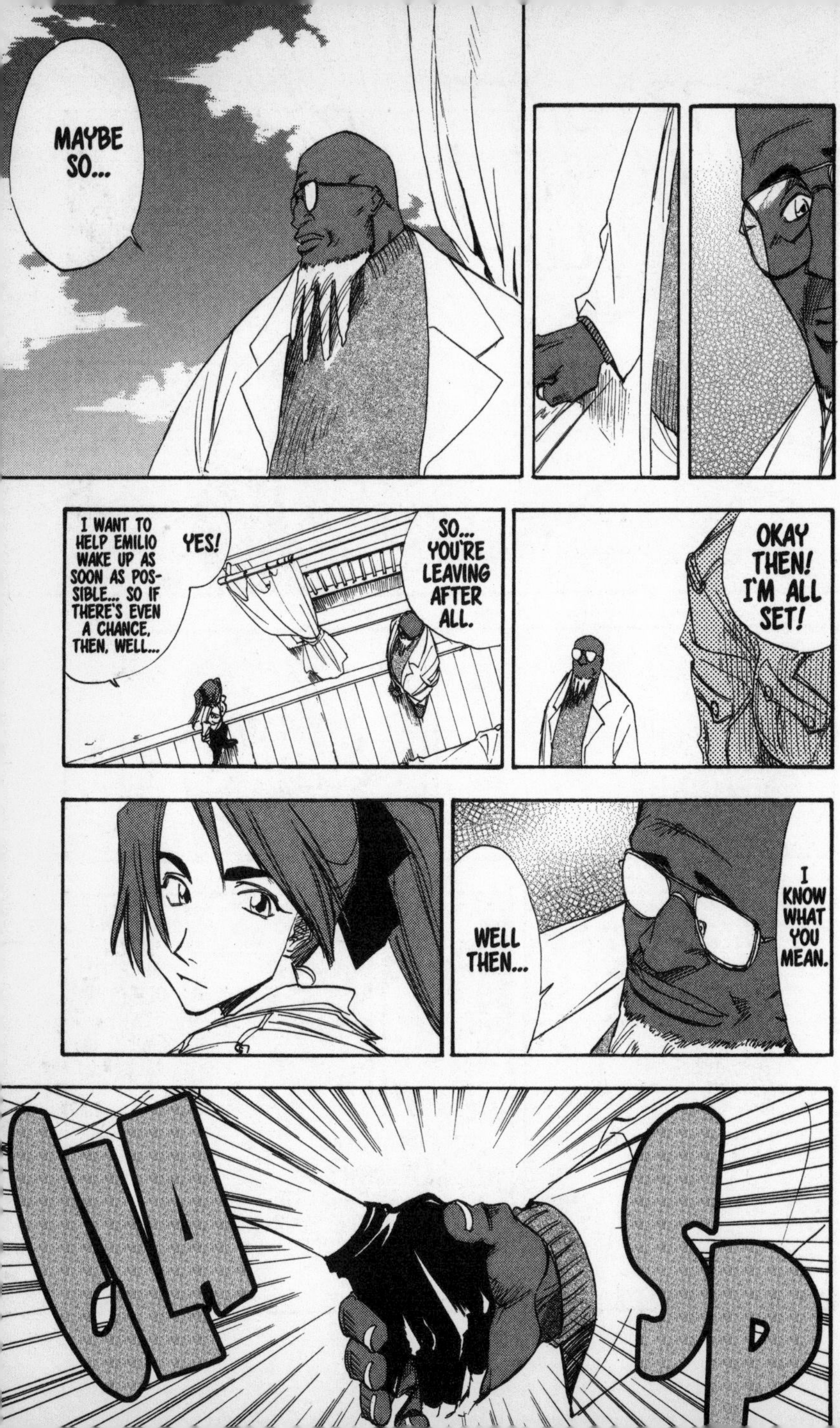
MAYBE SO...
OKAY THEN! I'M ALL SET!
SO... YOU'RE LEAVING AFTER ALL.
YES!
I WANT TO HELP EMILIO WAKE UP AS SOON AS POS-SIBLE... SO IF THERE'S EVEN A CHANCE, THEN, WELL...
I KNOW WHAT YOU MEAN.
WELL THEN...
CLA SP

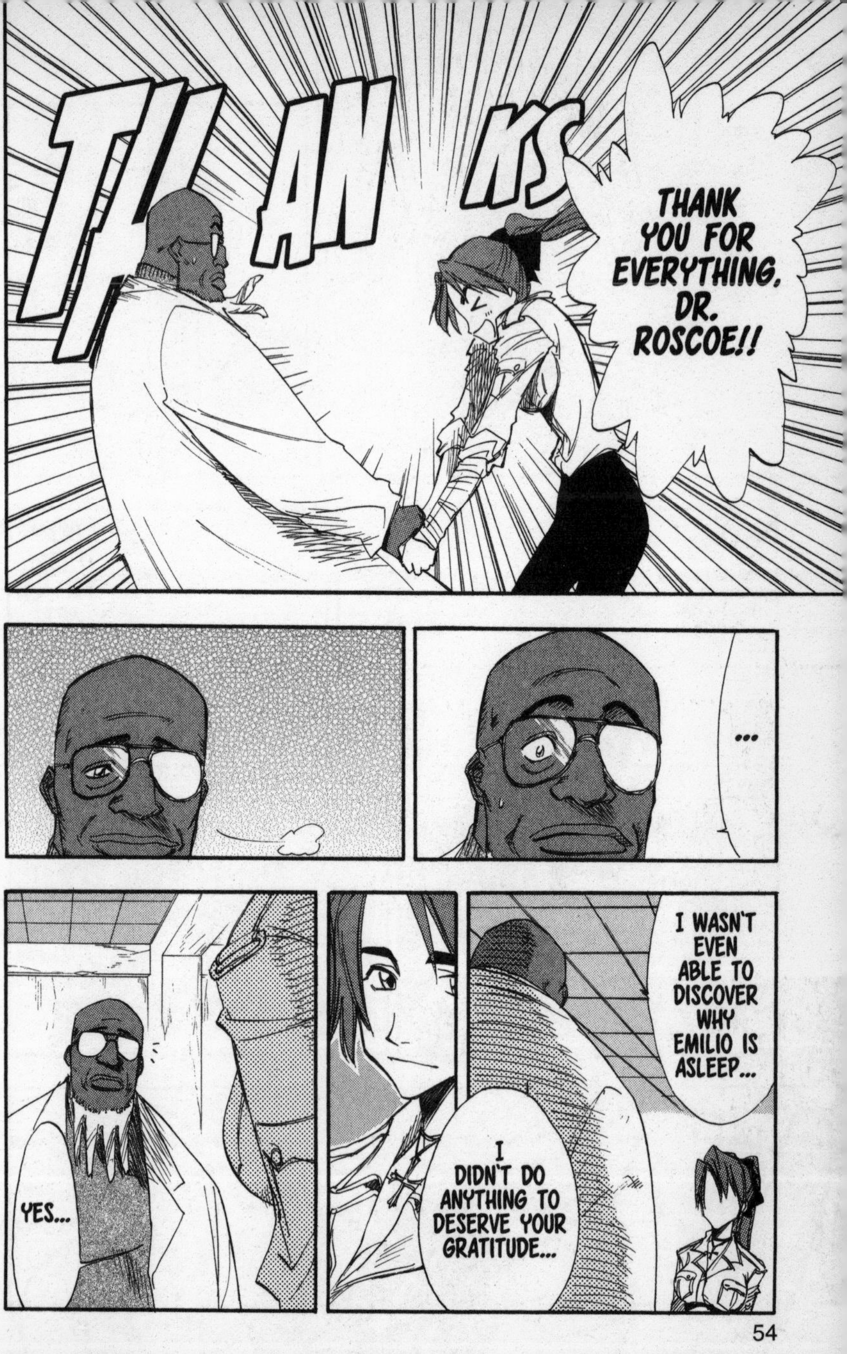
THANKS
THANK YOU FOR EVERYTHING, DR. ROSCOE!!
...
I WASN'T EVEN ABLE TO DISCOVER WHY EMILIO IS ASLEEP...
I DIDN'T DO ANYTHING TO DESERVE YOUR GRATITUDE...
YES...

THAT'S WHY...

I'M THANK-ING YOU.

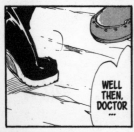

WELL THEN, DOCTOR ...

HUH ...?

DID YOU SAY SOME-THING?

JUST ONE MORE...

WOLFINA !

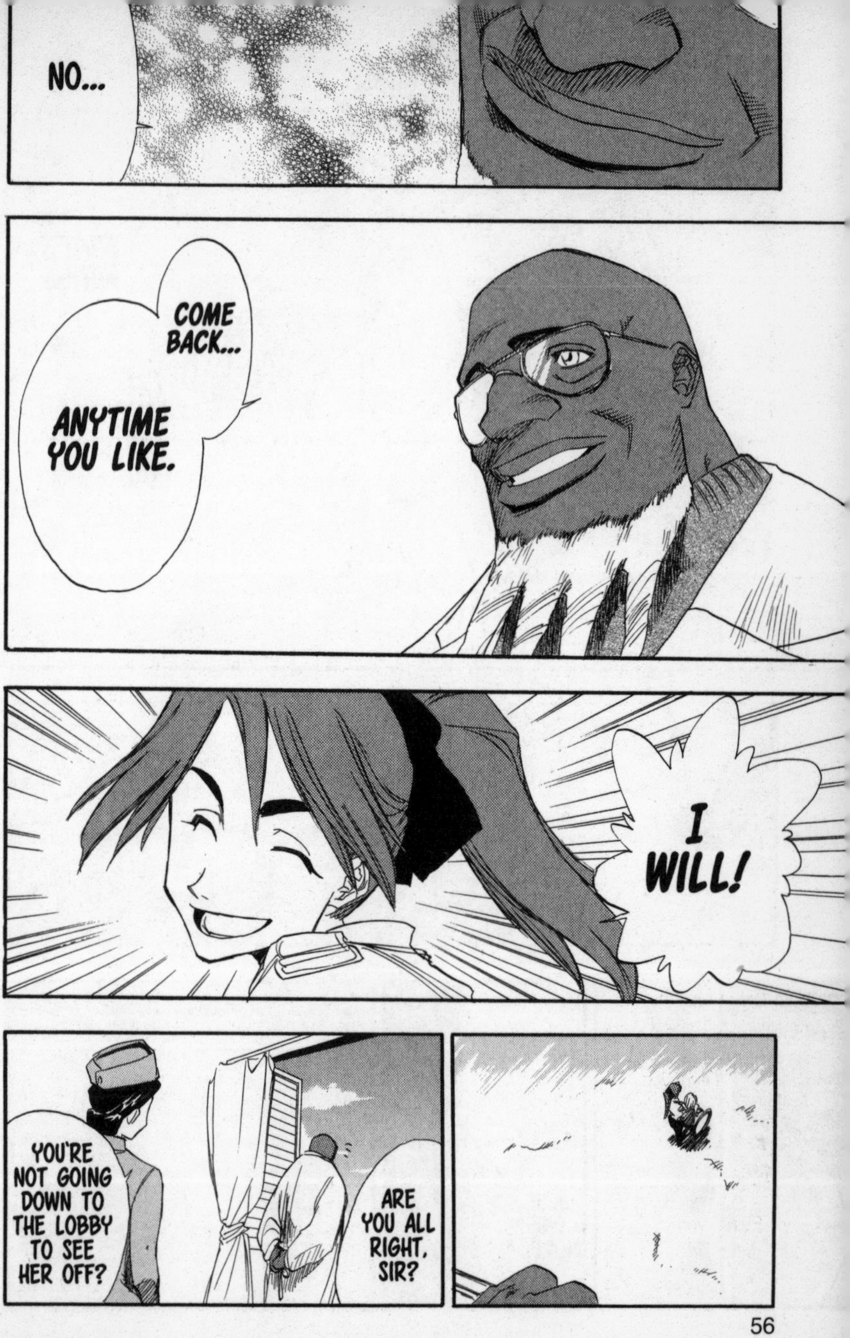
NO...
COME BACK...
ANYTIME YOU LIKE.
I WILL!
ARE YOU ALL RIGHT, SIR?
YOU'RE NOT GOING DOWN TO THE LOBBY TO SEE HER OFF?

READ THIS WAY

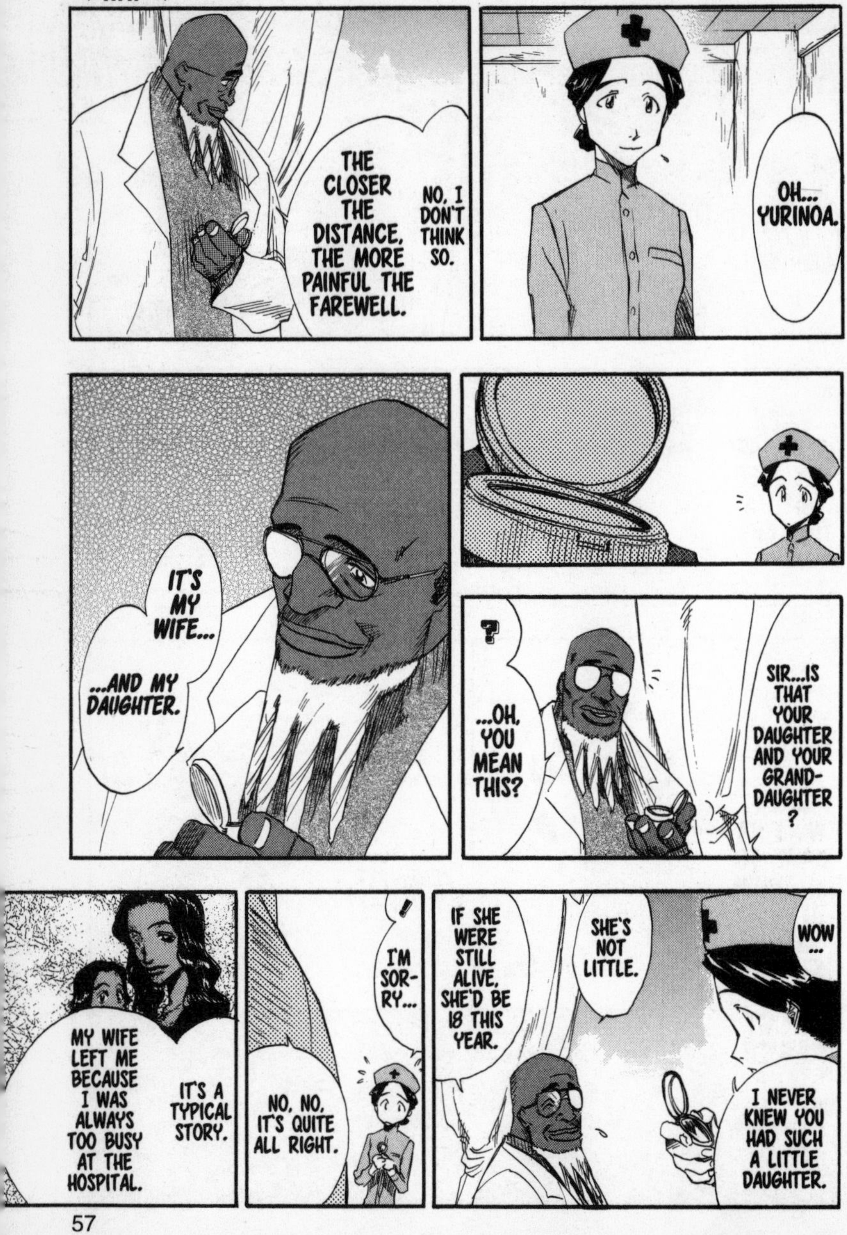
OH... YURINOA.
NO, I DON'T THINK SO.
THE CLOSER THE DISTANCE, THE MORE PAINFUL THE FAREWELL.
SIR...IS THAT YOUR DAUGHTER AND YOUR GRAND-DAUGHTER?
?
...OH, YOU MEAN THIS?
IT'S MY WIFE...
...AND MY DAUGHTER.
WOW...
I NEVER KNEW YOU HAD SUCH A LITTLE DAUGHTER.
SHE'S NOT LITTLE.
IF SHE WERE STILL ALIVE, SHE'D BE 18 THIS YEAR.
!
I'M SOR-RY...
NO, NO, IT'S QUITE ALL RIGHT.
IT'S A TYPICAL STORY.
MY WIFE LEFT ME BECAUSE I WAS ALWAYS TOO BUSY AT THE HOSPITAL.

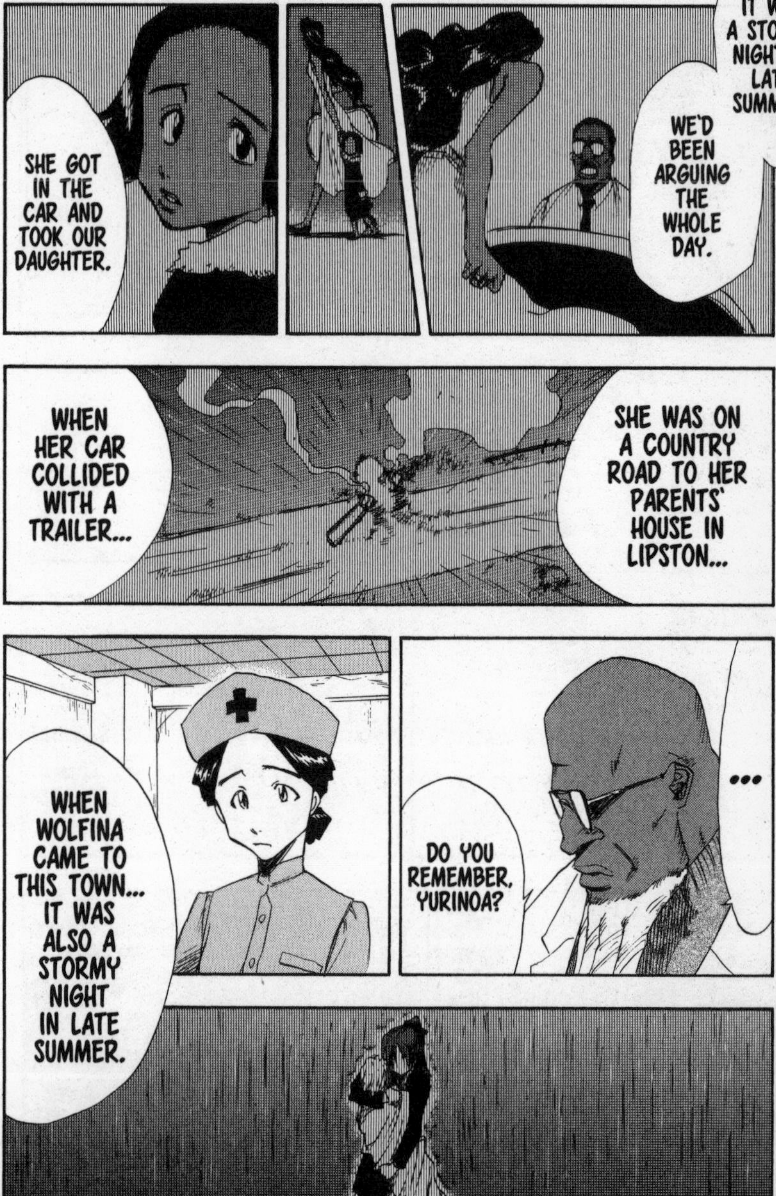
IT WAS A STORMY NIGHT IN LATE SUMMER.
WE'D BEEN ARGUING THE WHOLE DAY.
SHE GOT IN THE CAR AND TOOK OUR DAUGHTER.
SHE WAS ON A COUNTRY ROAD TO HER PARENTS' HOUSE IN LIPSTON...
WHEN HER CAR COLLIDED WITH A TRAILER...
...
DO YOU REMEMBER, YURINOA?
WHEN WOLFINA CAME TO THIS TOWN... IT WAS ALSO A STORMY NIGHT IN LATE SUMMER.

READ THIS WAY

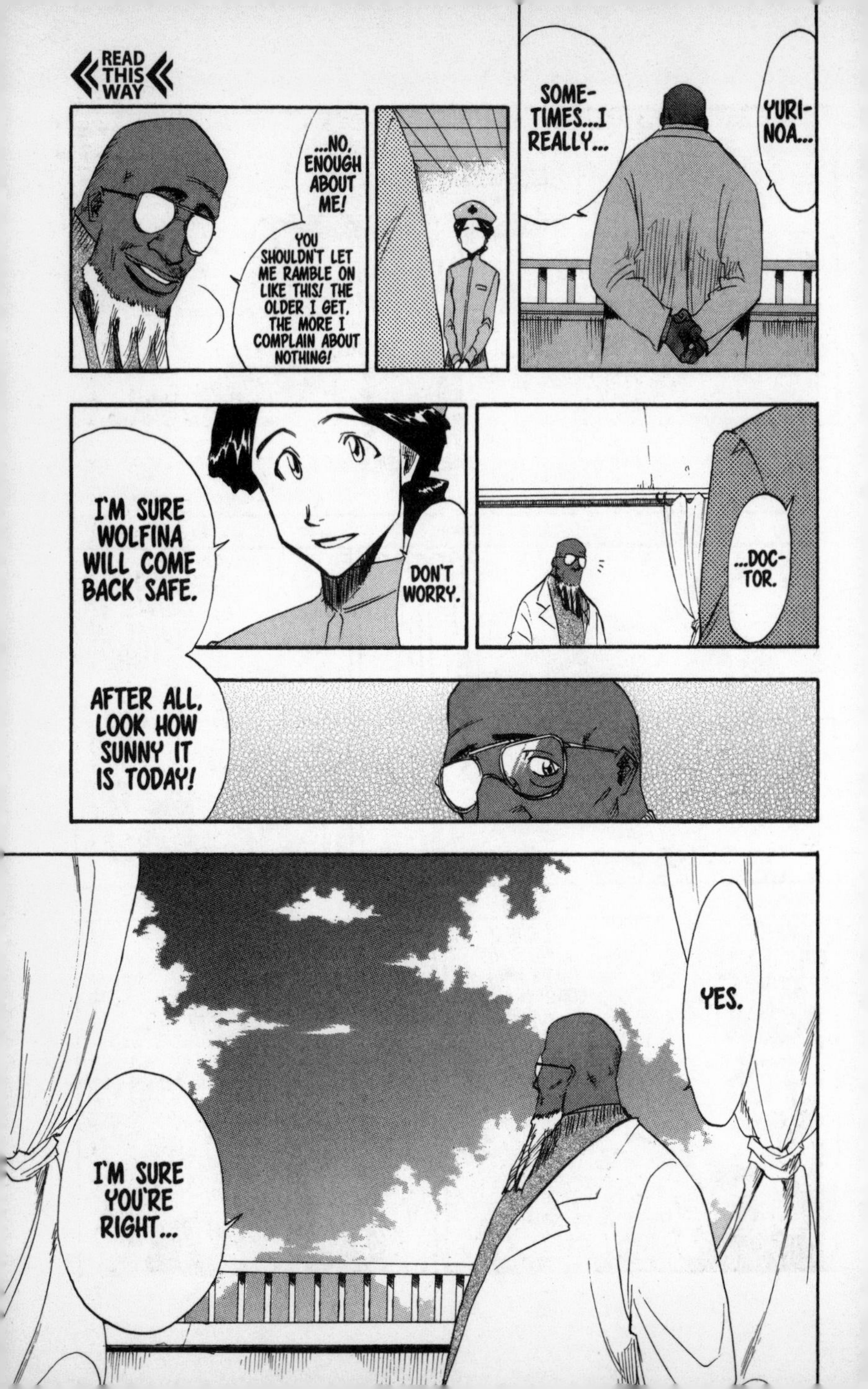
YURI-NOA...
SOME-TIMES...I REALLY...
...NO, ENOUGH ABOUT ME!
YOU SHOULDN'T LET ME RAMBLE ON LIKE THIS! THE OLDER I GET, THE MORE I COMPLAIN ABOUT NOTHING!
...DOC-TOR.
DON'T WORRY.
I'M SURE WOLFINA WILL COME BACK SAFE.
AFTER ALL, LOOK HOW SUNNY IT IS TODAY!
YES.
I'M SURE YOU'RE RIGHT...

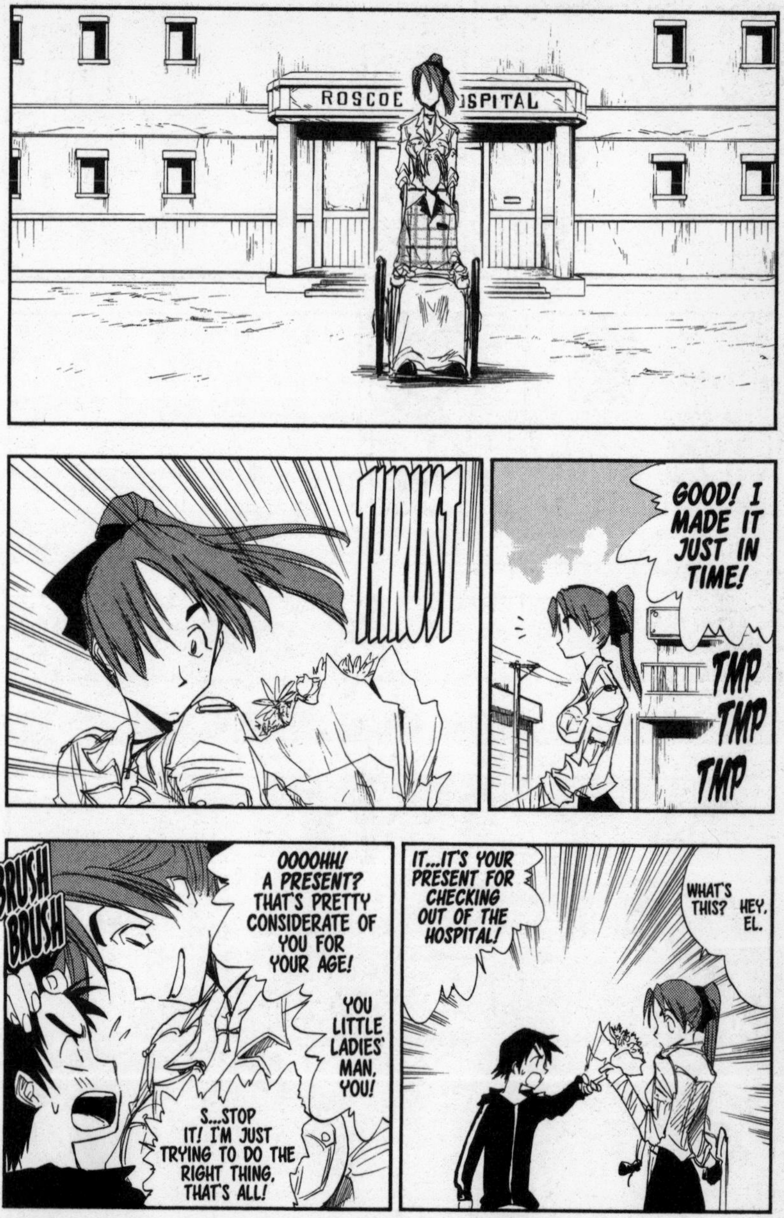
ROSCOE HOSPITAL
GOOD! I MADE IT JUST IN TIME!
TMP TMP TMP
THRUST
WHAT'S THIS? HEY, EL.
IT...IT'S YOUR PRESENT FOR CHECKING OUT OF THE HOSPITAL!
OOOOHH! A PRESENT? THAT'S PRETTY CONSIDERATE OF YOU FOR YOUR AGE!
YOU LITTLE LADIES' MAN, YOU!
BRUSH BRUSH
S...STOP IT! I'M JUST TRYING TO DO THE RIGHT THING, THAT'S ALL!

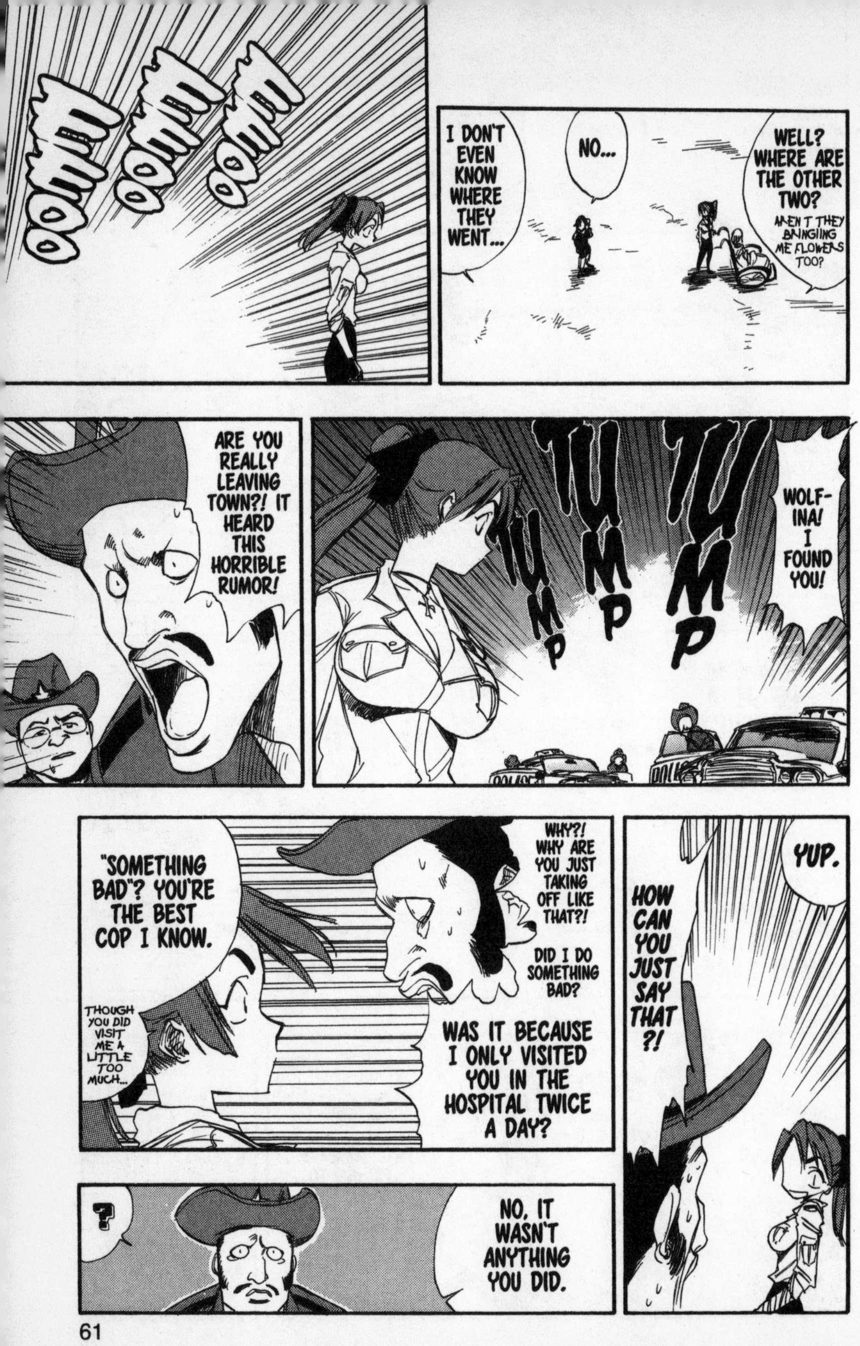
WELL? WHERE ARE THE OTHER TWO?
AREN'T THEY BRINGING ME FLOWERS TOO?
NO...
I DON'T EVEN KNOW WHERE THEY WENT...
WOLF-INA! I FOUND YOU!
TUMP
TUMP
TUMP
ARE YOU REALLY LEAVING TOWN?! IT HEARD THIS HORRIBLE RUMOR!
YUP.
HOW CAN YOU JUST SAY THAT?!
WHY?! WHY ARE YOU JUST TAKING OFF LIKE THAT?!
DID I DO SOMETHING BAD?
WAS IT BECAUSE I ONLY VISITED YOU IN THE HOSPITAL TWICE A DAY?
"SOMETHING BAD"? YOU'RE THE BEST COP I KNOW.
THOUGH YOU DID VISIT ME A LITTLE TOO MUCH...
NO, IT WASN'T ANYTHING YOU DID.
?

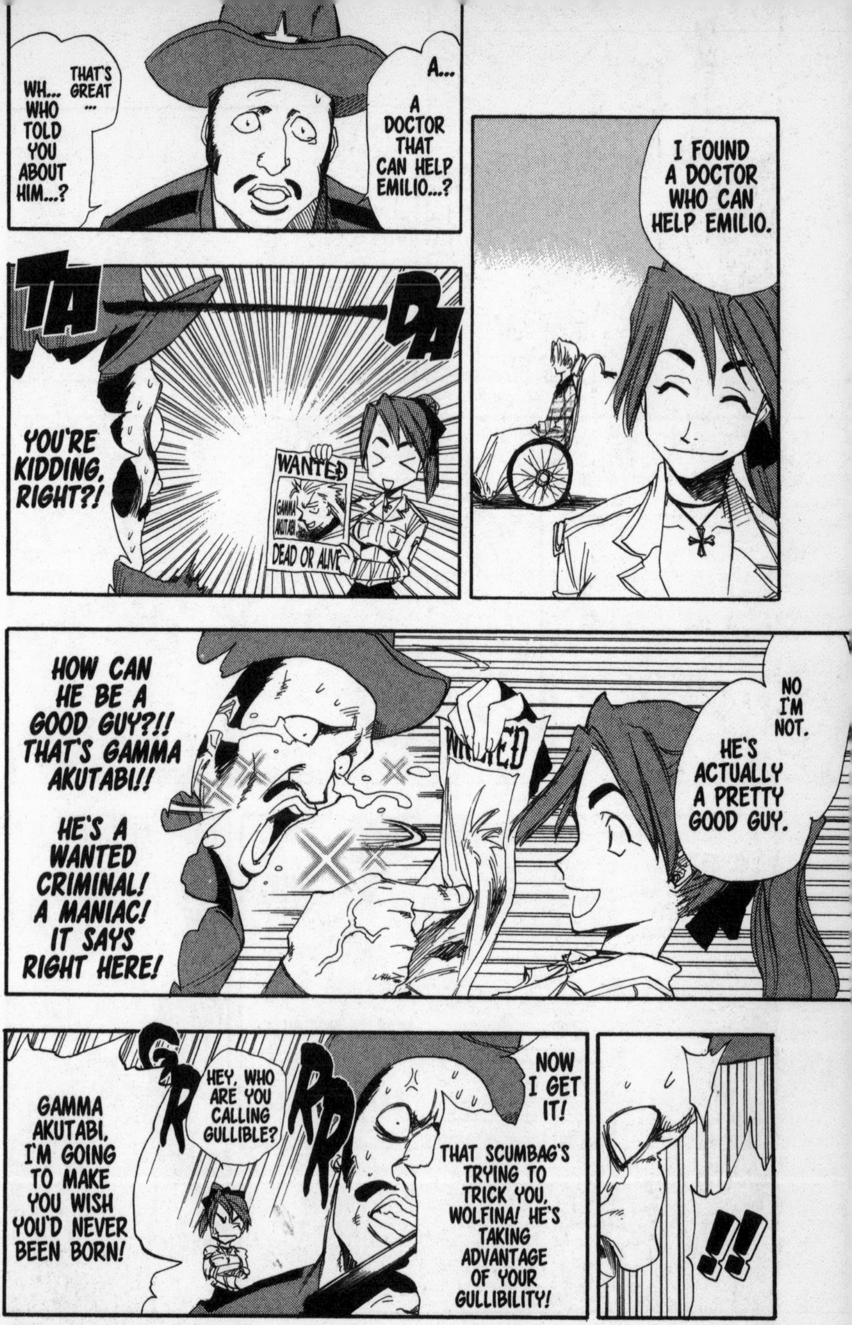
I FOUND A DOCTOR WHO CAN HELP EMILIO.
A... A DOCTOR THAT CAN HELP EMILIO...?
THAT'S GREAT ...
WH... WHO TOLD YOU ABOUT HIM...?
TA DA
WANTED
GAMMA AKUTABI
DEAD OR ALIVE
YOU'RE KIDDING, RIGHT?!
NO I'M NOT.
HE'S ACTUALLY A PRETTY GOOD GUY.
WANTED
HOW CAN HE BE A GOOD GUY?!! THAT'S GAMMA AKUTABI!!
HE'S A WANTED CRIMINAL! A MANIAC! IT SAYS RIGHT HERE!
!!
NOW I GET IT!
THAT SCUMBAG'S TRYING TO TRICK YOU, WOLFINA! HE'S TAKING ADVANTAGE OF YOUR GULLIBILITY!
GRRR
HEY, WHO ARE YOU CALLING GULLIBLE?
GAMMA AKUTABI, I'M GOING TO MAKE YOU WISH YOU'D NEVER BEEN BORN!

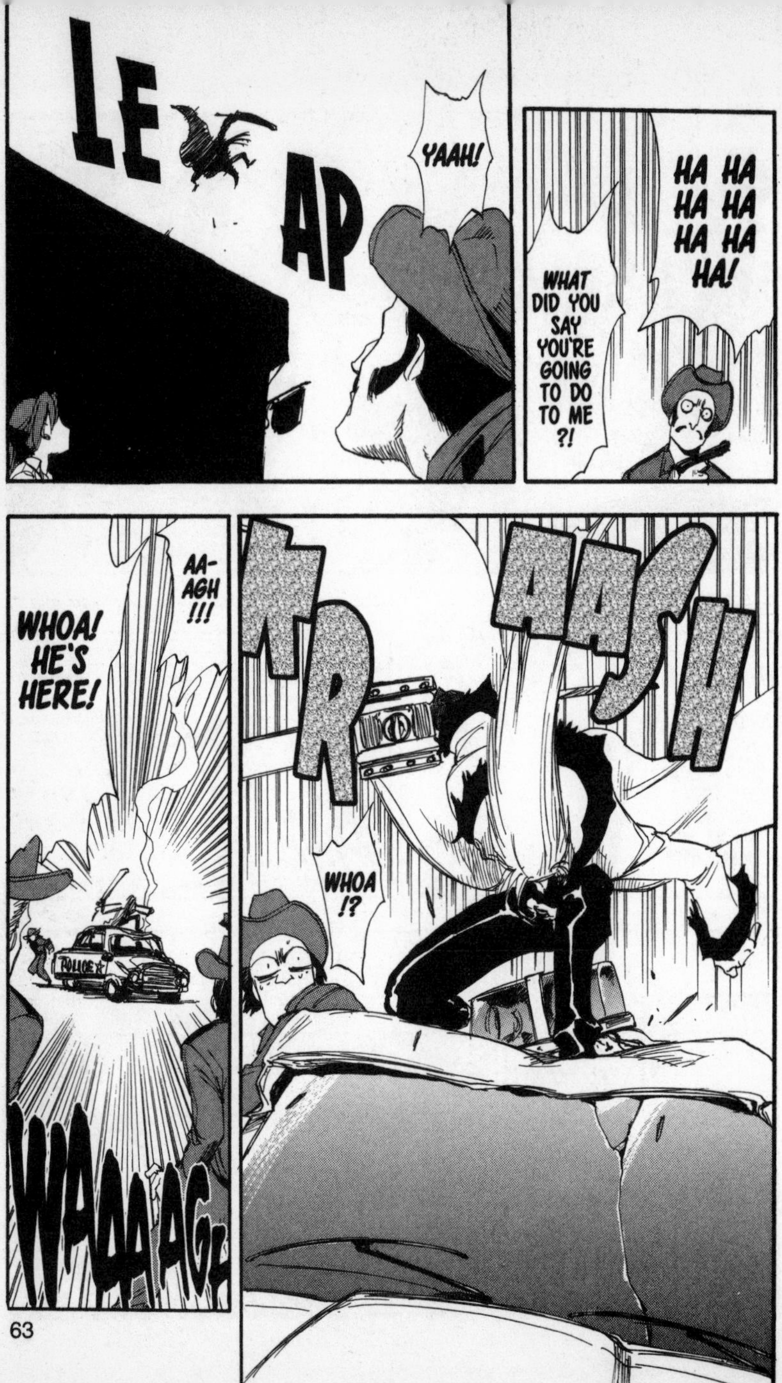
HA HA HA HA HA HA HA!
WHAT DID YOU SAY YOU'RE GOING TO DO TO ME ?!
YAAH!
LEAP
KR AASH
WHOA !?
AA-AGH !!!
WHOA! HE'S HERE!
WAAAAG

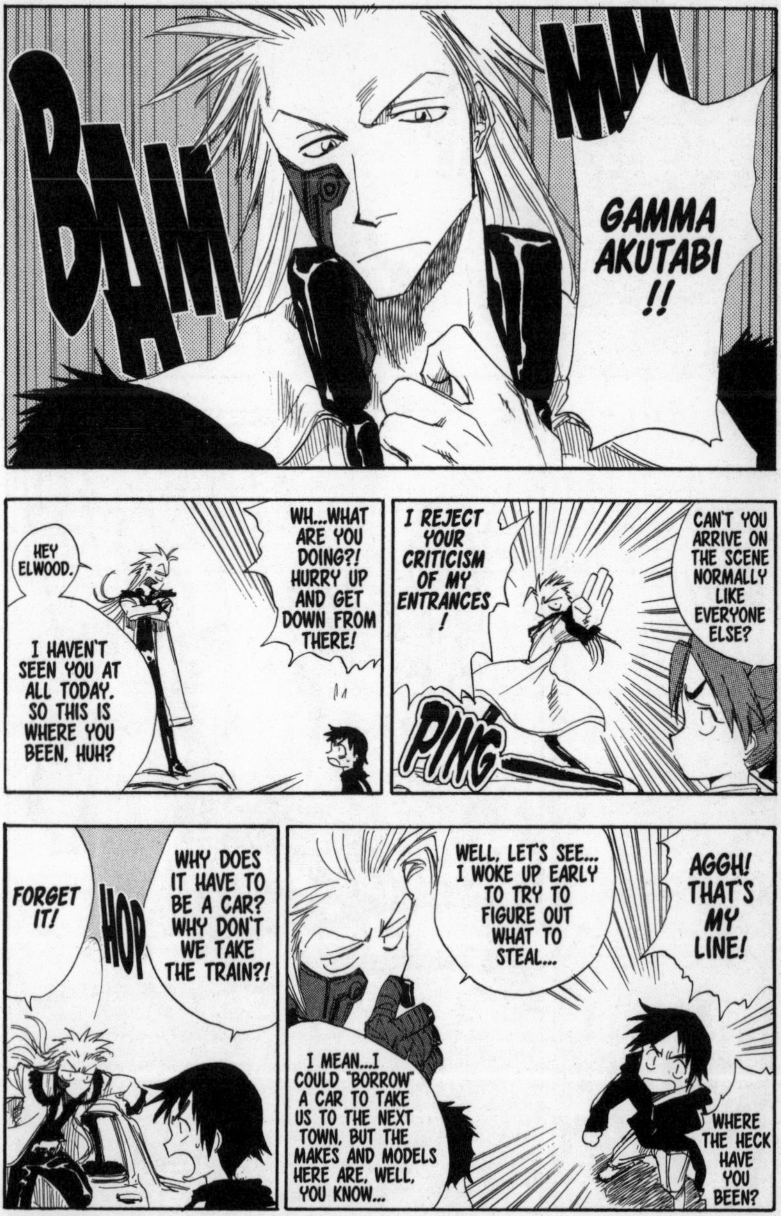
BAMMM
GAMMA AKUTABI !!
CAN'T YOU ARRIVE ON THE SCENE NORMALLY LIKE EVERYONE ELSE?
I REJECT YOUR CRITICISM OF MY ENTRANCES!
PING
WH...WHAT ARE YOU DOING?! HURRY UP AND GET DOWN FROM THERE!
HEY ELWOOD.
I HAVEN'T SEEN YOU AT ALL TODAY. SO THIS IS WHERE YOU BEEN, HUH?
AGGH! THAT'S MY LINE!
WHERE THE HECK HAVE YOU BEEN?
WELL, LET'S SEE... I WOKE UP EARLY TO TRY TO FIGURE OUT WHAT TO STEAL...
I MEAN...I COULD "BORROW" A CAR TO TAKE US TO THE NEXT TOWN, BUT THE MAKES AND MODELS HERE ARE, WELL, YOU KNOW...
WHY DOES IT HAVE TO BE A CAR? WHY DON'T WE TAKE THE TRAIN?!
HOP
FORGET IT!

READ THIS WAY

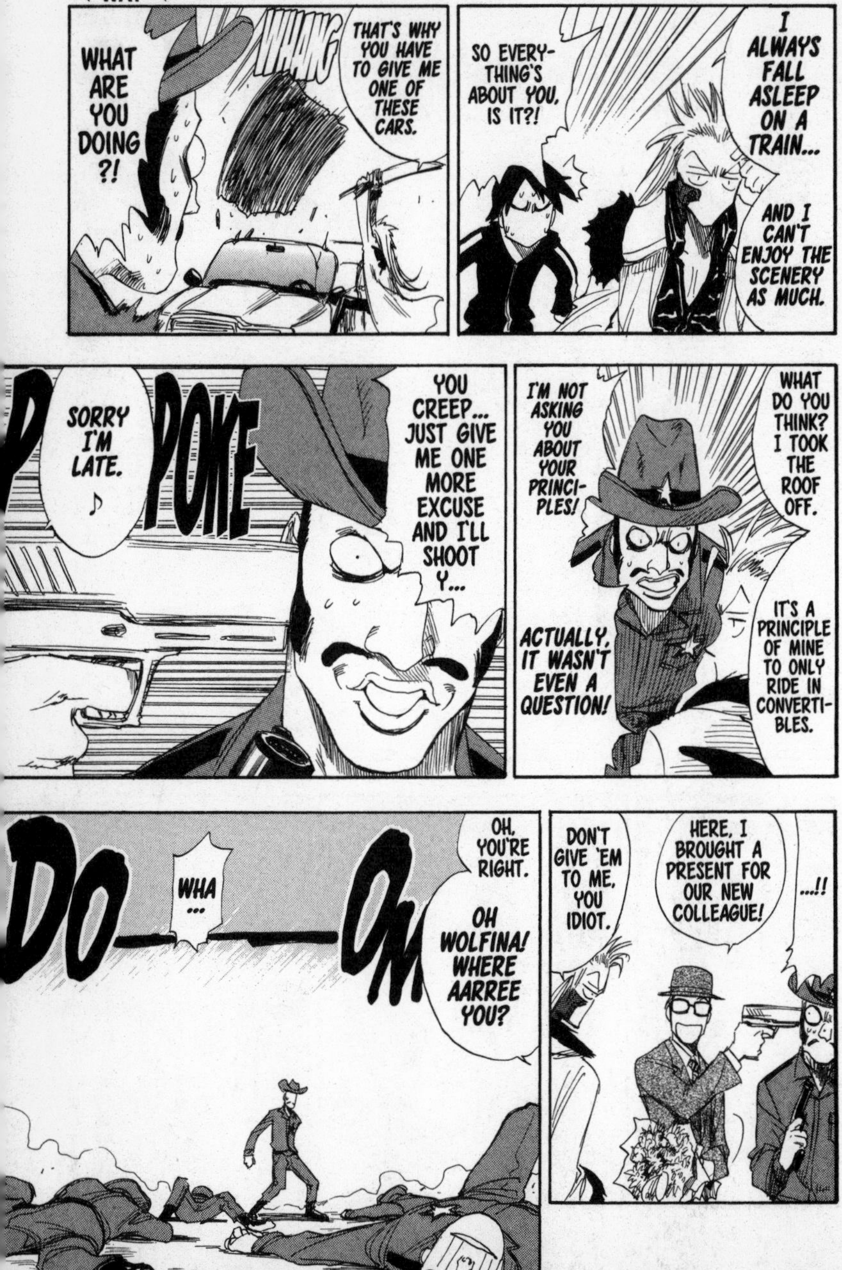
I ALWAYS FALL ASLEEP ON A TRAIN...
AND I CAN'T ENJOY THE SCENERY AS MUCH.
SO EVERY-THING'S ABOUT YOU, IS IT?!
THAT'S WHY YOU HAVE TO GIVE ME ONE OF THESE CARS.
WHANG
WHAT ARE YOU DOING?!
WHAT DO YOU THINK? I TOOK THE ROOF OFF.
I'M NOT ASKING YOU ABOUT YOUR PRINCI-PLES!
IT'S A PRINCIPLE OF MINE TO ONLY RIDE IN CONVERTI-BLES.
ACTUALLY, IT WASN'T EVEN A QUESTION!
YOU CREEP... JUST GIVE ME ONE MORE EXCUSE AND I'LL SHOOT Y...
POKE
SORRY I'M LATE. ♪
...!!
HERE, I BROUGHT A PRESENT FOR OUR NEW COLLEAGUE!
DON'T GIVE 'EM TO ME, YOU IDIOT.
OH, YOU'RE RIGHT.
OH WOLFINA! WHERE AARREE YOU?
WHA...
DO—

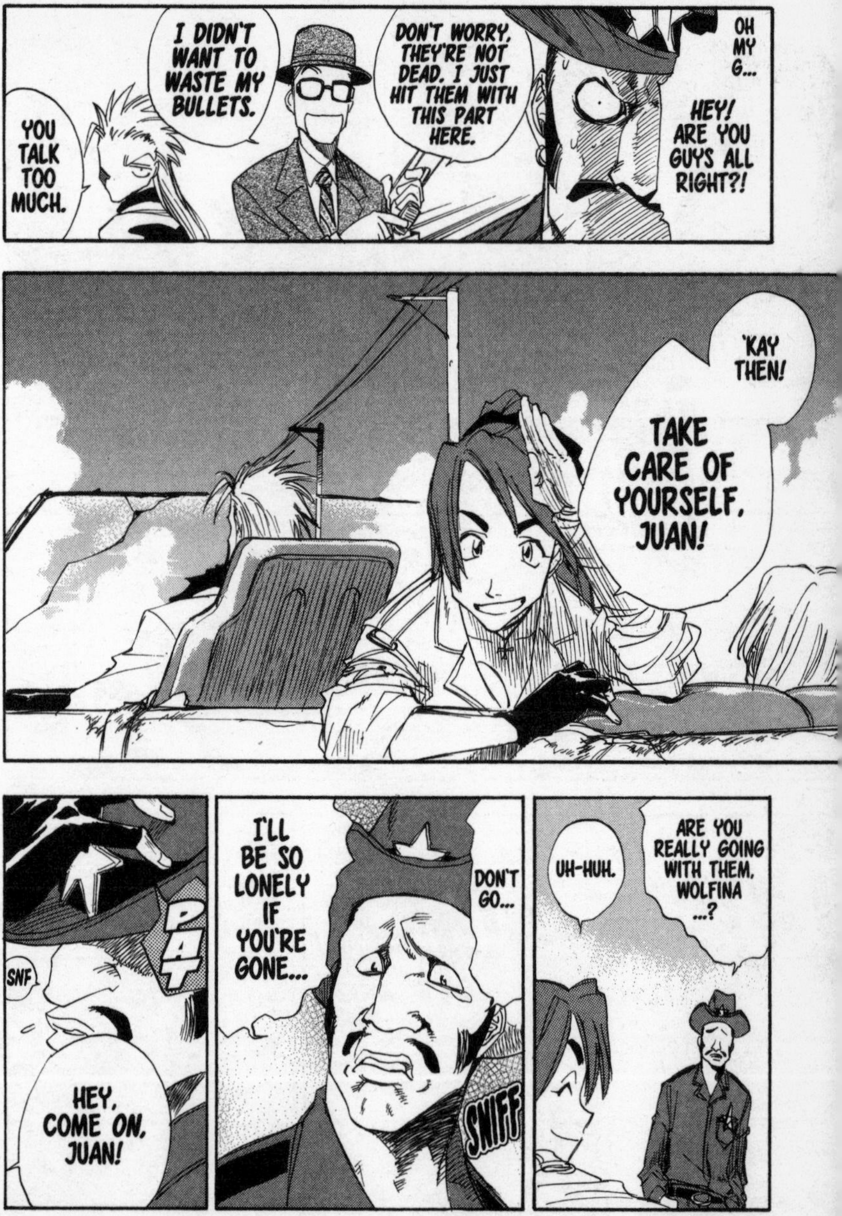
OH MY G...
HEY! ARE YOU GUYS ALL RIGHT?!
DON'T WORRY, THEY'RE NOT DEAD. I JUST HIT THEM WITH THIS PART HERE.
I DIDN'T WANT TO WASTE MY BULLETS.
YOU TALK TOO MUCH.
'KAY THEN!
TAKE CARE OF YOURSELF, JUAN!
ARE YOU REALLY GOING WITH THEM, WOLFINA ...?
UH-HUH.
DON'T GO...
I'LL BE SO LONELY IF YOU'RE GONE...
SNIFF
PAT
SNF
HEY, COME ON, JUAN!

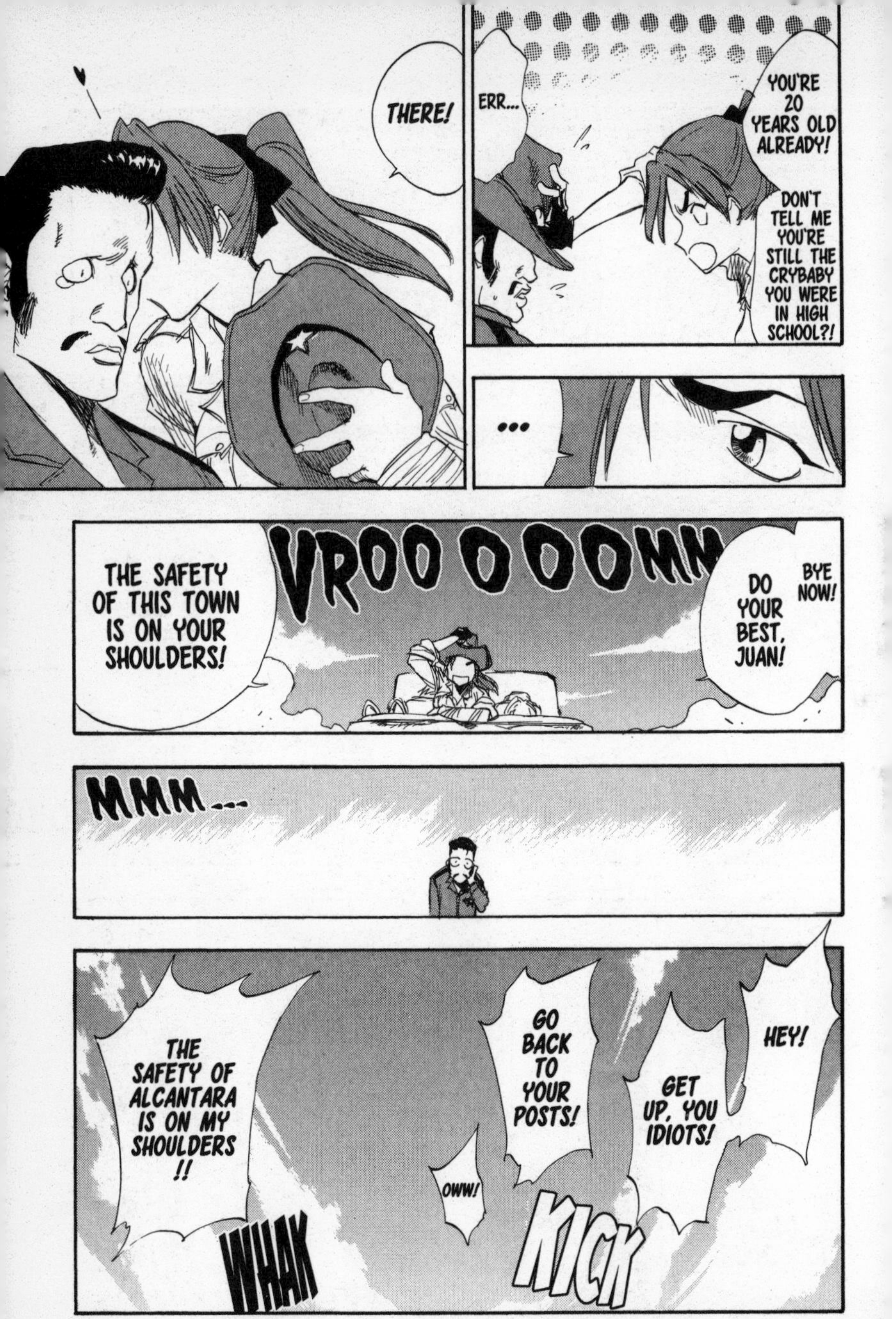
YOU'RE 20 YEARS OLD ALREADY!
DON'T TELL ME YOU'RE STILL THE CRYBABY YOU WERE IN HIGH SCHOOL?!
ERR...
...
THERE!
BYE NOW!
DO YOUR BEST, JUAN!
VROOOOOMN
THE SAFETY OF THIS TOWN IS ON YOUR SHOULDERS!
MMM...
HEY!
GET UP, YOU IDIOTS!
GO BACK TO YOUR POSTS!
KICK
OWW!
THE SAFETY OF ALCANTARA IS ON MY SHOULDERS!!
WHAK

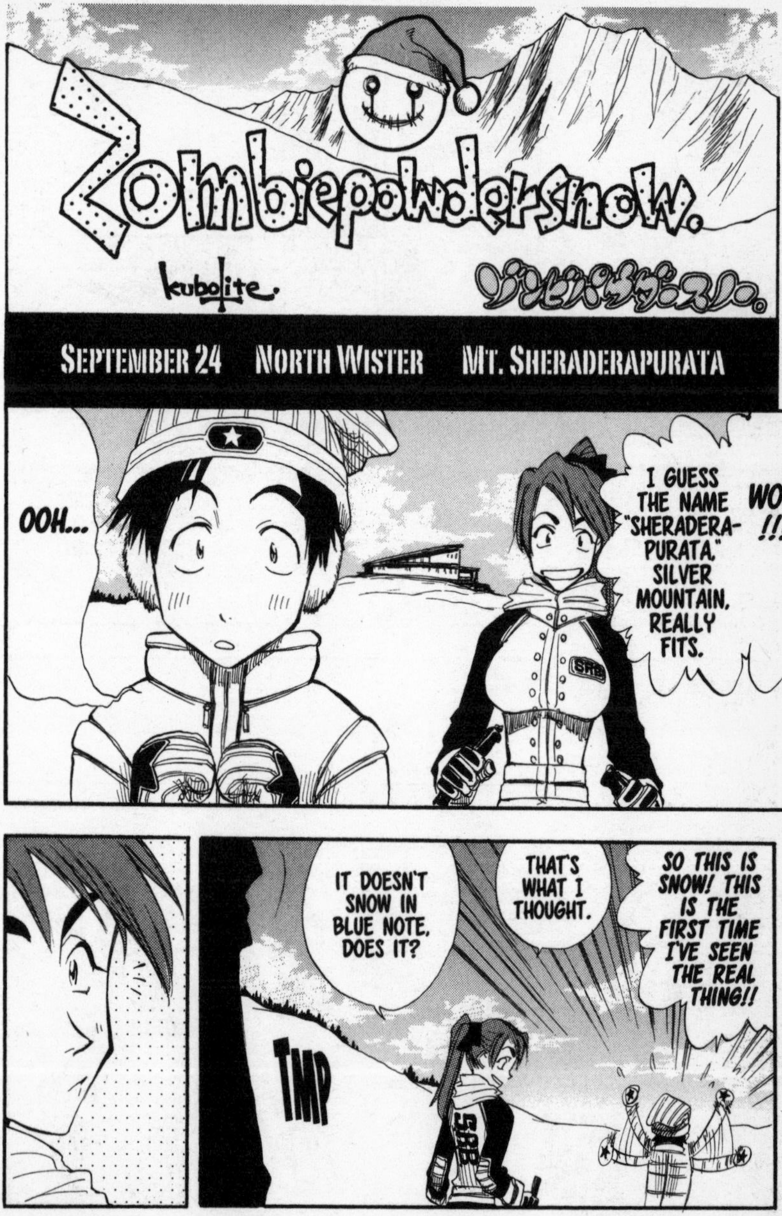
Zombiepowdersnow.
kubotite.
ゾンビパウダースノー。
SEPTEMBER 24 NORTH WISTER MT. SHERADERAPURATA
WOW!!!
I GUESS THE NAME "SHERADERA-PURATA," SILVER MOUNTAIN, REALLY FITS.
OOH...
SO THIS IS SNOW! THIS IS THE FIRST TIME I'VE SEEN THE REAL THING!!
THAT'S WHAT I THOUGHT.
IT DOESN'T SNOW IN BLUE NOTE, DOES IT?
TMP

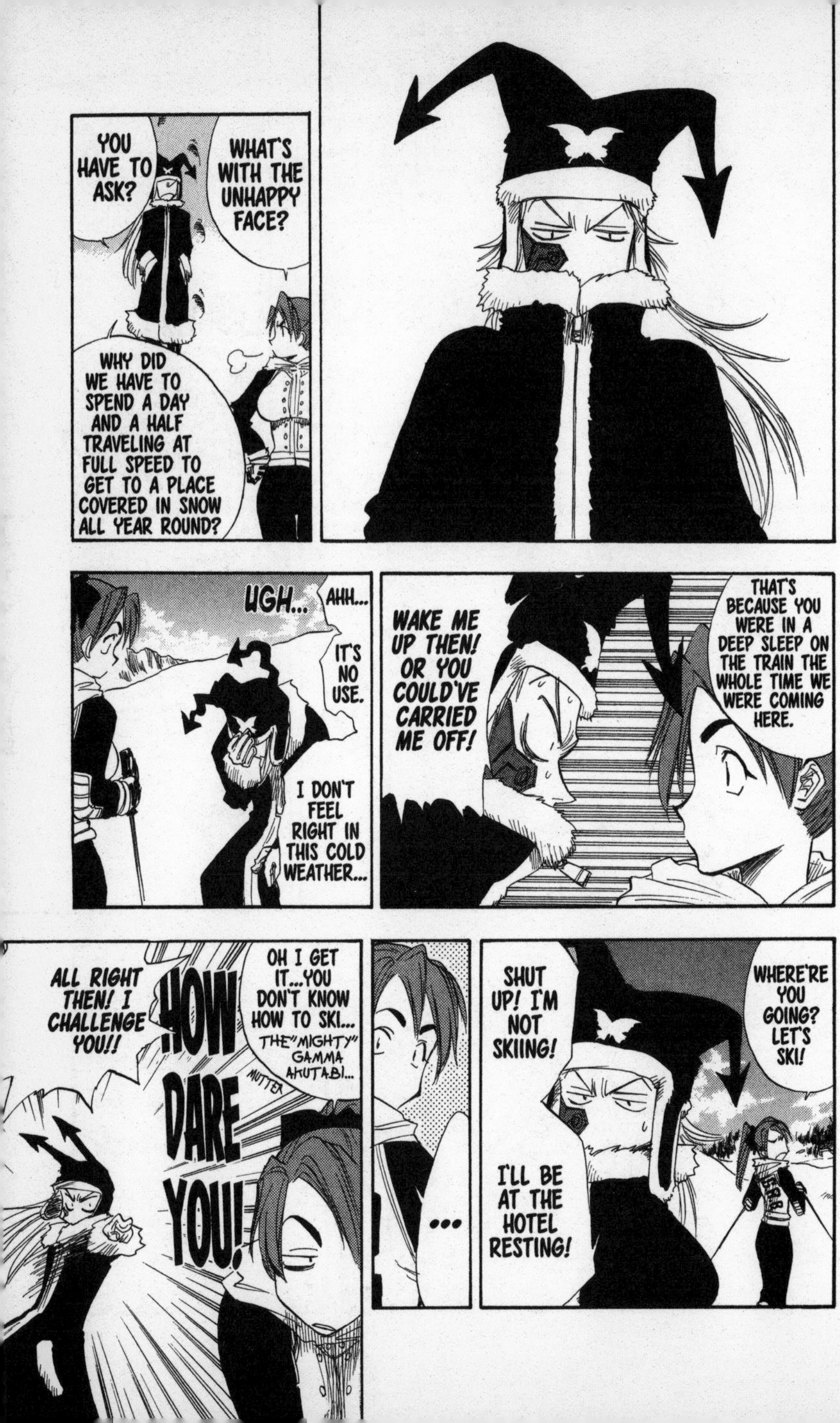
WHAT'S WITH THE UNHAPPY FACE?
YOU HAVE TO ASK?
WHY DID WE HAVE TO SPEND A DAY AND A HALF TRAVELING AT FULL SPEED TO GET TO A PLACE COVERED IN SNOW ALL YEAR ROUND?
THAT'S BECAUSE YOU WERE IN A DEEP SLEEP ON THE TRAIN THE WHOLE TIME WE WERE COMING HERE.
WAKE ME UP THEN! OR YOU COULD'VE CARRIED ME OFF!
AHH...
IT'S NO USE.
UGH...
I DON'T FEEL RIGHT IN THIS COLD WEATHER...
WHERE'RE YOU GOING? LET'S SKI!
SHUT UP! I'M NOT SKIING!
I'LL BE AT THE HOTEL RESTING!
...
OH I GET IT...YOU DON'T KNOW HOW TO SKI...
THE "MIGHTY" GAMMA AKUTABI...
MUTTER
HOW DARE YOU!
ALL RIGHT THEN! I CHALLENGE YOU!!

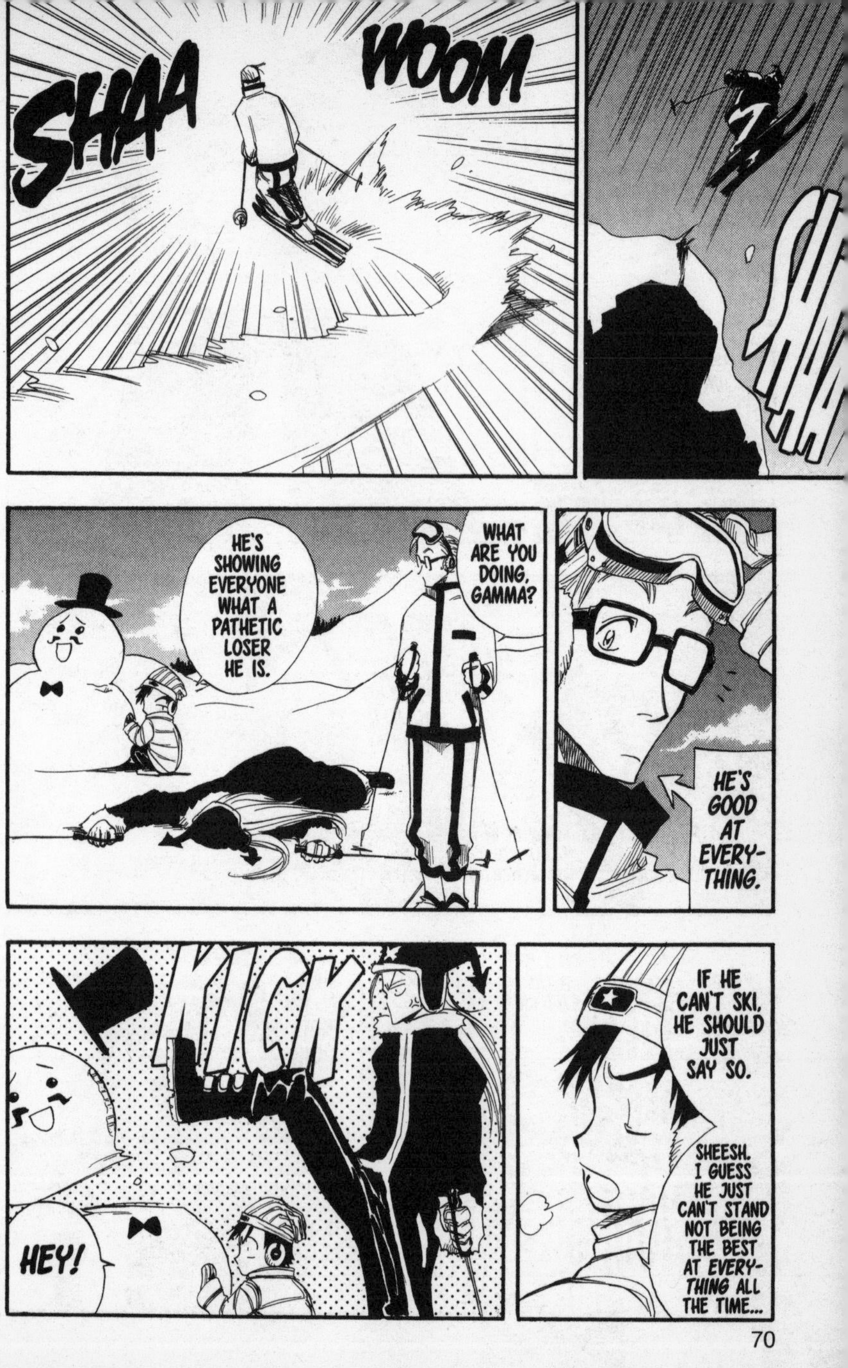
SHAA
SHAA
WOOM
HE'S GOOD AT EVERY-THING.
WHAT ARE YOU DOING, GAMMA?
HE'S SHOWING EVERYONE WHAT A PATHETIC LOSER HE IS.
IF HE CAN'T SKI, HE SHOULD JUST SAY SO.
SHEESH. I GUESS HE JUST CAN'T STAND NOT BEING THE BEST AT EVERY-THING ALL THE TIME...
KICK
HEY!

READ THIS WAY

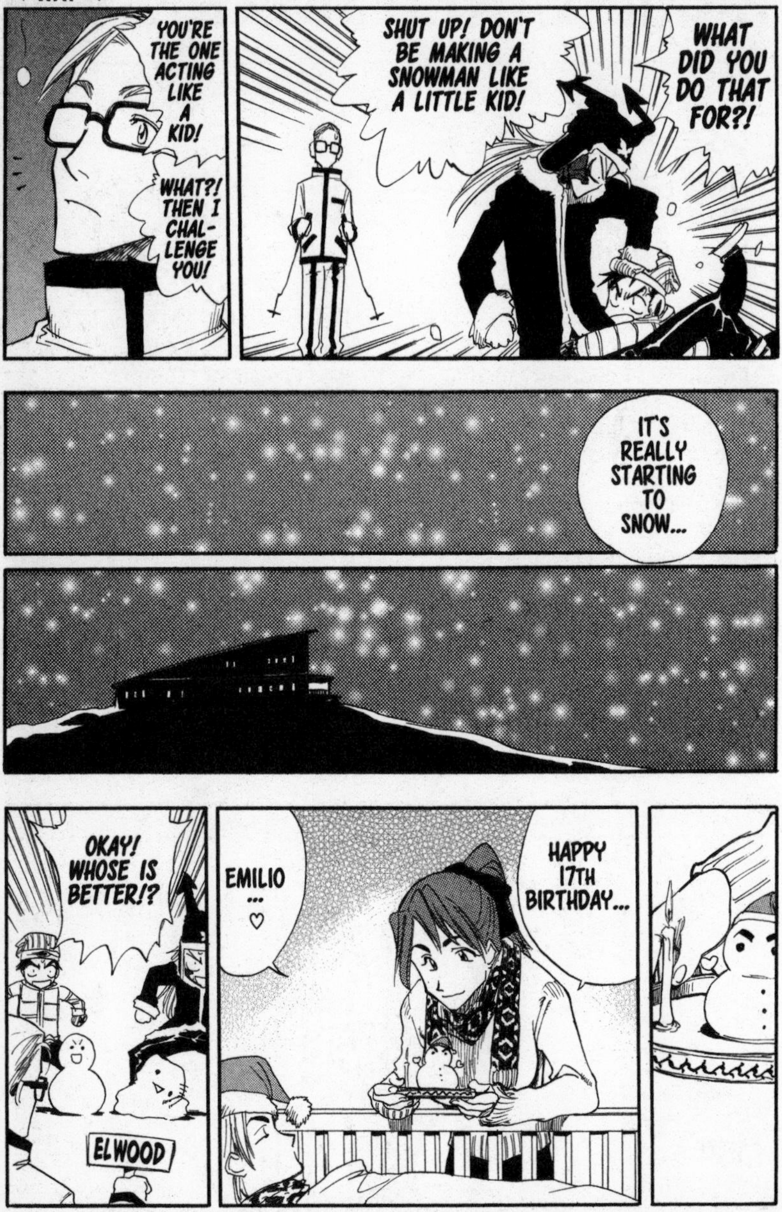
WHAT DID YOU DO THAT FOR?!
SHUT UP! DON'T BE MAKING A SNOWMAN LIKE A LITTLE KID!
YOU'RE THE ONE ACTING LIKE A KID!
WHAT?! THEN I CHAL-LENGE YOU!
IT'S REALLY STARTING TO SNOW...
HAPPY 17TH BIRTHDAY...
EMILIO ... ♡
OKAY! WHOSE IS BETTER!?
ELWOOD

B-side NAKED MONKEYS 16.

Geraldine Tickey & Ulrika Wismar

ジェラルディーン・ティッキー　ウルリカ・ウィスマール

Height: 166cm
Weight: 52kg
Date of Birth: 8/1
Age: 21
Blood Type: AB

Geraldine is an instructor for the Gemini Laboratory martial arts program as well as being in charge of managing the petty officers. She is the adjutant of "Gemini Force." Her hair color is a pale blonde and her eyes are blue with a slight sepia tint. Her favorite food is miso cutlet and her favorite cocktail is a Pina Colada. Her special abilities are playing the bass guitar and mental arithmetic. Things that she doesn't like include ghost stories and listening to Ulrika's poetry.

Height: 162cm
Weight: 46kg
Date of Birth: 1/19
Age: 24
Blood Type: AB

The black-haired, blue-eyed captain of "Gemini Force," the special combat unit of Gemini Laboratory. Ulrika is always in the company of Nazna and takes care of all her personal needs. She likes Marron Glacé, the skin shed by a Cicada, and reciting poetry. But she can't eat chocolate because she's allergic to it.

TRACK 25: BADFINGER/BITCHANGEL

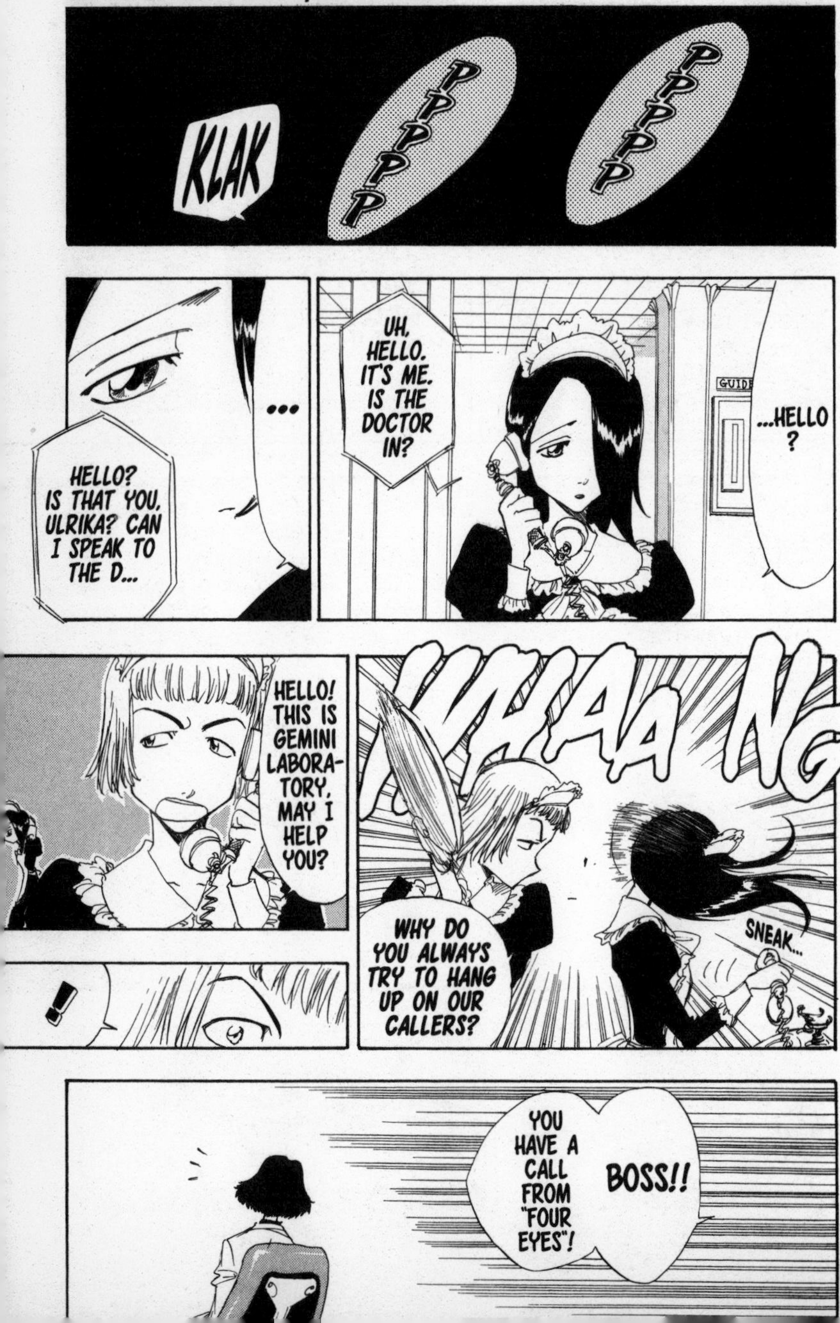
PPPPP
PPPPP
KLAK
...HELLO?
UH, HELLO. IT'S ME. IS THE DOCTOR IN?
GUIDE
...
HELLO? IS THAT YOU, ULRIKA? CAN I SPEAK TO THE D...
WHAANG
SNEAK...
WHY DO YOU ALWAYS TRY TO HANG UP ON OUR CALLERS?
HELLO! THIS IS GEMINI LABORATORY, MAY I HELP YOU?
!
BOSS!!
YOU HAVE A CALL FROM "FOUR EYES"!

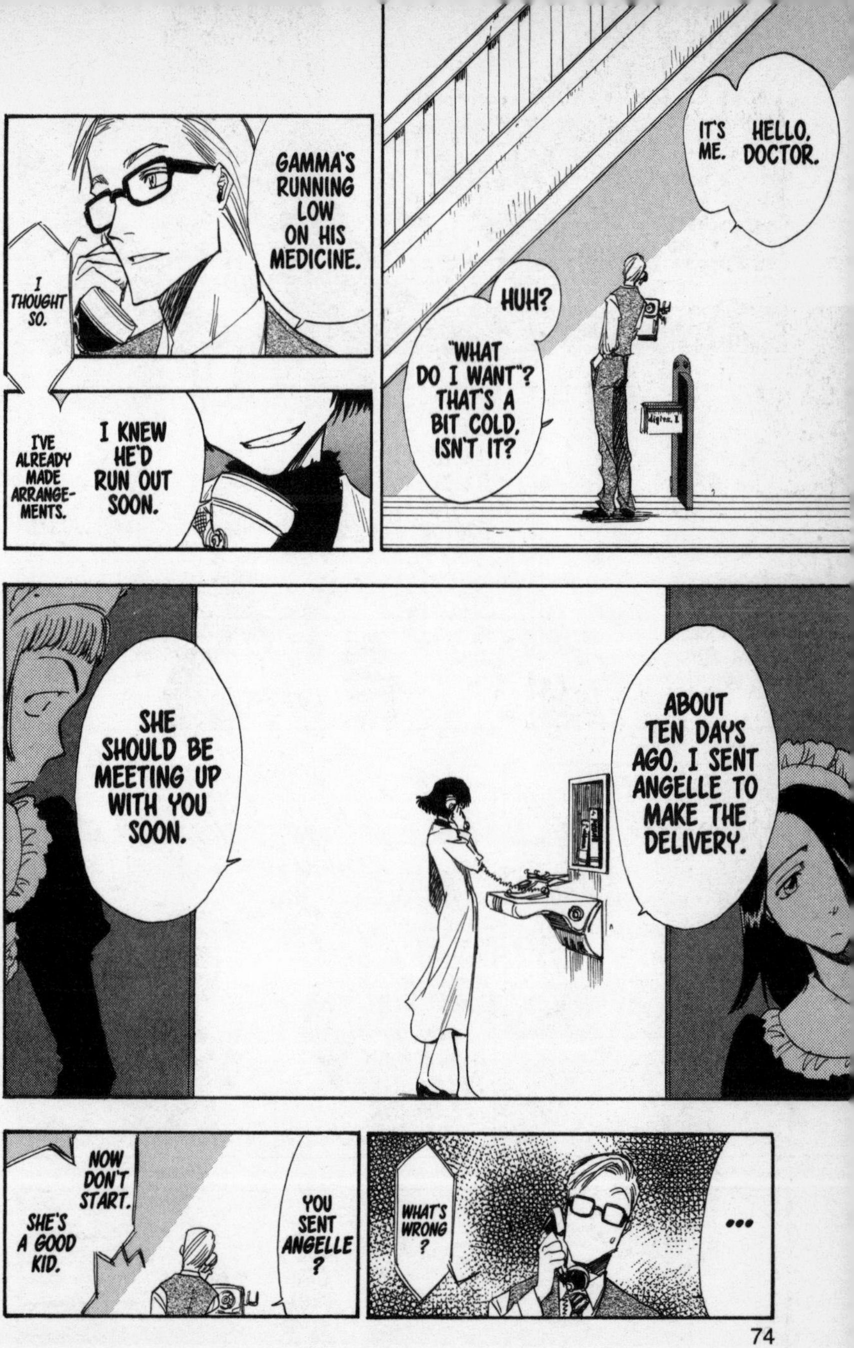
HELLO, DOCTOR.
IT'S ME.
HUH?
"WHAT DO I WANT"? THAT'S A BIT COLD, ISN'T IT?
GAMMA'S RUNNING LOW ON HIS MEDICINE.
I THOUGHT SO.
I KNEW HE'D RUN OUT SOON.
I'VE ALREADY MADE ARRANGE-MENTS.
ABOUT TEN DAYS AGO, I SENT ANGELLE TO MAKE THE DELIVERY.
SHE SHOULD BE MEETING UP WITH YOU SOON.
...
WHAT'S WRONG?
YOU SENT ANGELLE?
NOW DON'T START.
SHE'S A GOOD KID.

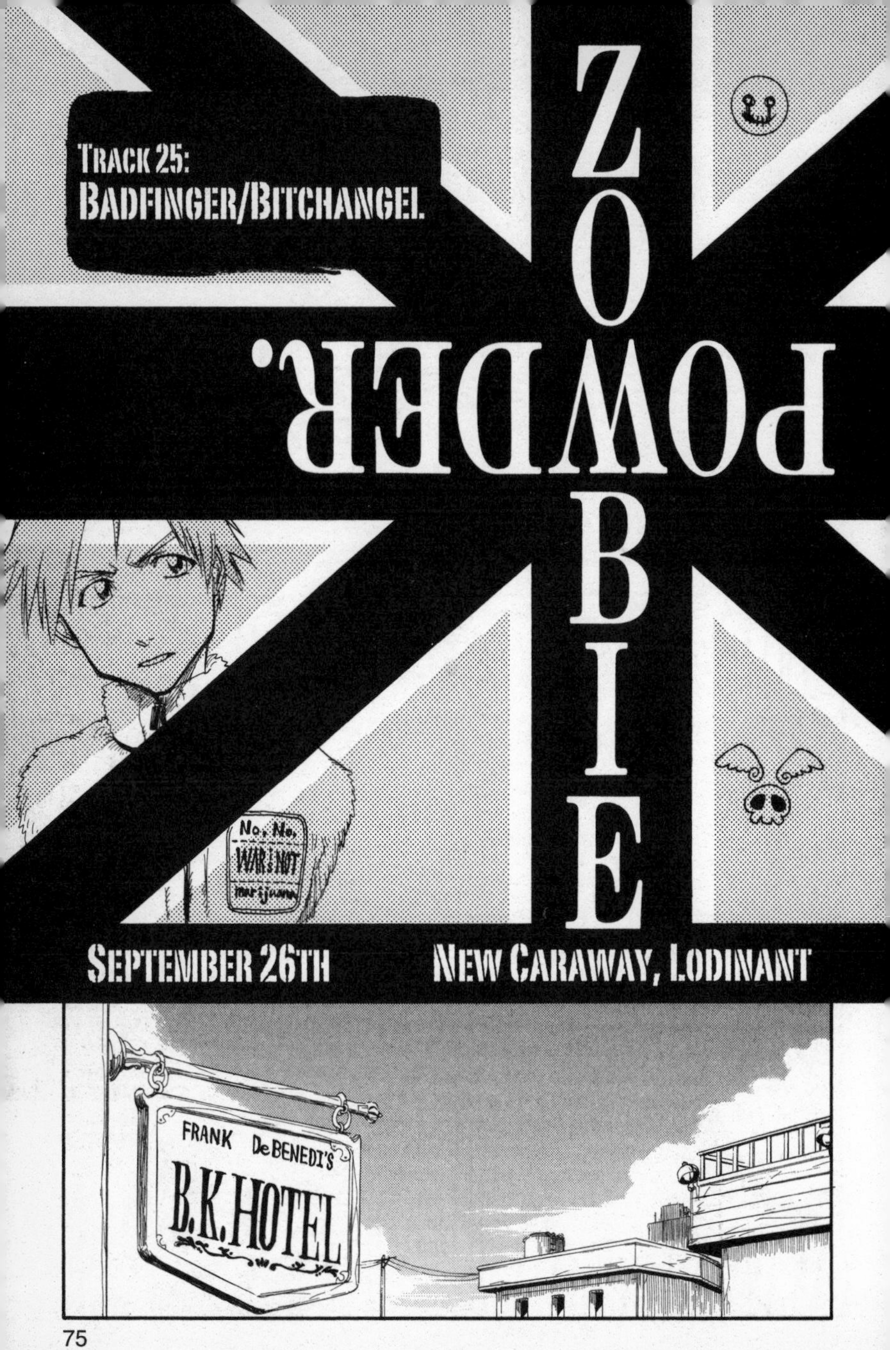
TRACK 25:
BADFINGER/BITCHANGEL
ZOMBIE POWDER.
SEPTEMBER 26TH
NEW CARAWAY, LODINANT
FRANK DeBENEDI'S
B.K. HOTEL

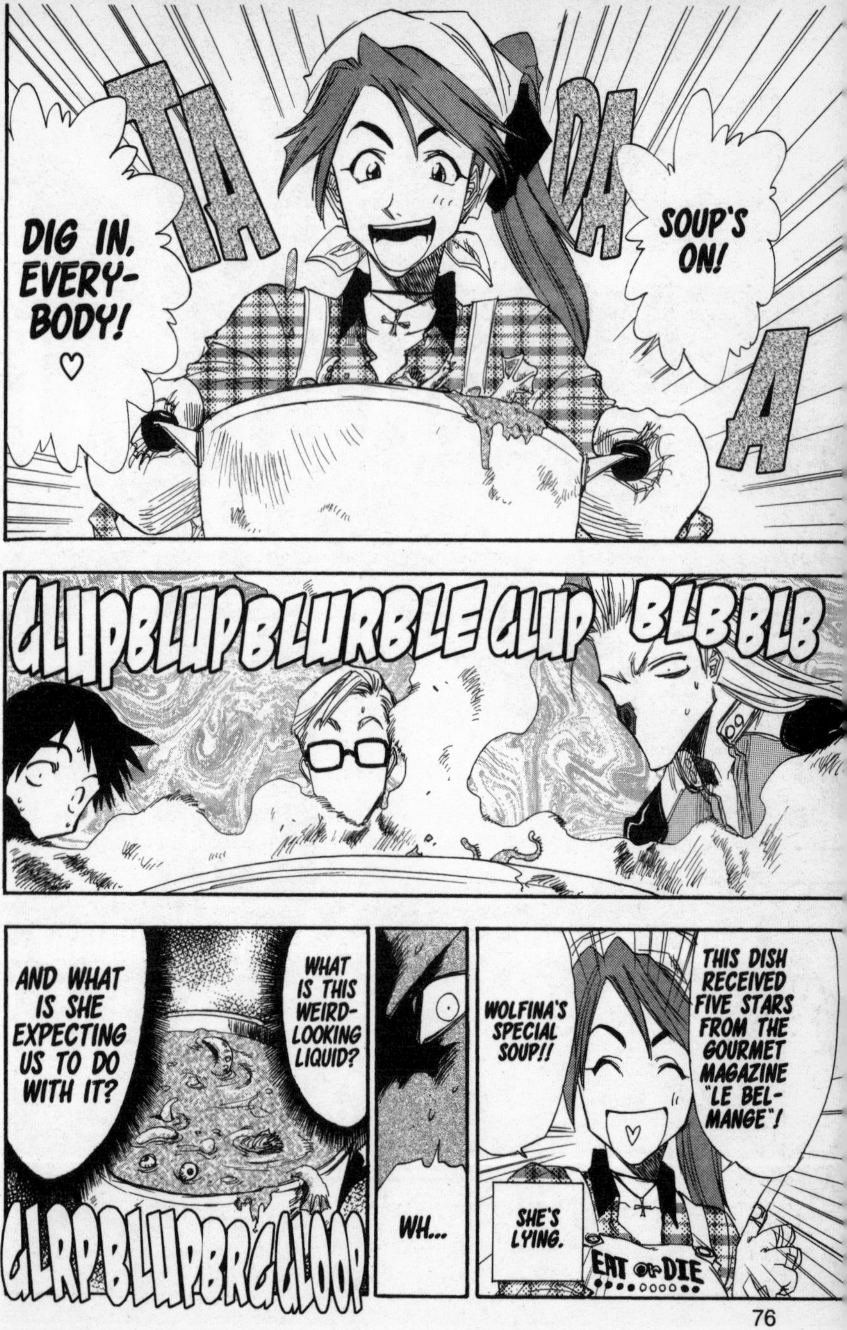
TA
DA
A
SOUP'S ON!
DIG IN, EVERY-BODY! ♡
BLB BLB
GLUPBLUPBLURBLE GLUP
THIS DISH RECEIVED FIVE STARS FROM THE GOURMET MAGAZINE "LE BEL-MANGE"!
WOLFINA'S SPECIAL SOUP!!
SHE'S LYING.
EAT or DIE
WH...
WHAT IS THIS WEIRD-LOOKING LIQUID?
AND WHAT IS SHE EXPECTING US TO DO WITH IT?
GLRPBLUPBRGGLOOP

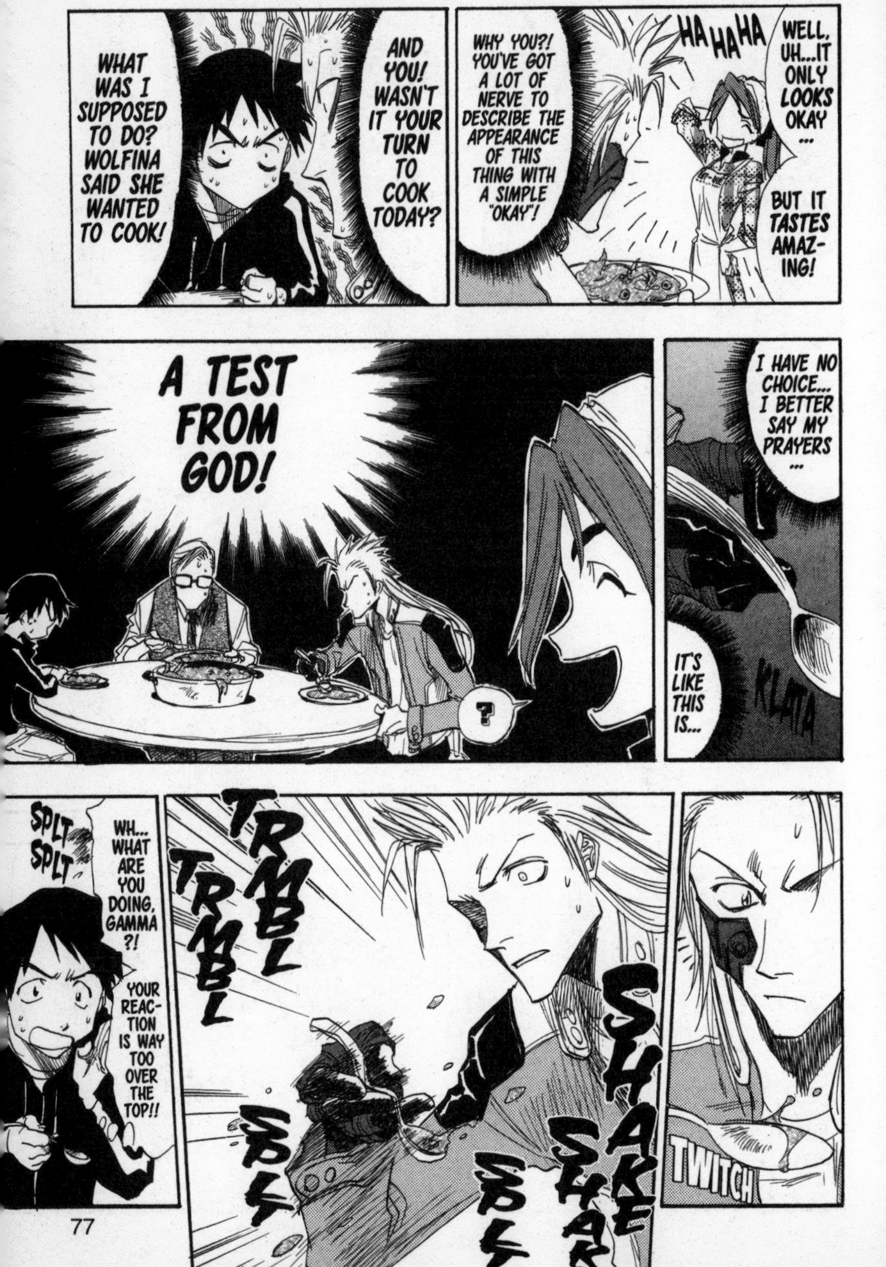
WELL, UH...IT ONLY LOOKS OKAY...
HA HA HA
BUT IT TASTES AMAZ-ING!
WHY YOU?! YOU'VE GOT A LOT OF NERVE TO DESCRIBE THE APPEARANCE OF THIS THING WITH A SIMPLE "OKAY"!
AND YOU! WASN'T IT YOUR TURN TO COOK TODAY?
WHAT WAS I SUPPOSED TO DO? WOLFINA SAID SHE WANTED TO COOK!
I HAVE NO CHOICE... I BETTER SAY MY PRAYERS...
KLATA
IT'S LIKE THIS IS...
A TEST FROM GOD!
?
TWITCH
TRMBL TRMBL
SHAKE SHAKE
SPLT SPLT
SPLT SPLT
WH... WHAT ARE YOU DOING, GAMMA?!
YOUR REACTION IS WAY TOO OVER THE TOP!!

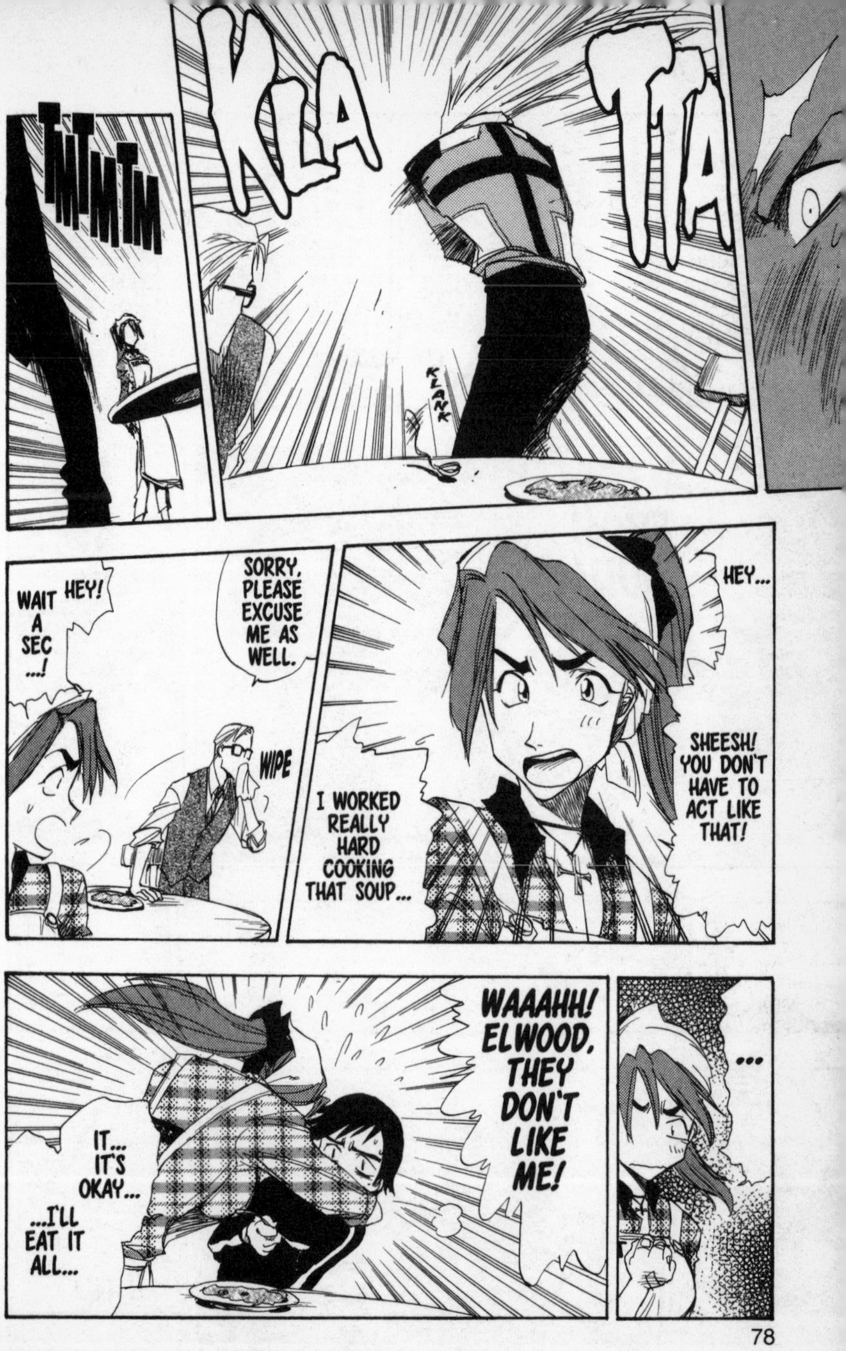
KLATTA
KLANK
TMTMTM
HEY...
SHEESH! YOU DON'T HAVE TO ACT LIKE THAT!
I WORKED REALLY HARD COOKING THAT SOUP...
SORRY, PLEASE EXCUSE ME AS WELL.
HEY! WAIT A SEC...!
WIPE
...
WAAAHH! ELWOOD, THEY DON'T LIKE ME!
IT... IT'S OKAY...
...I'LL EAT IT ALL...

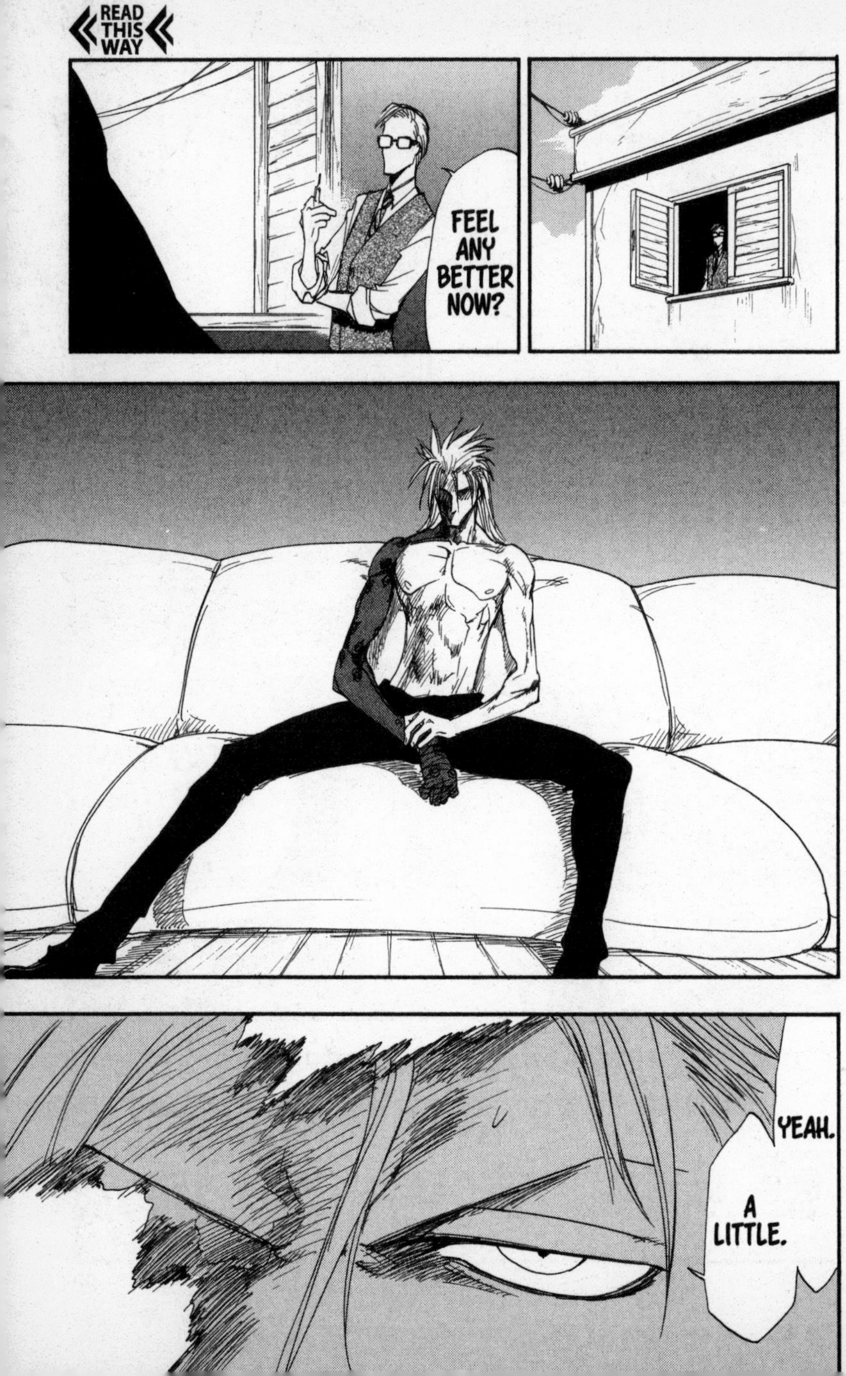
READ THIS WAY
FEEL ANY BETTER NOW?
YEAH.
A LITTLE.

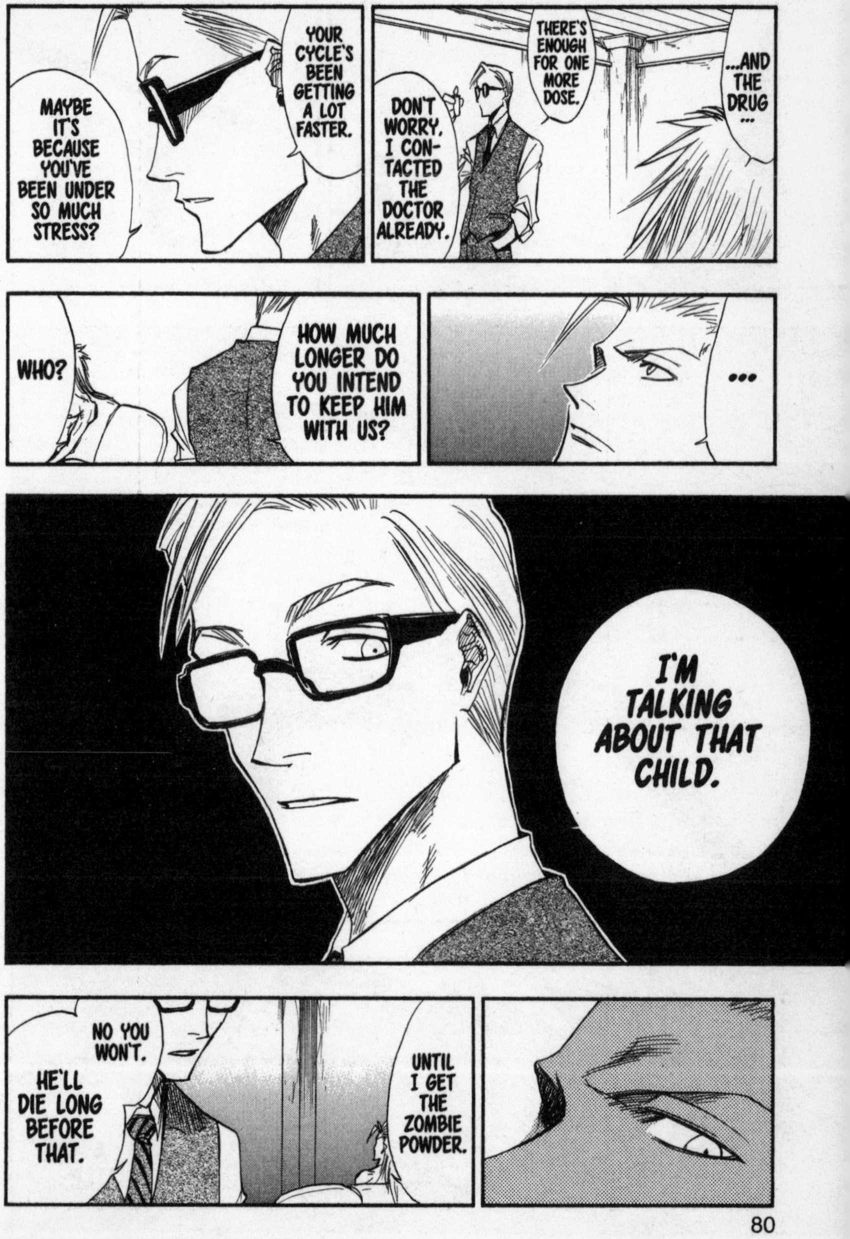
...AND THE DRUG...
THERE'S ENOUGH FOR ONE MORE DOSE.
DON'T WORRY, I CON-TACTED THE DOCTOR ALREADY.
YOUR CYCLE'S BEEN GETTING A LOT FASTER.
MAYBE IT'S BECAUSE YOU'VE BEEN UNDER SO MUCH STRESS?
...
HOW MUCH LONGER DO YOU INTEND TO KEEP HIM WITH US?
WHO?
I'M TALKING ABOUT THAT CHILD.
UNTIL I GET THE ZOMBIE POWDER.
NO YOU WON'T.
HE'LL DIE LONG BEFORE THAT.

READ THIS WAY

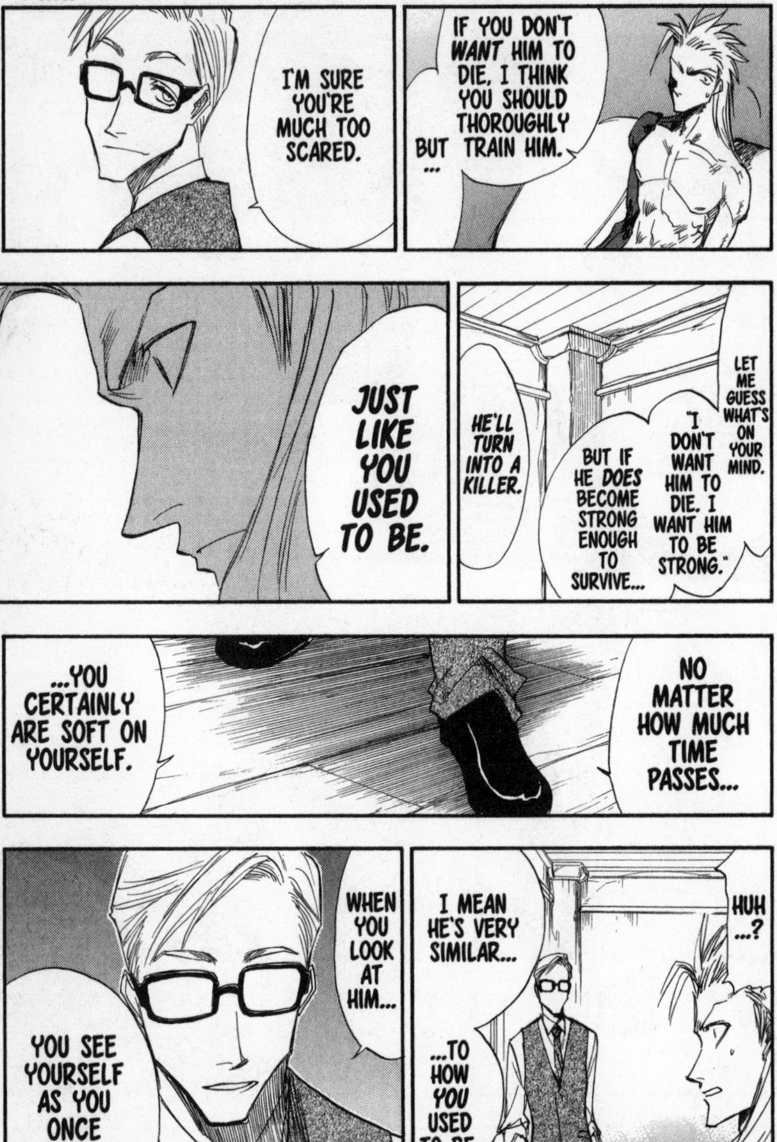
IF YOU DON'T WANT HIM TO DIE, I THINK YOU SHOULD THOROUGHLY TRAIN HIM.
BUT ...
I'M SURE YOU'RE MUCH TOO SCARED.
LET ME GUESS WHAT'S ON YOUR MIND.
"I DON'T WANT HIM TO DIE. I WANT HIM TO BE STRONG."
BUT IF HE DOES BECOME STRONG ENOUGH TO SURVIVE...
HE'LL TURN INTO A KILLER.
JUST LIKE YOU USED TO BE.
NO MATTER HOW MUCH TIME PASSES...
...YOU CERTAINLY ARE SOFT ON YOURSELF.
HUH ...?
I MEAN HE'S VERY SIMILAR...
...TO HOW YOU USED TO BE.
WHEN YOU LOOK AT HIM...
YOU SEE YOURSELF AS YOU ONCE WERE.

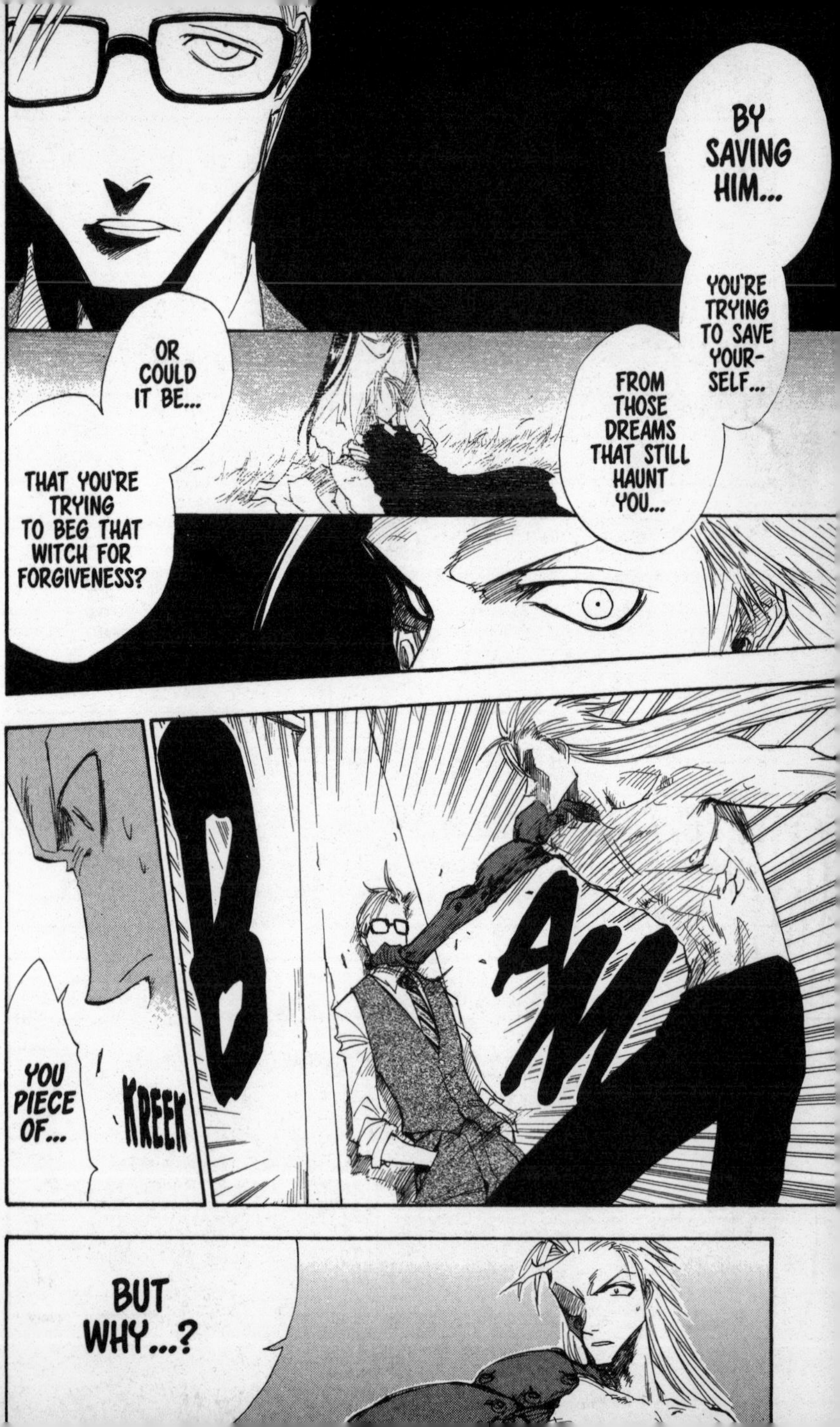
BY SAVING HIM...
YOU'RE TRYING TO SAVE YOUR-SELF...
FROM THOSE DREAMS THAT STILL HAUNT YOU...
OR COULD IT BE...
THAT YOU'RE TRYING TO BEG THAT WITCH FOR FORGIVENESS?
BAM
KREEK
YOU PIECE OF...
BUT WHY...?

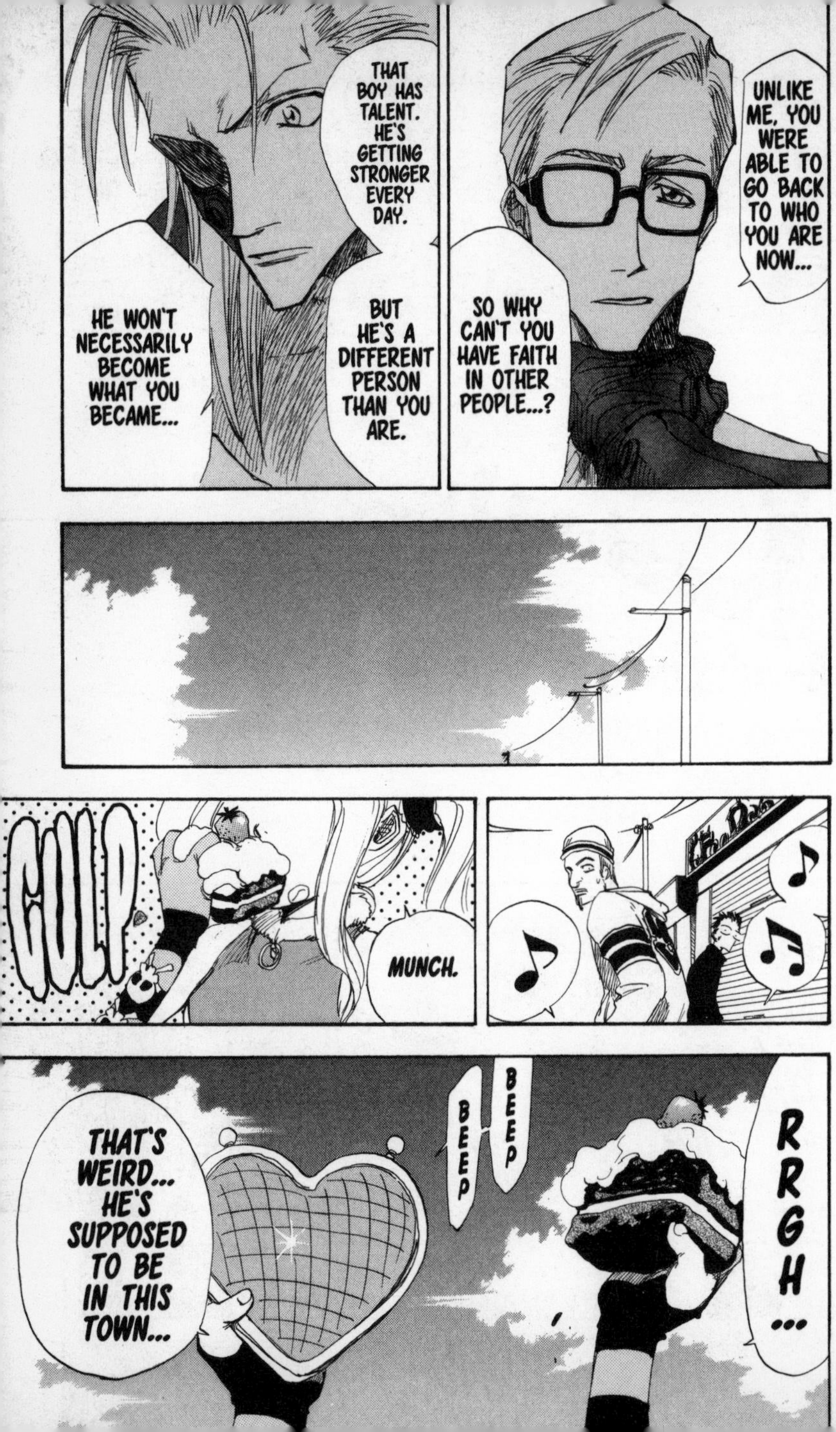
UNLIKE ME, YOU WERE ABLE TO GO BACK TO WHO YOU ARE NOW...
SO WHY CAN'T YOU HAVE FAITH IN OTHER PEOPLE...?
THAT BOY HAS TALENT. HE'S GETTING STRONGER EVERY DAY.
BUT HE'S A DIFFERENT PERSON THAN YOU ARE.
HE WON'T NECESSARILY BECOME WHAT YOU BECAME...
MUNCH.
GULP
RRGH...
BEEP
BEEP
THAT'S WEIRD... HE'S SUPPOSED TO BE IN THIS TOWN...

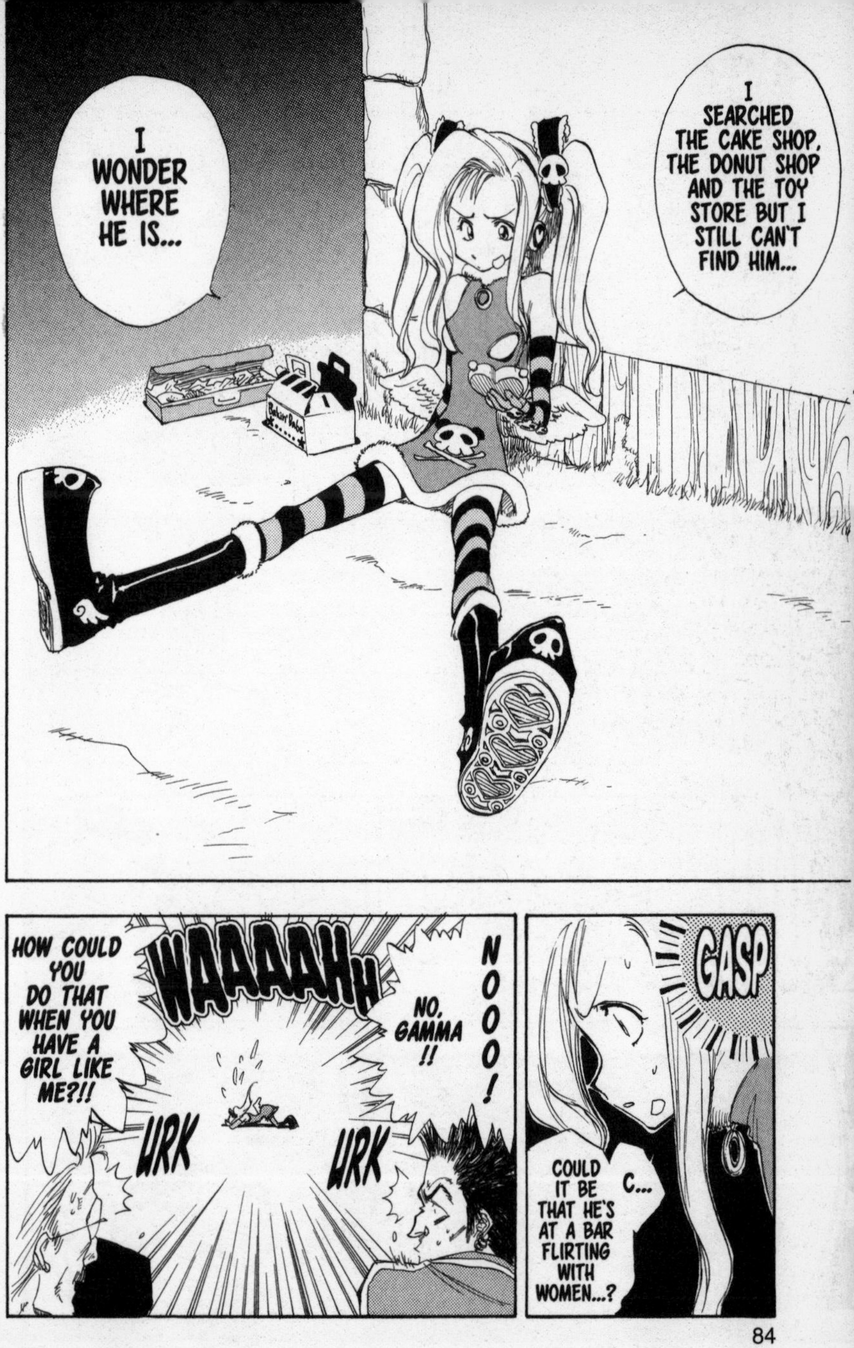
I SEARCHED THE CAKE SHOP, THE DONUT SHOP AND THE TOY STORE BUT I STILL CAN'T FIND HIM...
I WONDER WHERE HE IS...
GASP
C...
COULD IT BE THAT HE'S AT A BAR FLIRTING WITH WOMEN...?
NOOOO!
NO, GAMMA!!
WAAAAHH
HOW COULD YOU DO THAT WHEN YOU HAVE A GIRL LIKE ME?!!
URK
URK

READ THIS WAY

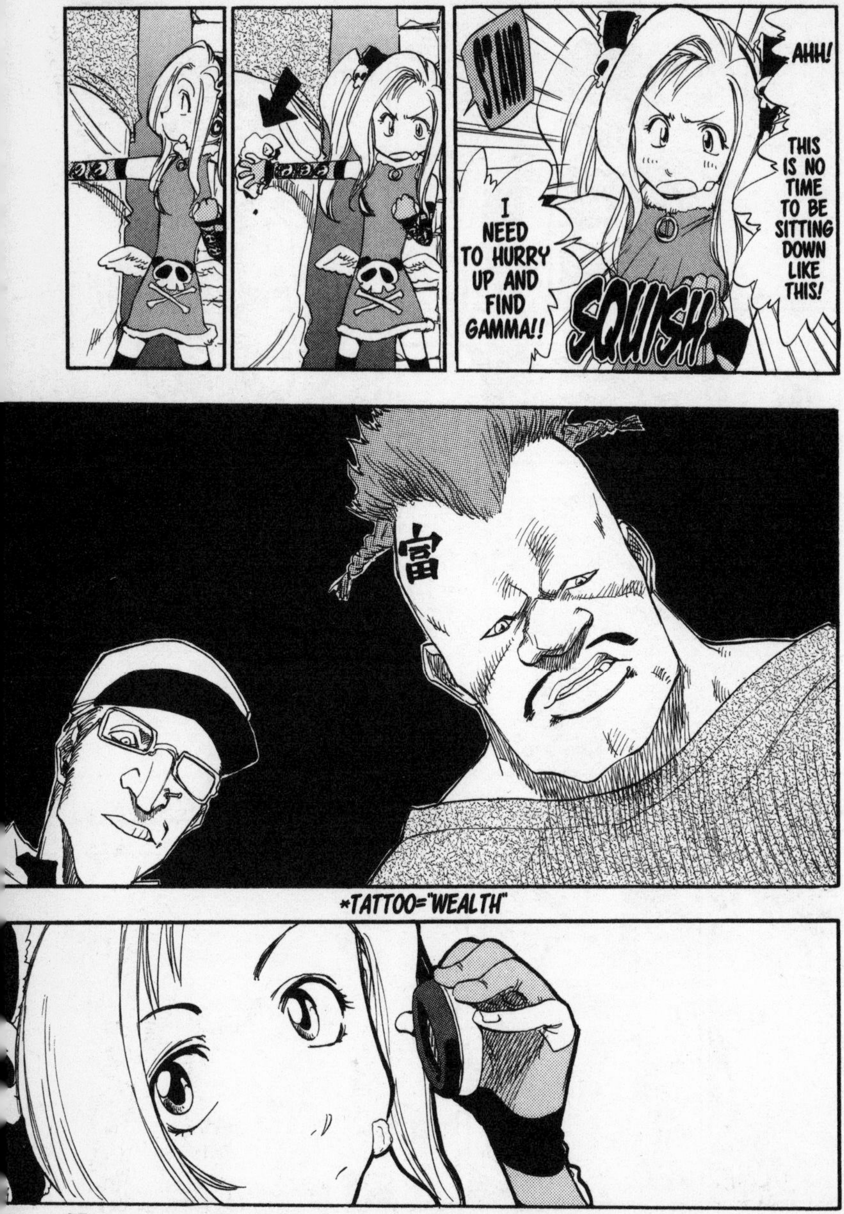
AHH!
THIS IS NO TIME TO BE SITTING DOWN LIKE THIS!
STAND
I NEED TO HURRY UP AND FIND GAMMA!!
SQUISH
富
*TATTOO="WEALTH"

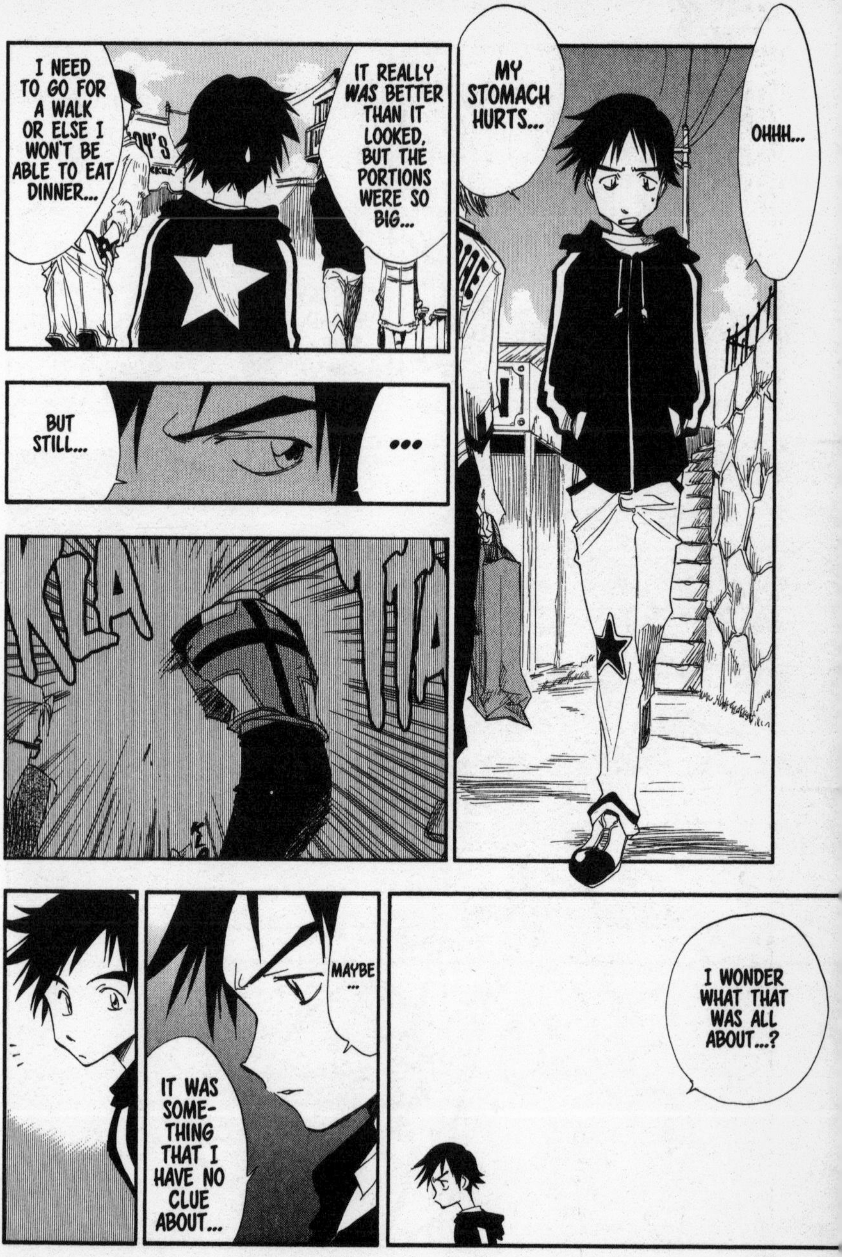
OHHH...
MY STOMACH HURTS...
IT REALLY WAS BETTER THAN IT LOOKED, BUT THE PORTIONS WERE SO BIG...
I NEED TO GO FOR A WALK OR ELSE I WON'T BE ABLE TO EAT DINNER...
...
BUT STILL...
I WONDER WHAT THAT WAS ALL ABOUT...?
MAYBE...
IT WAS SOME-THING THAT I HAVE NO CLUE ABOUT...

READ THIS WAY

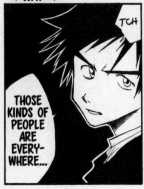

TCH
THOSE KINDS OF PEOPLE ARE EVERYWHERE...
YAWN...
I'M SOOOOOO SORRY.
WH-WHY YOU?! YOU CALL THAT AN APOLOGY?!
I SAID I WAS SORRY.
DON'T YOU UNDERSTAND WHAT "SORRY" MEANS? WAS THAT WORD TOO HARD FOR YOU TO UNDERSTAND?
YOU LITTLE BRAT...!
GRR
GRR
DO YOU WANT ME TO TEACH YOU ONE WORD AT A TIME?
OKAY, REPEAT AFTER ME:
"I'M."

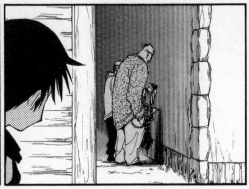

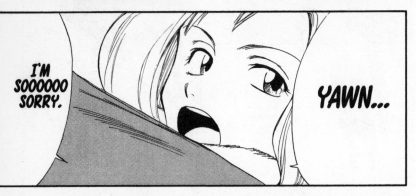

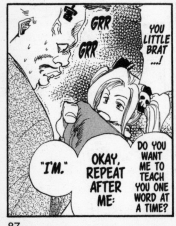

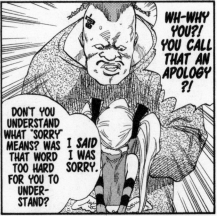

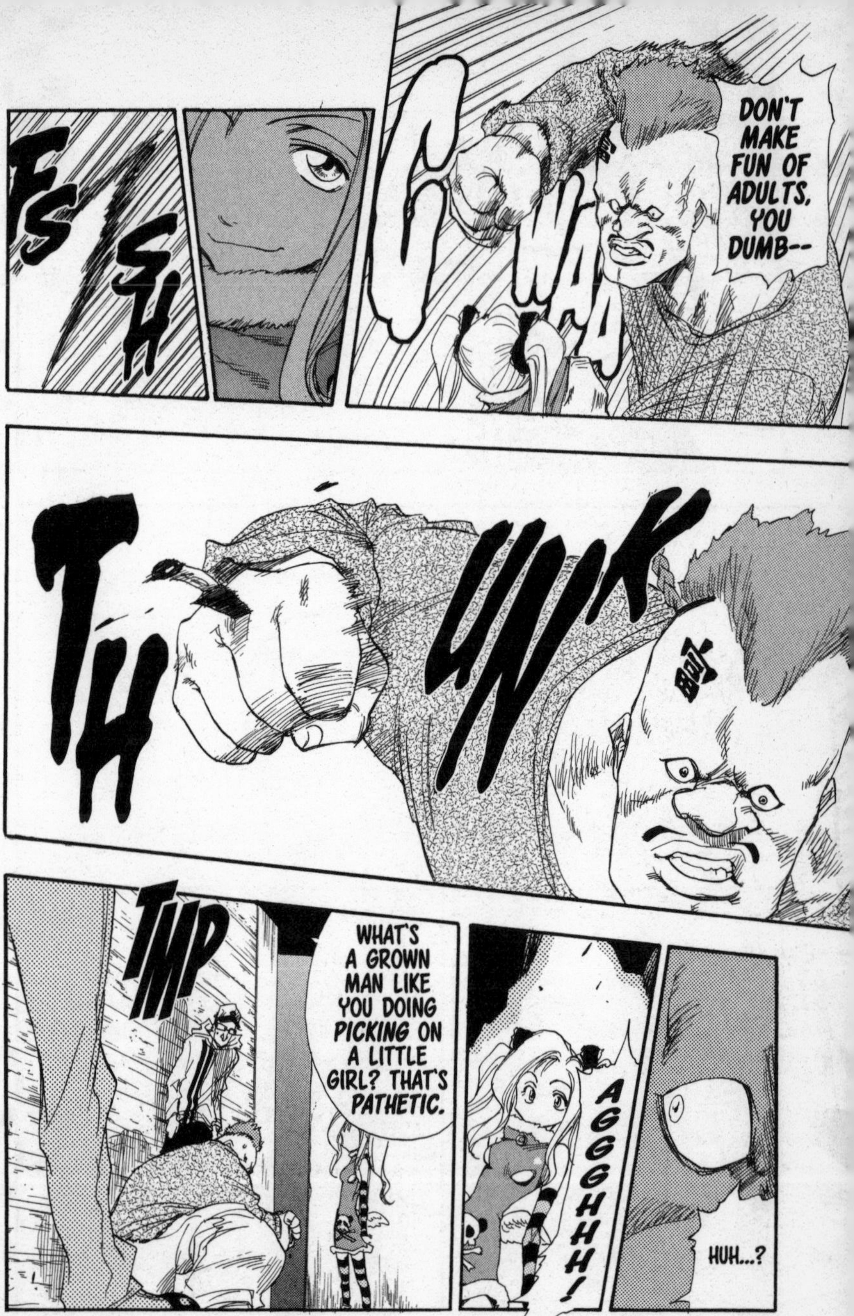

DON'T MAKE FUN OF ADULTS, YOU DUMB--
FSSH
THUNK
HUH...?
AGGGHHH!
WHAT'S A GROWN MAN LIKE YOU DOING PICKING ON A LITTLE GIRL? THAT'S PATHETIC.
TMP

READ THIS WAY

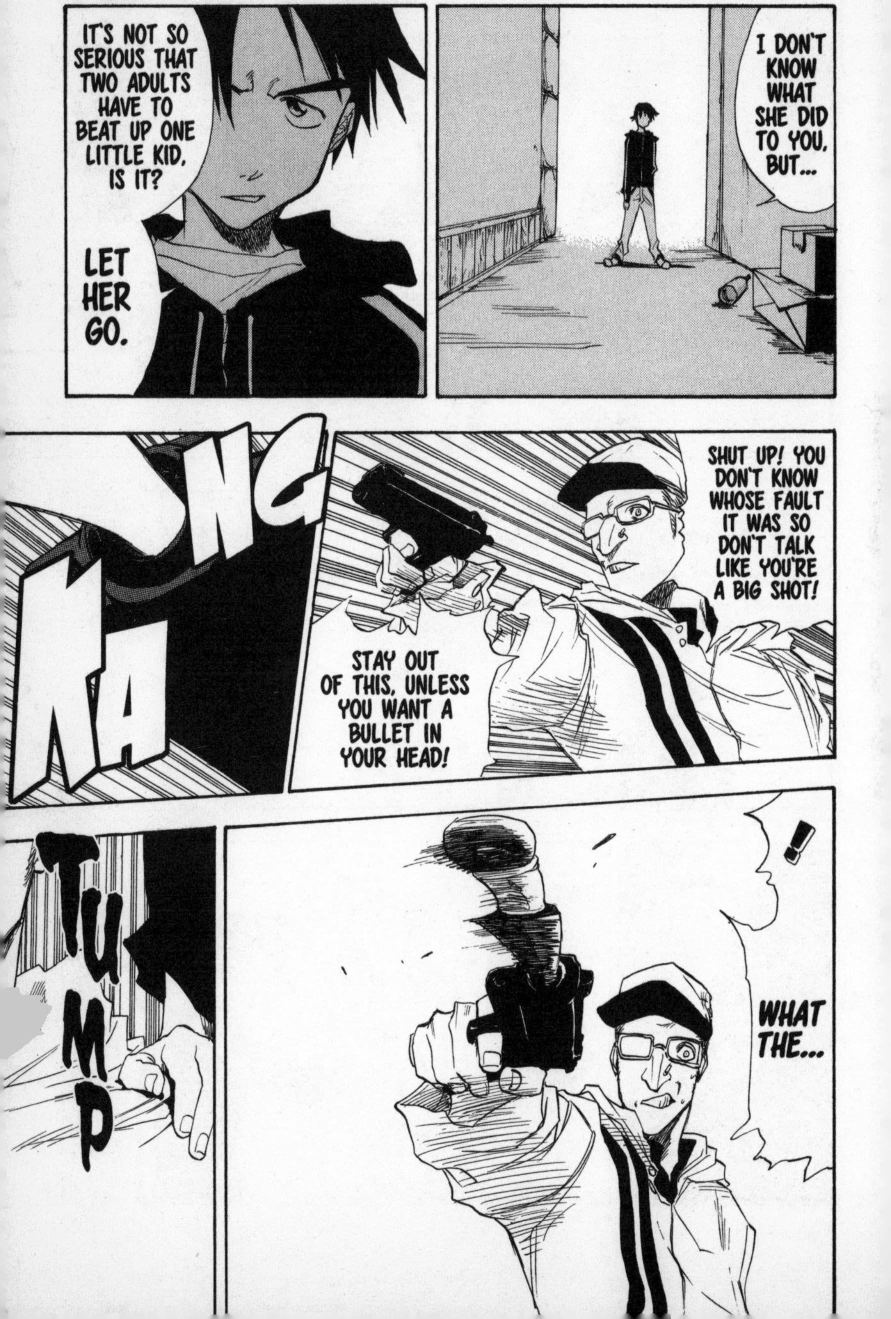
I DON'T KNOW WHAT SHE DID TO YOU, BUT...
IT'S NOT SO SERIOUS THAT TWO ADULTS HAVE TO BEAT UP ONE LITTLE KID, IS IT?
LET HER GO.
SHUT UP! YOU DON'T KNOW WHOSE FAULT IT WAS SO DON'T TALK LIKE YOU'RE A BIG SHOT!
STAY OUT OF THIS, UNLESS YOU WANT A BULLET IN YOUR HEAD!
NG
KA
!
WHAT THE...
TUMP

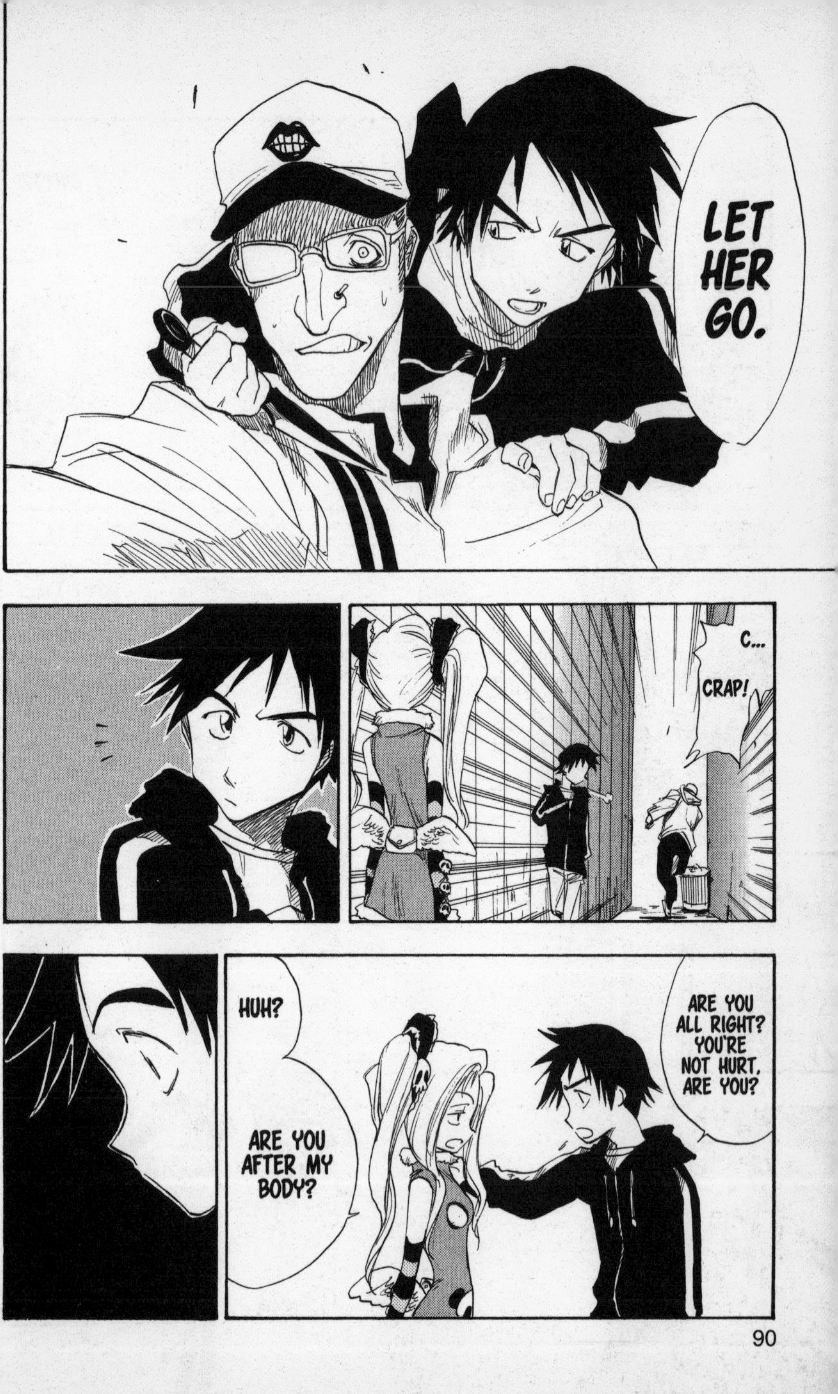
LET HER GO.
C...
CRAP!
ARE YOU ALL RIGHT? YOU'RE NOT HURT, ARE YOU?
HUH?
ARE YOU AFTER MY BODY?

READ THIS WAY

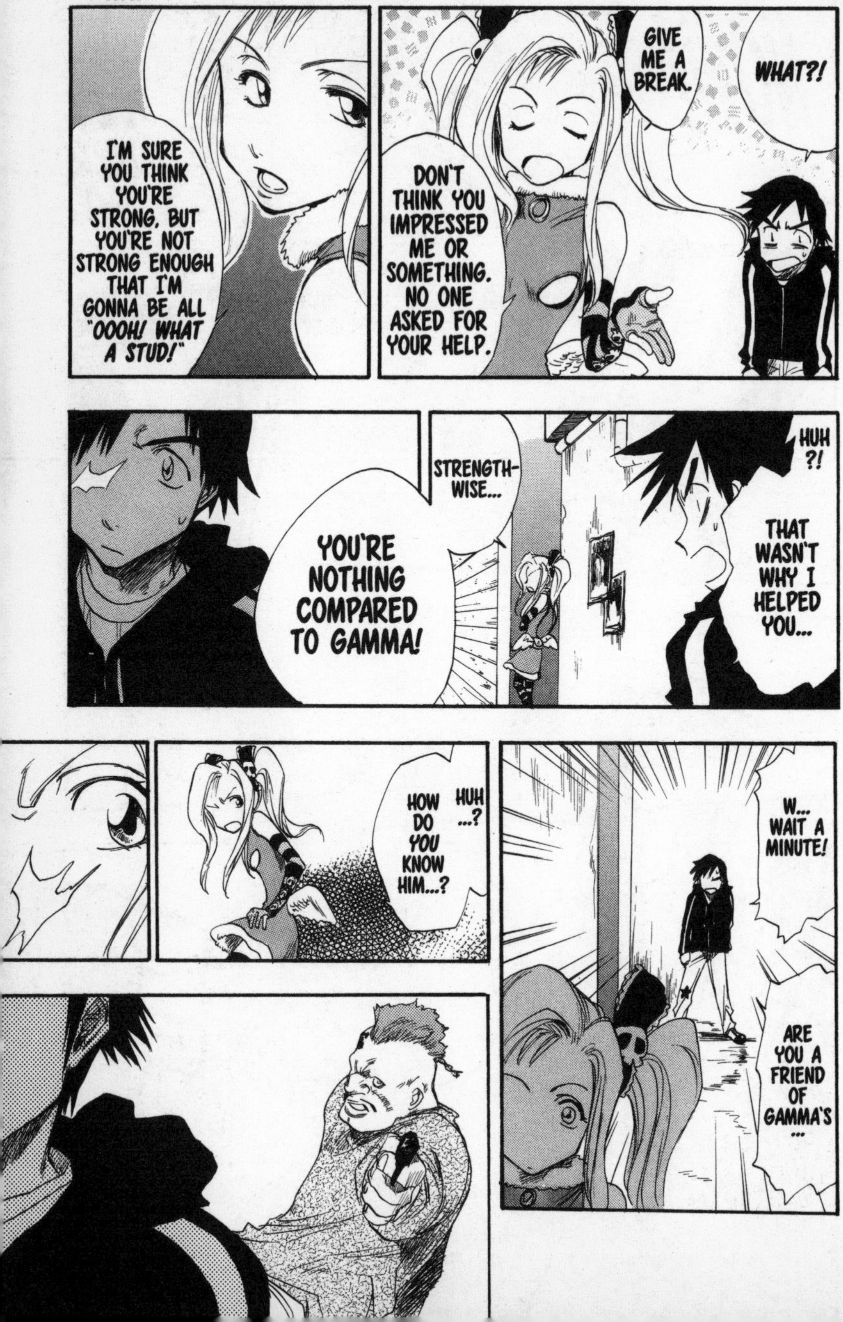
WHAT?!
GIVE ME A BREAK.
DON'T THINK YOU IMPRESSED ME OR SOMETHING. NO ONE ASKED FOR YOUR HELP.
I'M SURE YOU THINK YOU'RE STRONG, BUT YOU'RE NOT STRONG ENOUGH THAT I'M GONNA BE ALL "OOOH! WHAT A STUD!"
HUH?!
THAT WASN'T WHY I HELPED YOU...
STRENGTH-WISE...
YOU'RE NOTHING COMPARED TO GAMMA!
W... WAIT A MINUTE!
ARE YOU A FRIEND OF GAMMA'S ...
HUH ...?
HOW DO YOU KNOW HIM...?

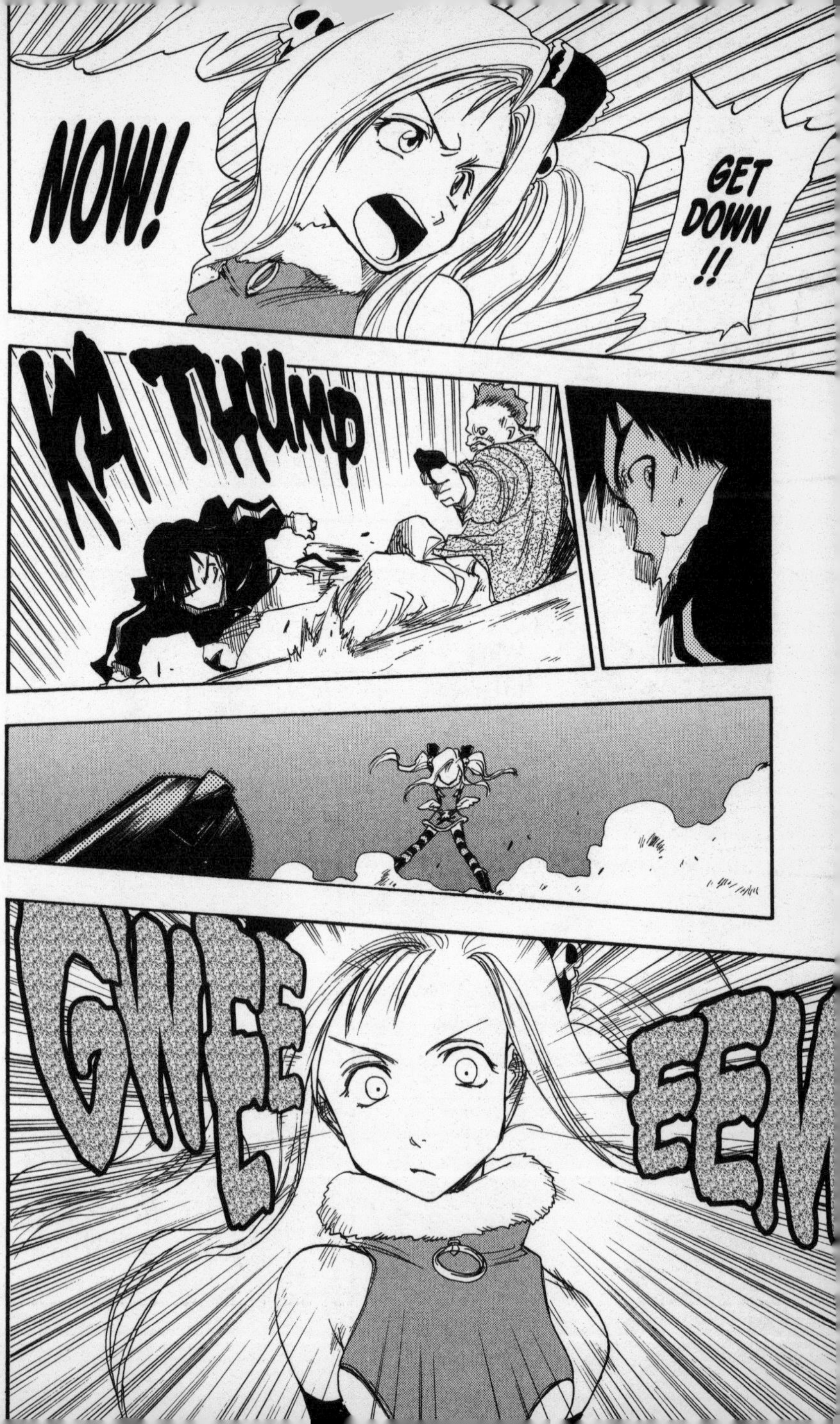
GET DOWN !!
NOW!
KA THUMP
GWEE
EEM

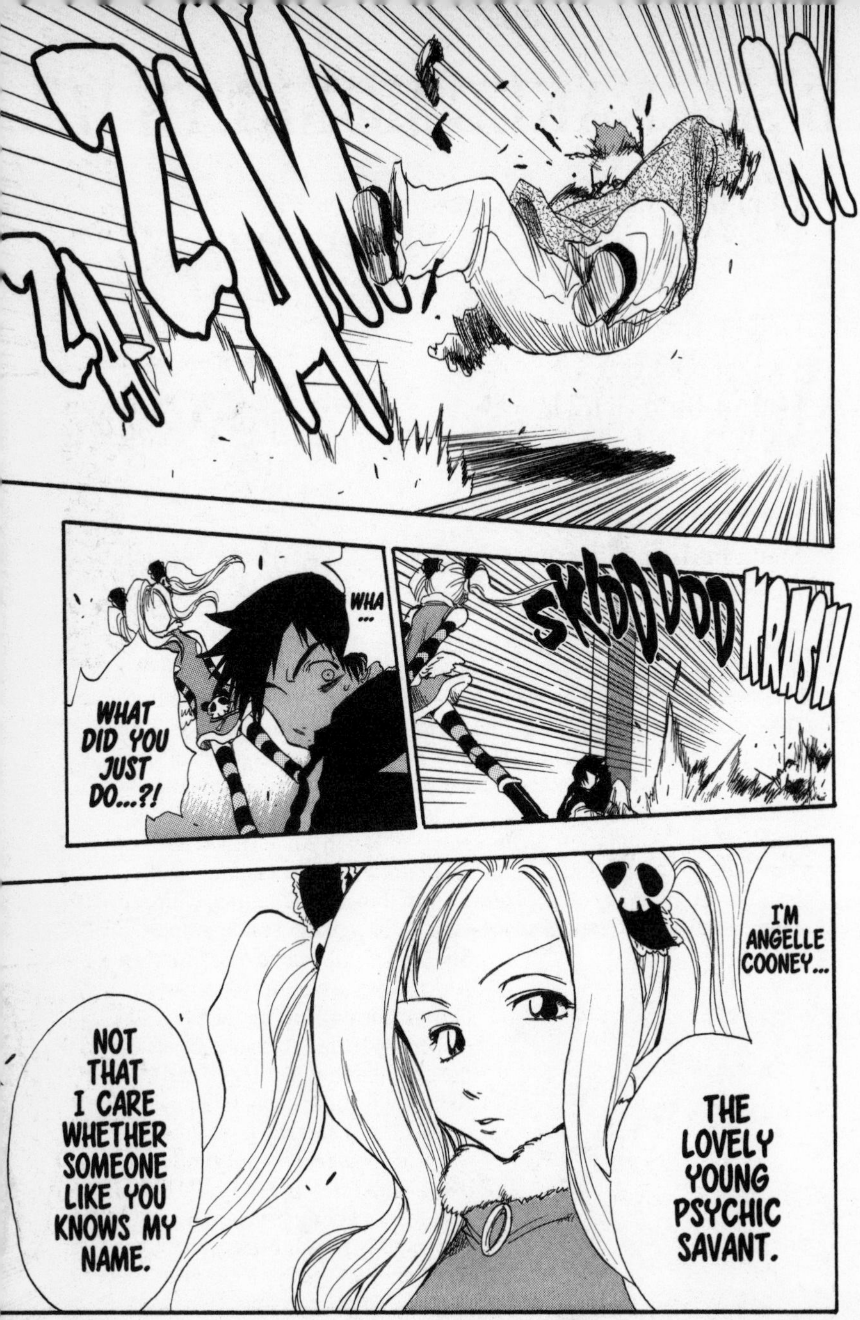
ZWAM
SKIDDDDD
KRASH
WHA...
WHAT DID YOU JUST DO...?!
I'M ANGELLE COONEY...
THE LOVELY YOUNG PSYCHIC SAVANT.
NOT THAT I CARE WHETHER SOMEONE LIKE YOU KNOWS MY NAME.

B-side NAKED MONKEYS 17.

Angelle Belle Rose Cooney
エンジェル・ベル・ローズ・クーニー

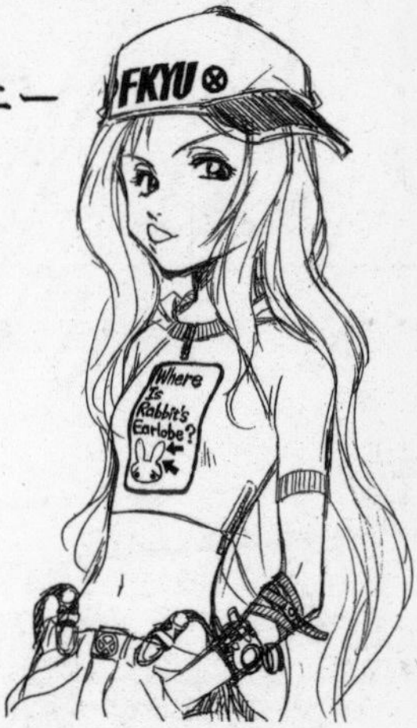
FKYU
Where Is Rabbit's Earlobe?

Height : 145cm
Weight : 36kg
Date of Birth : 11/24
Age : 11
Blood Type : AO
Hometown :
Santa Ferrica, Clikemear
Academic Career : None

From Santa Ferrica, Clikemear. The child of the unknown painter Claude Christopher Cooney and Julia Tiffany Rose, the former Miss Clikemear. She is a beautiful young girl with pale white skin, deep blue eyes and honey blonde hair. Angelle's mother disappeared when she was two years old. Her father is currently serving a prison sentence for locking up and committing violent acts against a minor; he has three years and two months left on his sentence. When Angelle was seven years old she went to the Gemini Laboratory and met Gamma, and she's adored him ever since. Her favorite things are Gamma, whipped cream, strawberry flavored snacks, the color pink and photographs. She doesn't like dogs (because they bark), news programs (because they're boring), sitting with her legs tucked under her (because it cuts off the circulation in her legs), garlic (because it stinks), and onions and carrots (because they taste gross). She uses powers that are similar to psychic abilities and she calls herself "the lovely young psychic savant" but actually her abilities aren't psychic; it's something closer to Gamma's "chain arts."

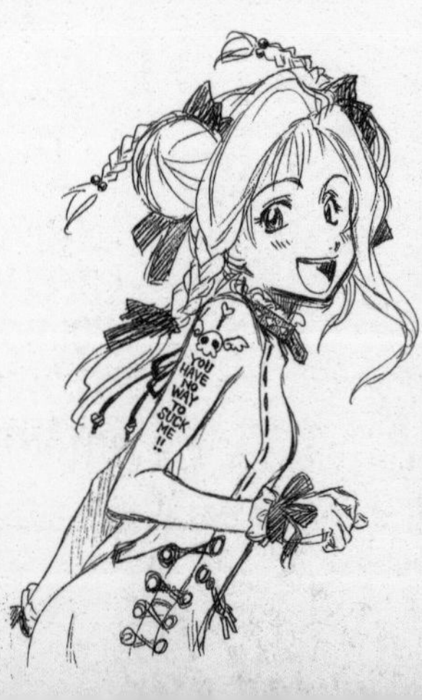
YOU HAVE NO WAY TO SUCK ME!!

TRACK 26: BELIEVE

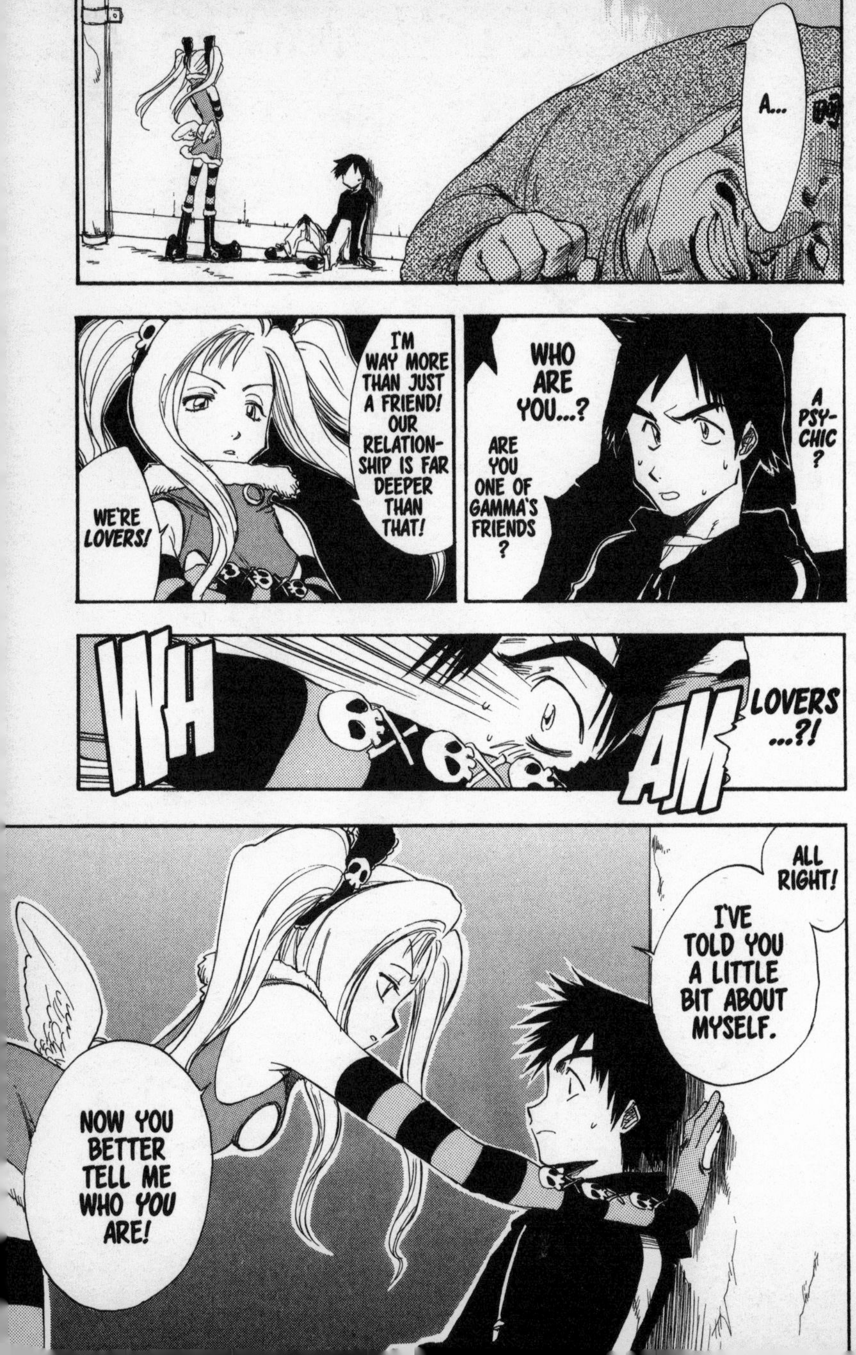
A...
WHO ARE YOU...?
ARE YOU ONE OF GAMMA'S FRIENDS?
A PSYCHIC?
I'M WAY MORE THAN JUST A FRIEND! OUR RELATIONSHIP IS FAR DEEPER THAN THAT!
WE'RE LOVERS!
WHAM
LOVERS...?!
ALL RIGHT!
I'VE TOLD YOU A LITTLE BIT ABOUT MYSELF.
NOW YOU BETTER TELL ME WHO YOU ARE!

TRACK 26: BELIEVE

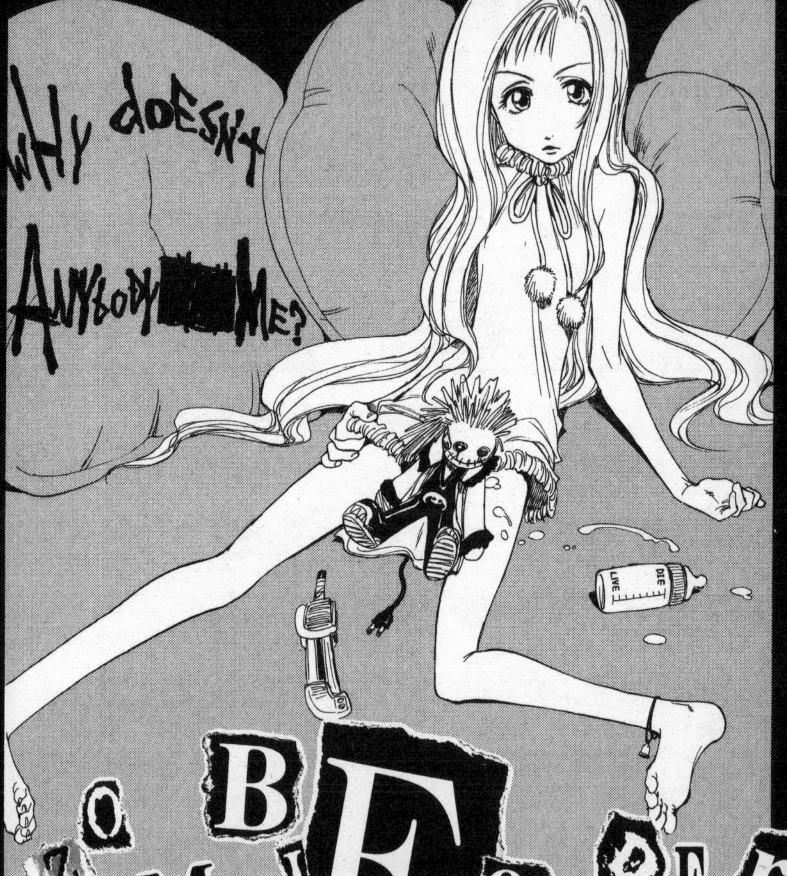
WHY DOESN'T ANYBODY [redacted] ME?
LIVE
DIE
ZOMBIE POWDER.

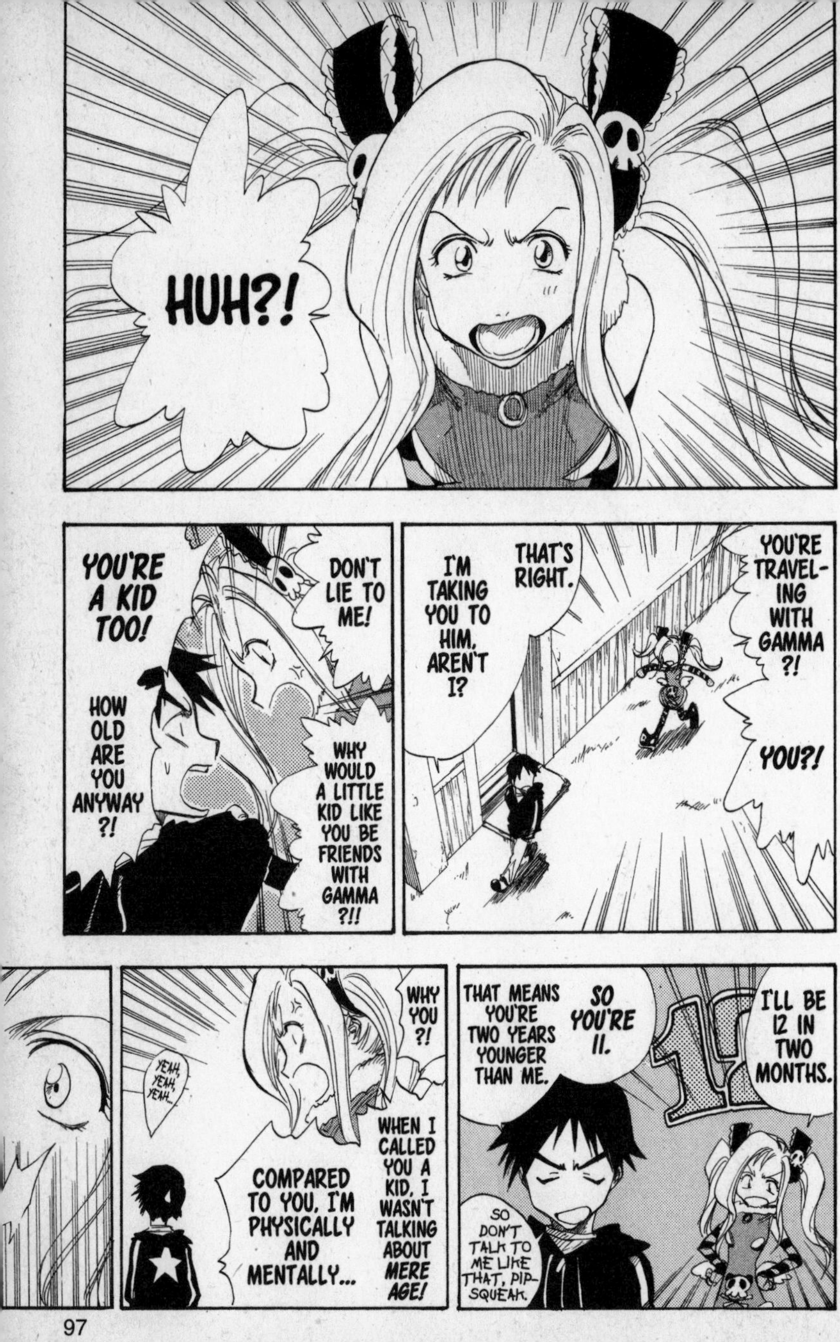
HUH?!
YOU'RE TRAVEL-ING WITH GAMMA?!
YOU?!
THAT'S RIGHT.
I'M TAKING YOU TO HIM, AREN'T I?
DON'T LIE TO ME!
YOU'RE A KID TOO!
WHY WOULD A LITTLE KID LIKE YOU BE FRIENDS WITH GAMMA?!!
HOW OLD ARE YOU ANYWAY?!
I'LL BE 12 IN TWO MONTHS.
SO YOU'RE 11.
THAT MEANS YOU'RE TWO YEARS YOUNGER THAN ME.
SO DON'T TALK TO ME LIKE THAT, PIP-SQUEAK.
WHY YOU?!
YEAH, YEAH, YEAH...
WHEN I CALLED YOU A KID, I WASN'T TALKING ABOUT MERE AGE!
COMPARED TO YOU, I'M PHYSICALLY AND MENTALLY...

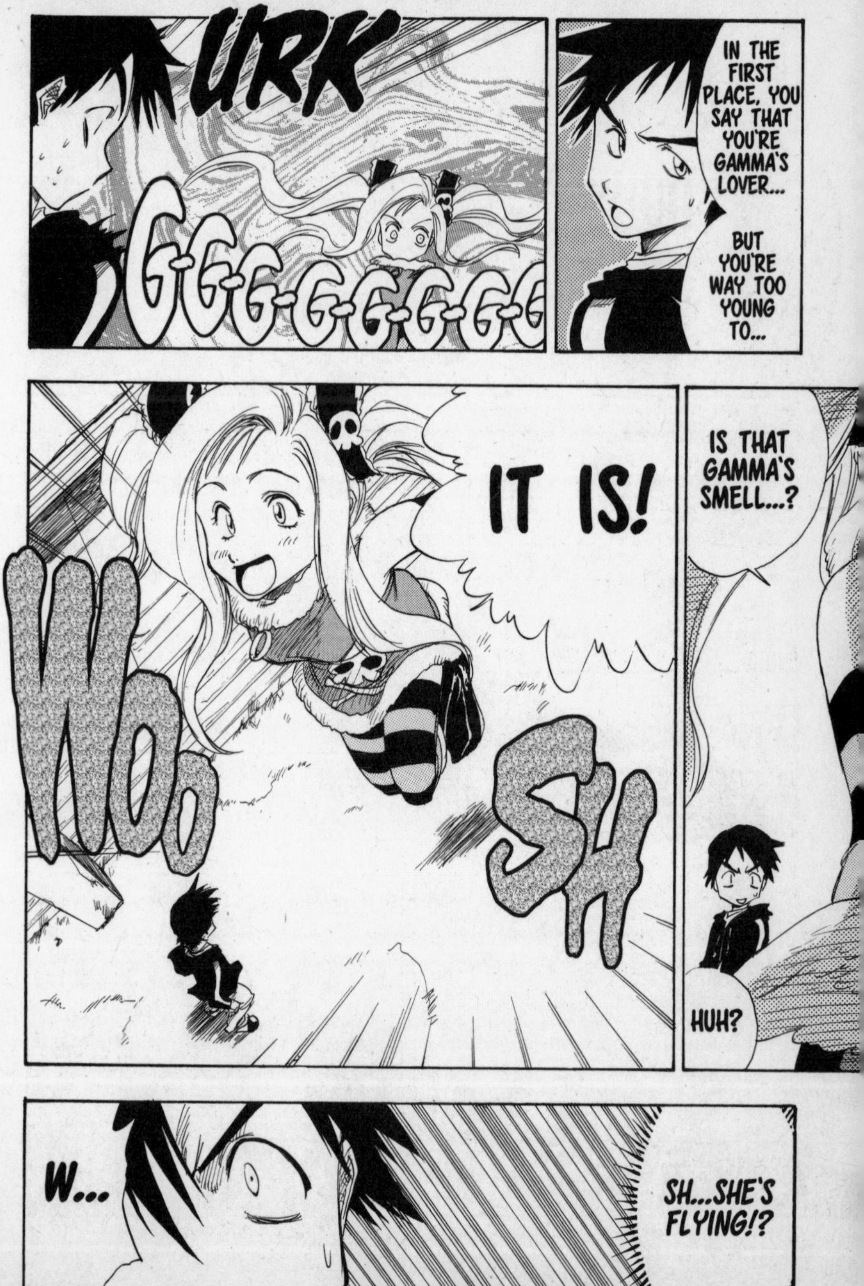
IN THE FIRST PLACE, YOU SAY THAT YOU'RE GAMMA'S LOVER...
BUT YOU'RE WAY TOO YOUNG TO...
URK
G-G-G-G-G-G-G-G
IS THAT GAMMA'S SMELL...?
HUH?
IT IS!
WOOSH
SH...SHE'S FLYING!?
W...

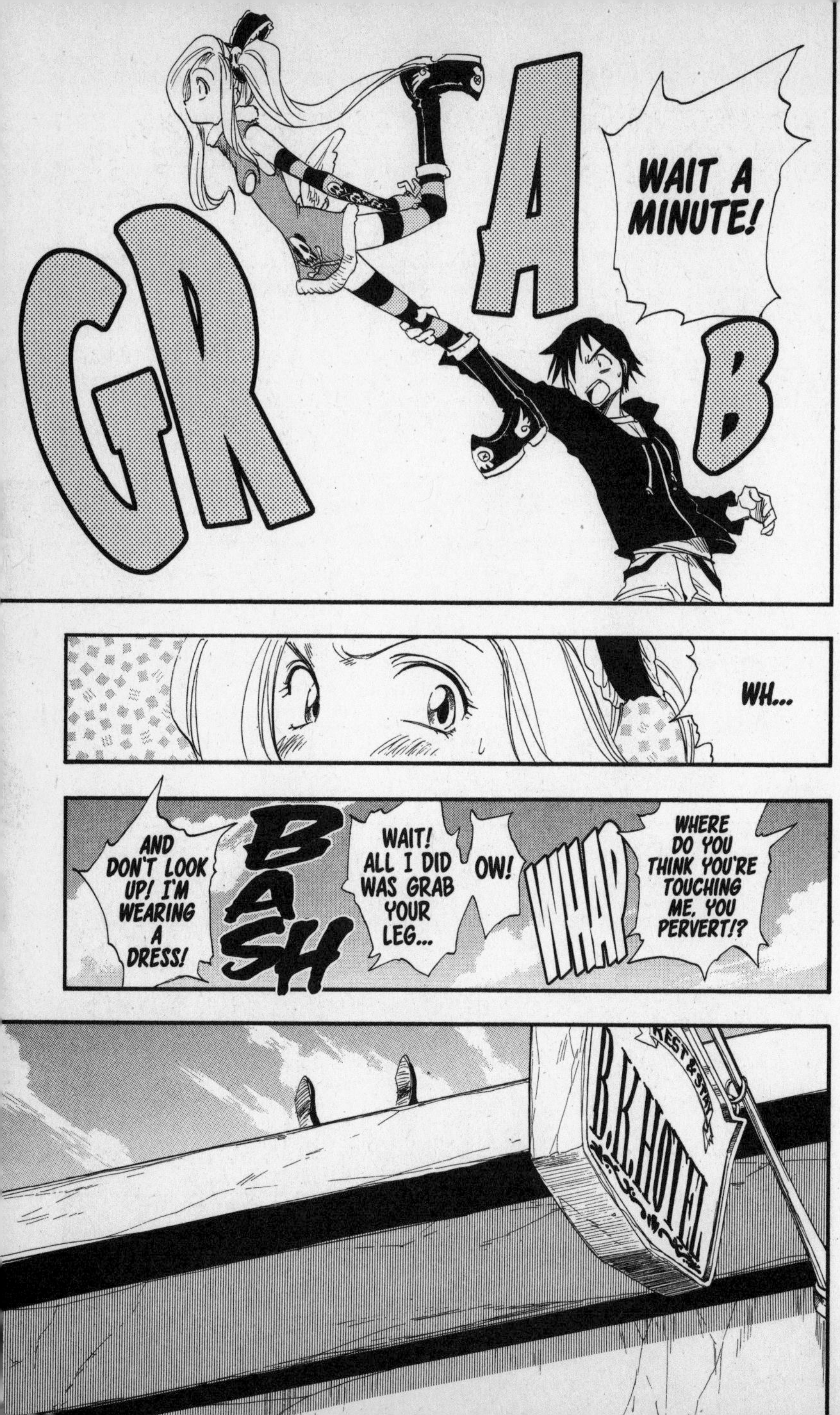
WAIT A MINUTE!
GRAB
WH...
WHERE DO YOU THINK YOU'RE TOUCHING ME, YOU PERVERT!?
WHAP
OW!
WAIT! ALL I DID WAS GRAB YOUR LEG...
BASH
AND DON'T LOOK UP! I'M WEARING A DRESS!
REST & STAY
B.K. HOTEL

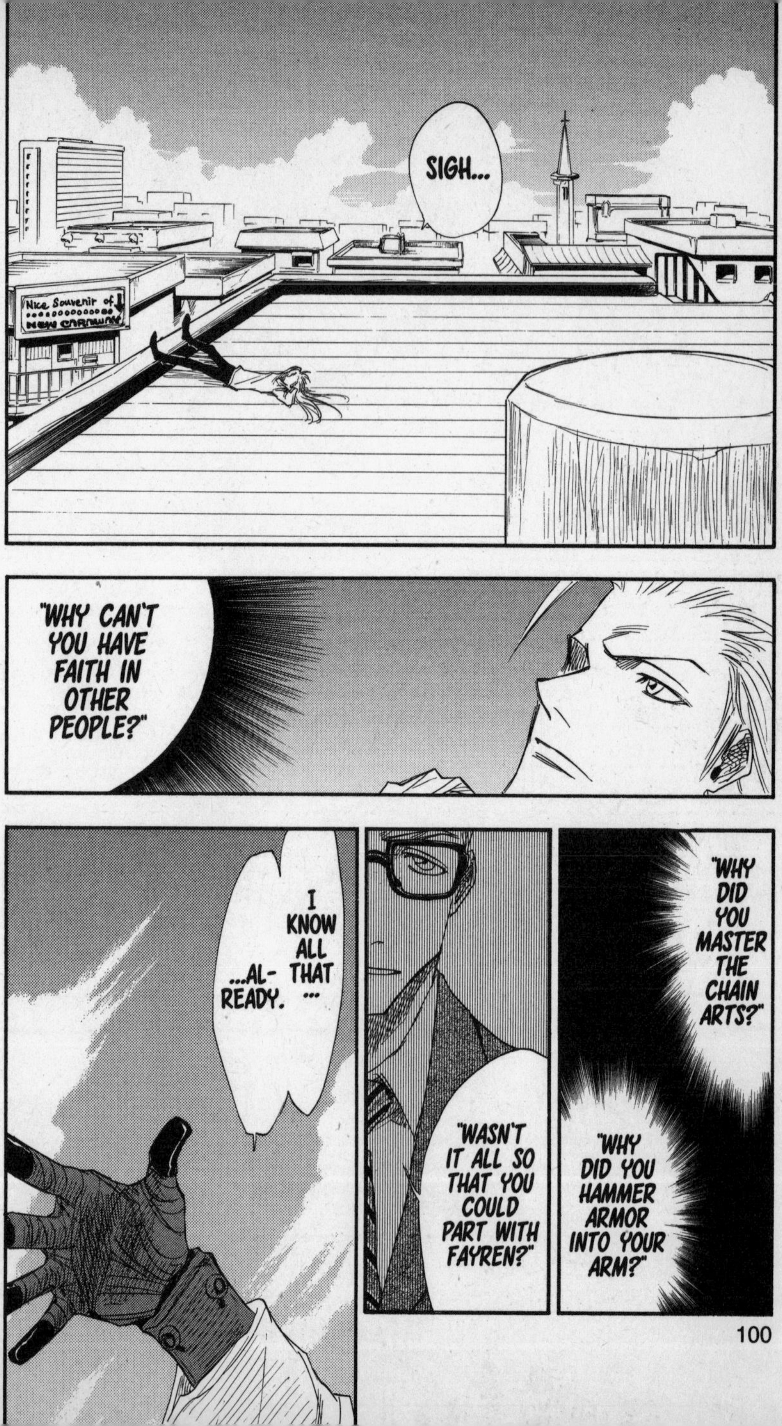
SIGH...
Nice Souvenir of
"WHY CAN'T YOU HAVE FAITH IN OTHER PEOPLE?"
"WHY DID YOU MASTER THE CHAIN ARTS?"
"WHY DID YOU HAMMER ARMOR INTO YOUR ARM?"
"WASN'T IT ALL SO THAT YOU COULD PART WITH FAYREN?"
I KNOW ALL THAT ...
...ALREADY.

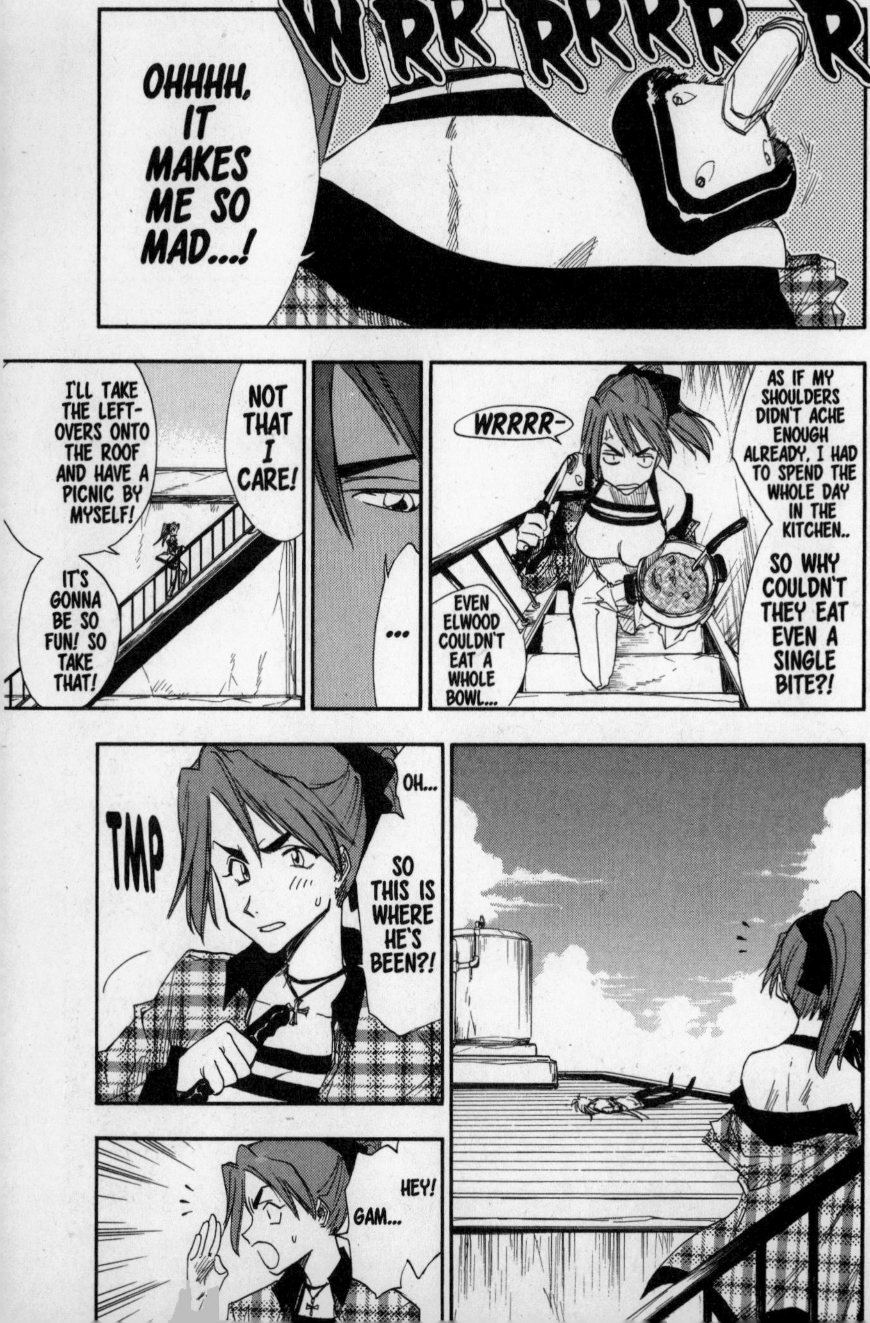
WRR RRRRR R
OHHHH, IT MAKES ME SO MAD...!
AS IF MY SHOULDERS DIDN'T ACHE ENOUGH ALREADY, I HAD TO SPEND THE WHOLE DAY IN THE KITCHEN..
SO WHY COULDN'T THEY EAT EVEN A SINGLE BITE?!
WRRRR-
EVEN ELWOOD COULDN'T EAT A WHOLE BOWL...
...
NOT THAT I CARE!
I'LL TAKE THE LEFT-OVERS ONTO THE ROOF AND HAVE A PICNIC BY MYSELF!
IT'S GONNA BE SO FUN! SO TAKE THAT!
OH...
SO THIS IS WHERE HE'S BEEN?!
TMP
HEY!
GAM...

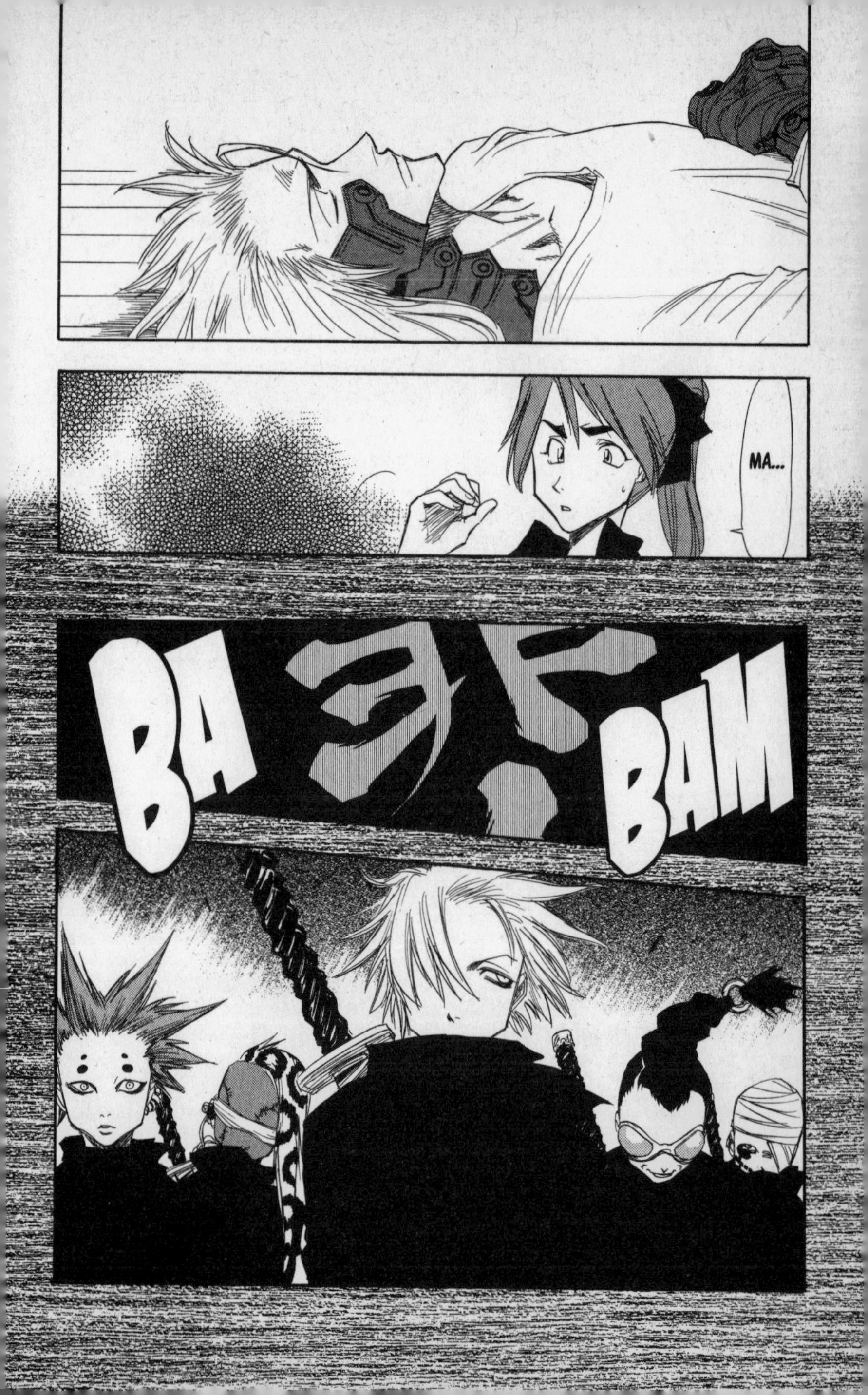
MA...
BA
BAM

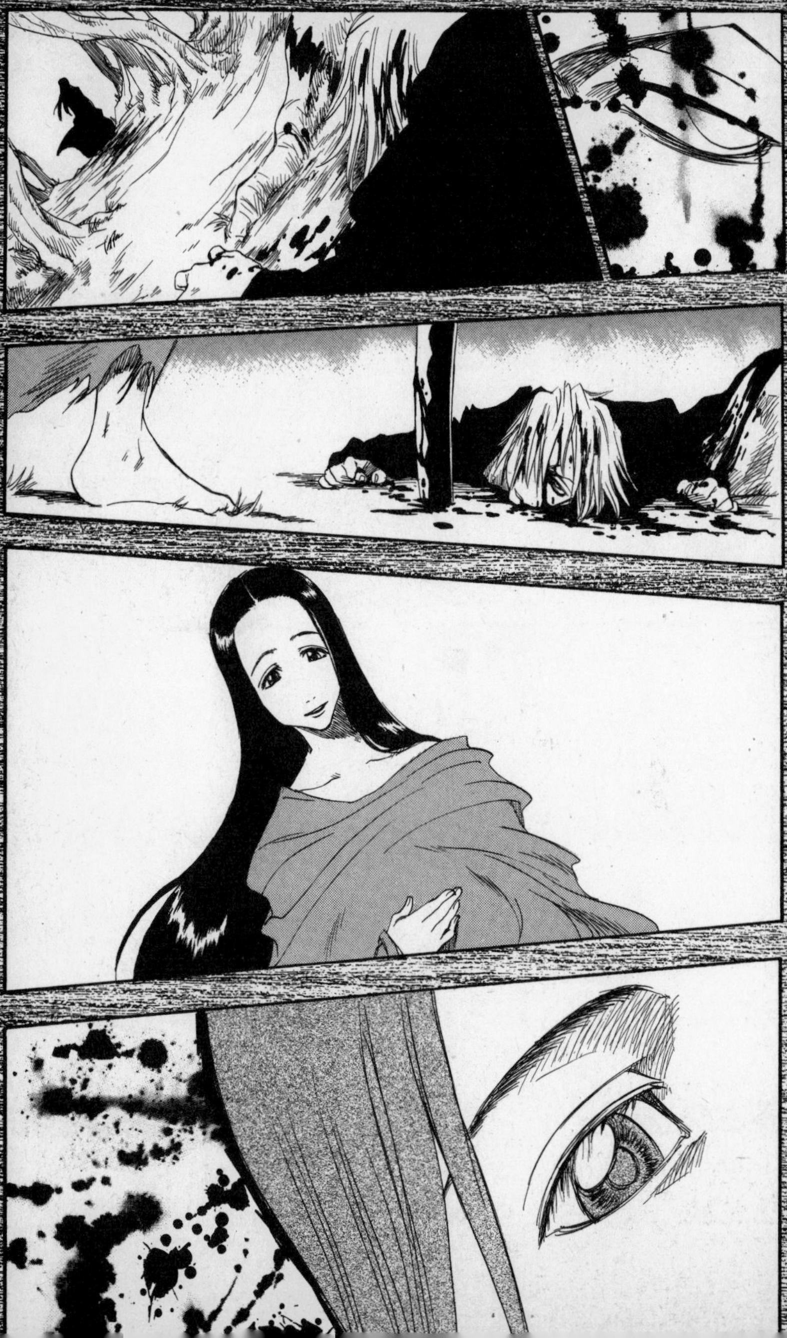

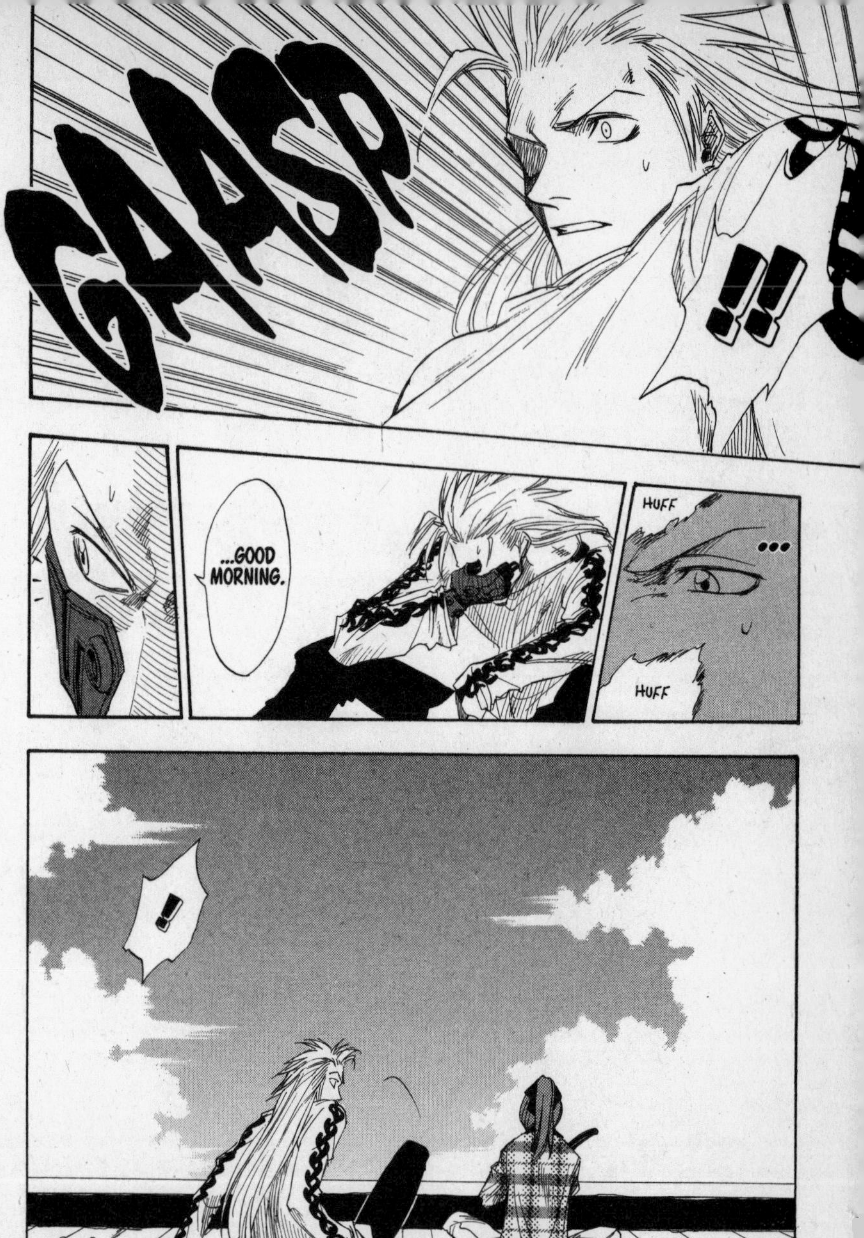
!!
GASP
HUFF
...
HUFF
...GOOD MORNING.
!

READ THIS WAY

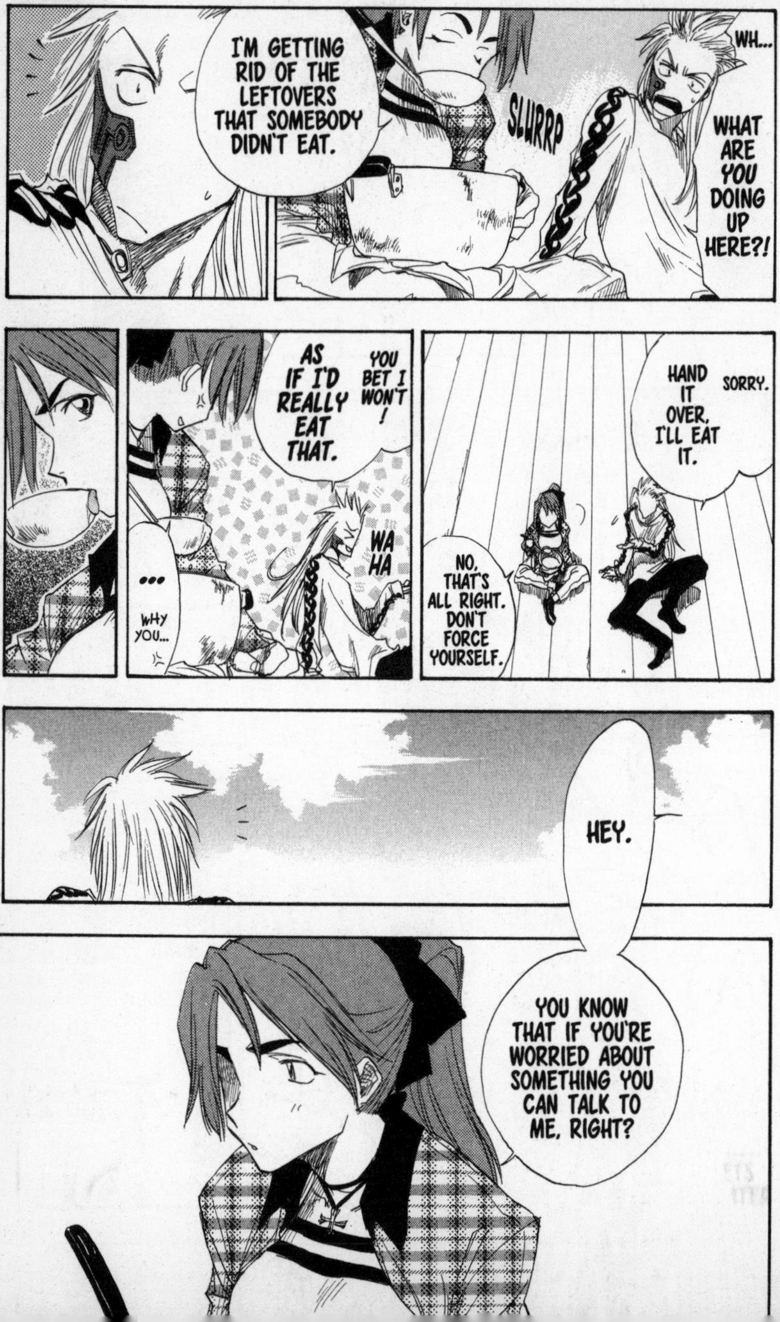
WH...
WHAT ARE YOU DOING UP HERE?!
SLURRP
I'M GETTING RID OF THE LEFTOVERS THAT SOMEBODY DIDN'T EAT.
SORRY.
HAND IT OVER, I'LL EAT IT.
NO, THAT'S ALL RIGHT. DON'T FORCE YOURSELF.
YOU BET I WON'T!
AS IF I'D REALLY EAT THAT.
WA HA
...
WHY YOU...
HEY.
YOU KNOW THAT IF YOU'RE WORRIED ABOUT SOMETHING YOU CAN TALK TO ME, RIGHT?

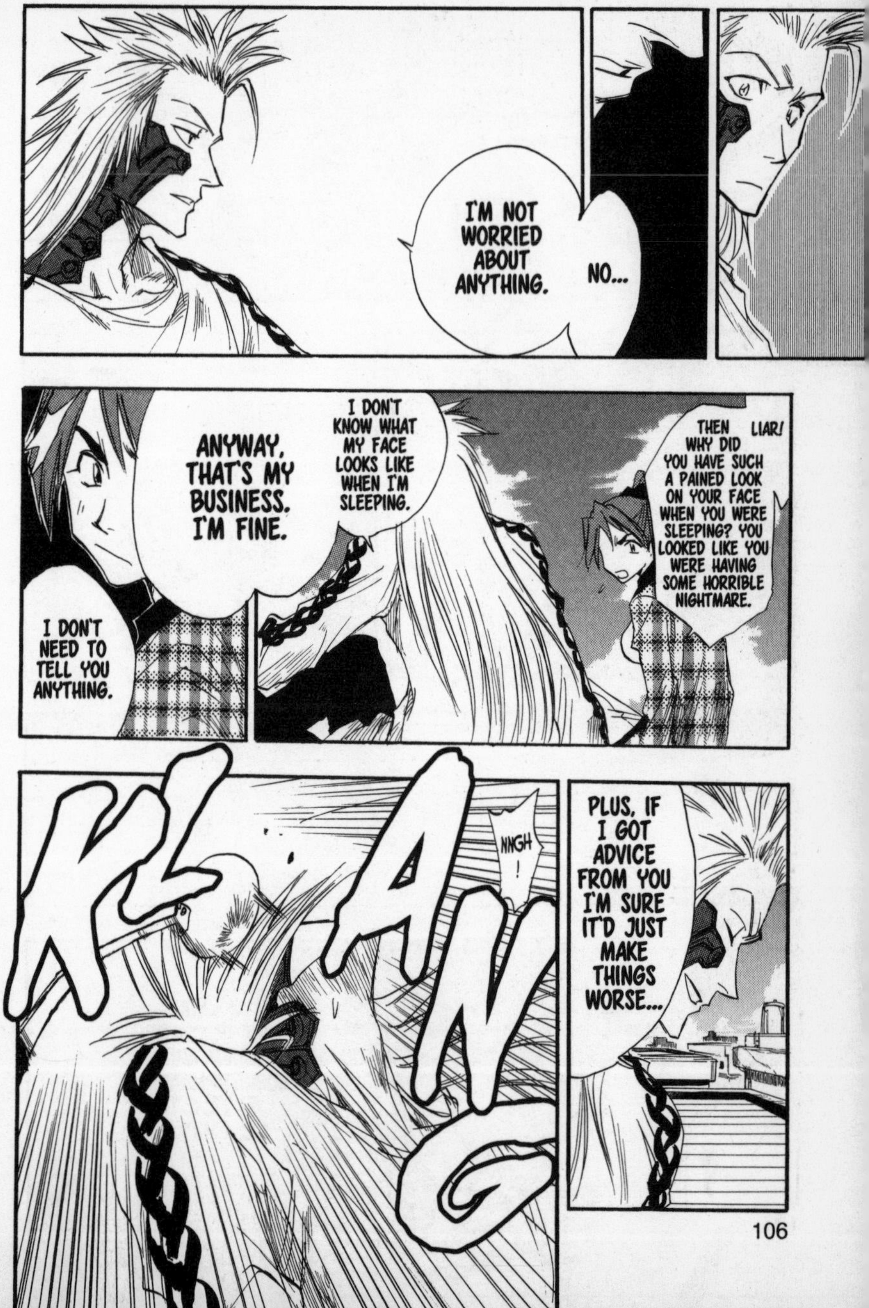
NO...
I'M NOT WORRIED ABOUT ANYTHING.
LIAR!
THEN WHY DID YOU HAVE SUCH A PAINED LOOK ON YOUR FACE WHEN YOU WERE SLEEPING? YOU LOOKED LIKE YOU WERE HAVING SOME HORRIBLE NIGHTMARE.
I DON'T KNOW WHAT MY FACE LOOKS LIKE WHEN I'M SLEEPING.
ANYWAY, THAT'S MY BUSINESS. I'M FINE.
I DON'T NEED TO TELL YOU ANYTHING.
PLUS, IF I GOT ADVICE FROM YOU I'M SURE IT'D JUST MAKE THINGS WORSE...
NNGH!
KLANG

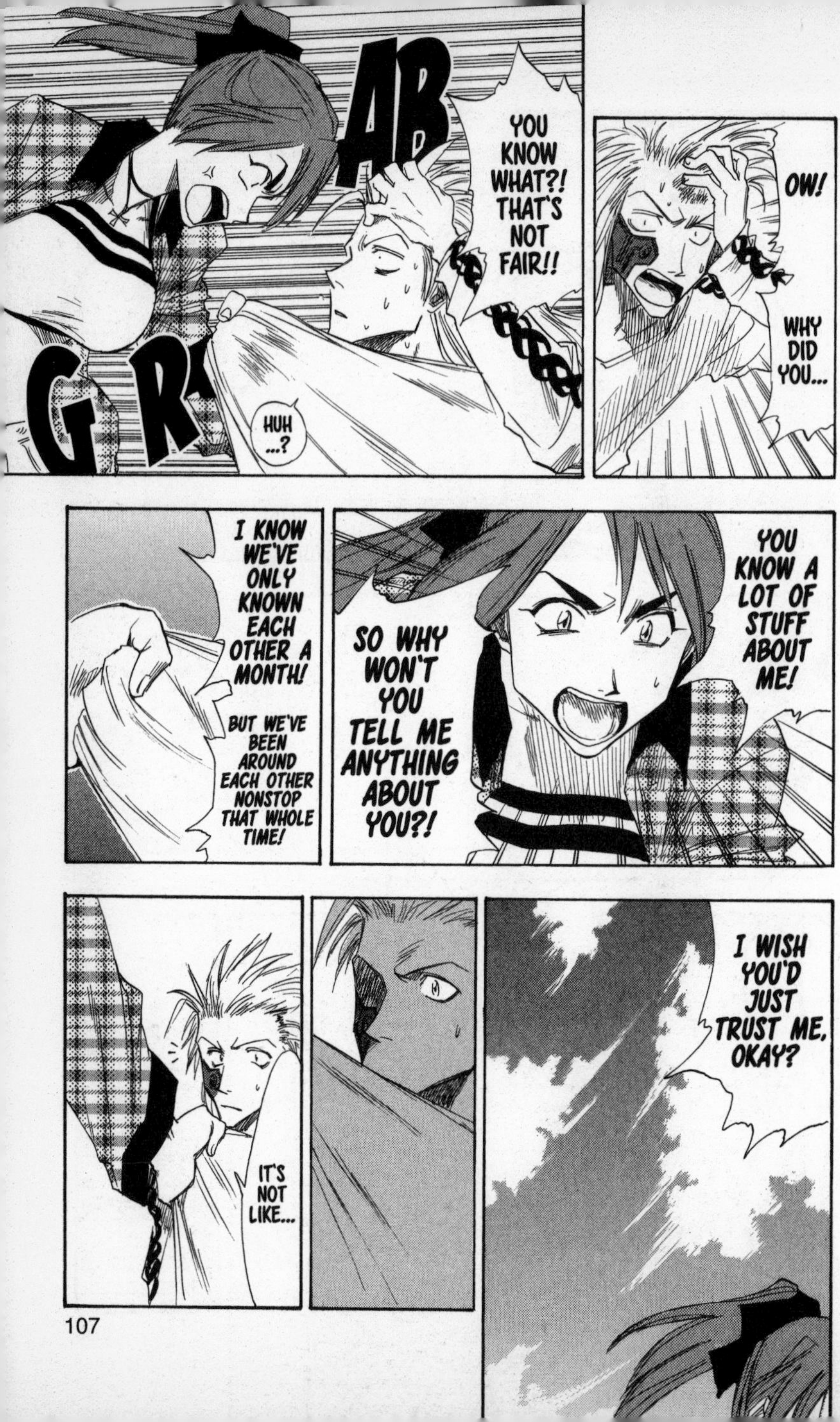
OW!
WHY DID YOU...
YOU KNOW WHAT?! THAT'S NOT FAIR!!
GRAB
HUH ...?
YOU KNOW A LOT OF STUFF ABOUT ME!
SO WHY WON'T YOU TELL ME ANYTHING ABOUT YOU?!
I KNOW WE'VE ONLY KNOWN EACH OTHER A MONTH!
BUT WE'VE BEEN AROUND EACH OTHER NONSTOP THAT WHOLE TIME!
I WISH YOU'D JUST TRUST ME, OKAY?
IT'S NOT LIKE...

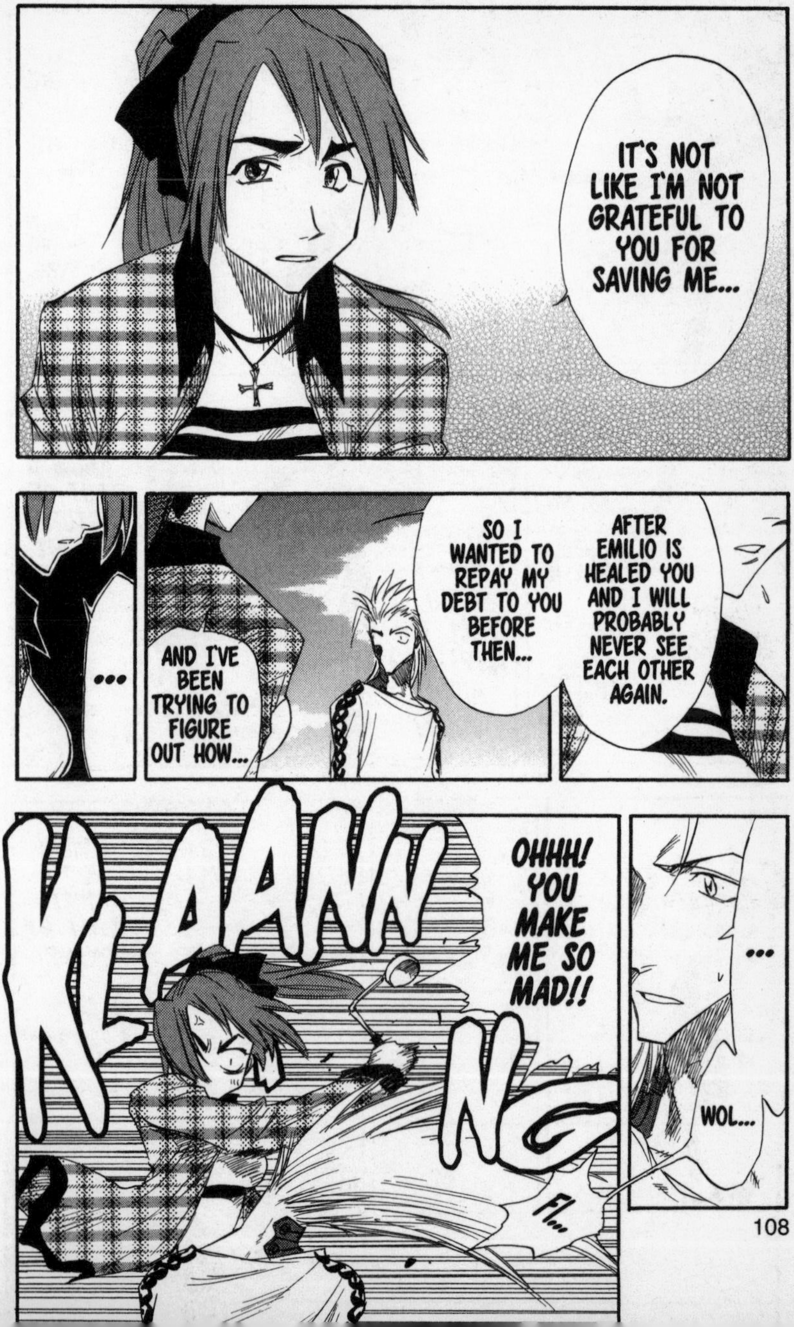
IT'S NOT LIKE I'M NOT GRATEFUL TO YOU FOR SAVING ME...
AFTER EMILIO IS HEALED YOU AND I WILL PROBABLY NEVER SEE EACH OTHER AGAIN.
SO I WANTED TO REPAY MY DEBT TO YOU BEFORE THEN...
AND I'VE BEEN TRYING TO FIGURE OUT HOW...
...
...
WOL...
OHHH! YOU MAKE ME SO MAD!!
KLAANNNG
FL...

READ THIS WAY

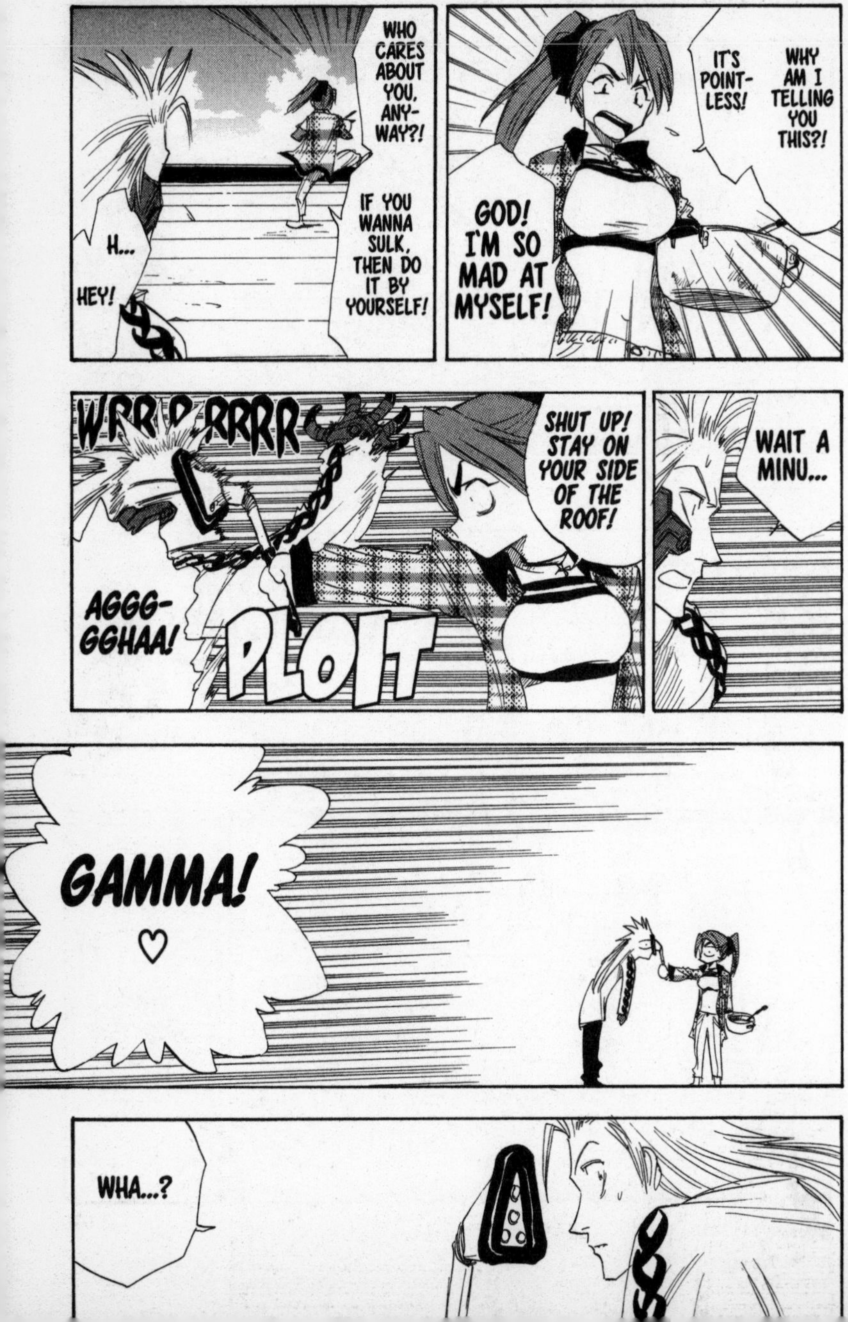
WHY AM I TELLING YOU THIS?!
IT'S POINT-LESS!
GOD! I'M SO MAD AT MYSELF!
WHO CARES ABOUT YOU, ANY-WAY?!
IF YOU WANNA SULK, THEN DO IT BY YOURSELF!
H...
HEY!
WAIT A MINU...
SHUT UP! STAY ON YOUR SIDE OF THE ROOF!
WRRRRRRRR
PLOIT
AGGG-GGHAA!
GAMMA! ♡
WHA...?

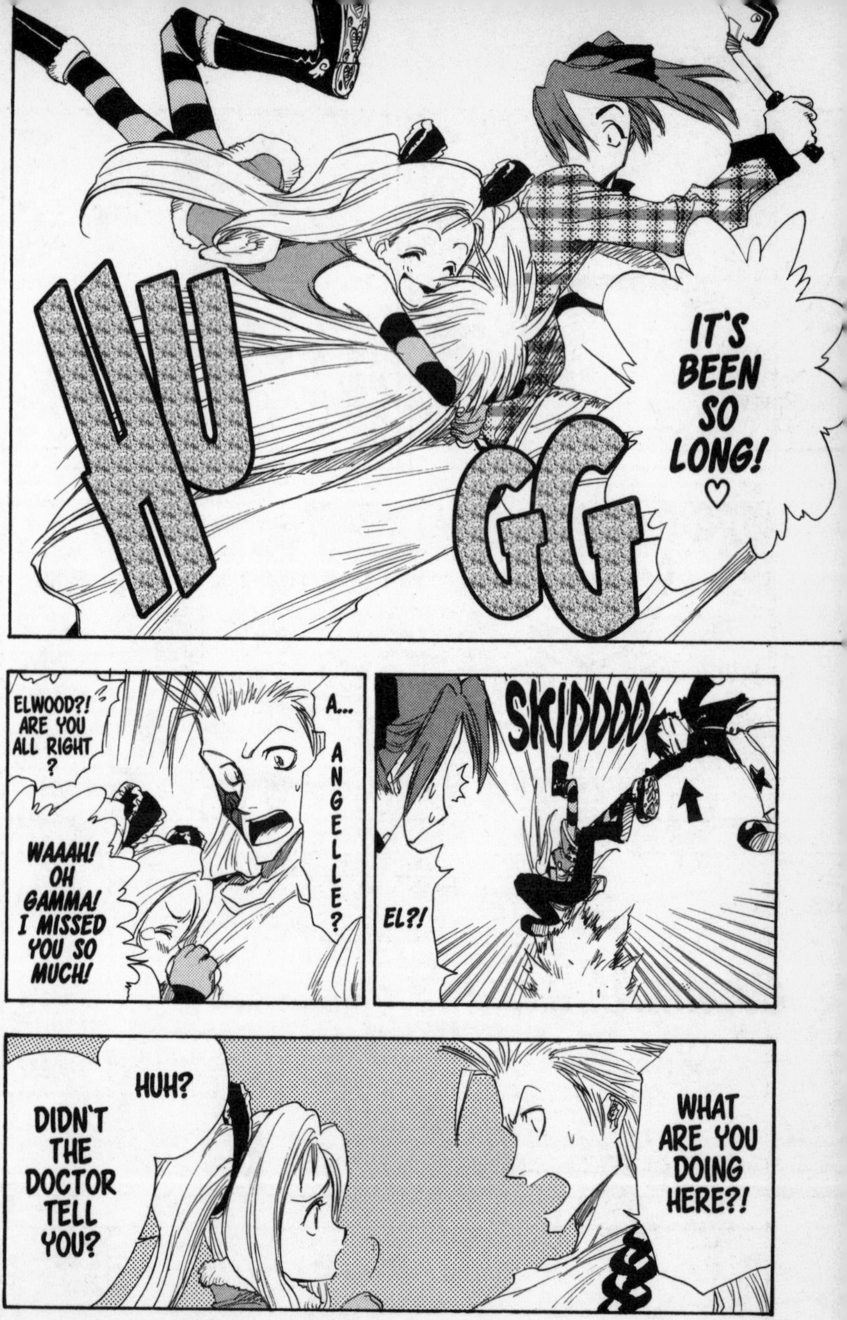
IT'S BEEN SO LONG! ♡
HUGG
SKIDDDD
EL?!
A... ANGELLE?
ELWOOD?! ARE YOU ALL RIGHT?
WAAAH! OH GAMMA! I MISSED YOU SO MUCH!
WHAT ARE YOU DOING HERE?!
HUH?
DIDN'T THE DOCTOR TELL YOU?

READ THIS WAY

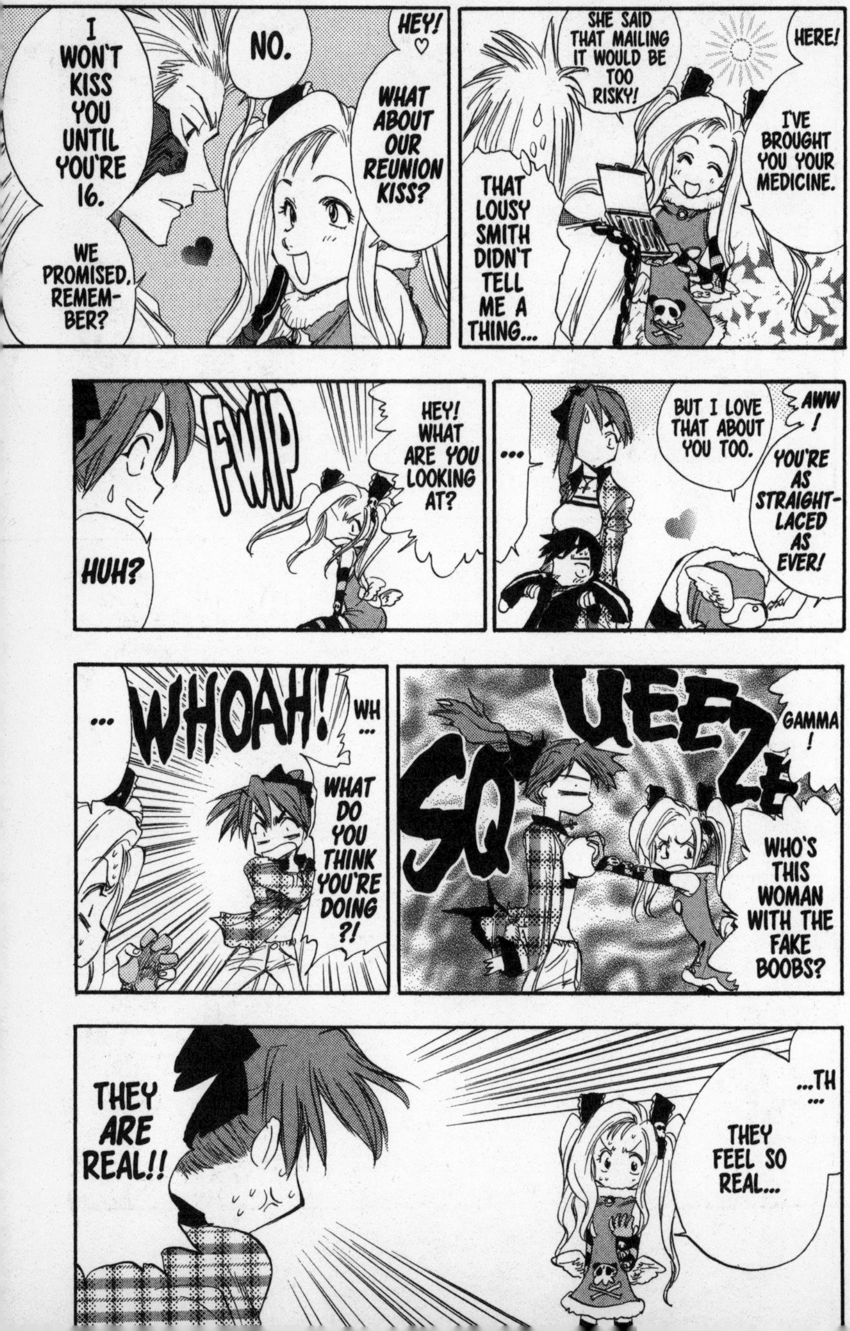

HERE!
I'VE BROUGHT YOU YOUR MEDICINE.
SHE SAID THAT MAILING IT WOULD BE TOO RISKY!
THAT LOUSY SMITH DIDN'T TELL ME A THING...
HEY! ♡
WHAT ABOUT OUR REUNION KISS?
NO.
I WON'T KISS YOU UNTIL YOU'RE 16.
WE PROMISED, REMEMBER?
AWW!
YOU'RE AS STRAIGHT-LACED AS EVER!
BUT I LOVE THAT ABOUT YOU TOO.
...
HEY! WHAT ARE YOU LOOKING AT?
FWIP
HUH?
GAMMA!
WHO'S THIS WOMAN WITH THE FAKE BOOBS?
SQUEEZE
WH...
WHAT DO YOU THINK YOU'RE DOING?!
WHOAH!
...
...TH...
THEY FEEL SO REAL...
THEY ARE REAL!!

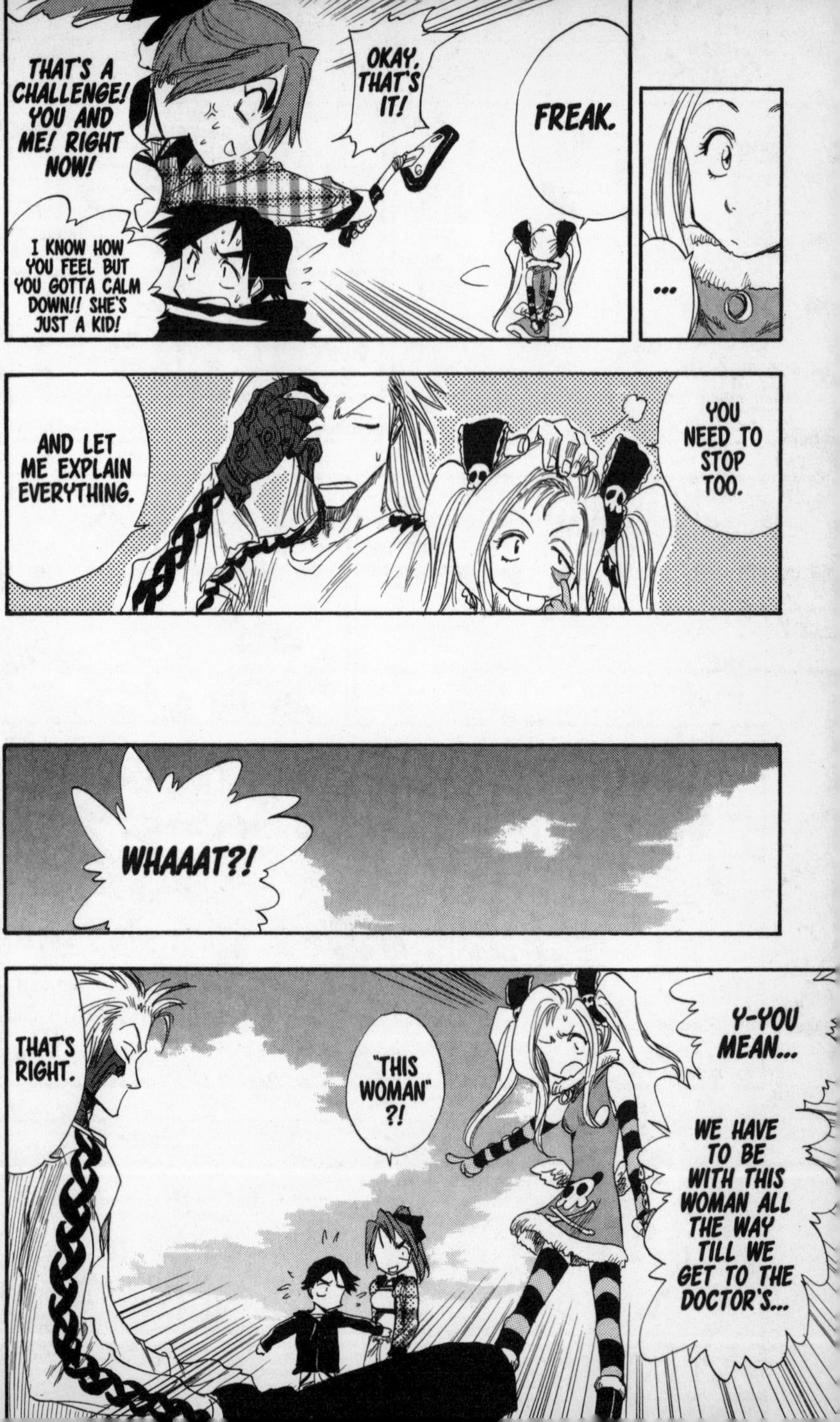
...
FREAK.
OKAY, THAT'S IT!
THAT'S A CHALLENGE! YOU AND ME! RIGHT NOW!
I KNOW HOW YOU FEEL BUT YOU GOTTA CALM DOWN!! SHE'S JUST A KID!
YOU NEED TO STOP TOO.
AND LET ME EXPLAIN EVERYTHING.
WHAAAT?!
Y-YOU MEAN...
WE HAVE TO BE WITH THIS WOMAN ALL THE WAY TILL WE GET TO THE DOCTOR'S...
"THIS WOMAN" ?!
THAT'S RIGHT.

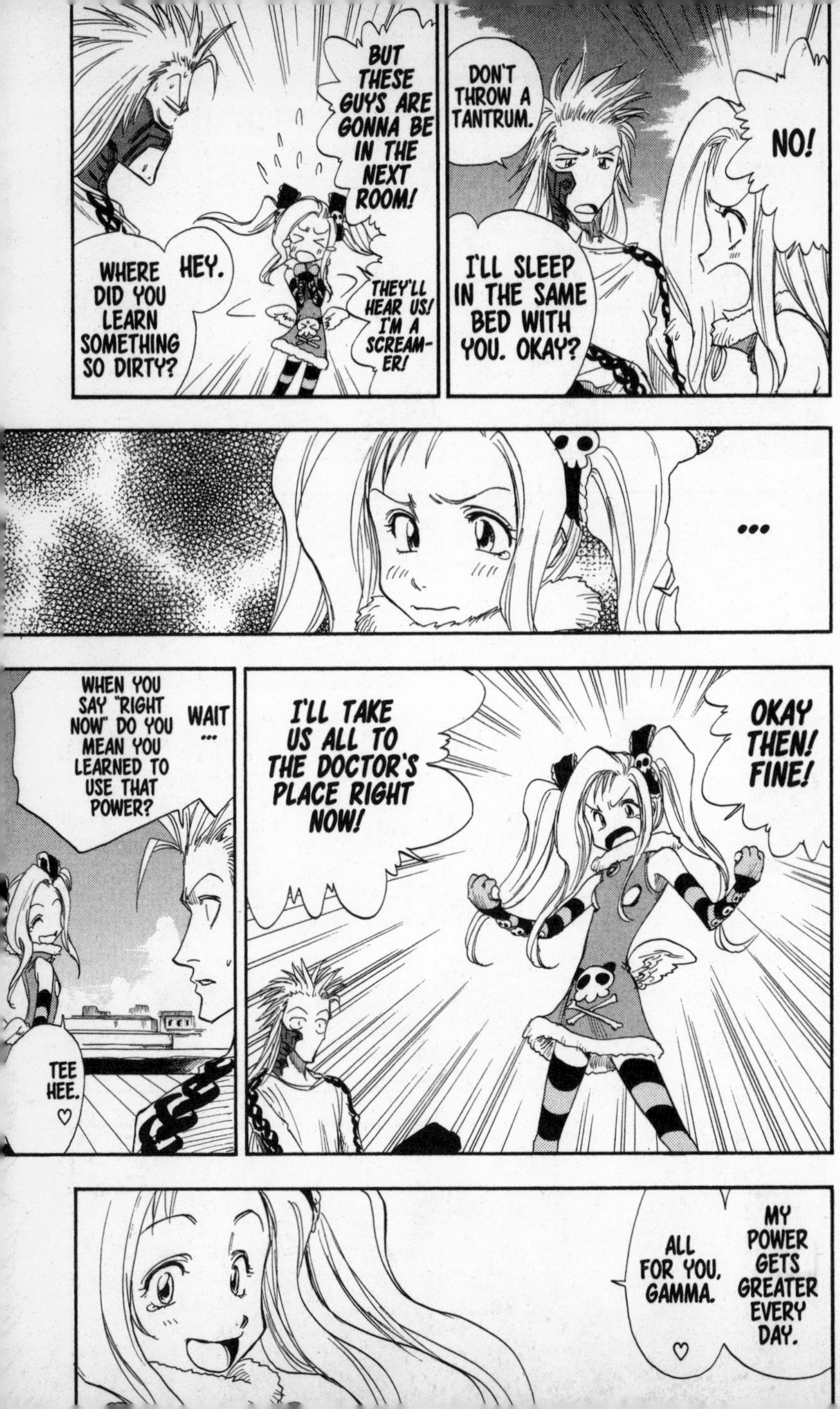
NO!
DON'T THROW A TANTRUM.
I'LL SLEEP IN THE SAME BED WITH YOU. OKAY?
BUT THESE GUYS ARE GONNA BE IN THE NEXT ROOM!
THEY'LL HEAR US! I'M A SCREAMER!
HEY.
WHERE DID YOU LEARN SOMETHING SO DIRTY?
...
OKAY THEN! FINE!
I'LL TAKE US ALL TO THE DOCTOR'S PLACE RIGHT NOW!
WAIT...
WHEN YOU SAY "RIGHT NOW" DO YOU MEAN YOU LEARNED TO USE THAT POWER?
TEE HEE. ♡
MY POWER GETS GREATER EVERY DAY.
ALL FOR YOU, GAMMA. ♡

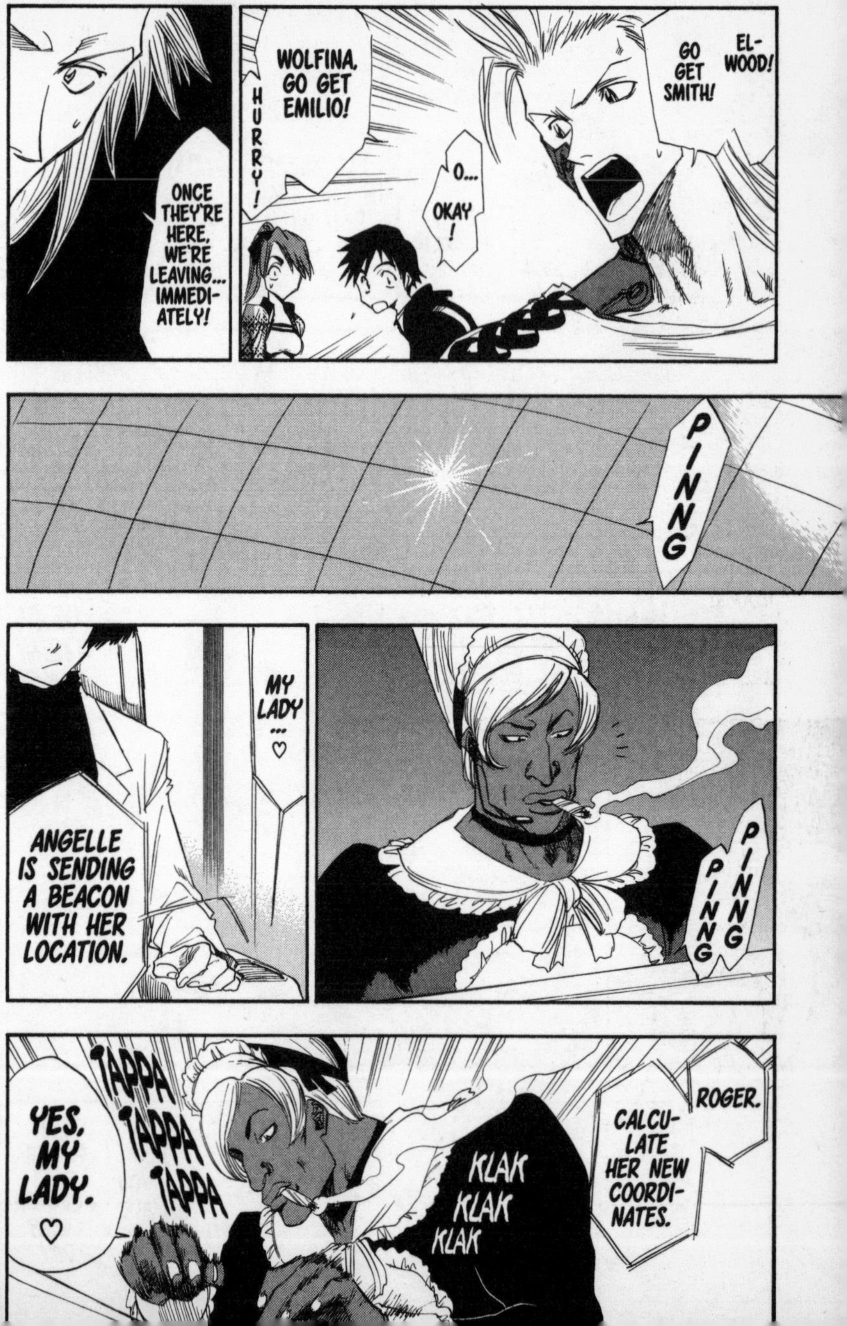
EL-WOOD!
GO GET SMITH!
O... OKAY!
WOLFINA, GO GET EMILIO!
HURRY!
ONCE THEY'RE HERE, WE'RE LEAVING... IMMEDIATELY!
PINNG
PINNG
PINNG
MY LADY... ♡
ANGELLE IS SENDING A BEACON WITH HER LOCATION.
ROGER.
CALCULATE HER NEW COORDINATES.
KLAK KLAK KLAK
TAPPA TAPPA TAPPA
YES, MY LADY. ♡

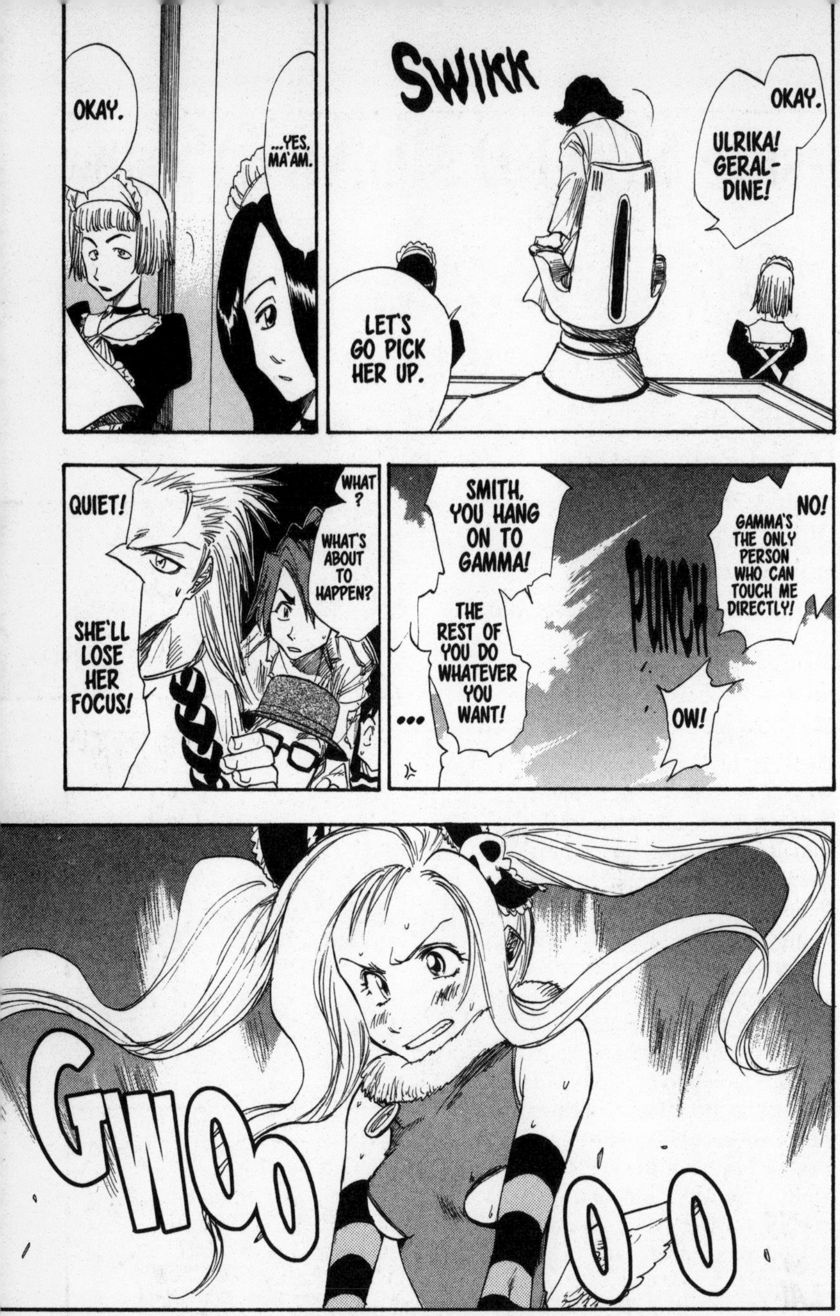

SWIKK
OKAY.
ULRIKA! GERAL-DINE!
LET'S GO PICK HER UP.
...YES, MA'AM.
OKAY.
NO!
GAMMA'S THE ONLY PERSON WHO CAN TOUCH ME DIRECTLY!
PUNCH
OW!
SMITH, YOU HANG ON TO GAMMA!
THE REST OF YOU DO WHATEVER YOU WANT!
...
WHAT?
WHAT'S ABOUT TO HAPPEN?
QUIET!
SHE'LL LOSE HER FOCUS!
GWOOOO-O-O

B-side NAKED MONKEYS 18.

Nazna Gemini
ナズナ・ジェミニ

Height : 153cm
Weight : 40kg
Date of Birth : 11/4
Age : unknown
Blood Type : unknown
Hometown : unknown
Academic Career : unknown

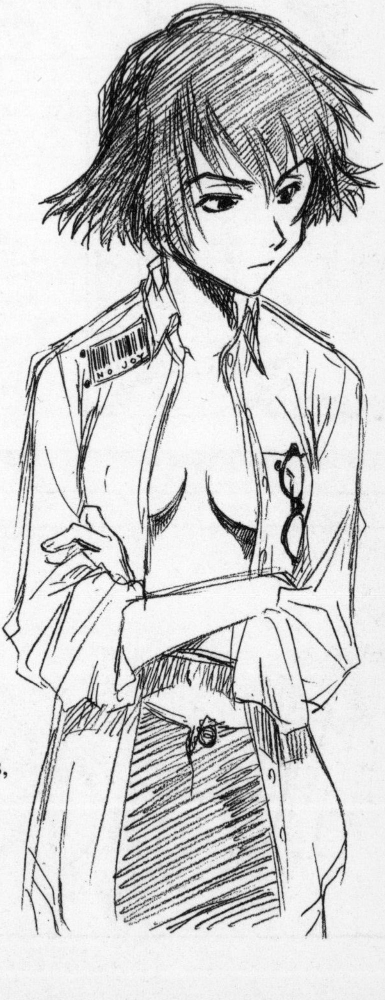
NO JOY

The head of Gemini Laboratory. She has been involved in many federal crimes, all of which she maliciously blames on Gamma. She lives with Angelle, five maids, and many strange creatures. Her area of expertise, as well as her primary hobby, is surgery. Apart from surgery, her interests are fickle and change frequently, to the inconvenience of her maids who are forced to go along with her latest hobby. Her favorite things are coconuts, white asparagus, meat dishes other than chicken, pointing out the faults of others and bullying the weak. Her dislikes include okra, cheese and frogs.

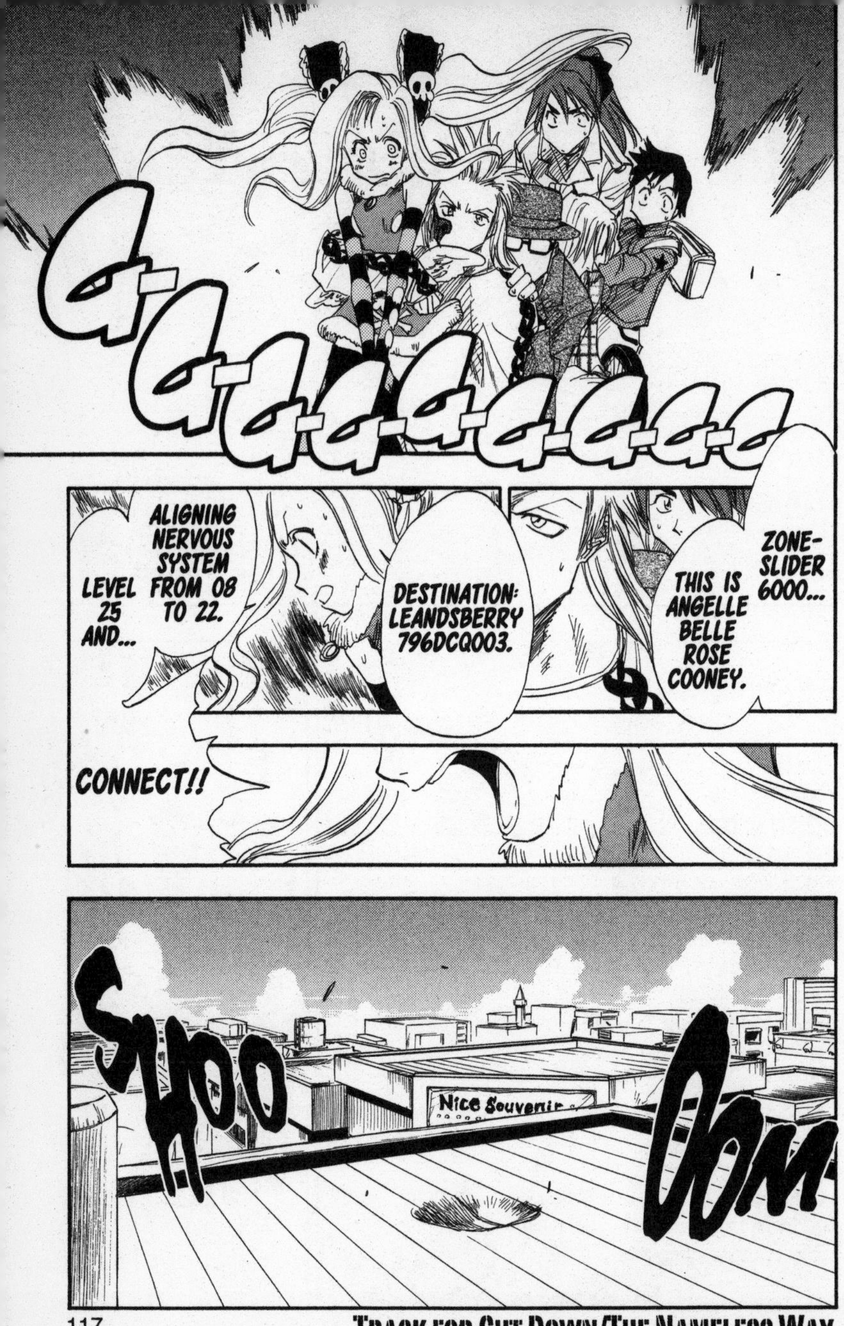

G-G-G-G-G-G-G-G-G-G
ZONE-SLIDER 6000...
THIS IS ANGELLE BELLE ROSE COONEY.
DESTINATION: LEANDSBERRY 796DCQ003.
ALIGNING NERVOUS SYSTEM FROM 08 TO 22.
LEVEL 25 AND...
CONNECT!!
SHOO
OOM
Nice Souvenir

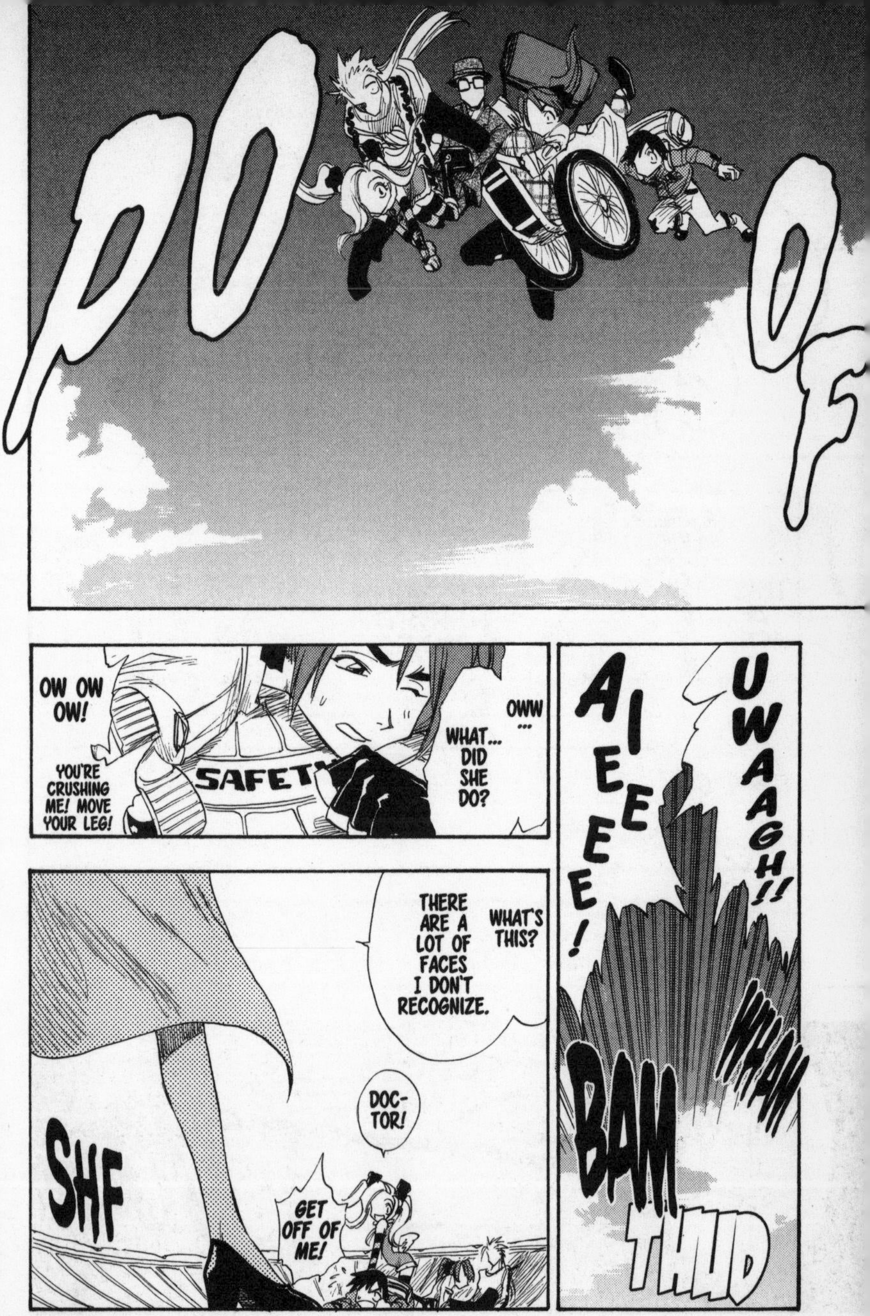
POOOF
UWAAGH!!
AIEEEE!
WHAM
BAM
THUD
OWW...
WHAT... DID SHE DO?
OW OW OW!
YOU'RE CRUSHING ME! MOVE YOUR LEG!
SAFET
WHAT'S THIS?
THERE ARE A LOT OF FACES I DON'T RECOGNIZE.
DOC-TOR!
GET OFF OF ME!
SHF

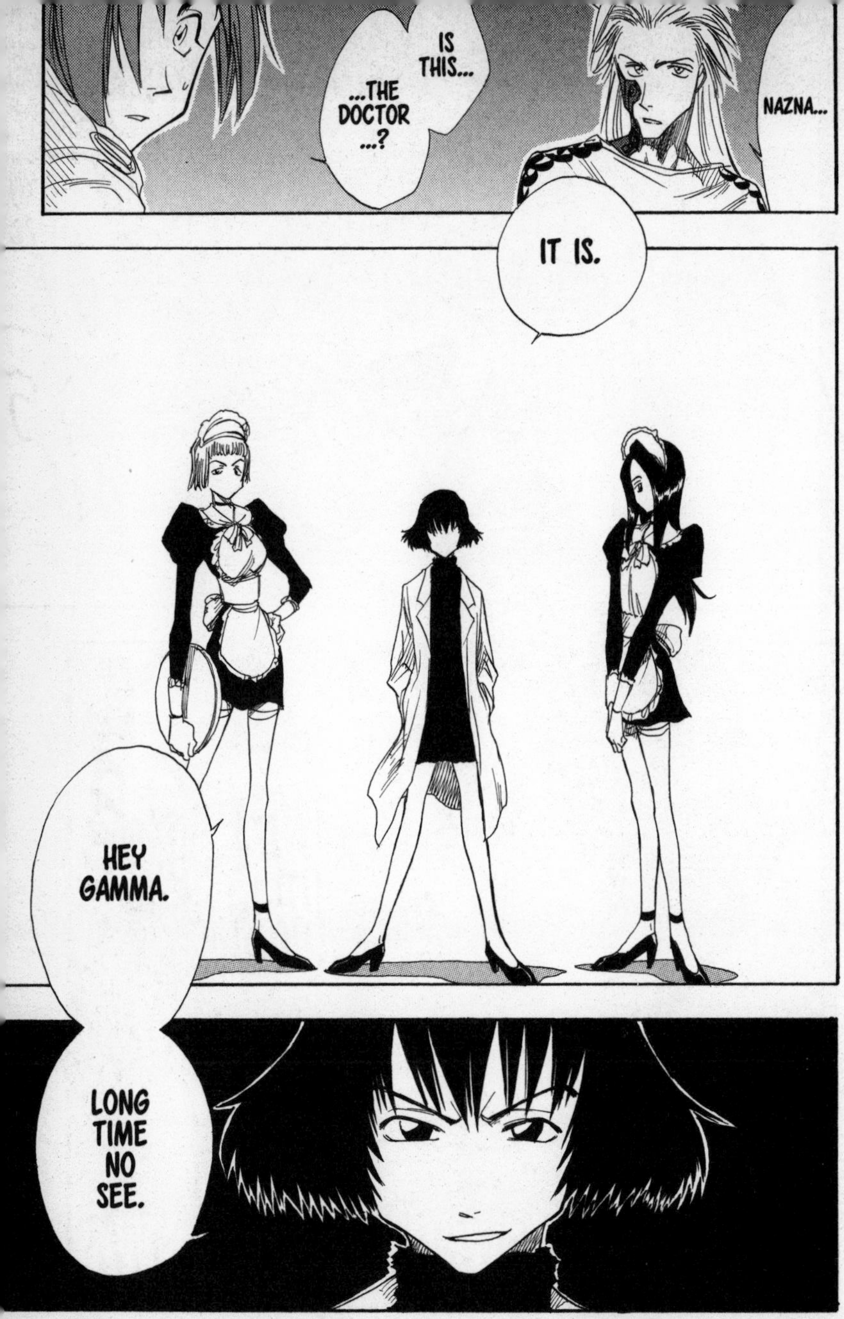
NAZNA...
IS THIS... ...THE DOCTOR ...?
IT IS.
HEY GAMMA.
LONG TIME NO SEE.

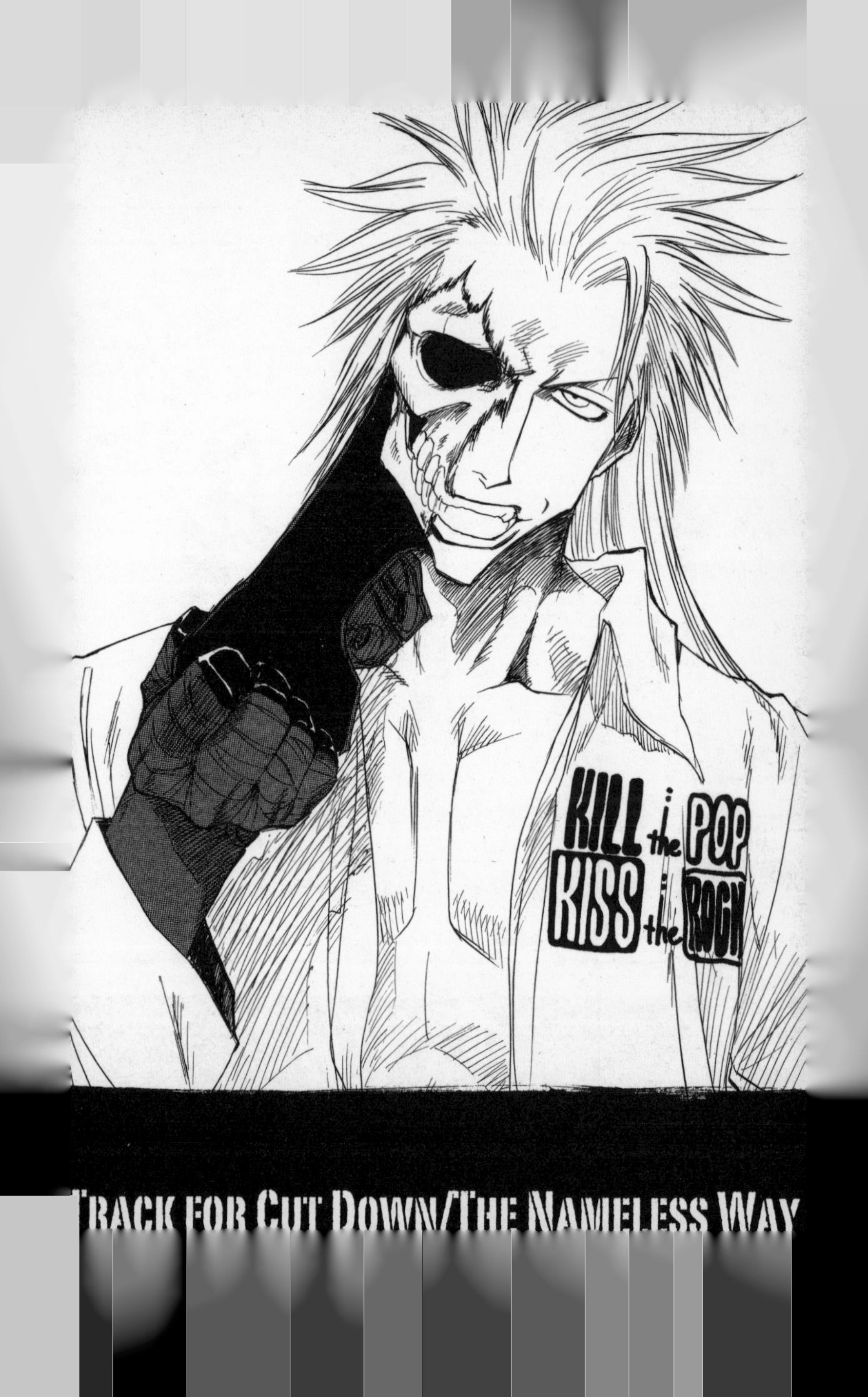
KILL the POP
KISS the ROCK

Track for Cut Down/The Nameless Way

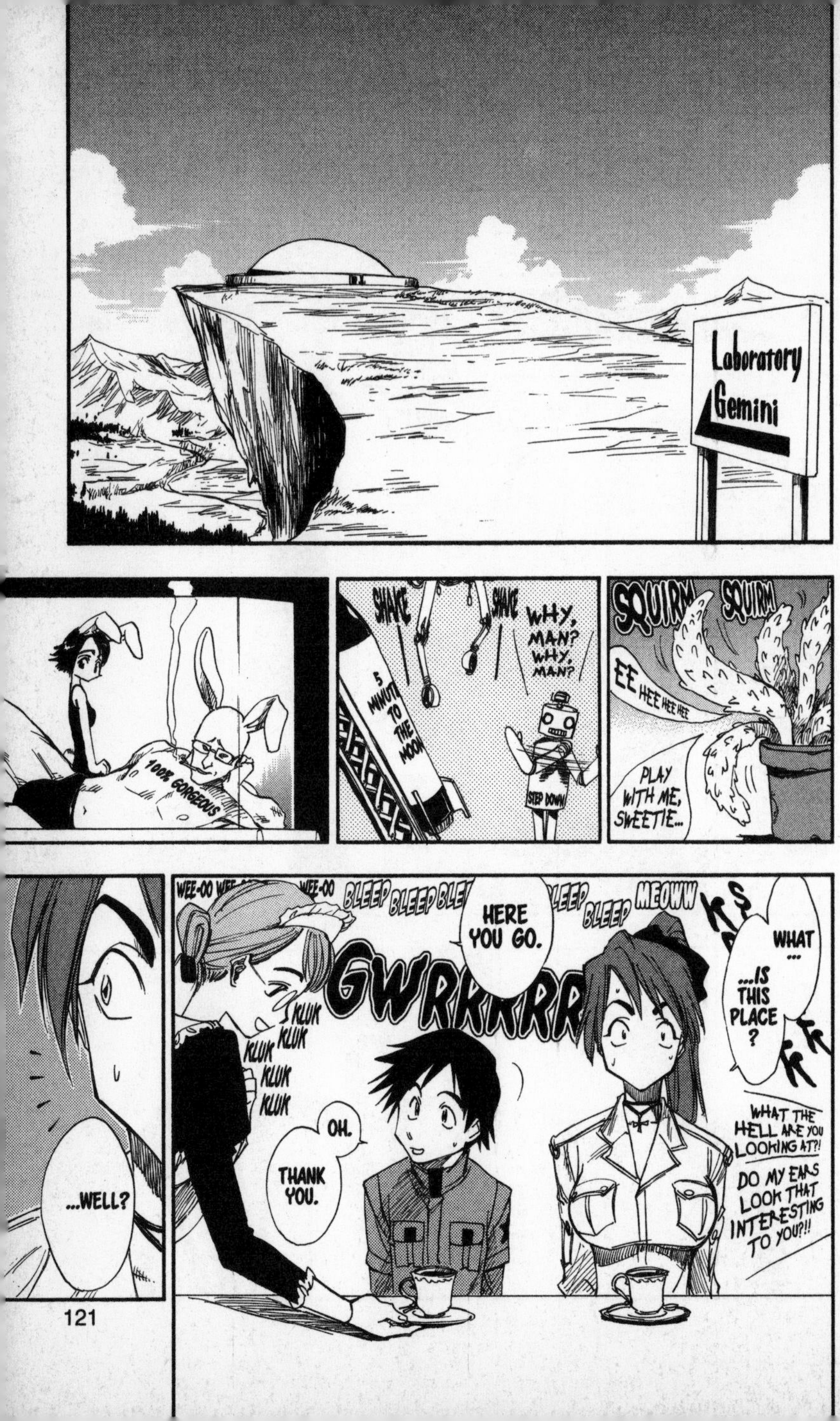
Laboratory Gemini
SQUIRM SQUIRM
EE HEE HEE HEE
PLAY WITH ME, SWEETIE...
SHAKE SHAKE
WHY, MAN? WHY, MAN?
5 MINUTE TO THE MOON
STEP DOWN
100% GORGEOUS
WHAT ...
...IS THIS PLACE?
MEOWW
BLEEP BLEEP
HERE YOU GO.
BLEEP BLEEP BLE
WEE-OO WEE-OO
GWRRRRR
WHAT THE HELL ARE YOU LOOKING AT?!
DO MY EARS LOOK THAT INTERESTING TO YOU?!!
KLUK KLUK KLUK KLUK KLUK
OH.
THANK YOU.
...WELL?

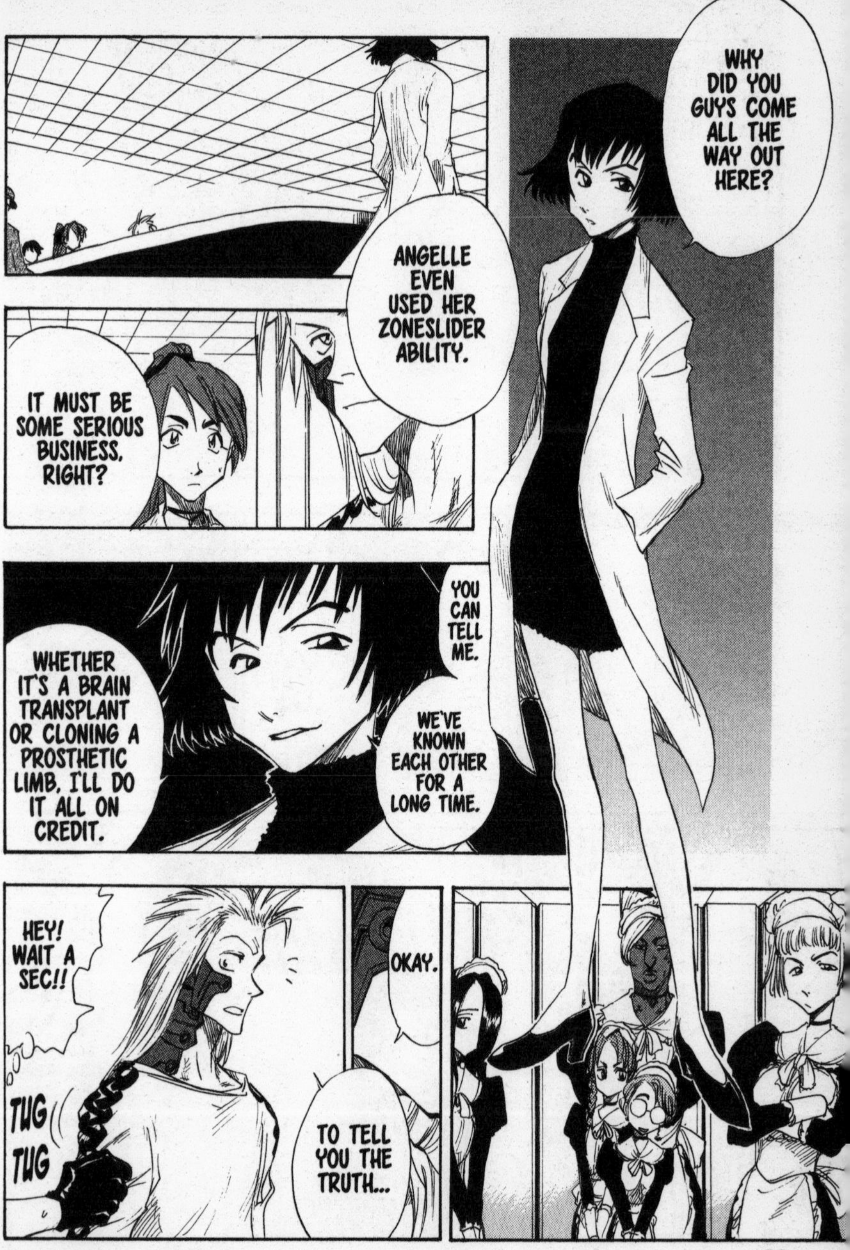
WHY DID YOU GUYS COME ALL THE WAY OUT HERE?
ANGELLE EVEN USED HER ZONESLIDER ABILITY.
IT MUST BE SOME SERIOUS BUSINESS, RIGHT?
YOU CAN TELL ME.
WE'VE KNOWN EACH OTHER FOR A LONG TIME.
WHETHER IT'S A BRAIN TRANSPLANT OR CLONING A PROSTHETIC LIMB, I'LL DO IT ALL ON CREDIT.
OKAY.
TO TELL YOU THE TRUTH...
HEY! WAIT A SEC!!
TUG TUG

READ THIS WAY

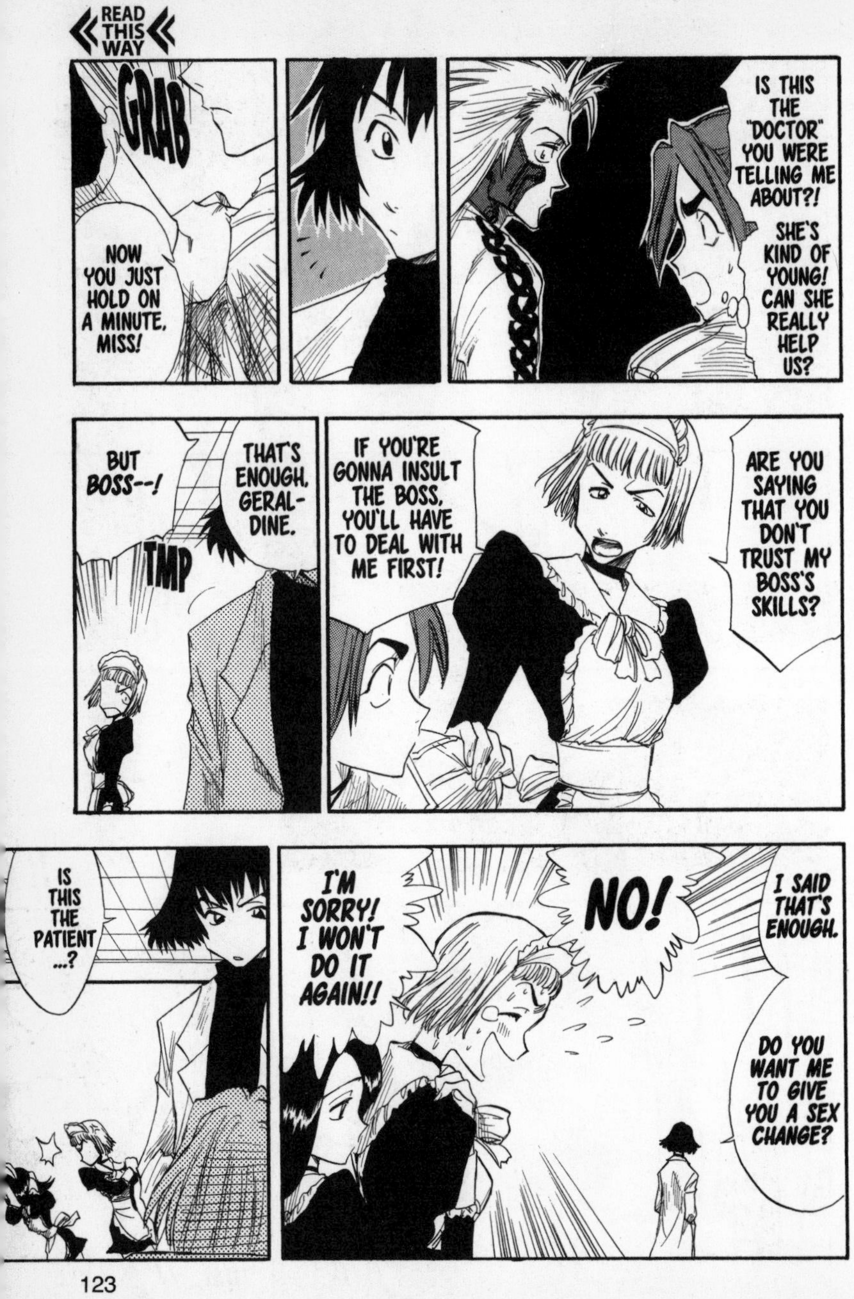
IS THIS THE "DOCTOR" YOU WERE TELLING ME ABOUT?!
SHE'S KIND OF YOUNG! CAN SHE REALLY HELP US?
GRAB
NOW YOU JUST HOLD ON A MINUTE, MISS!
ARE YOU SAYING THAT YOU DON'T TRUST MY BOSS'S SKILLS?
IF YOU'RE GONNA INSULT THE BOSS, YOU'LL HAVE TO DEAL WITH ME FIRST!
THAT'S ENOUGH, GERAL-DINE.
BUT BOSS--!
TMP
I SAID THAT'S ENOUGH.
DO YOU WANT ME TO GIVE YOU A SEX CHANGE?
NO!
I'M SORRY! I WON'T DO IT AGAIN!!
IS THIS THE PATIENT ...?

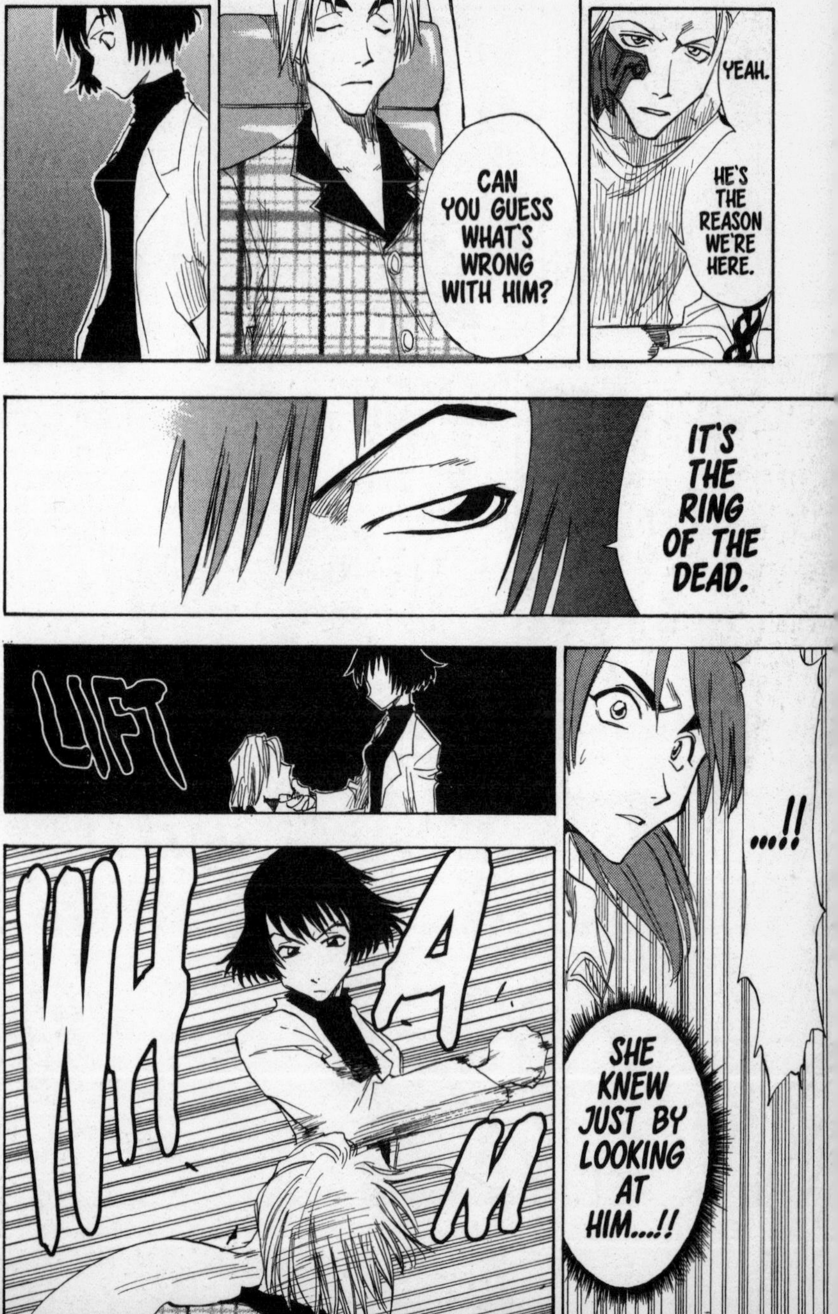
YEAH.
HE'S THE REASON WE'RE HERE.
CAN YOU GUESS WHAT'S WRONG WITH HIM?
IT'S THE RING OF THE DEAD.
...!!
SHE KNEW JUST BY LOOKING AT HIM...!!
LIFT
WHAM

READ THIS WAY

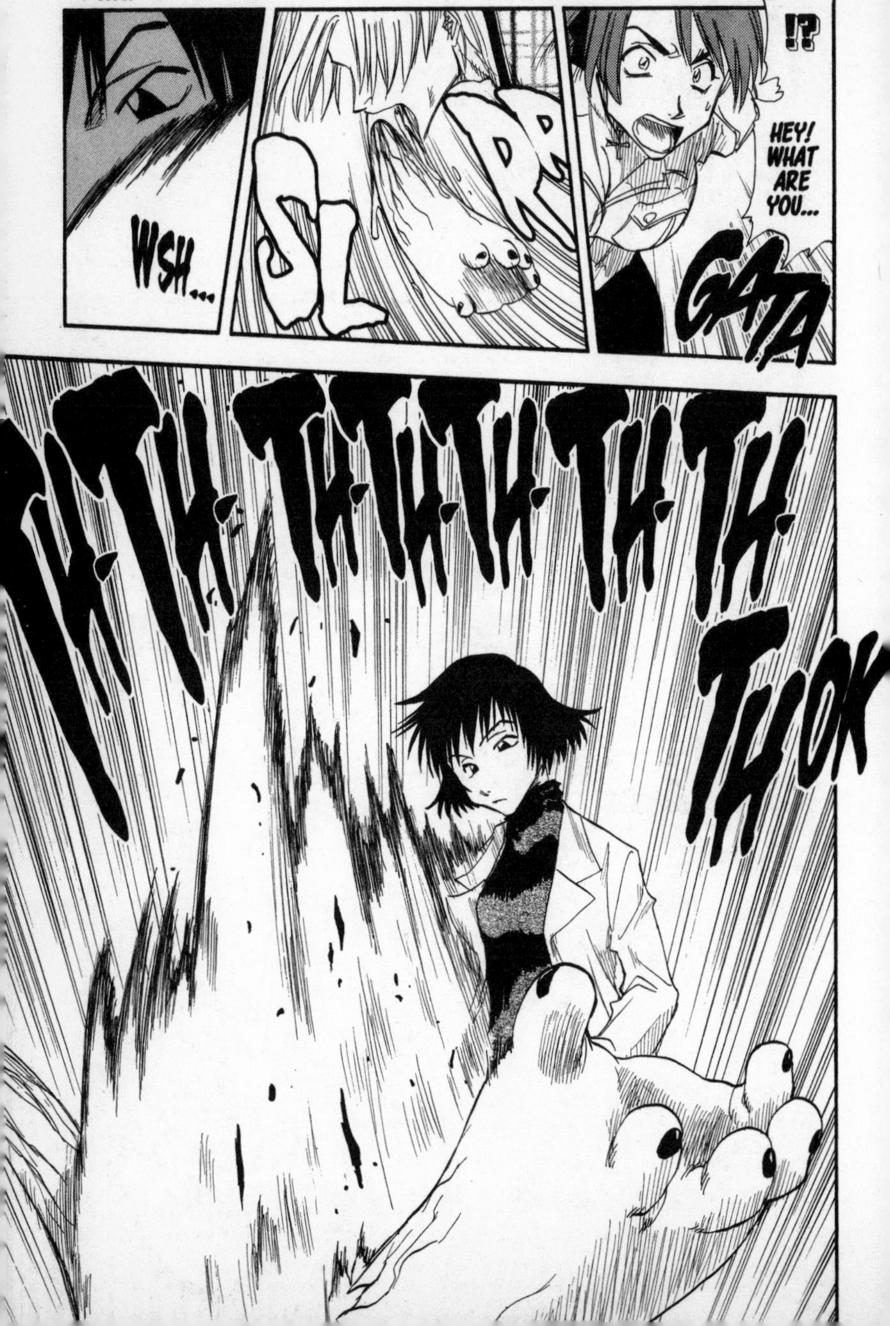
!?
HEY! WHAT ARE YOU...
GATA
SLRP
WSH...
TH-TH- TH-TH-TH-TH-TH-TH-TH-
THOK

WSH

!!

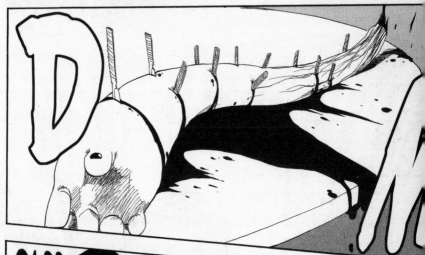

D

GLSS SSH ...

SEVEN
YEARS...

IT'S
FAIRLY
DEEP...

NO,
IT'S BEEN
AT LEAST
EIGHT YEARS.

READ THIS WAY

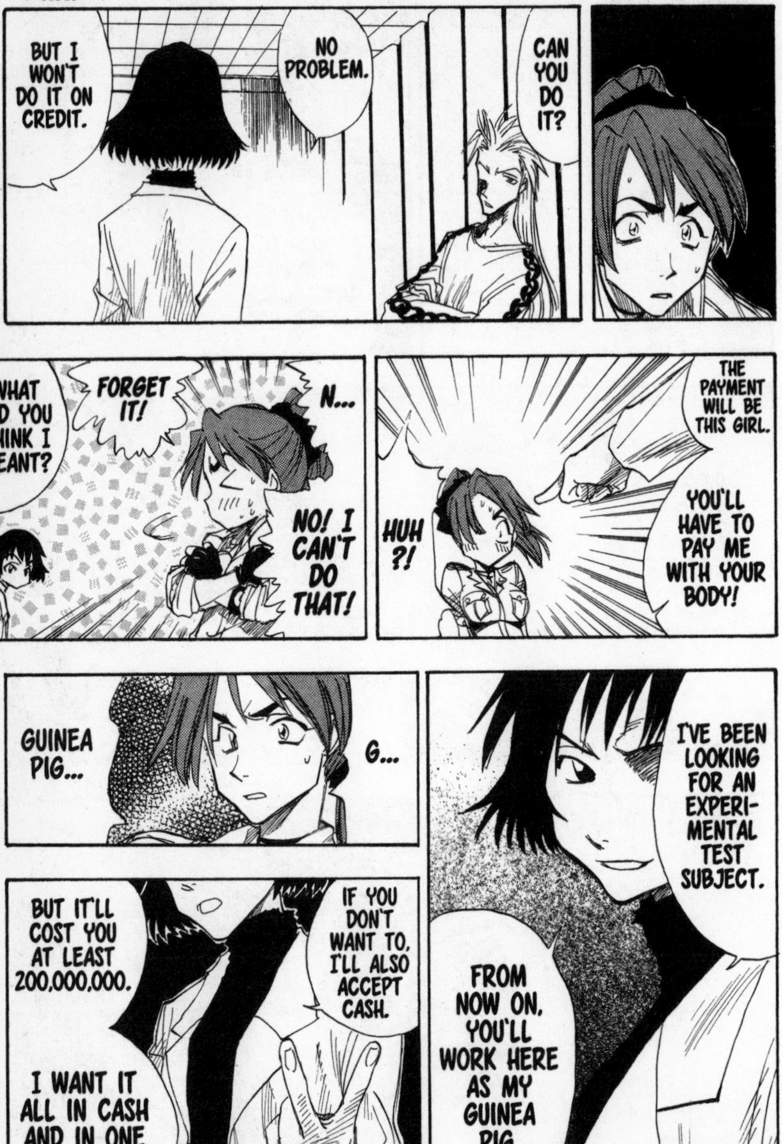
CAN YOU DO IT?
NO PROBLEM.
BUT I WON'T DO IT ON CREDIT.
THE PAYMENT WILL BE THIS GIRL.
YOU'LL HAVE TO PAY ME WITH YOUR BODY!
HUH?!
N...
NO! I CAN'T DO THAT!
WHAT DID YOU THINK I MEANT?
FORGET IT!
I'VE BEEN LOOKING FOR AN EXPERIMENTAL TEST SUBJECT.
FROM NOW ON, YOU'LL WORK HERE AS MY GUINEA PIG.
G...
GUINEA PIG...
IF YOU DON'T WANT TO, I'LL ALSO ACCEPT CASH.
BUT IT'LL COST YOU AT LEAST 200,000,000.
I WANT IT ALL IN CASH AND IN ONE PAYMENT.

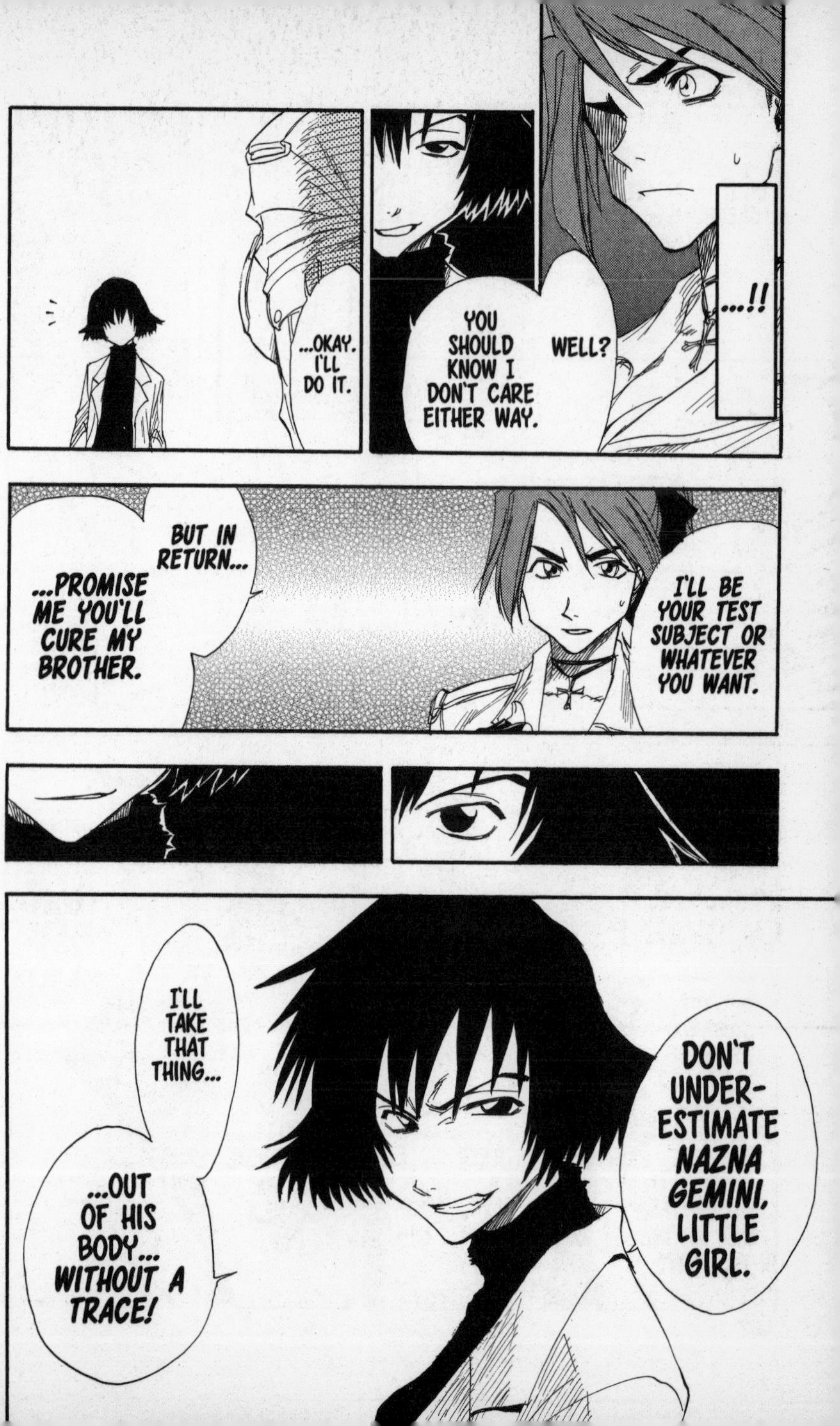
...!!
WELL?
YOU SHOULD KNOW I DON'T CARE EITHER WAY.
...OKAY. I'LL DO IT.
I'LL BE YOUR TEST SUBJECT OR WHATEVER YOU WANT.
BUT IN RETURN...
...PROMISE ME YOU'LL CURE MY BROTHER.
DON'T UNDER-ESTIMATE NAZNA GEMINI, LITTLE GIRL.
I'LL TAKE THAT THING...
...OUT OF HIS BODY... WITHOUT A TRACE!

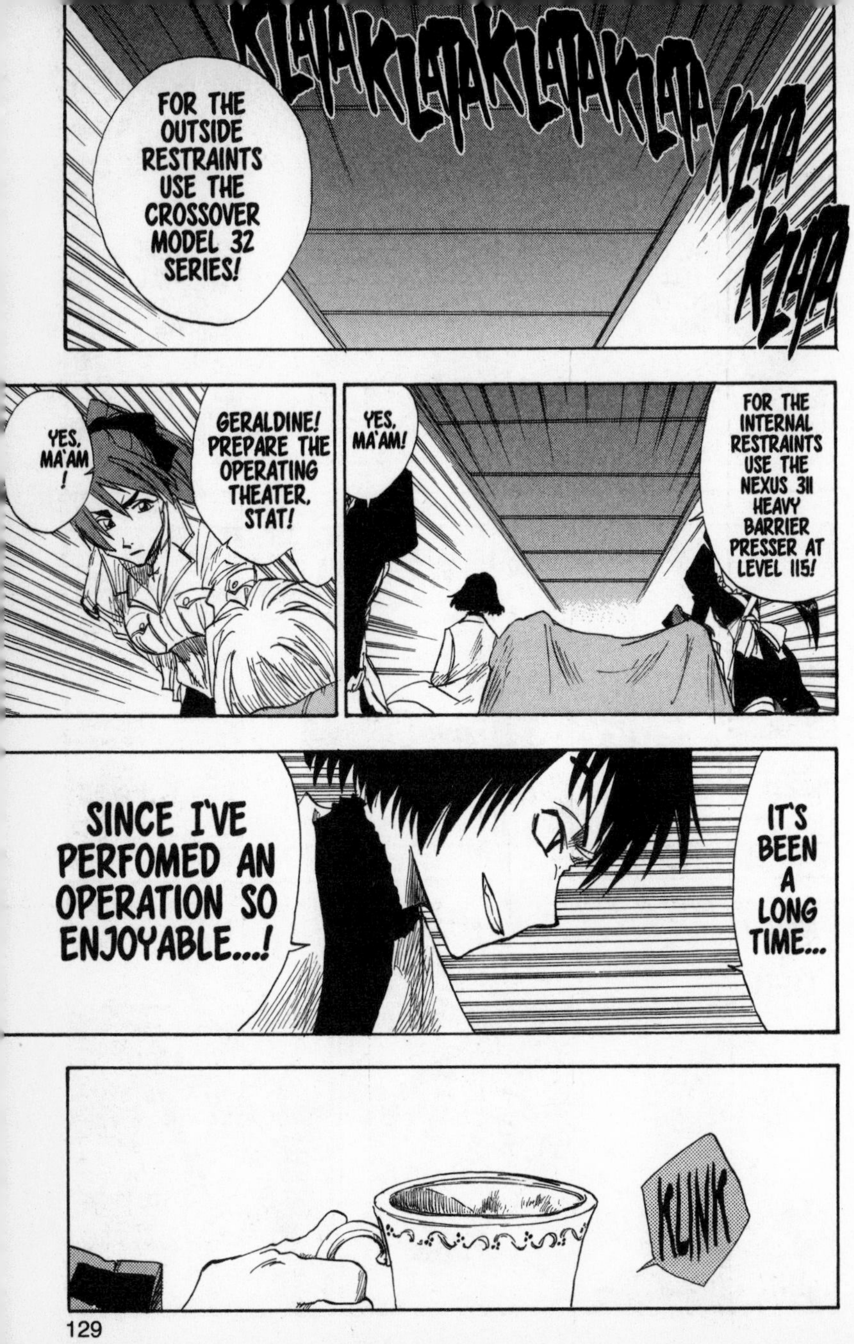
KLATAKLATAKLATAKLATA
KLATA KLATA
FOR THE OUTSIDE RESTRAINTS USE THE CROSSOVER MODEL 32 SERIES!
FOR THE INTERNAL RESTRAINTS USE THE NEXUS 311 HEAVY BARRIER PRESSER AT LEVEL 115!
YES, MA'AM!
GERALDINE! PREPARE THE OPERATING THEATER, STAT!
YES, MA'AM!
IT'S BEEN A LONG TIME...
SINCE I'VE PERFOMED AN OPERATION SO ENJOYABLE...!
KLINK

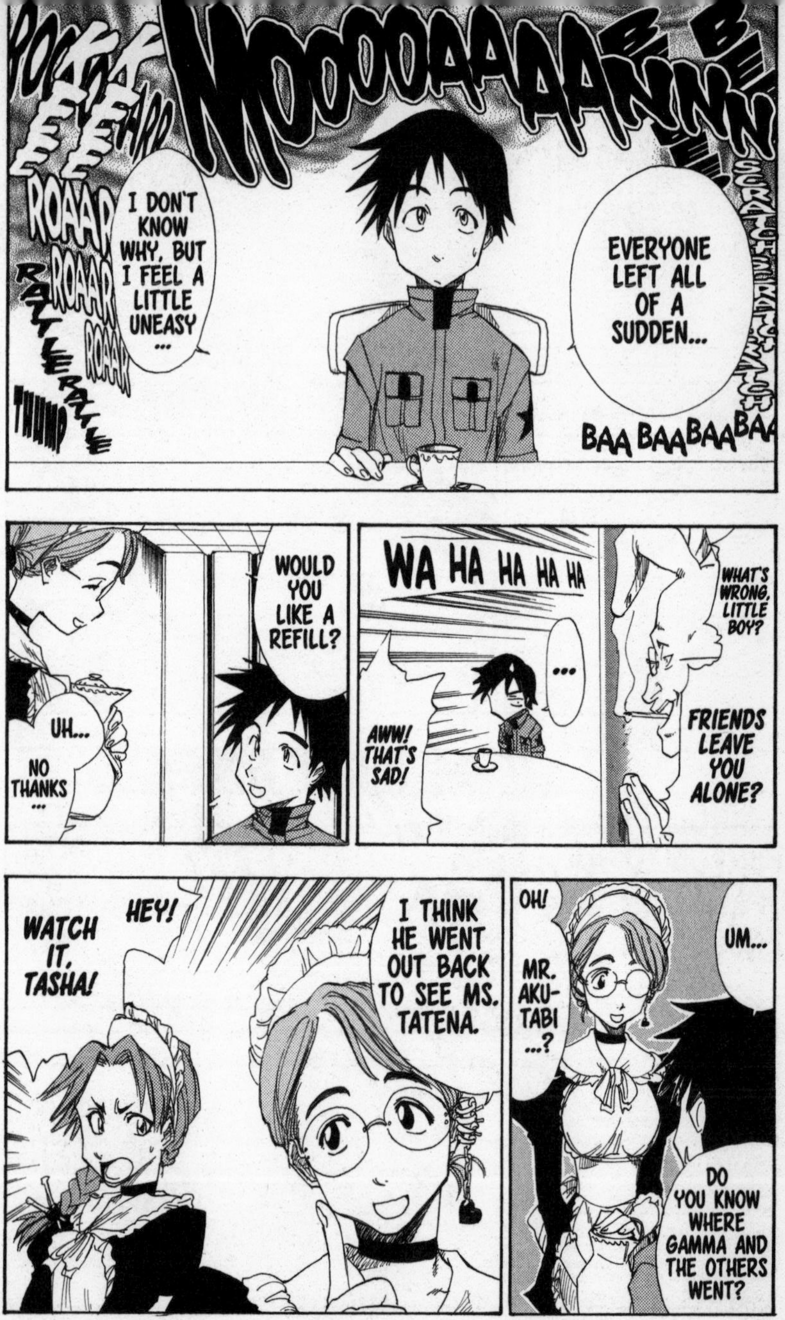
MOOOOAAAAANNN
EVERYONE LEFT ALL OF A SUDDEN...
BAA BAA BAA BAA
I DON'T KNOW WHY, BUT I FEEL A LITTLE UNEASY ...
ROAAR ROAAR ROAAR ROAAR
THUMP
WA HA HA HA HA
WHAT'S WRONG, LITTLE BOY?
FRIENDS LEAVE YOU ALONE?
...
AWW! THAT'S SAD!
WOULD YOU LIKE A REFILL?
UH...
NO THANKS ...
UM...
OH!
MR. AKU-TABI ...?
DO YOU KNOW WHERE GAMMA AND THE OTHERS WENT?
I THINK HE WENT OUT BACK TO SEE MS. TATENA.
HEY!
WATCH IT, TASHA!

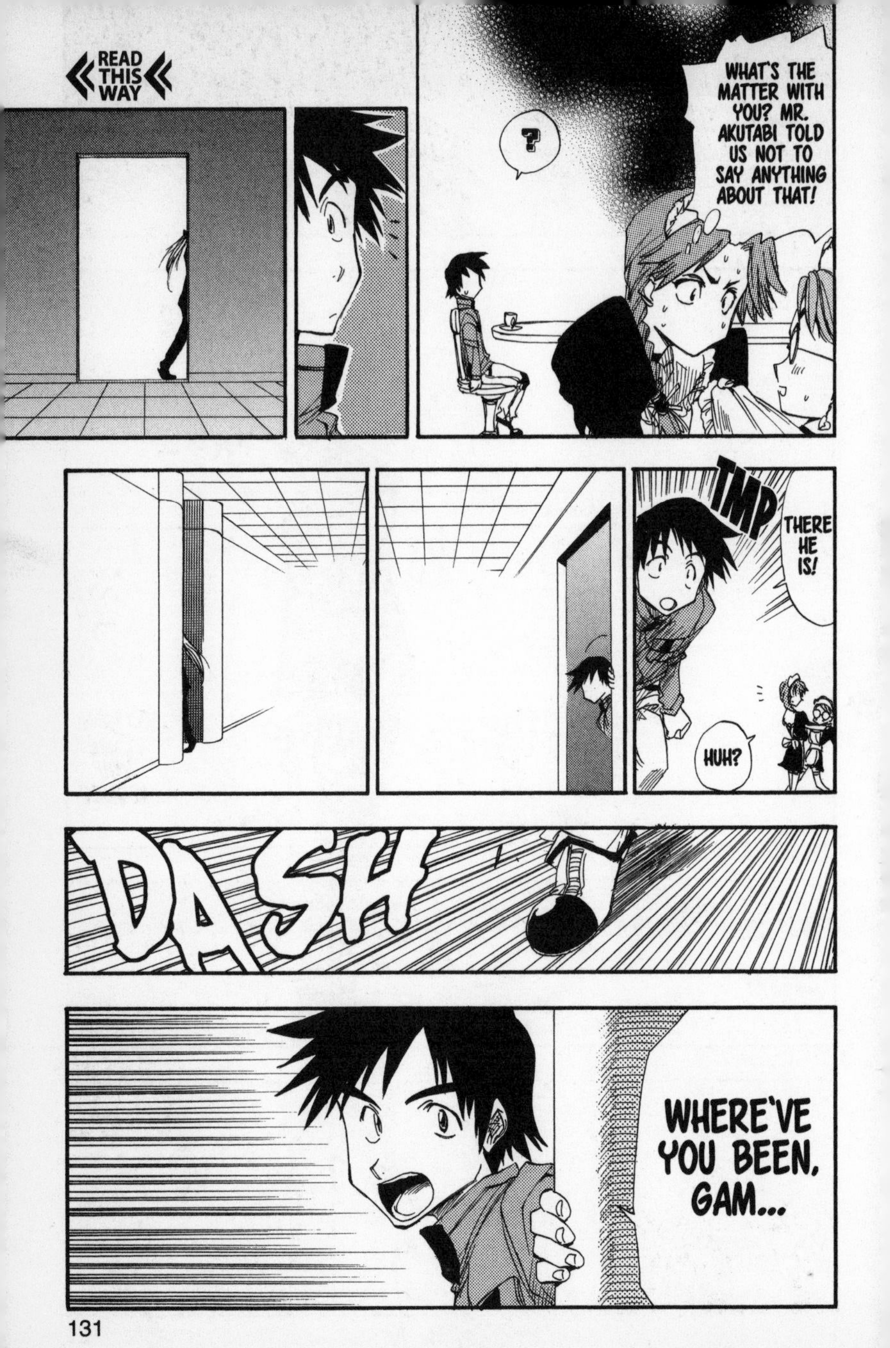
READ THIS WAY
WHAT'S THE MATTER WITH YOU? MR. AKUTABI TOLD US NOT TO SAY ANYTHING ABOUT THAT!
?
TMP
THERE HE IS!
HUH?
DASH
WHERE'VE YOU BEEN, GAM...

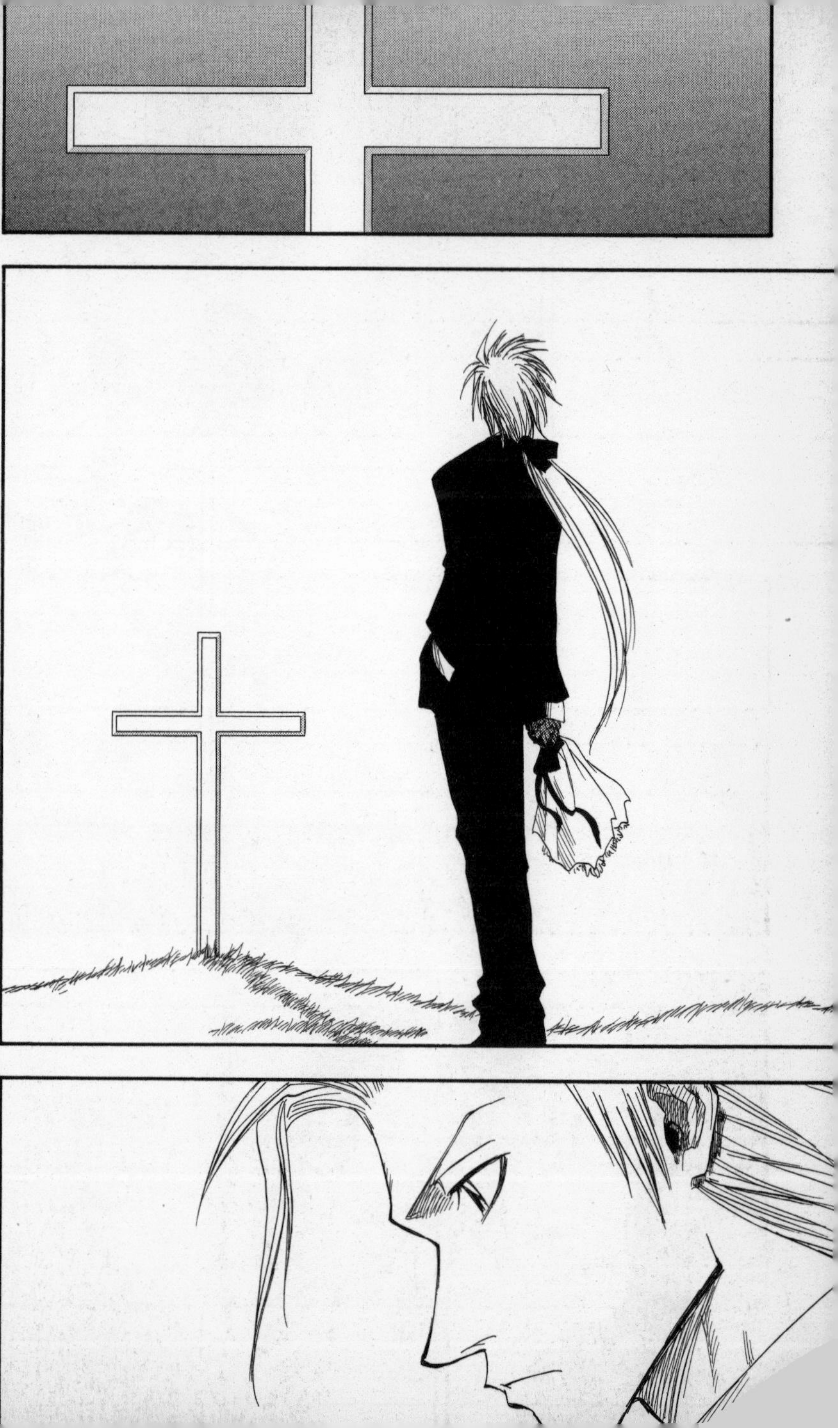

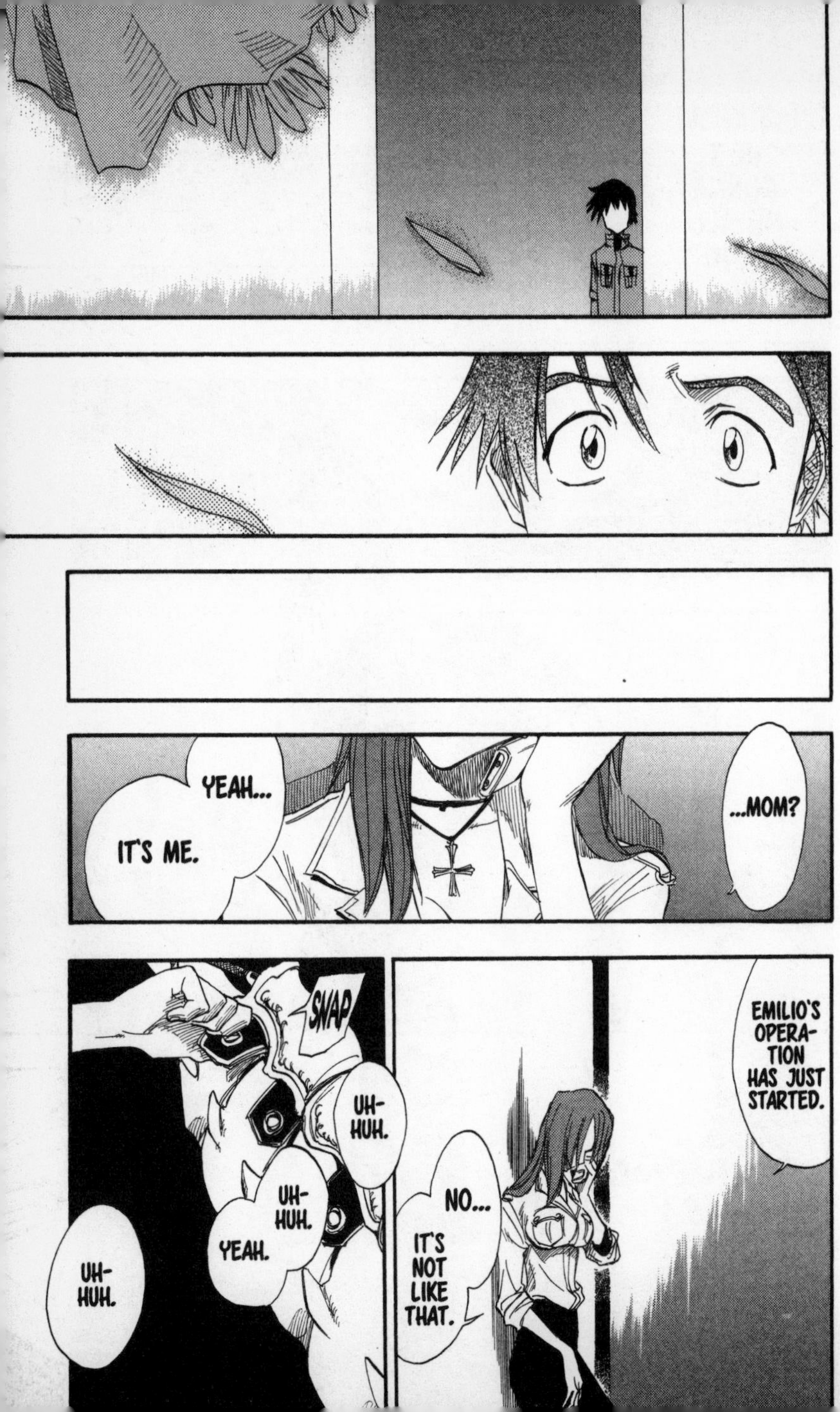
...MOM?
YEAH... IT'S ME.
EMILIO'S OPERATION HAS JUST STARTED.
NO... IT'S NOT LIKE THAT.
SNAP
UH-HUH.
UH-HUH. YEAH.
UH-HUH.

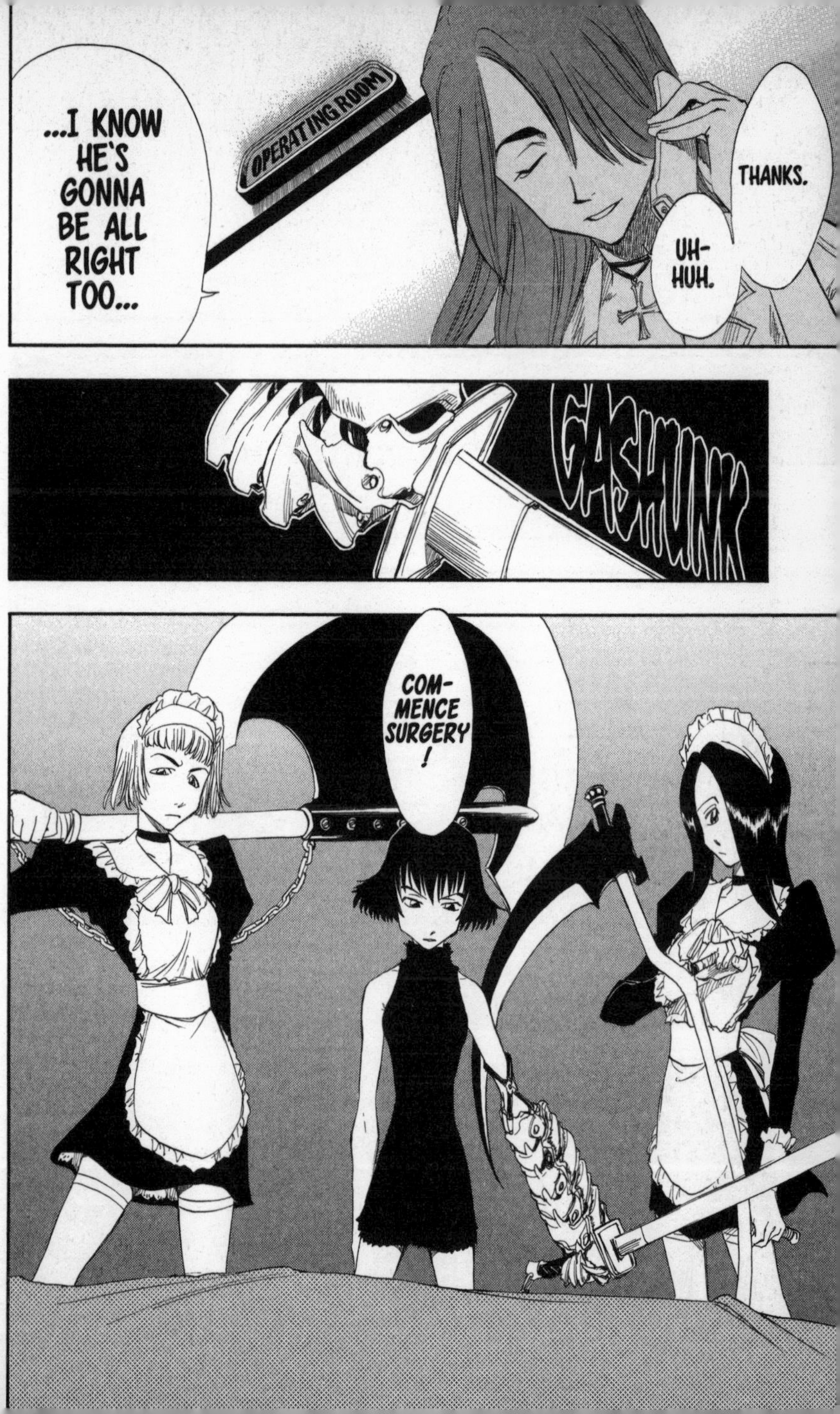
THANKS.
UH-HUH.
OPERATING ROOM
...I KNOW HE'S GONNA BE ALL RIGHT TOO...
GASHUNK
COM-MENCE SURGERY!

SNK...

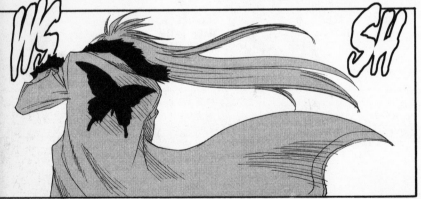

WS

SH

SO HAVE YOU MADE UP YOUR MIND?

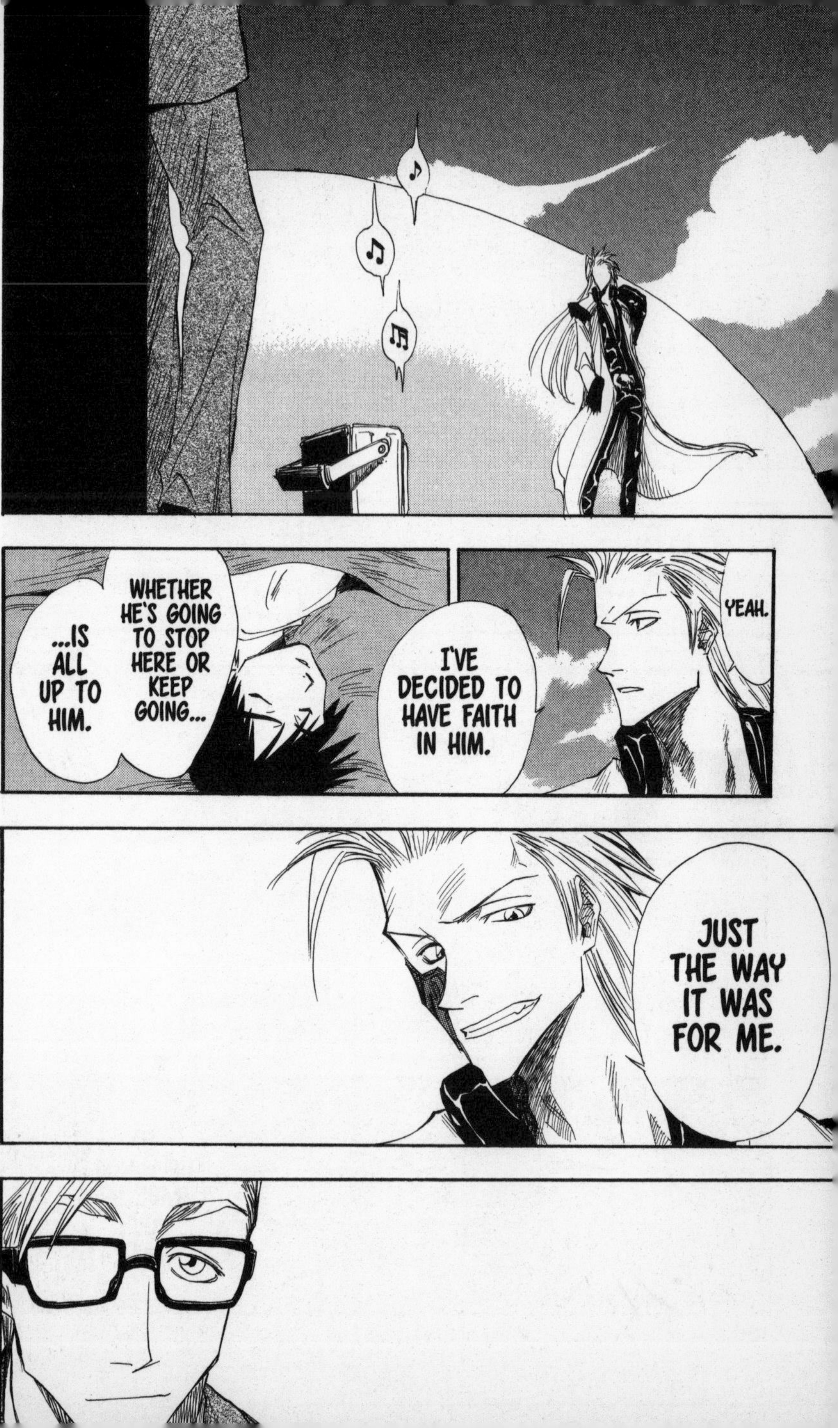
YEAH.
I'VE DECIDED TO HAVE FAITH IN HIM.
WHETHER HE'S GOING TO STOP HERE OR KEEP GOING...
...IS ALL UP TO HIM.
JUST THE WAY IT WAS FOR ME.

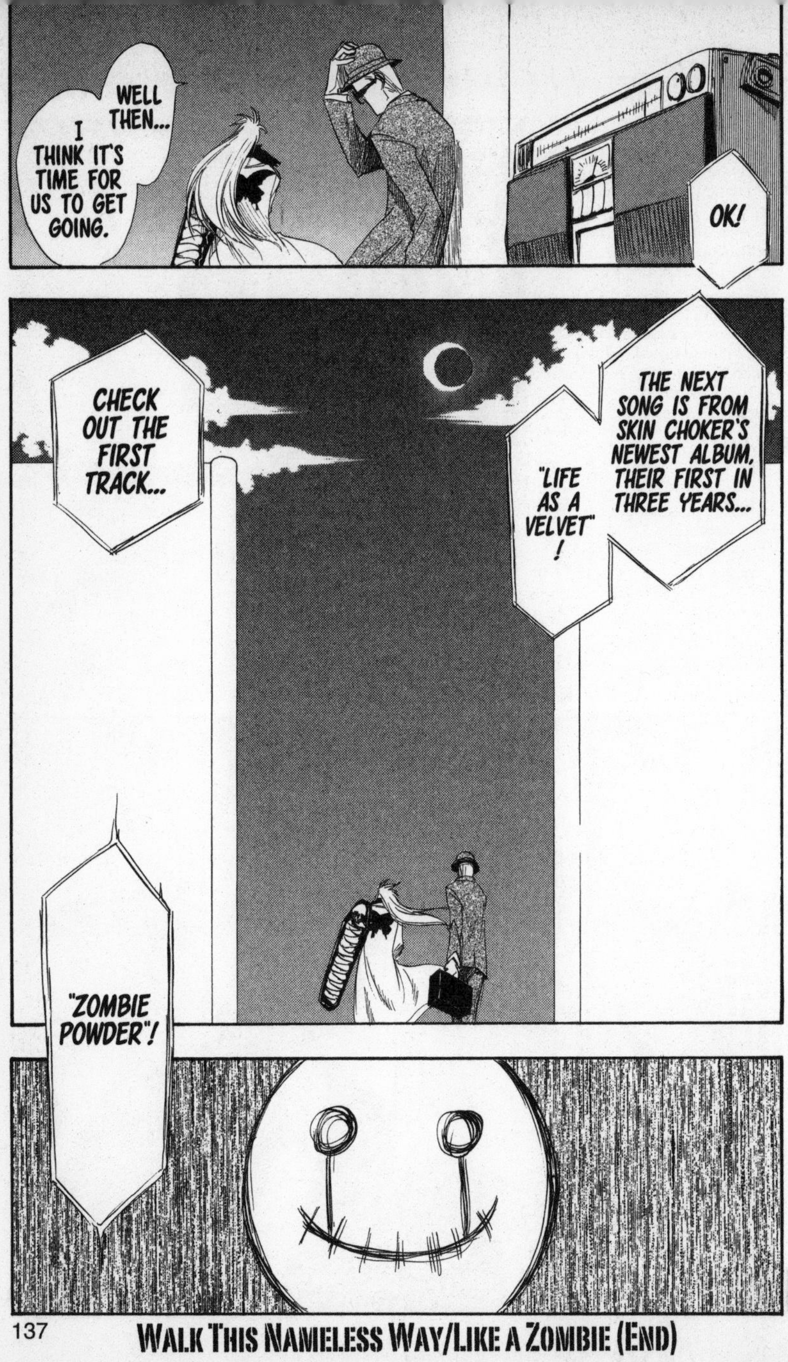
OK!
WELL THEN... I THINK IT'S TIME FOR US TO GET GOING.
THE NEXT SONG IS FROM SKIN CHOKER'S NEWEST ALBUM, THEIR FIRST IN THREE YEARS...
"LIFE AS A VELVET"!
CHECK OUT THE FIRST TRACK...
"ZOMBIE POWDER"!

WALK THIS NAMELESS WAY/LIKE A ZOMBIE (END)

Autumn 1997. This next comic, "BAD SHIELD UNITED," is from when I was around 20 years old. I remember that I had very little time and took on the impossible task of completing it in just three weeks. At the time I didn't like this piece because it came out of such a painful work schedule but now I really love it. I'm thinking that eventually I'd like to do a series of short stories based on it.

BAD $HIELD UNITED

● ● ● ◎ ○

Belrin Richard Sherwood (42)	Mille Cerenfoht (23)	Richard Steadler Krisien (19)	Rachel Ramirez (18)
ベルリン・リチャード・シャーウッド	ミレ・ツェレンフォート	リチャード・ステッドラー・クリシェン	レイチェル・ラミレス
187cm 78kg	157cm 47kg	178cm 65kg	155cm 44kg
Born in 1.19.	Born in 6.12.	Born in 5.15.	Born in 1.4.

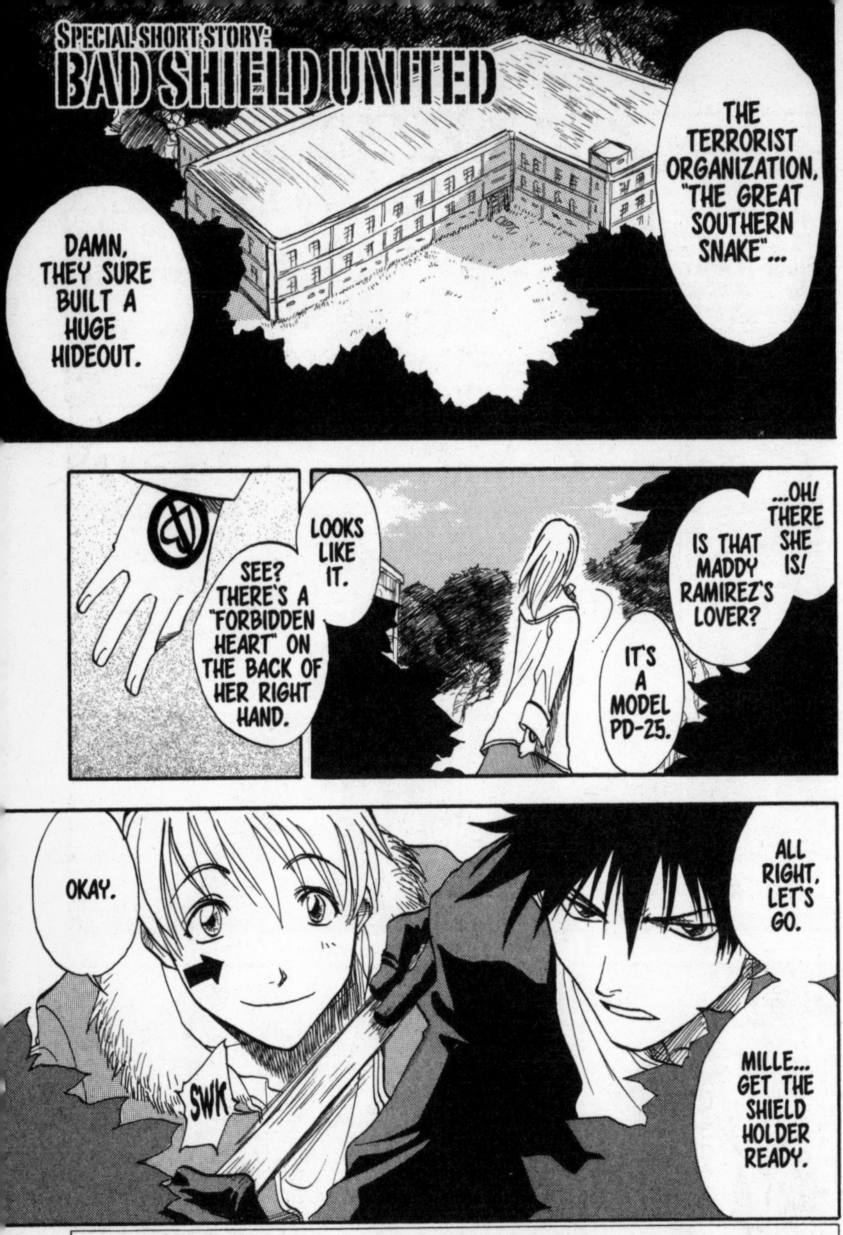
SPECIAL SHORT STORY:
BAD SHIELD UNITED
THE TERRORIST ORGANIZATION, "THE GREAT SOUTHERN SNAKE"...
DAMN, THEY SURE BUILT A HUGE HIDEOUT.
...OH! THERE SHE IS!
IS THAT MADDY RAMIREZ'S LOVER?
IT'S A MODEL PD-25.
LOOKS LIKE IT.
SEE? THERE'S A "FORBIDDEN HEART" ON THE BACK OF HER RIGHT HAND.
ALL RIGHT, LET'S GO.
MILLE... GET THE SHIELD HOLDER READY.
OKAY.
SWK
AUTOMATED COMBAT ANDROID. COMMON NAME: "SHIELD."

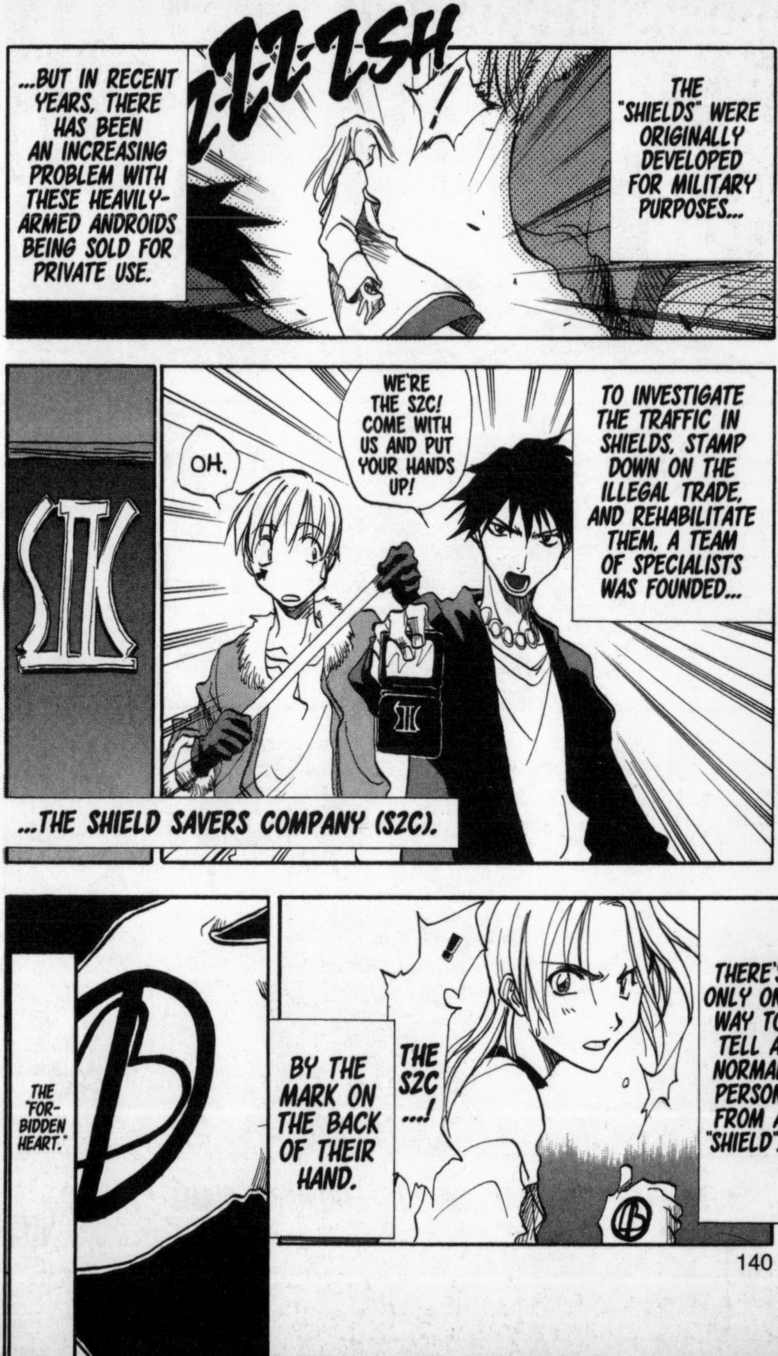
THE "SHIELDS" WERE ORIGINALLY DEVELOPED FOR MILITARY PURPOSES...
ZZZZZSH
...BUT IN RECENT YEARS, THERE HAS BEEN AN INCREASING PROBLEM WITH THESE HEAVILY-ARMED ANDROIDS BEING SOLD FOR PRIVATE USE.
TO INVESTIGATE THE TRAFFIC IN SHIELDS, STAMP DOWN ON THE ILLEGAL TRADE, AND REHABILITATE THEM, A TEAM OF SPECIALISTS WAS FOUNDED...
WE'RE THE S2C! COME WITH US AND PUT YOUR HANDS UP!
OH.
...THE SHIELD SAVERS COMPANY (S2C).
THERE'S ONLY ONE WAY TO TELL A NORMAL PERSON FROM A "SHIELD"...
!
THE S2C...!
BY THE MARK ON THE BACK OF THEIR HAND.
THE "FOR-BIDDEN HEART."

SPECIAL SHORT STORY

BAD SHIELD UNITED

バッド シールド ユナイテッド

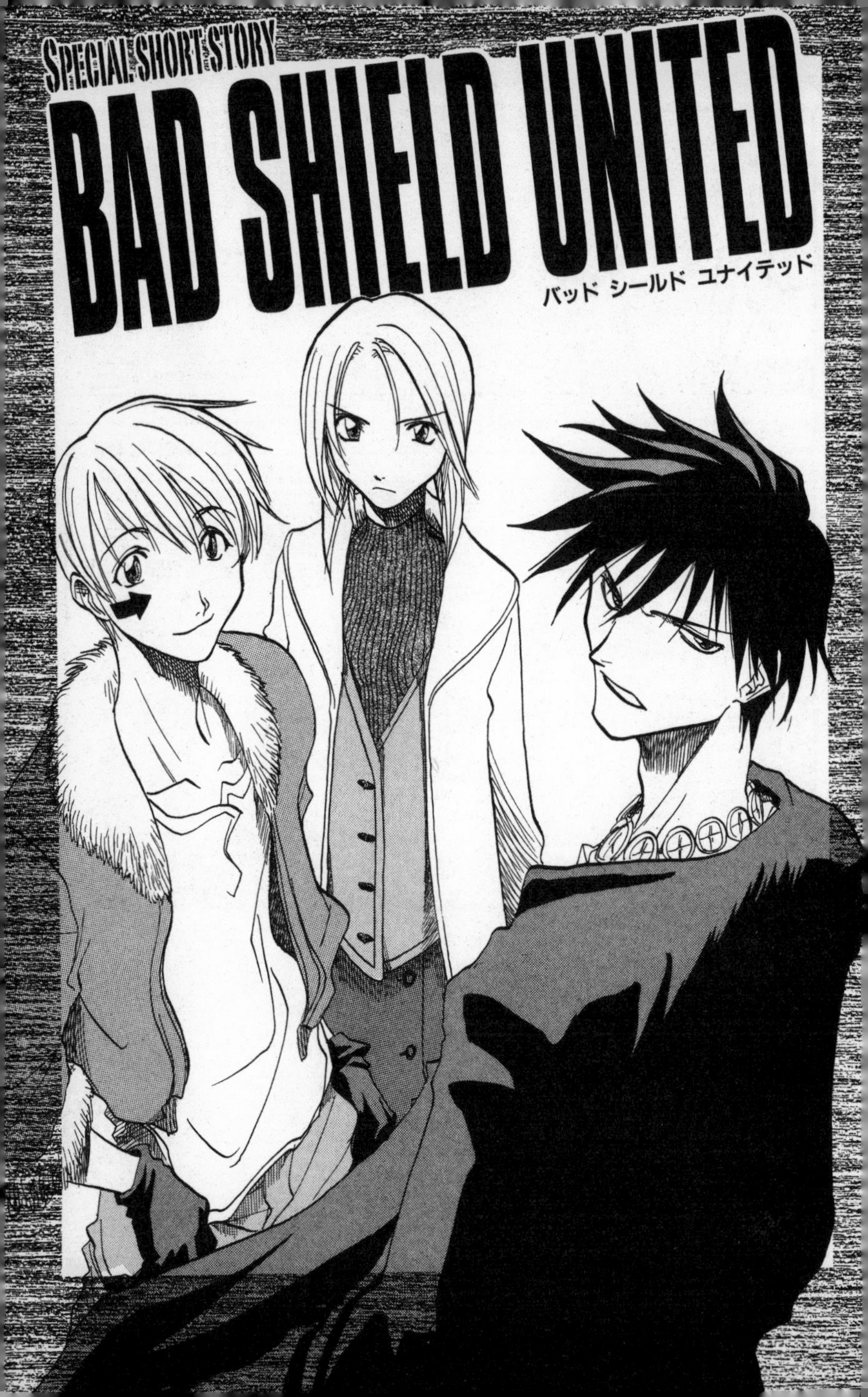

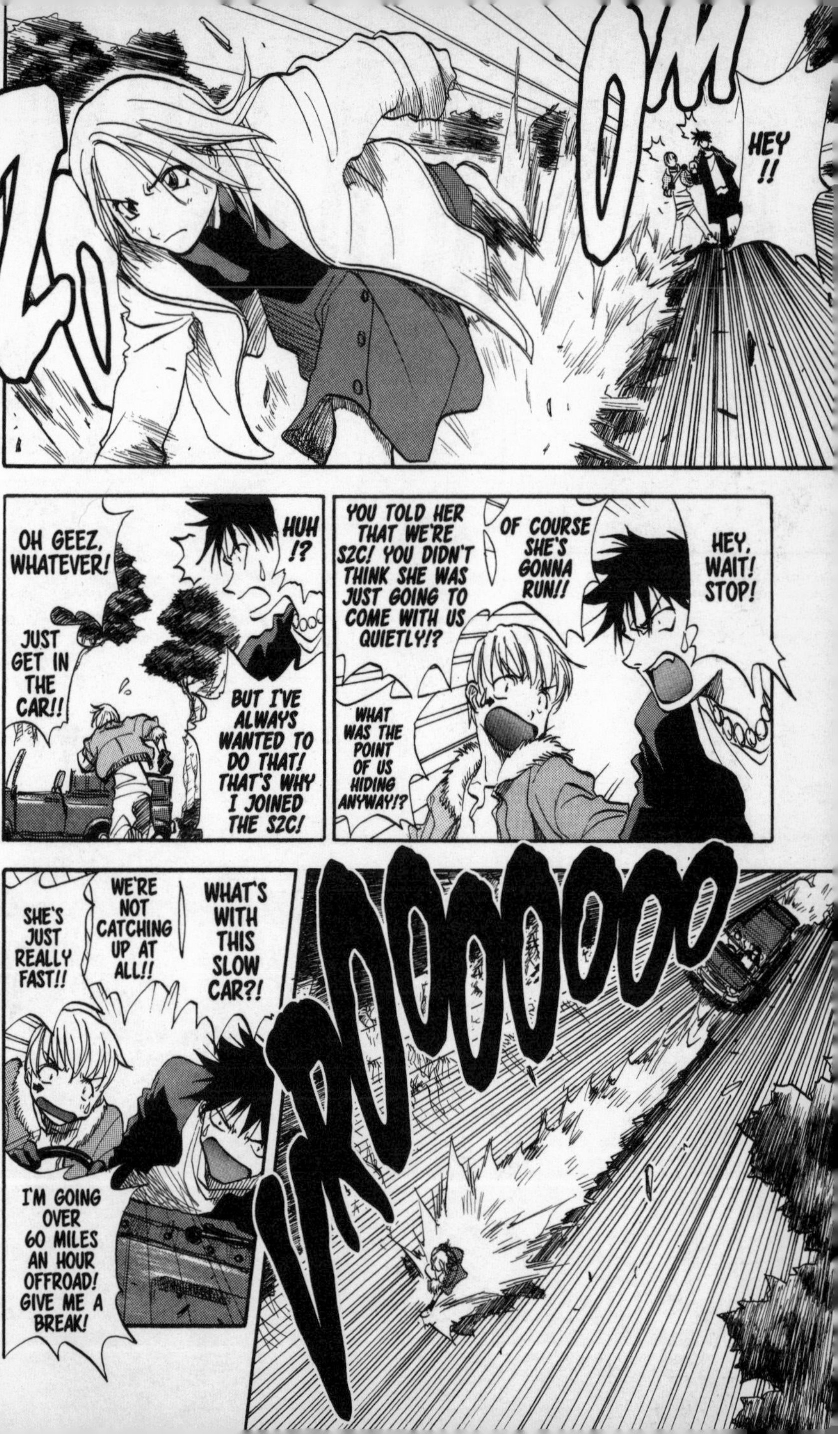
HEY !!
HEY, WAIT! STOP!
OF COURSE SHE'S GONNA RUN!!
YOU TOLD HER THAT WE'RE S2C! YOU DIDN'T THINK SHE WAS JUST GOING TO COME WITH US QUIETLY!?
WHAT WAS THE POINT OF US HIDING ANYWAY!?
HUH !?
OH GEEZ, WHATEVER!
JUST GET IN THE CAR!!
BUT I'VE ALWAYS WANTED TO DO THAT! THAT'S WHY I JOINED THE S2C!
WHAT'S WITH THIS SLOW CAR?!
WE'RE NOT CATCHING UP AT ALL!!
SHE'S JUST REALLY FAST!!
I'M GOING OVER 60 MILES AN HOUR OFFROAD! GIVE ME A BREAK!

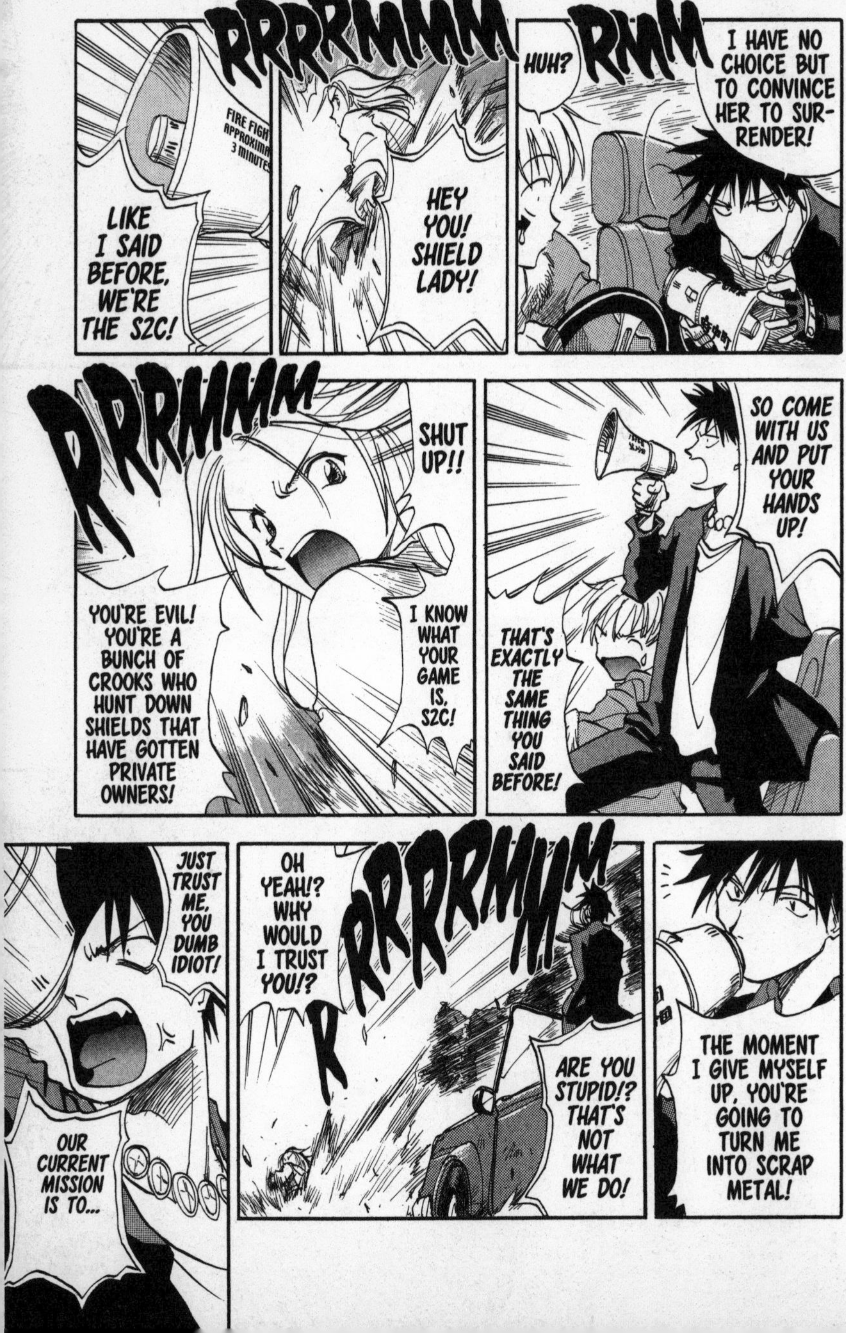
I HAVE NO CHOICE BUT TO CONVINCE HER TO SURRENDER!
RMM
HUH?
RRRRMMMM
HEY YOU! SHIELD LADY!
LIKE I SAID BEFORE, WE'RE THE S2C!
SO COME WITH US AND PUT YOUR HANDS UP!
THAT'S EXACTLY THE SAME THING YOU SAID BEFORE!
RRRMMM
SHUT UP!!
I KNOW WHAT YOUR GAME IS, S2C!
YOU'RE EVIL! YOU'RE A BUNCH OF CROOKS WHO HUNT DOWN SHIELDS THAT HAVE GOTTEN PRIVATE OWNERS!
THE MOMENT I GIVE MYSELF UP, YOU'RE GOING TO TURN ME INTO SCRAP METAL!
RRRRMMM
OH YEAH!? WHY WOULD I TRUST YOU!?
ARE YOU STUPID!? THAT'S NOT WHAT WE DO!
JUST TRUST ME, YOU DUMB IDIOT!
OUR CURRENT MISSION IS TO...

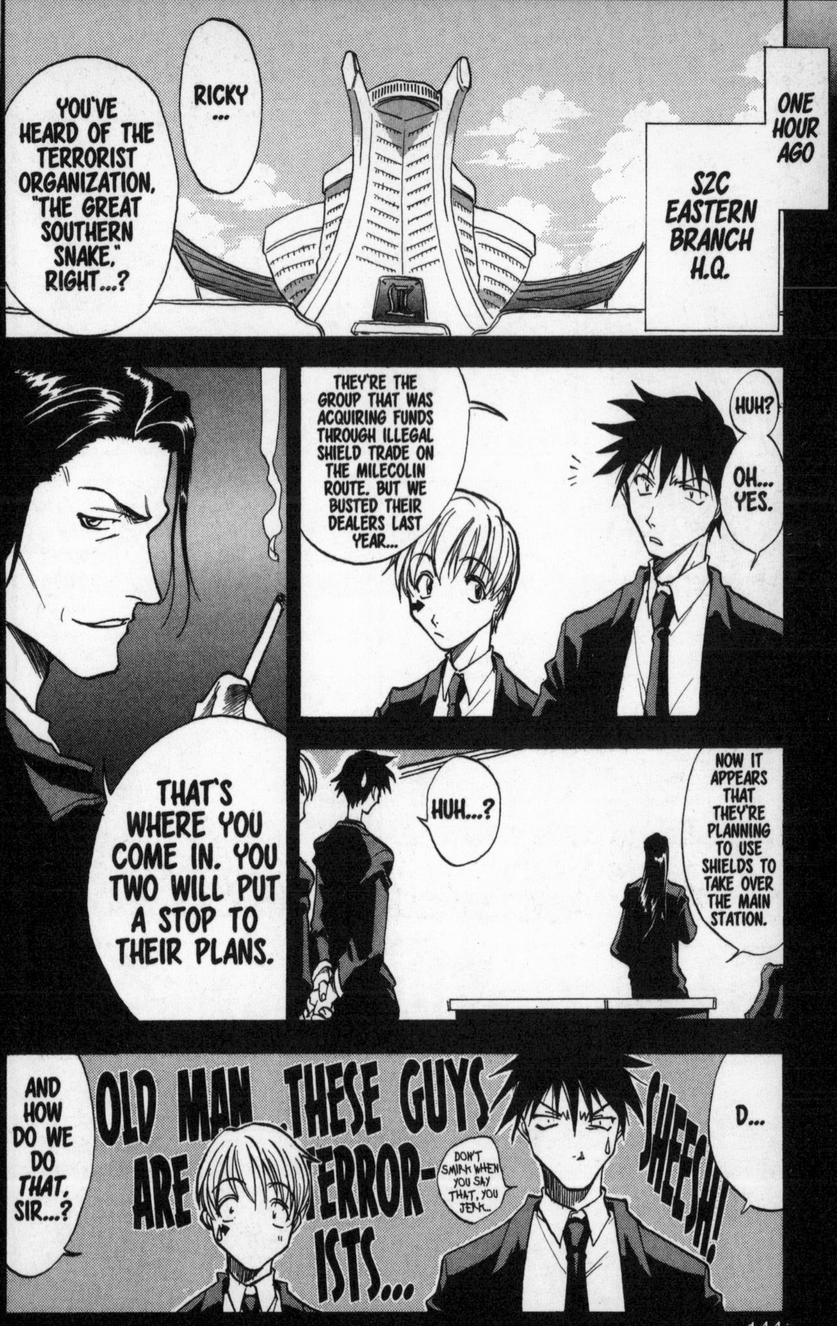
ONE HOUR AGO
S2C EASTERN BRANCH H.Q.
RICKY...
YOU'VE HEARD OF THE TERRORIST ORGANIZATION, "THE GREAT SOUTHERN SNAKE," RIGHT...?
HUH?
OH... YES.
THEY'RE THE GROUP THAT WAS ACQUIRING FUNDS THROUGH ILLEGAL SHIELD TRADE ON THE MILECOLIN ROUTE. BUT WE BUSTED THEIR DEALERS LAST YEAR...
NOW IT APPEARS THAT THEY'RE PLANNING TO USE SHIELDS TO TAKE OVER THE MAIN STATION.
HUH...?
THAT'S WHERE YOU COME IN. YOU TWO WILL PUT A STOP TO THEIR PLANS.
D...
SHEESH!
DON'T SMIRK WHEN YOU SAY THAT, YOU JERK...
OLD MAN...THESE GUYS ARE TERROR-ISTS...
AND HOW DO WE DO THAT, SIR...?

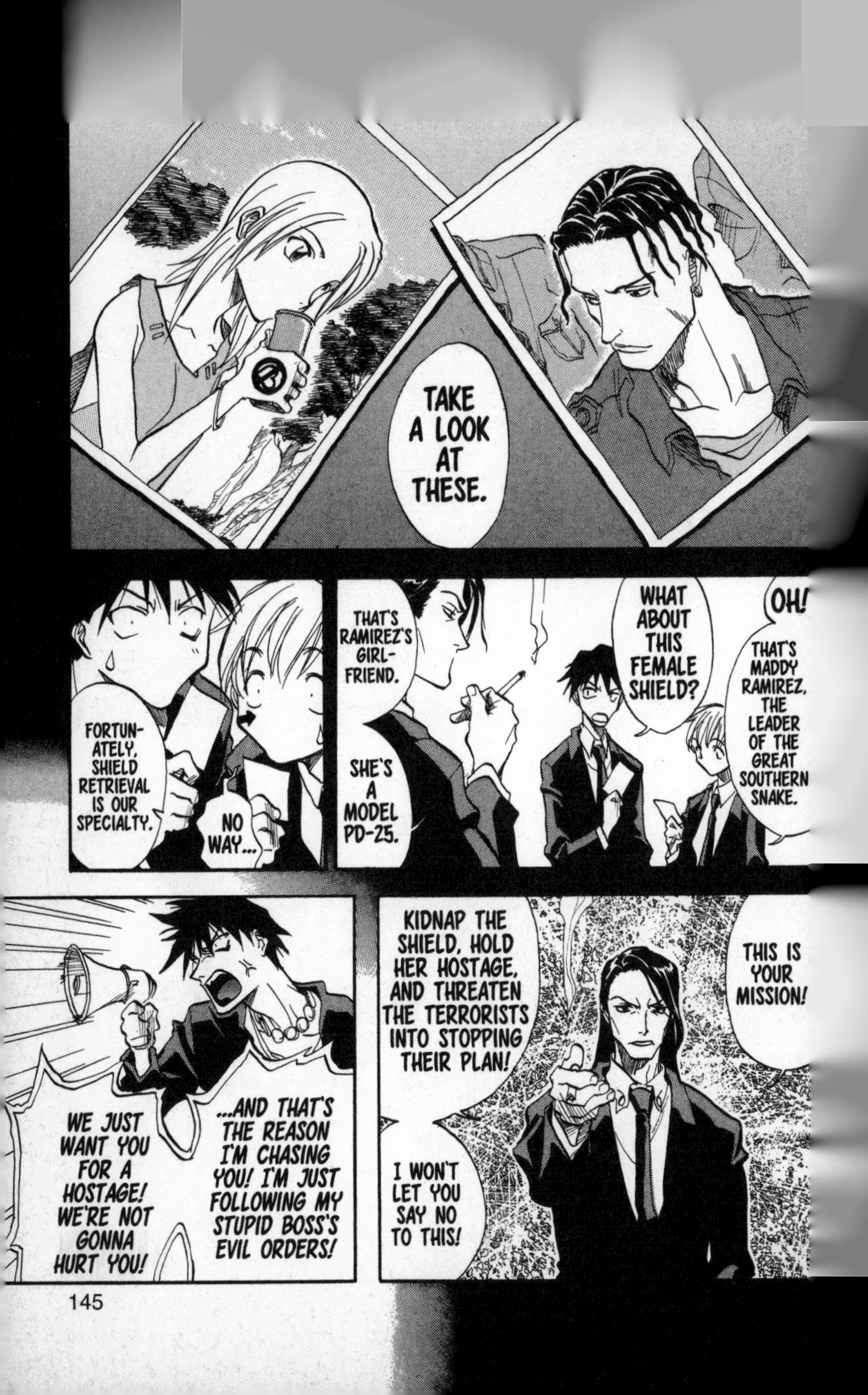
TAKE A LOOK AT THESE.
OH!
THAT'S MADDY RAMIREZ, THE LEADER OF THE GREAT SOUTHERN SNAKE.
WHAT ABOUT THIS FEMALE SHIELD?
THAT'S RAMIREZ'S GIRL-FRIEND.
SHE'S A MODEL PD-25.
FORTUN-ATELY, SHIELD RETRIEVAL IS OUR SPECIALTY.
NO WAY...
KIDNAP THE SHIELD, HOLD HER HOSTAGE, AND THREATEN THE TERRORISTS INTO STOPPING THEIR PLAN!
THIS IS YOUR MISSION!
I WON'T LET YOU SAY NO TO THIS!
...AND THAT'S THE REASON I'M CHASING YOU! I'M JUST FOLLOWING MY STUPID BOSS'S EVIL ORDERS!
WE JUST WANT YOU FOR A HOSTAGE! WE'RE NOT GONNA HURT YOU!

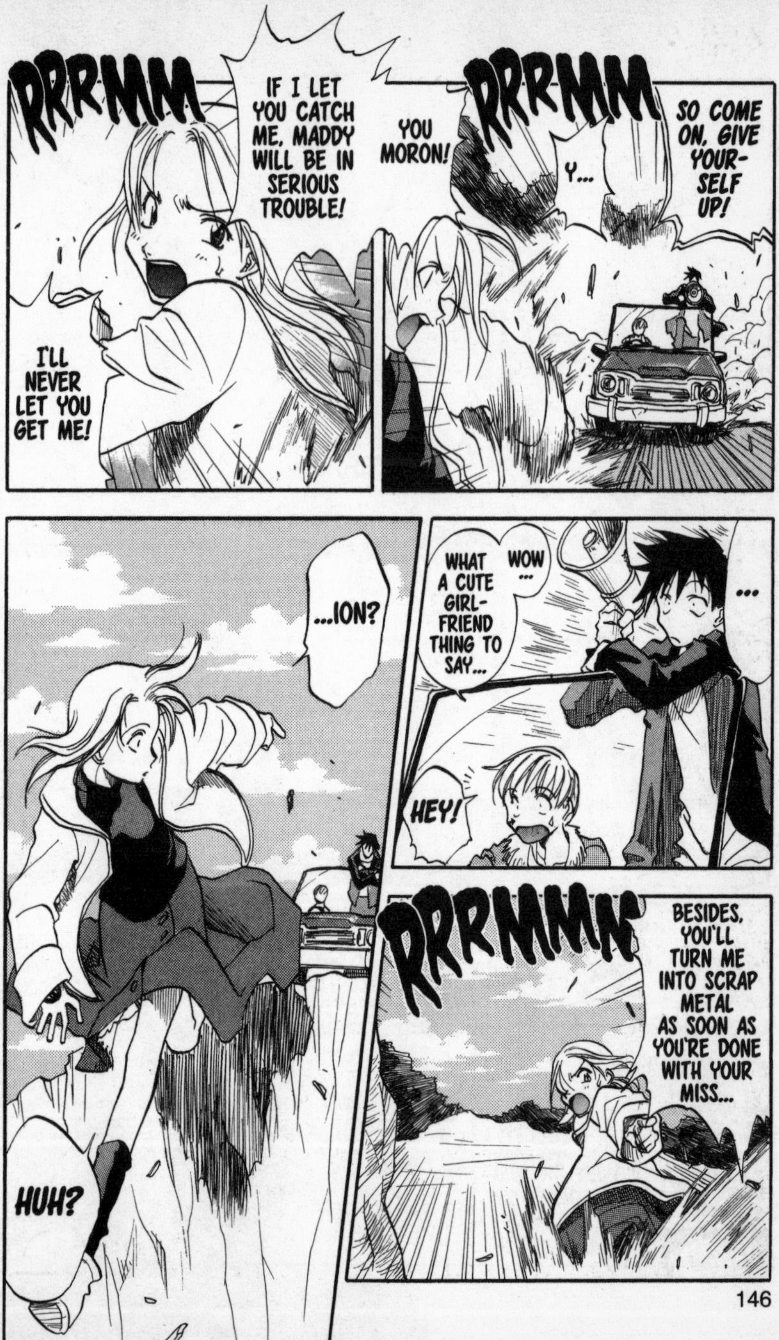
RRRMM
SO COME ON, GIVE YOUR-SELF UP!
Y...
YOU MORON!
RRRMM
IF I LET YOU CATCH ME, MADDY WILL BE IN SERIOUS TROUBLE!
I'LL NEVER LET YOU GET ME!
...
WOW ...
WHAT A CUTE GIRL-FRIEND THING TO SAY...
HEY!
RRRMMN
BESIDES, YOU'LL TURN ME INTO SCRAP METAL AS SOON AS YOU'RE DONE WITH YOUR MISS...
...ION?
HUH?

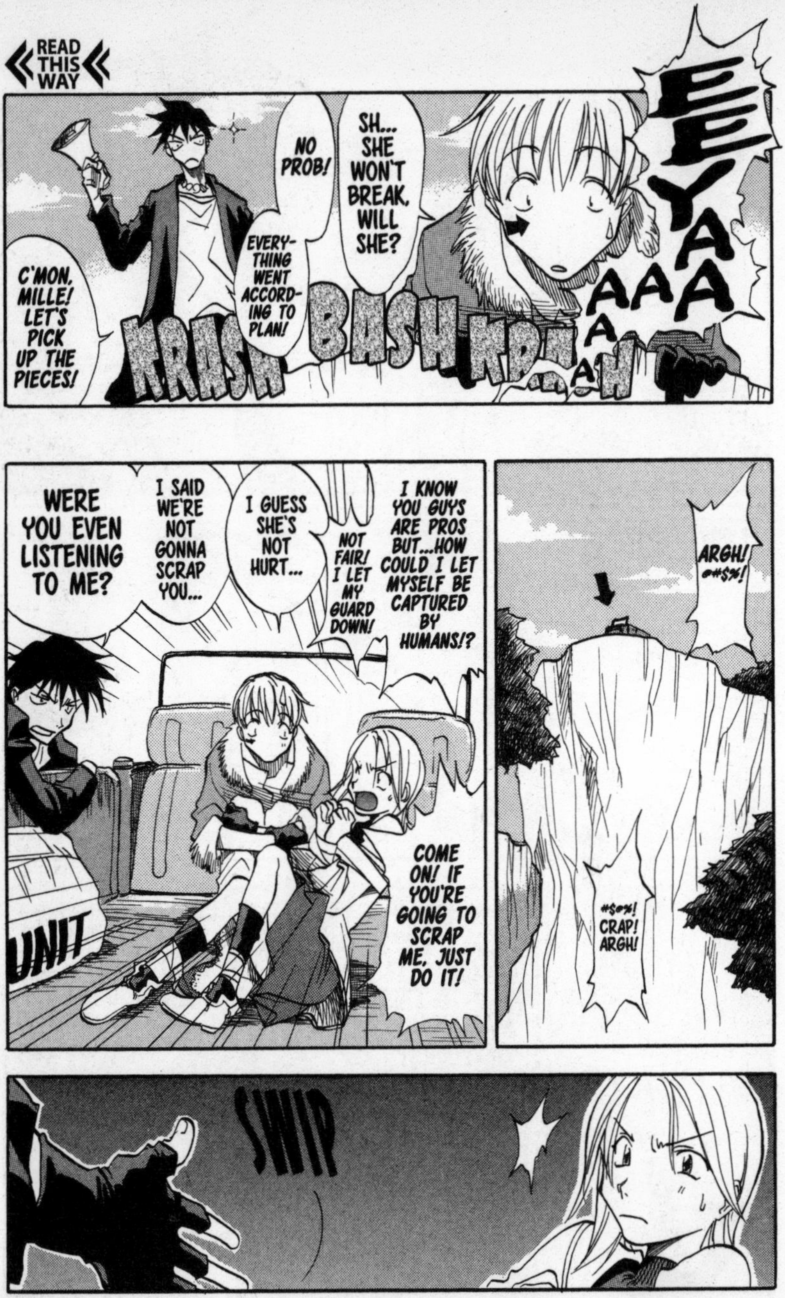
READ THIS WAY
EEYAAAAAAAH
SH... SHE WON'T BREAK, WILL SHE?
NO PROB!
EVERYTHING WENT ACCORDING TO PLAN!
C'MON, MILLE! LET'S PICK UP THE PIECES!
BASH
KRASH
ARGH! @#$%!
#$%! CRAP! ARGH!
I KNOW YOU GUYS ARE PROS BUT...HOW COULD I LET MYSELF BE CAPTURED BY HUMANS!?
NOT FAIR! I LET MY GUARD DOWN!
I GUESS SHE'S NOT HURT...
I SAID WE'RE NOT GONNA SCRAP YOU...
WERE YOU EVEN LISTENING TO ME?
COME ON! IF YOU'RE GOING TO SCRAP ME, JUST DO IT!
UNIT
SWIP

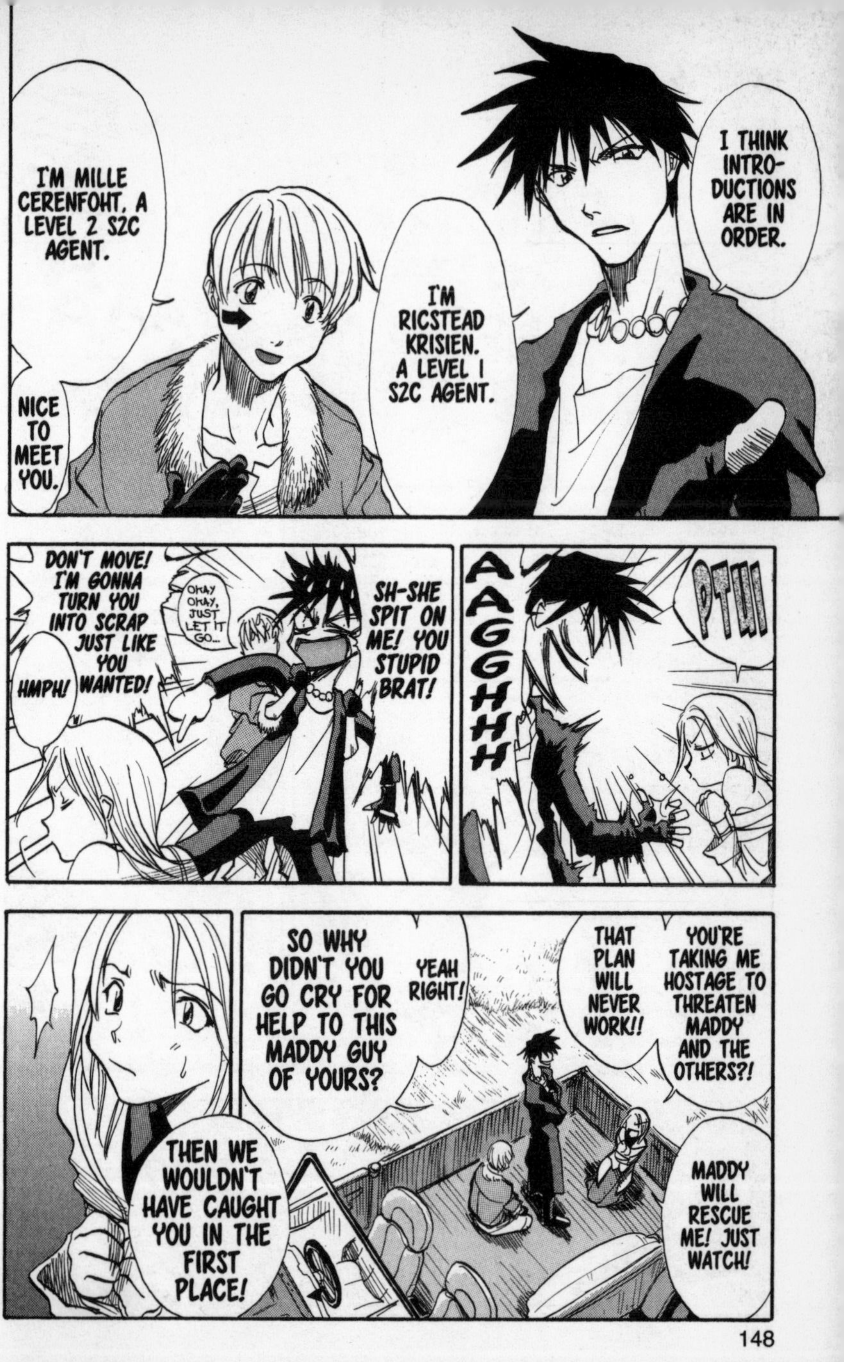
I THINK INTRODUCTIONS ARE IN ORDER.
I'M RICSTEAD KRISIEN. A LEVEL 1 S2C AGENT.
I'M MILLE CERENFOHT, A LEVEL 2 S2C AGENT.
NICE TO MEET YOU.
PTWI
AAGGHHH
SH-SHE SPIT ON ME! YOU STUPID BRAT!
OKAY OKAY, JUST LET IT GO...
DON'T MOVE! I'M GONNA TURN YOU INTO SCRAP JUST LIKE YOU WANTED!
HMPH!
YOU'RE TAKING ME HOSTAGE TO THREATEN MADDY AND THE OTHERS?!
THAT PLAN WILL NEVER WORK!!
YEAH RIGHT!
SO WHY DIDN'T YOU GO CRY FOR HELP TO THIS MADDY GUY OF YOURS?
MADDY WILL RESCUE ME! JUST WATCH!
THEN WE WOULDN'T HAVE CAUGHT YOU IN THE FIRST PLACE!

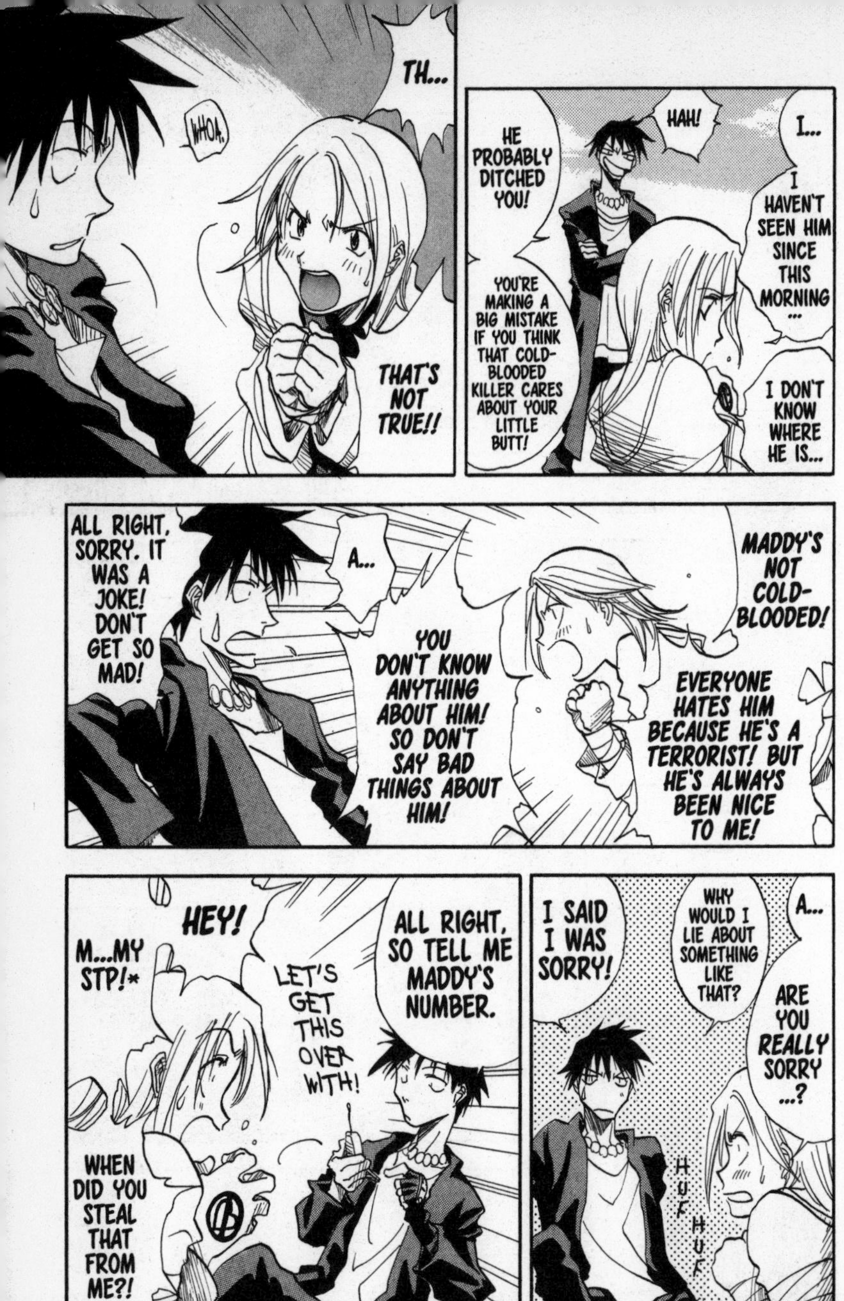
I...
I HAVEN'T SEEN HIM SINCE THIS MORNING...
HAH!
HE PROBABLY DITCHED YOU!
I DON'T KNOW WHERE HE IS...
YOU'RE MAKING A BIG MISTAKE IF YOU THINK THAT COLD-BLOODED KILLER CARES ABOUT YOUR LITTLE BUTT!
TH...
WHOA.
THAT'S NOT TRUE!!
MADDY'S NOT COLD-BLOODED!
EVERYONE HATES HIM BECAUSE HE'S A TERRORIST! BUT HE'S ALWAYS BEEN NICE TO ME!
YOU DON'T KNOW ANYTHING ABOUT HIM! SO DON'T SAY BAD THINGS ABOUT HIM!
A...
ALL RIGHT, SORRY. IT WAS A JOKE! DON'T GET SO MAD!
A...
WHY WOULD I LIE ABOUT SOMETHING LIKE THAT?
ARE YOU REALLY SORRY...?
I SAID I WAS SORRY!
HUF
HUF
ALL RIGHT, SO TELL ME MADDY'S NUMBER.
LET'S GET THIS OVER WITH!
HEY!
M...MY STP!*
WHEN DID YOU STEAL THAT FROM ME?!

*PHONE

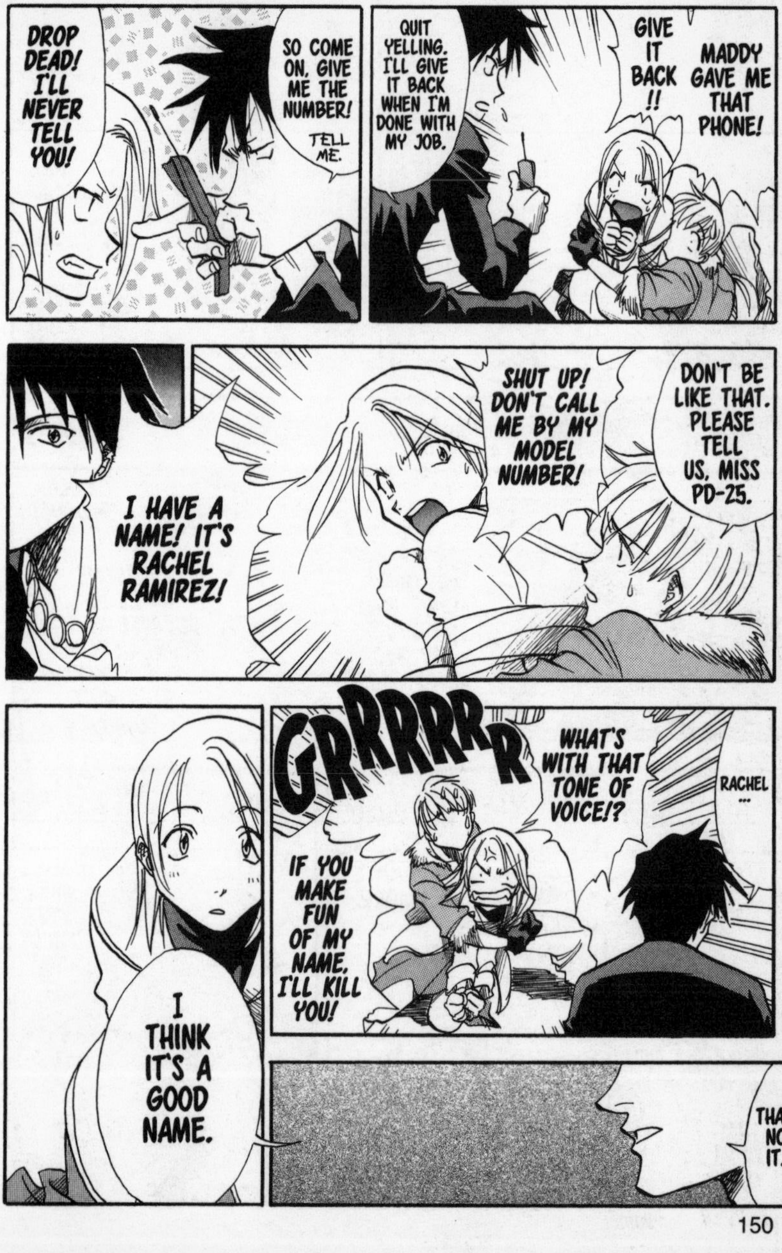
MADDY GAVE ME THAT PHONE!
GIVE IT BACK !!
QUIT YELLING. I'LL GIVE IT BACK WHEN I'M DONE WITH MY JOB.
SO COME ON, GIVE ME THE NUMBER!
TELL ME.
DROP DEAD! I'LL NEVER TELL YOU!
DON'T BE LIKE THAT. PLEASE TELL US, MISS PD-25.
SHUT UP! DON'T CALL ME BY MY MODEL NUMBER!
I HAVE A NAME! IT'S RACHEL RAMIREZ!
RACHEL ...
WHAT'S WITH THAT TONE OF VOICE!?
GRRRRRR
IF YOU MAKE FUN OF MY NAME, I'LL KILL YOU!
THAT'S NOT IT...
I THINK IT'S A GOOD NAME.

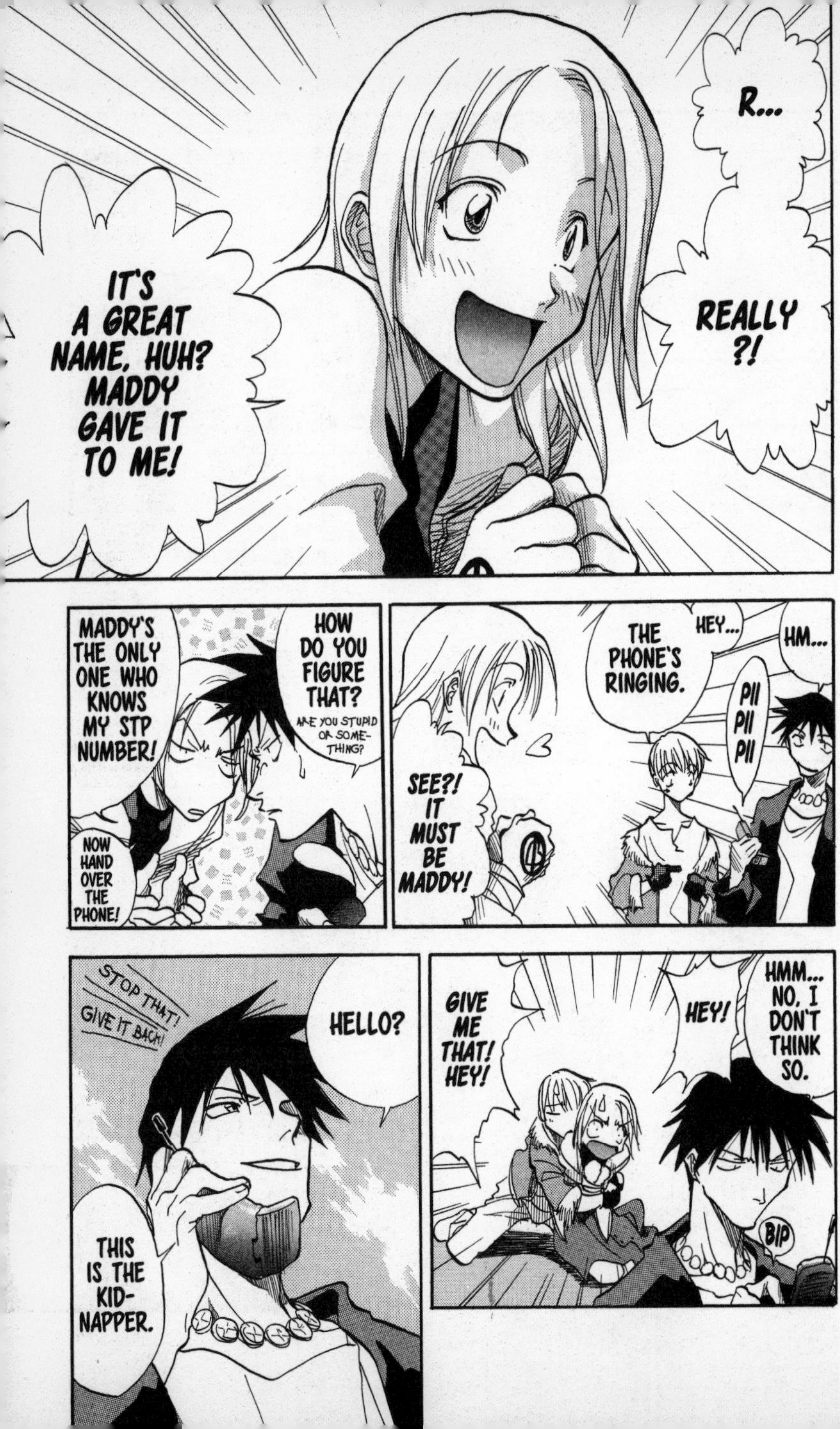
R...
REALLY?!
IT'S A GREAT NAME, HUH? MADDY GAVE IT TO ME!
HM...
HEY...
THE PHONE'S RINGING.
PII PII PII
SEE?! IT MUST BE MADDY!
HOW DO YOU FIGURE THAT?
ARE YOU STUPID OR SOME-THING?
MADDY'S THE ONLY ONE WHO KNOWS MY STP NUMBER!
NOW HAND OVER THE PHONE!
HMM... NO, I DON'T THINK SO.
HEY!
GIVE ME THAT! HEY!
BIP
HELLO?
STOP THAT!
GIVE IT BACK!
THIS IS THE KID-NAPPER.

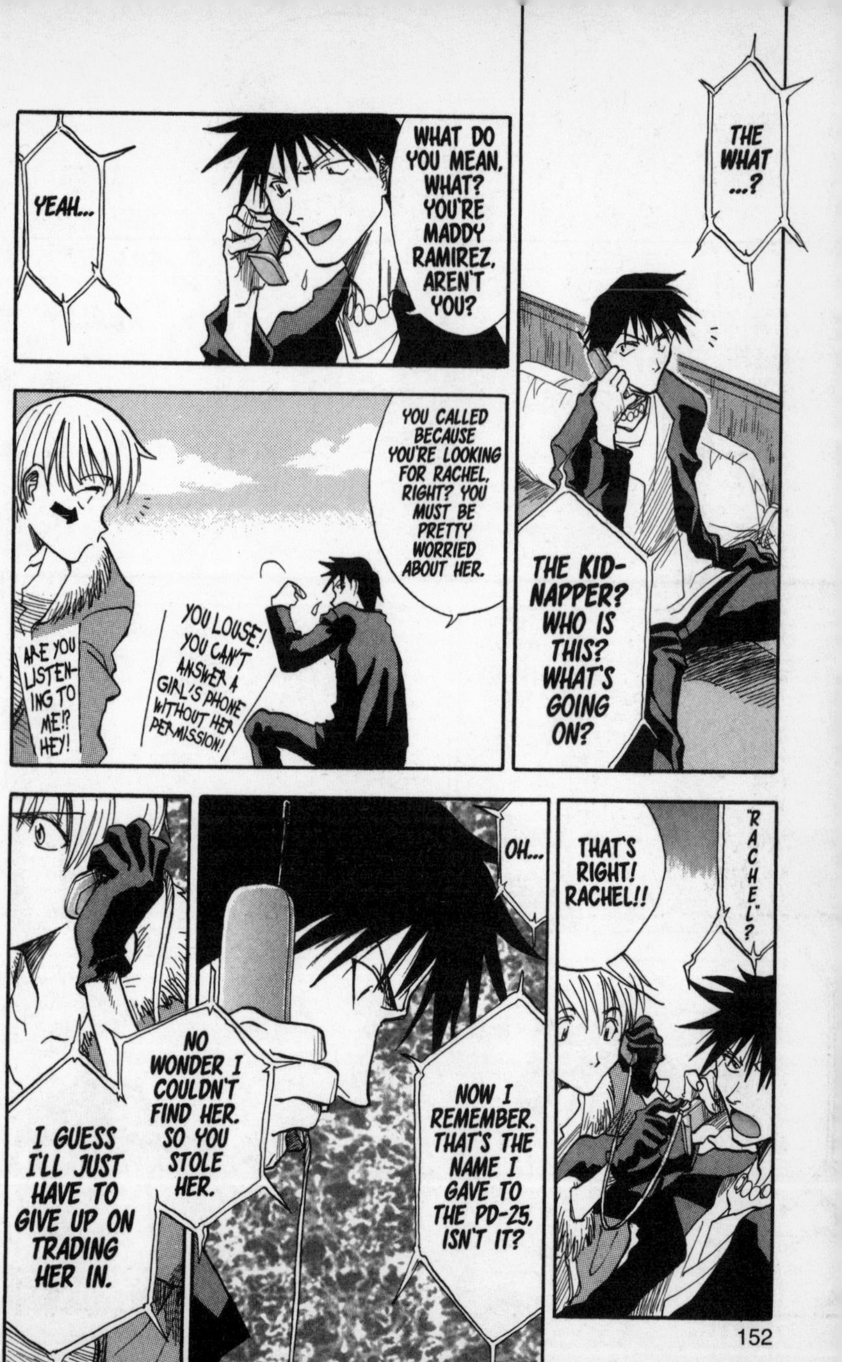
THE WHAT ...?
THE KID-NAPPER? WHO IS THIS? WHAT'S GOING ON?
WHAT DO YOU MEAN, WHAT? YOU'RE MADDY RAMIREZ, AREN'T YOU?
YEAH...
YOU CALLED BECAUSE YOU'RE LOOKING FOR RACHEL, RIGHT? YOU MUST BE PRETTY WORRIED ABOUT HER.
YOU LOUSE! YOU CAN'T ANSWER A GIRL'S PHONE WITHOUT HER PERMISSION!
ARE YOU LISTEN-ING TO ME!? HEY!
"RACHEL"?
THAT'S RIGHT! RACHEL!!
OH...
NOW I REMEMBER. THAT'S THE NAME I GAVE TO THE PD-25, ISN'T IT?
NO WONDER I COULDN'T FIND HER. SO YOU STOLE HER.
I GUESS I'LL JUST HAVE TO GIVE UP ON TRADING HER IN.

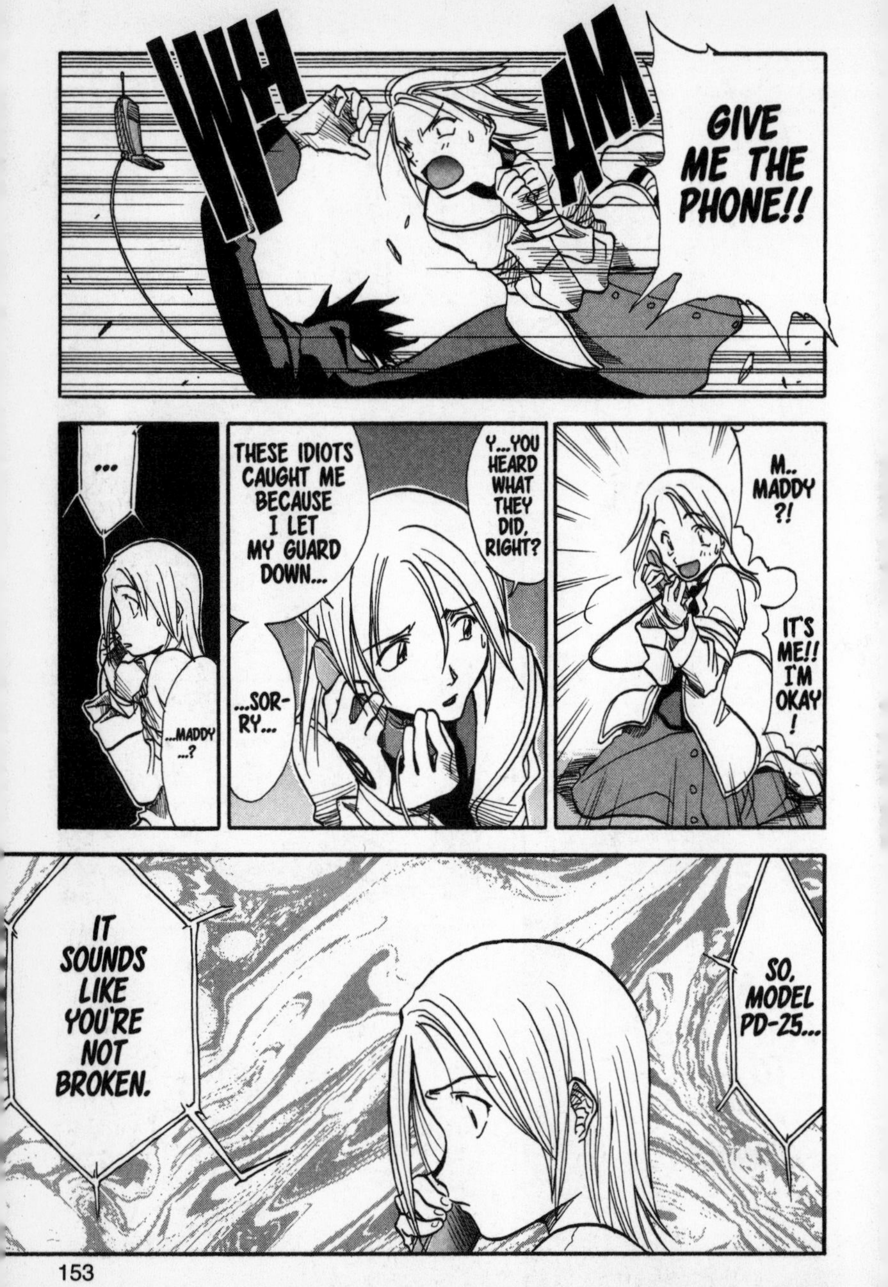
WHAM
GIVE ME THE PHONE!!
M.. MADDY?!
IT'S ME!! I'M OKAY!
Y...YOU HEARD WHAT THEY DID, RIGHT?
THESE IDIOTS CAUGHT ME BECAUSE I LET MY GUARD DOWN...
...SORRY...
...
...MADDY...?
SO, MODEL PD-25...
IT SOUNDS LIKE YOU'RE NOT BROKEN.

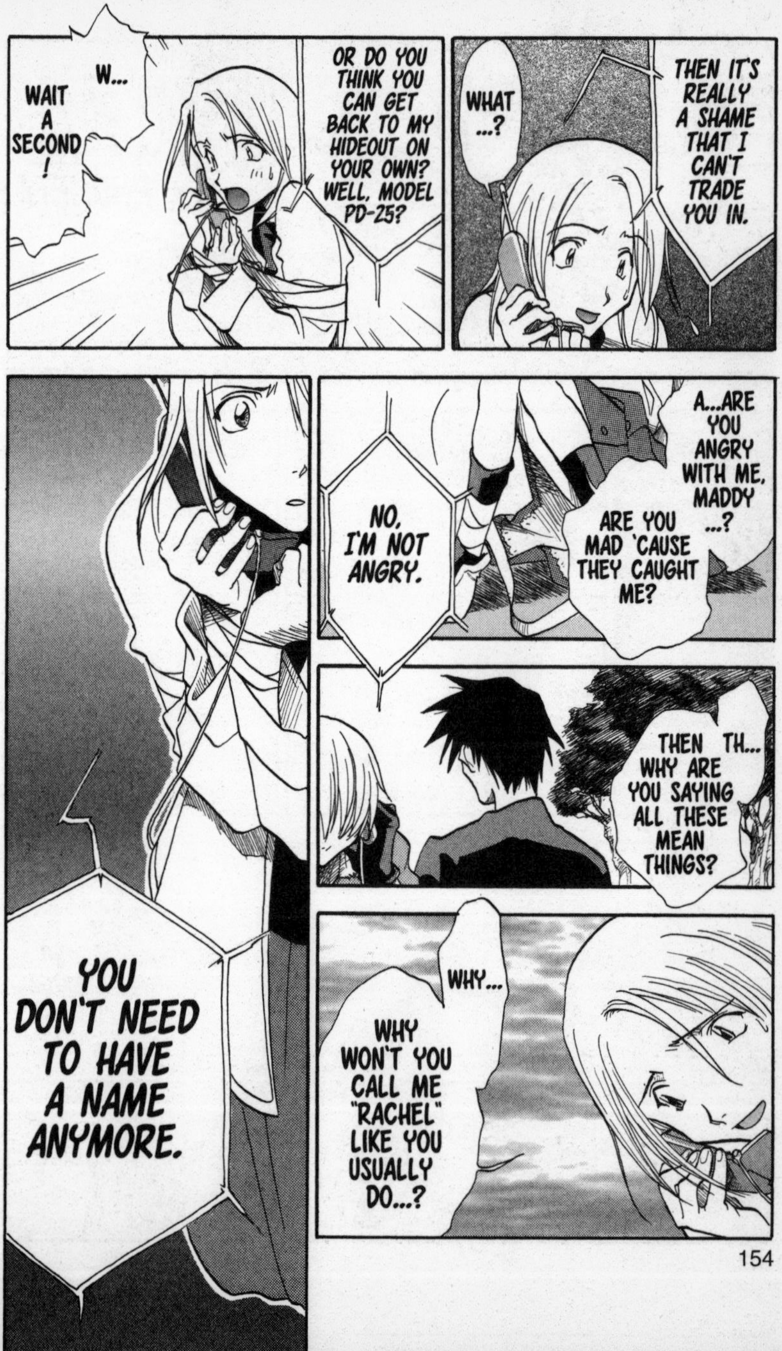
THEN IT'S REALLY A SHAME THAT I CAN'T TRADE YOU IN.
WHAT ...?
OR DO YOU THINK YOU CAN GET BACK TO MY HIDEOUT ON YOUR OWN? WELL, MODEL PD-25?
W...
WAIT A SECOND!
A...ARE YOU ANGRY WITH ME, MADDY ...?
ARE YOU MAD 'CAUSE THEY CAUGHT ME?
NO, I'M NOT ANGRY.
THEN TH... WHY ARE YOU SAYING ALL THESE MEAN THINGS?
WHY...
WHY WON'T YOU CALL ME "RACHEL" LIKE YOU USUALLY DO...?
YOU DON'T NEED TO HAVE A NAME ANYMORE.

READ THIS WAY

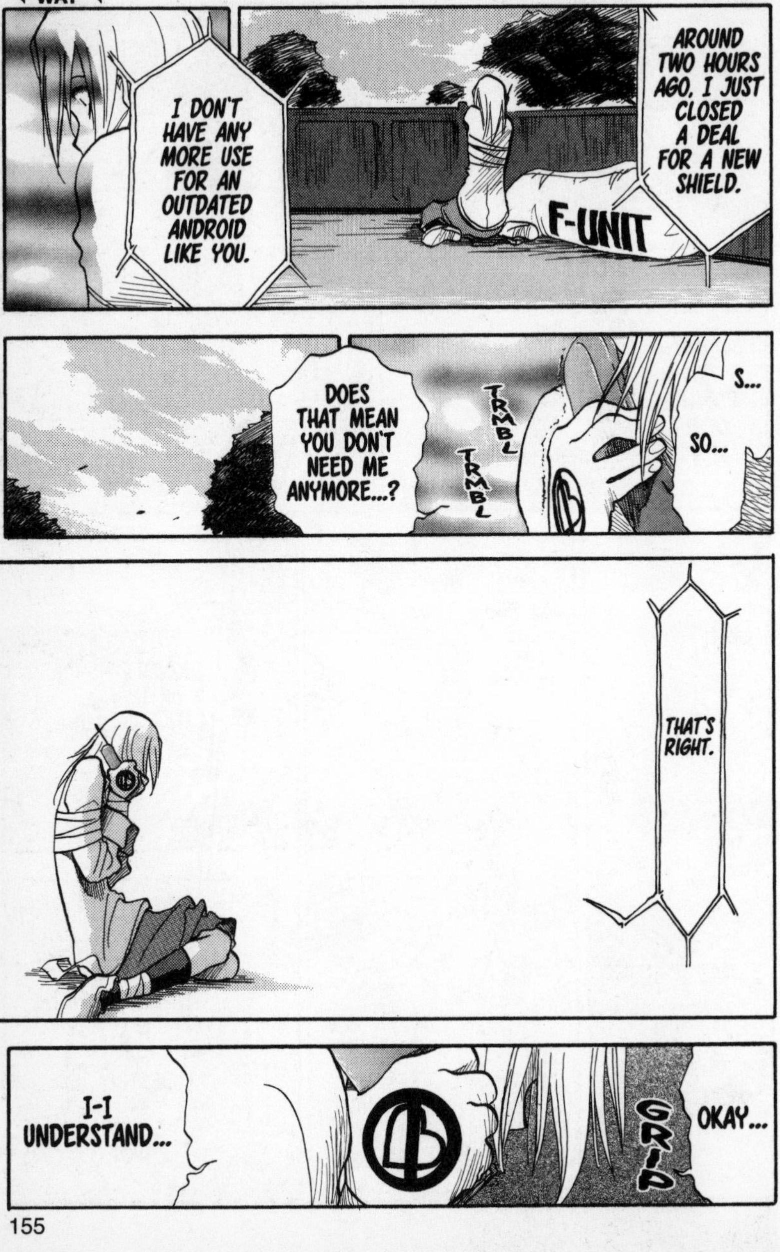
AROUND TWO HOURS AGO, I JUST CLOSED A DEAL FOR A NEW SHIELD.
F-UNIT
I DON'T HAVE ANY MORE USE FOR AN OUTDATED ANDROID LIKE YOU.
S...
SO...
TRMBL
TRMBL
DOES THAT MEAN YOU DON'T NEED ME ANYMORE...?
THAT'S RIGHT.
OKAY...
GRIP
I-I UNDERSTAND...

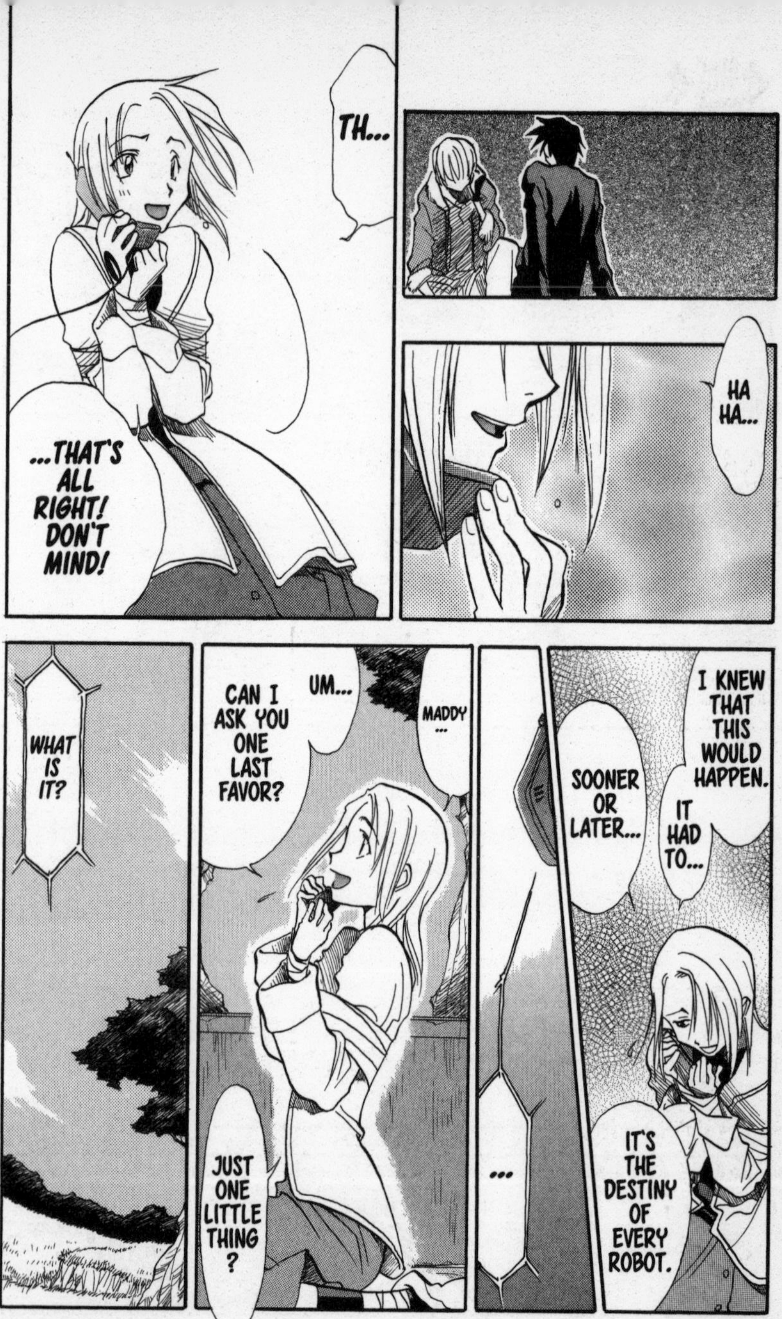
HA HA...
TH...
...THAT'S ALL RIGHT! DON'T MIND!
I KNEW THAT THIS WOULD HAPPEN.
IT HAD TO...
SOONER OR LATER...
IT'S THE DESTINY OF EVERY ROBOT.
...
MADDY...
UM...
CAN I ASK YOU ONE LAST FAVOR?
JUST ONE LITTLE THING?
WHAT IS IT?

READ THIS WAY

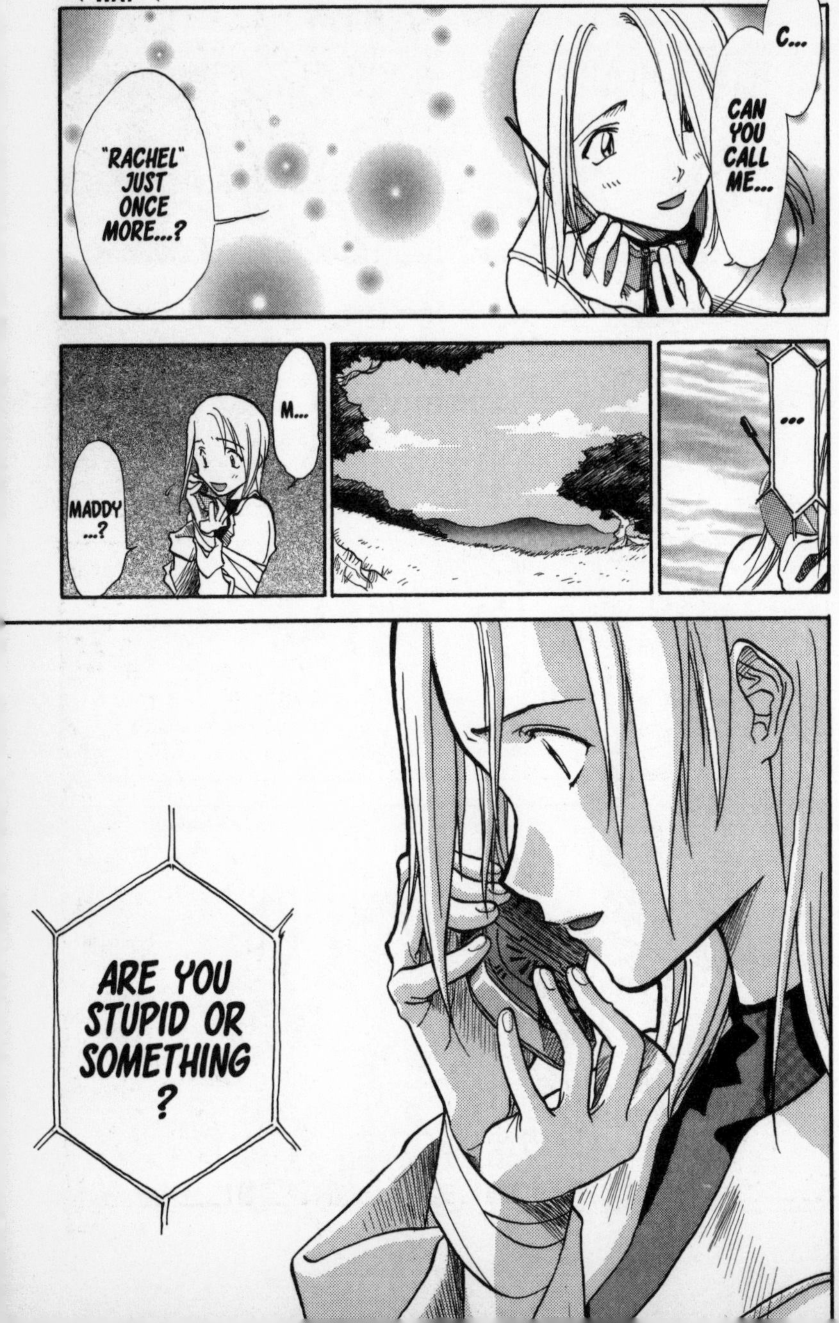

C...
CAN YOU CALL ME...
"RACHEL" JUST ONCE MORE...?
...
M...
MADDY ...?
ARE YOU STUPID OR SOMETHING ?

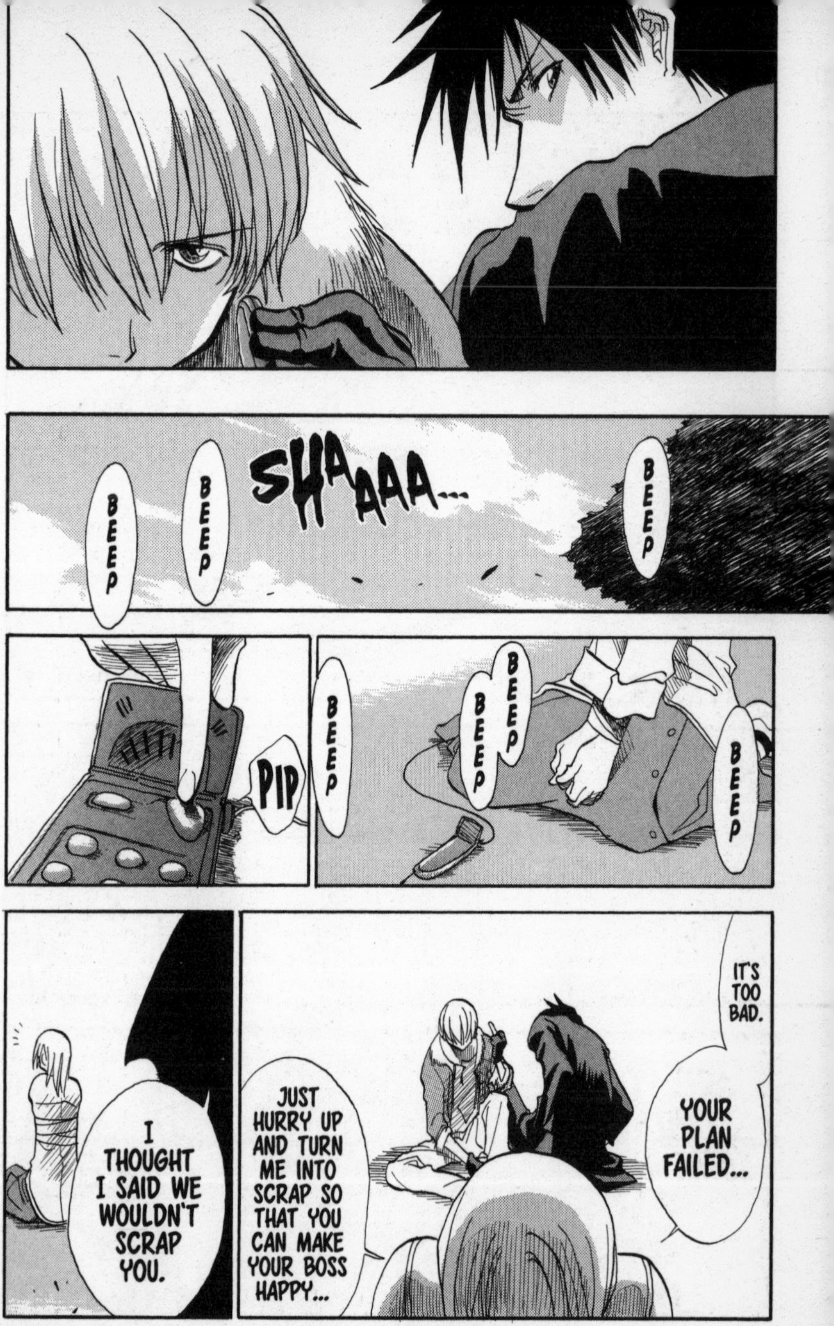
BEEP
SHAAAA...
BEEP
BEEP
BEEP
BEEP
BEEP
BEEP
PIP
IT'S TOO BAD.
YOUR PLAN FAILED...
JUST HURRY UP AND TURN ME INTO SCRAP SO THAT YOU CAN MAKE YOUR BOSS HAPPY...
I THOUGHT I SAID WE WOULDN'T SCRAP YOU.

READ THIS WAY

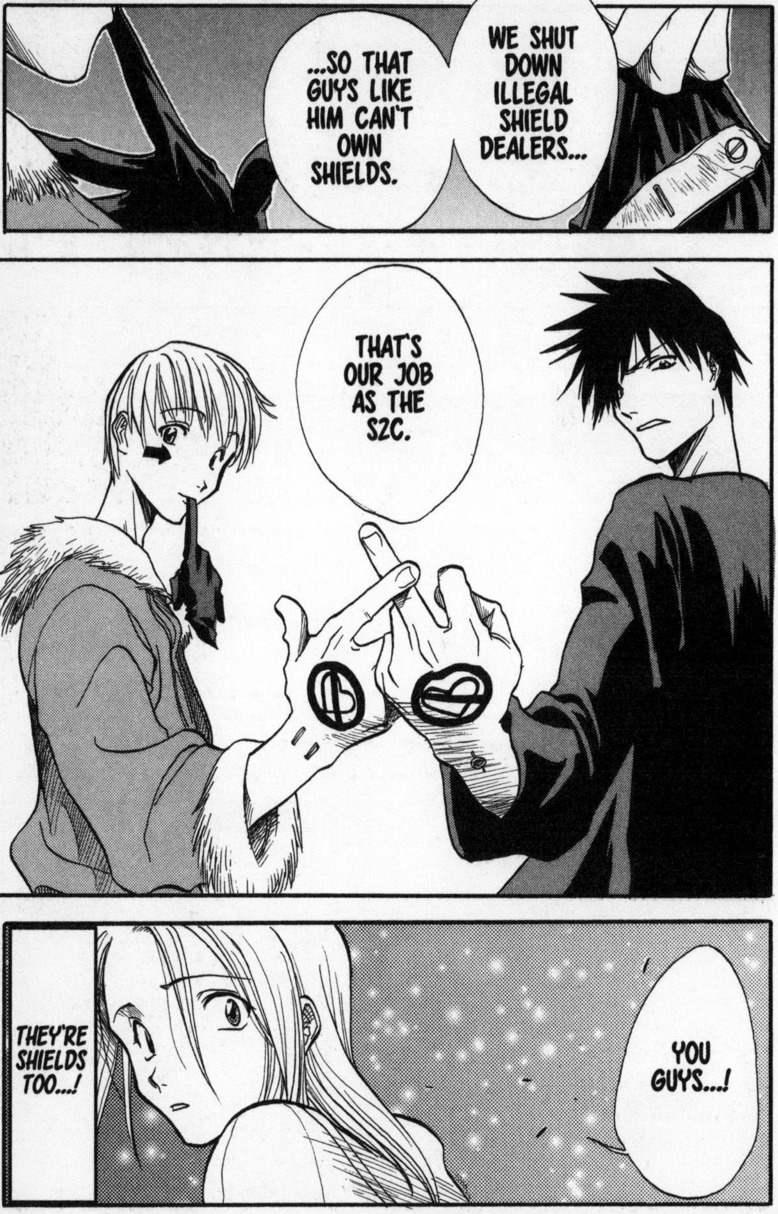
WE SHUT DOWN ILLEGAL SHIELD DEALERS...
...SO THAT GUYS LIKE HIM CAN'T OWN SHIELDS.
THAT'S OUR JOB AS THE S2C.
YOU GUYS...!
THEY'RE SHIELDS TOO...!

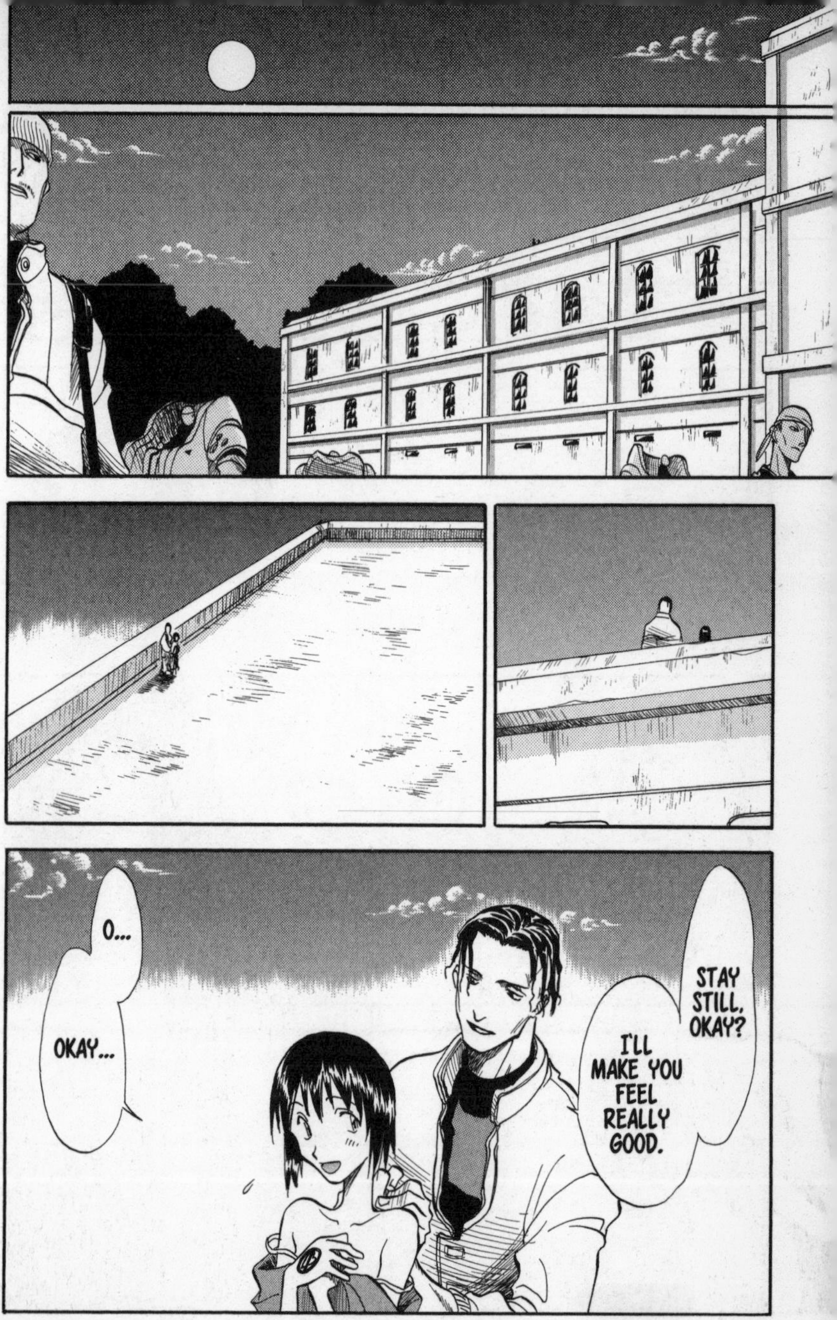
STAY STILL, OKAY?
I'LL MAKE YOU FEEL REALLY GOOD.
O...
OKAY...

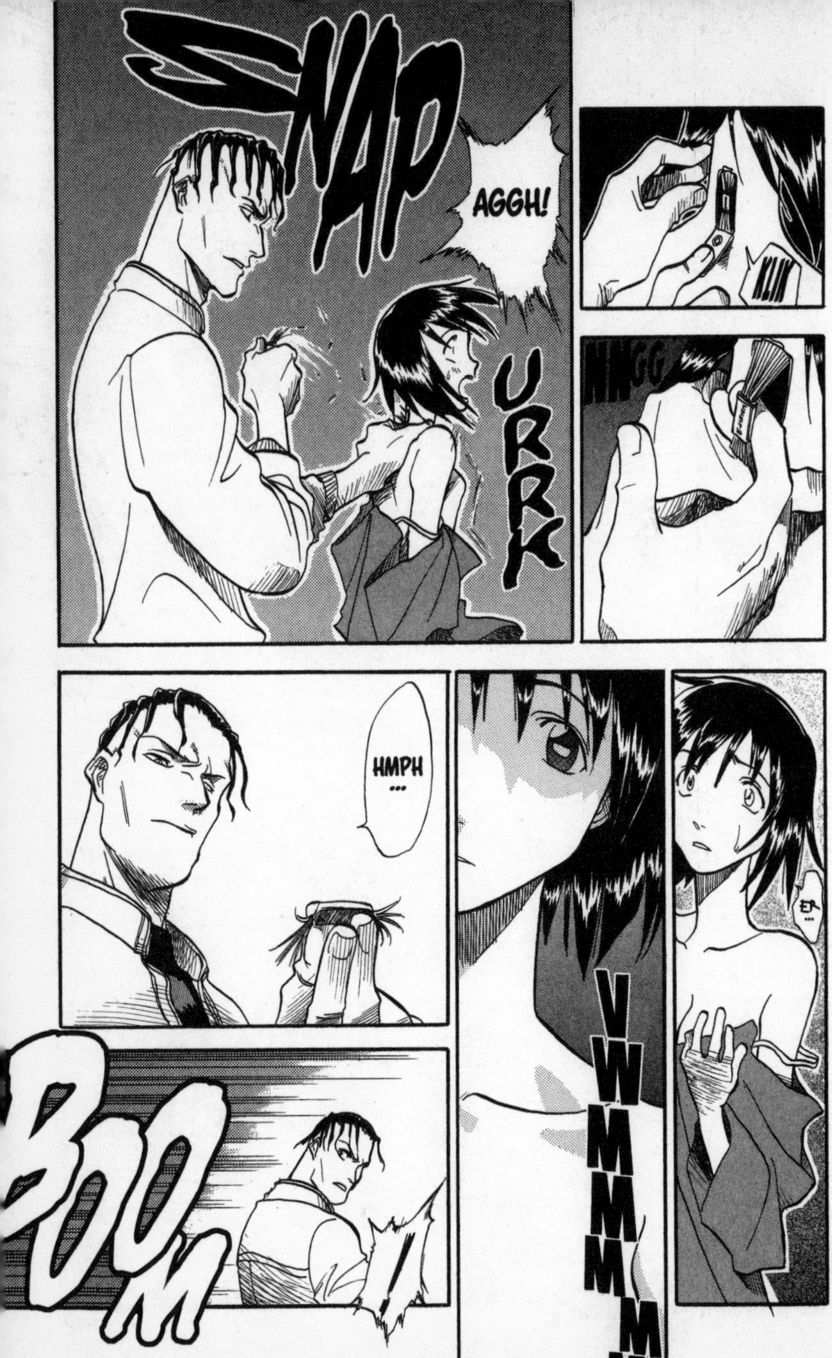
KLIK
NNGG
SNAP
AGGH!
URRK
VWMMMMM
HMPH...
BOOM
!

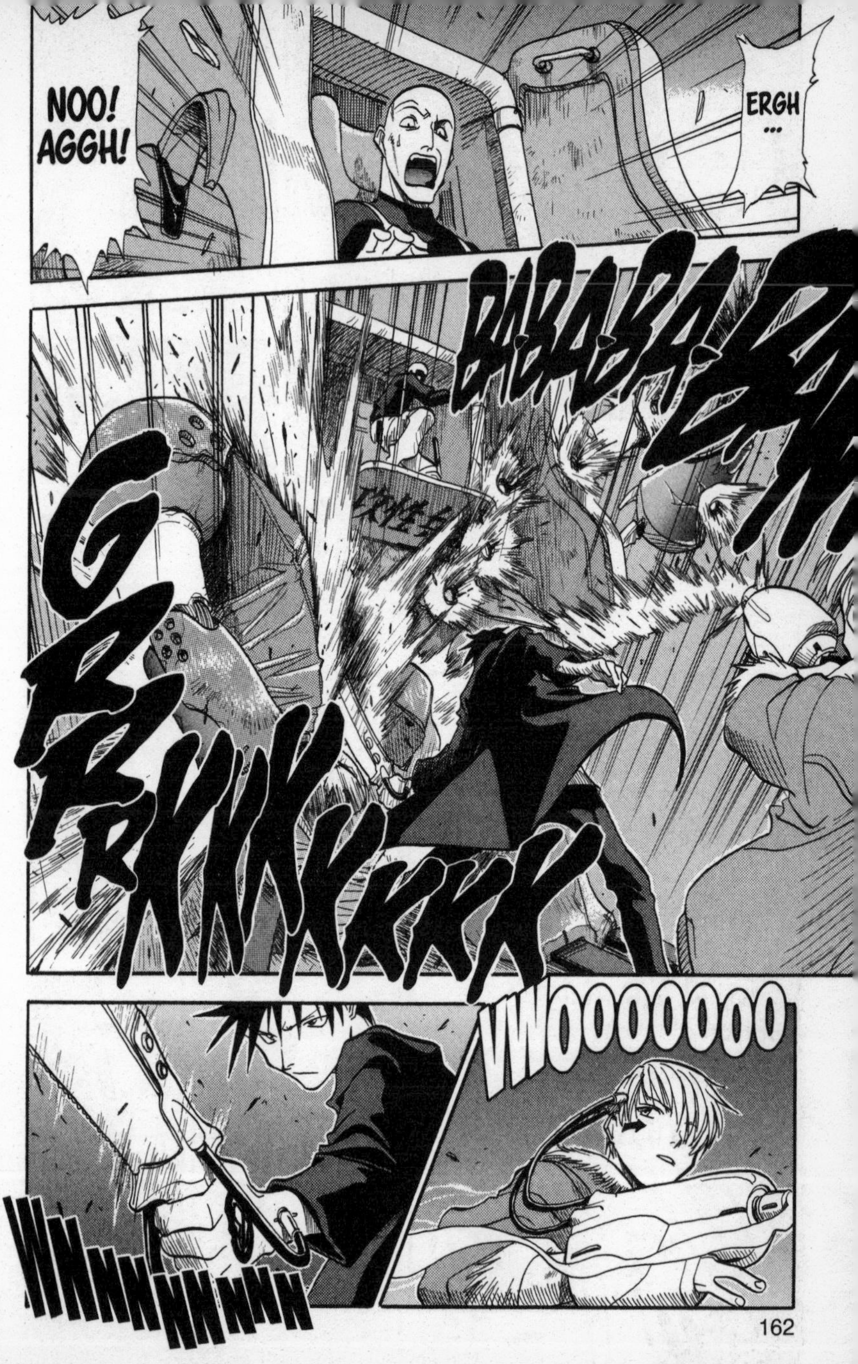
ERGH ...
NOO! AGGH!
BABABABA
GAZRKNKKKKKK
VWOOOOOOO
WNNNNNNNNNNN

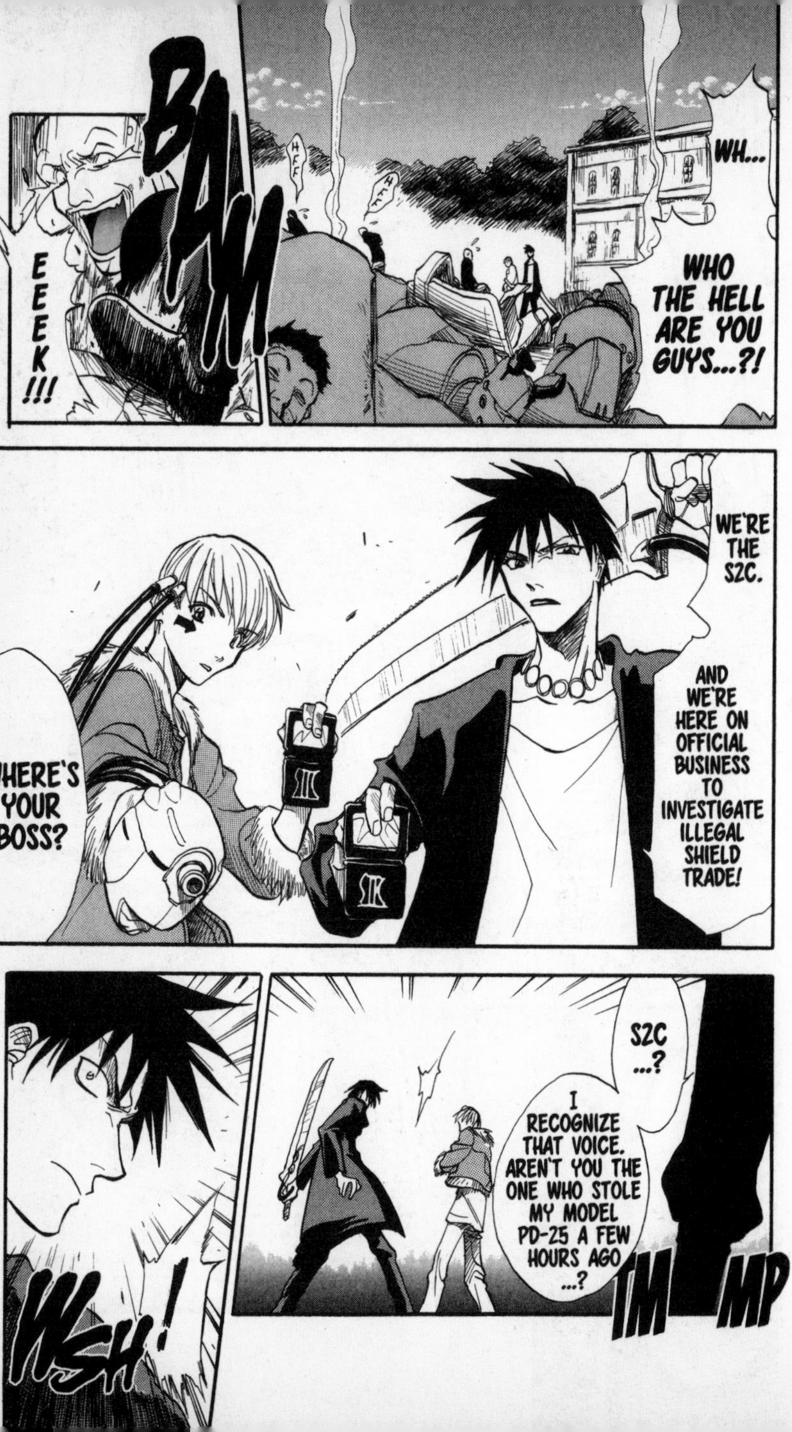
HFF
HFF
WH...
WHO THE HELL ARE YOU GUYS...?!
BAM
EEEK!!!
WE'RE THE S2C.
AND WE'RE HERE ON OFFICIAL BUSINESS TO INVESTIGATE ILLEGAL SHIELD TRADE!
WHERE'S YOUR BOSS?
S2C ...?
I RECOGNIZE THAT VOICE. AREN'T YOU THE ONE WHO STOLE MY MODEL PD-25 A FEW HOURS AGO ...?
TMMP
WSH!

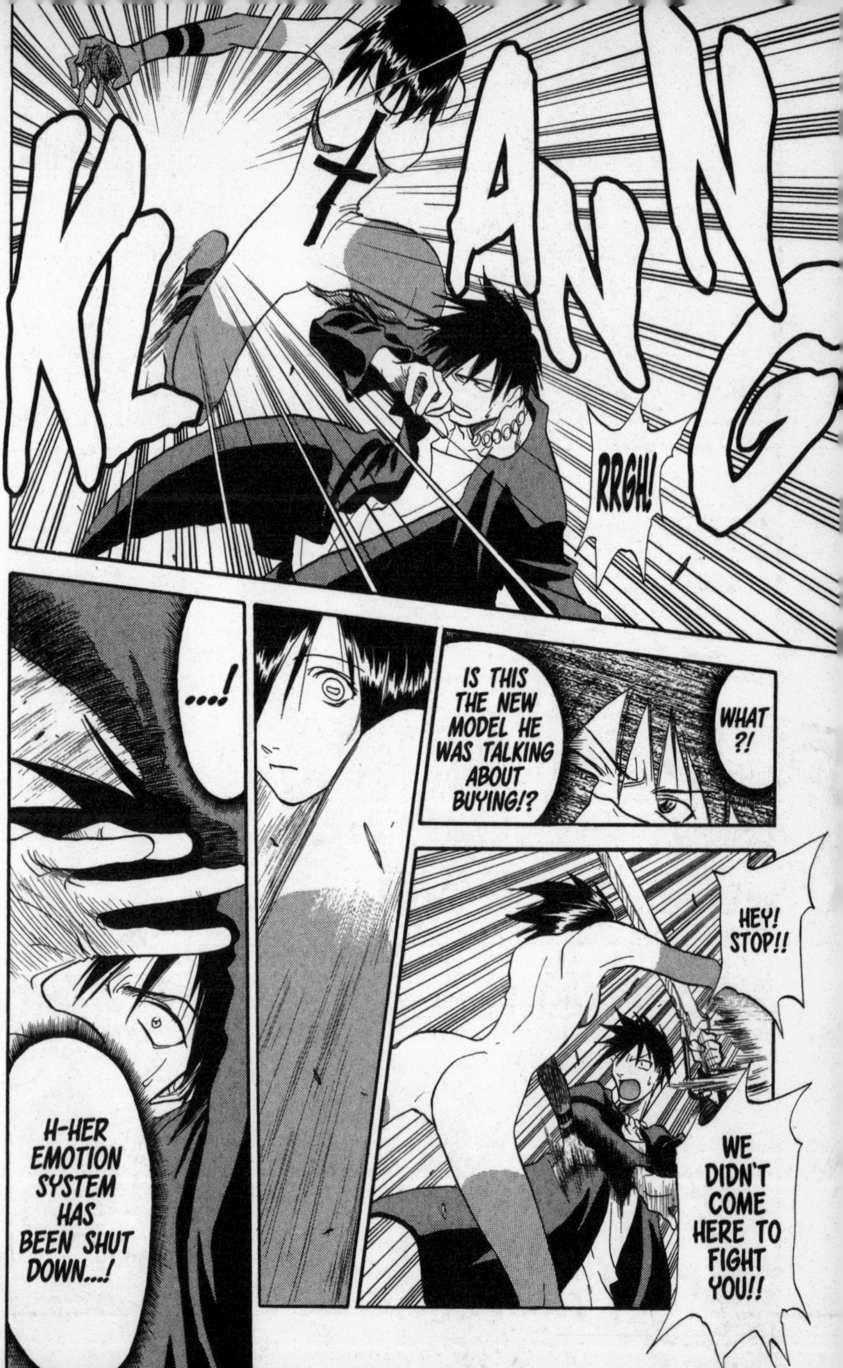
KLANNG
RRGH!
WHAT?!
IS THIS THE NEW MODEL HE WAS TALKING ABOUT BUYING!?
HEY! STOP!!
WE DIDN'T COME HERE TO FIGHT YOU!!
...!
H-HER EMOTION SYSTEM HAS BEEN SHUT DOWN...!

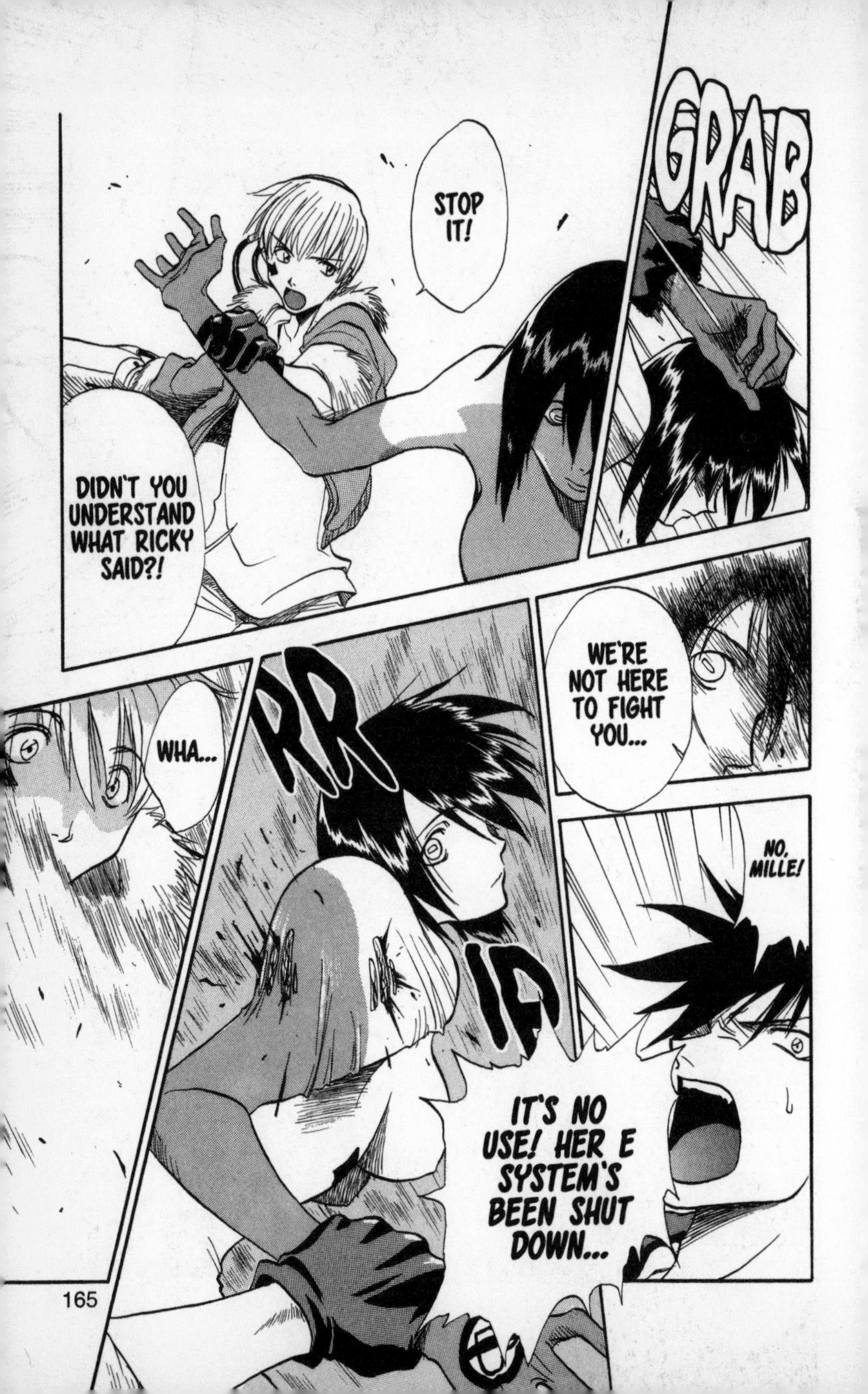
GRAB
STOP IT!
DIDN'T YOU UNDERSTAND WHAT RICKY SAID?!
WE'RE NOT HERE TO FIGHT YOU...
NO, MILLE!
IT'S NO USE! HER E SYSTEM'S BEEN SHUT DOWN...
RRIP
WHA...

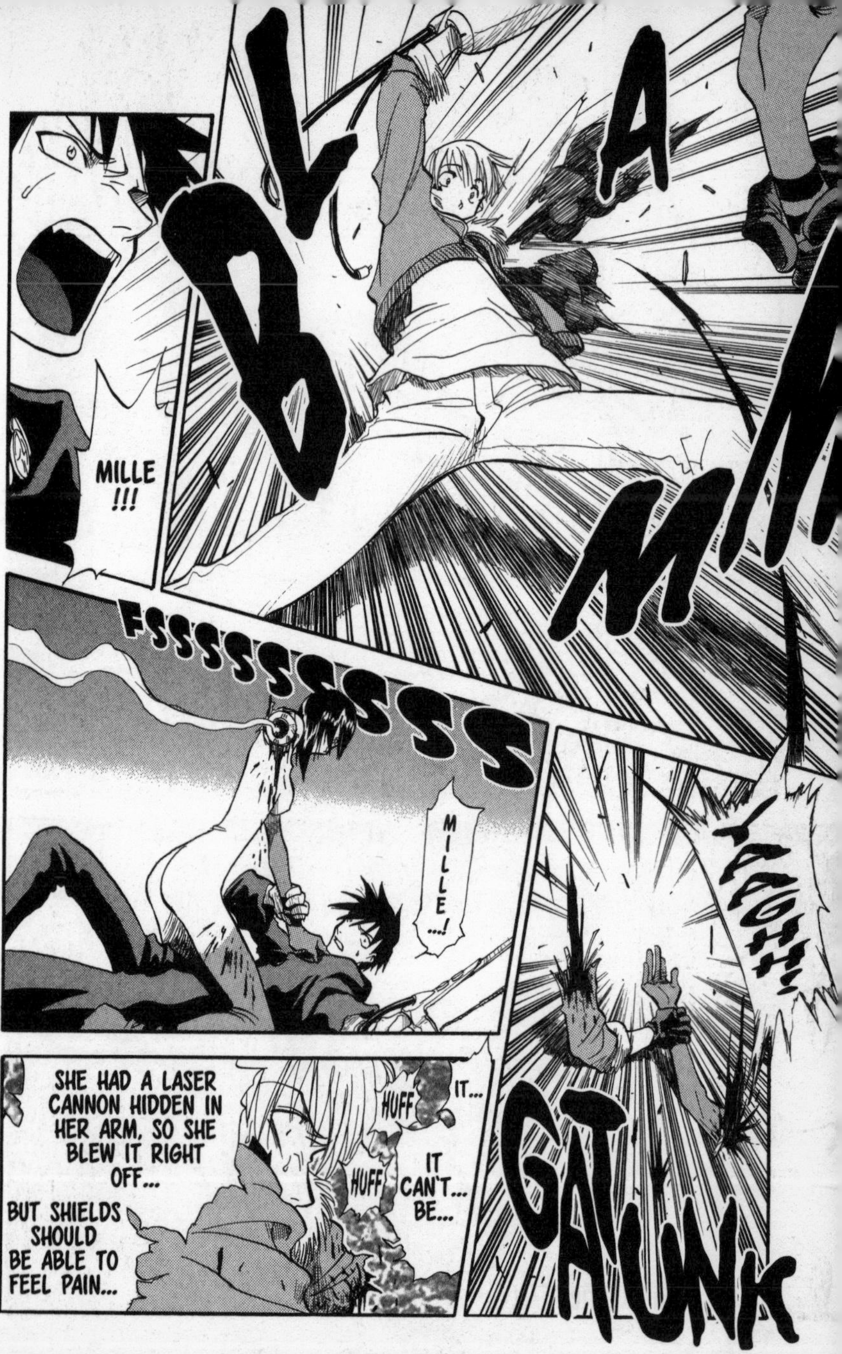
BLAM
MILLE !!!
YEAGHH!
GATUNK
FSSSSSSSSS
MILLE ...!
IT...
HUFF
IT CAN'T... BE...
HUFF
SHE HAD A LASER CANNON HIDDEN IN HER ARM, SO SHE BLEW IT RIGHT OFF...
BUT SHIELDS SHOULD BE ABLE TO FEEL PAIN...

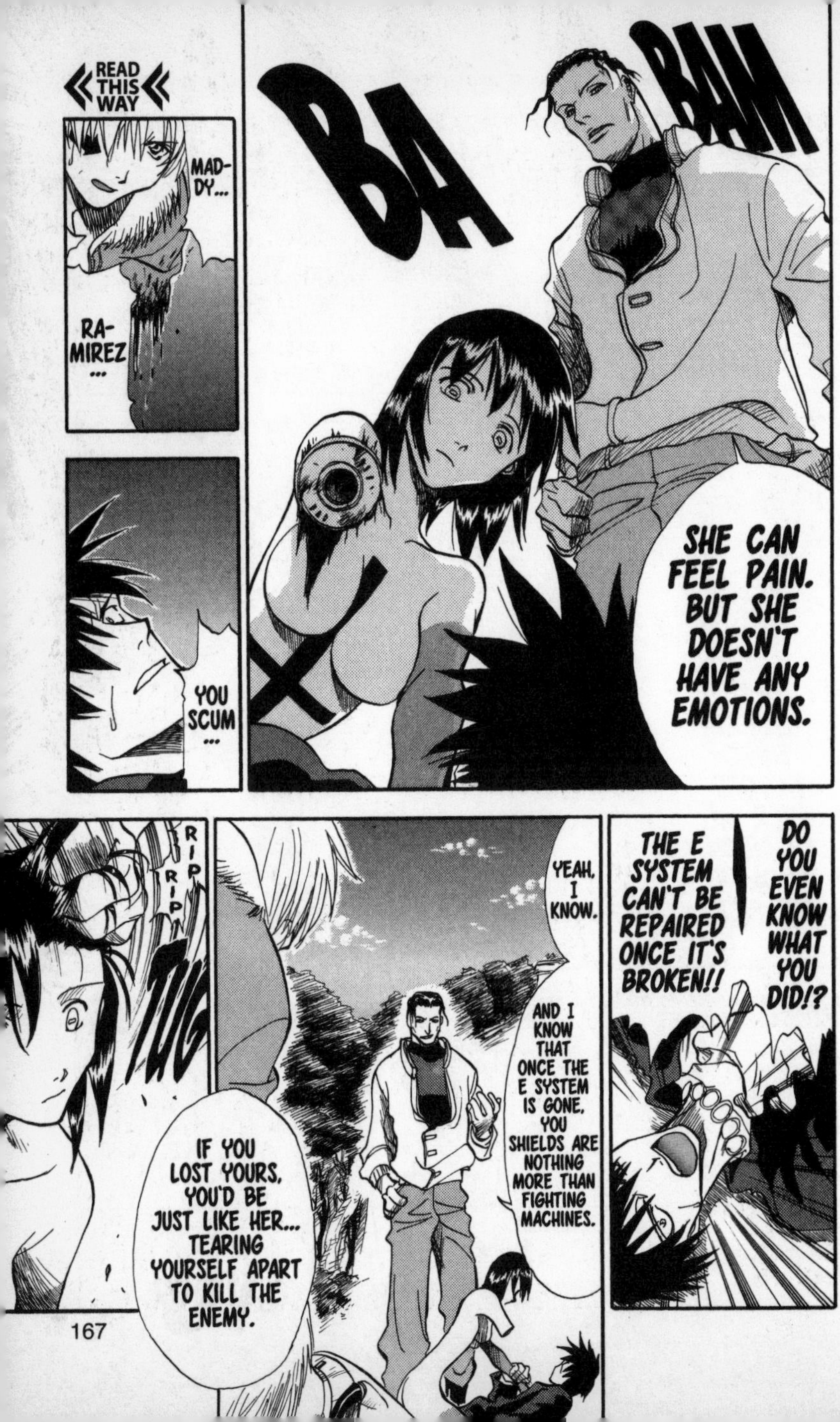
READ THIS WAY
BA BAM
SHE CAN FEEL PAIN. BUT SHE DOESN'T HAVE ANY EMOTIONS.
MAD-DY...
RA-MIREZ...
YOU SCUM...
DO YOU EVEN KNOW WHAT YOU DID!?
THE E SYSTEM CAN'T BE REPAIRED ONCE IT'S BROKEN!!
YEAH, I KNOW.
AND I KNOW THAT ONCE THE E SYSTEM IS GONE, YOU SHIELDS ARE NOTHING MORE THAN FIGHTING MACHINES.
IF YOU LOST YOURS, YOU'D BE JUST LIKE HER... TEARING YOURSELF APART TO KILL THE ENEMY.
RIP
RIP
TUG

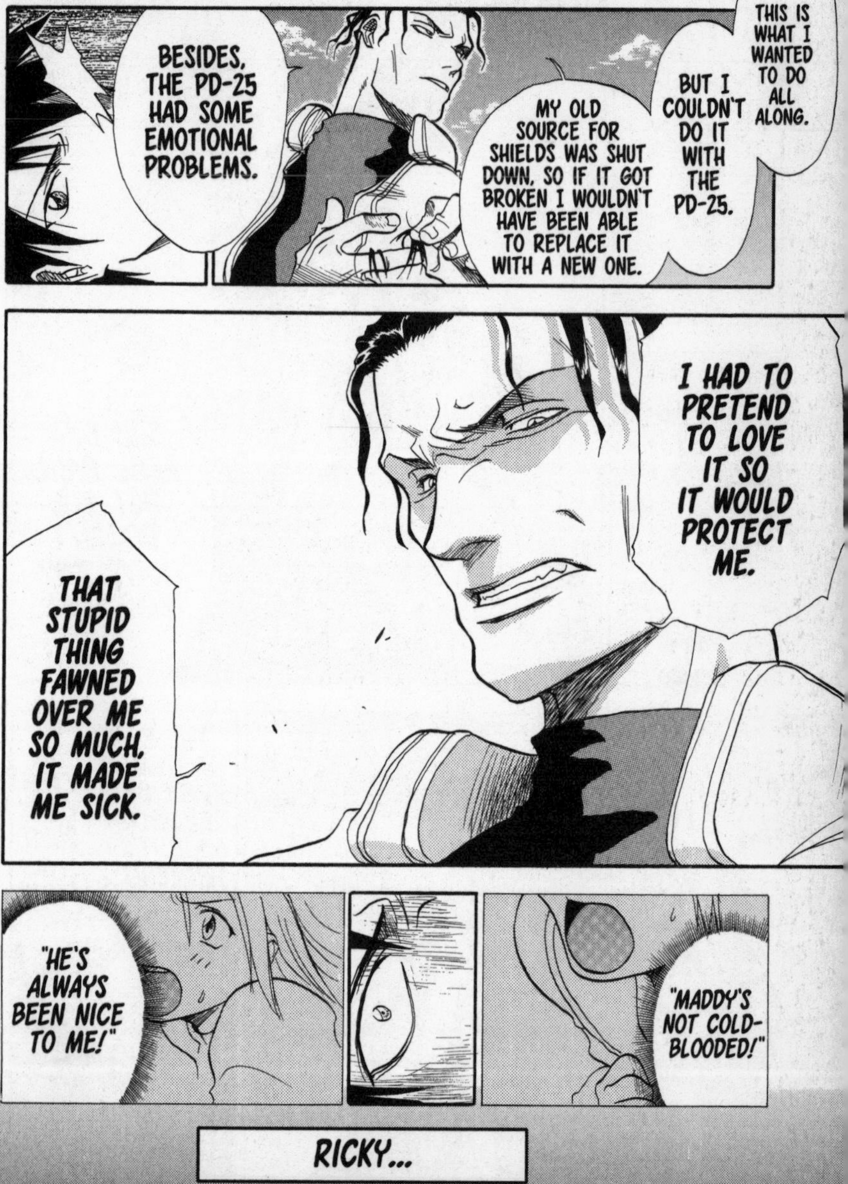
THIS IS WHAT I WANTED TO DO ALL ALONG.
BUT I COULDN'T DO IT WITH THE PD-25.
MY OLD SOURCE FOR SHIELDS WAS SHUT DOWN, SO IF IT GOT BROKEN I WOULDN'T HAVE BEEN ABLE TO REPLACE IT WITH A NEW ONE.
BESIDES, THE PD-25 HAD SOME EMOTIONAL PROBLEMS.
I HAD TO PRETEND TO LOVE IT SO IT WOULD PROTECT ME.
THAT STUPID THING FAWNED OVER ME SO MUCH, IT MADE ME SICK.
"MADDY'S NOT COLD-BLOODED!"
"HE'S ALWAYS BEEN NICE TO ME!"
RICKY...

READ THIS WAY

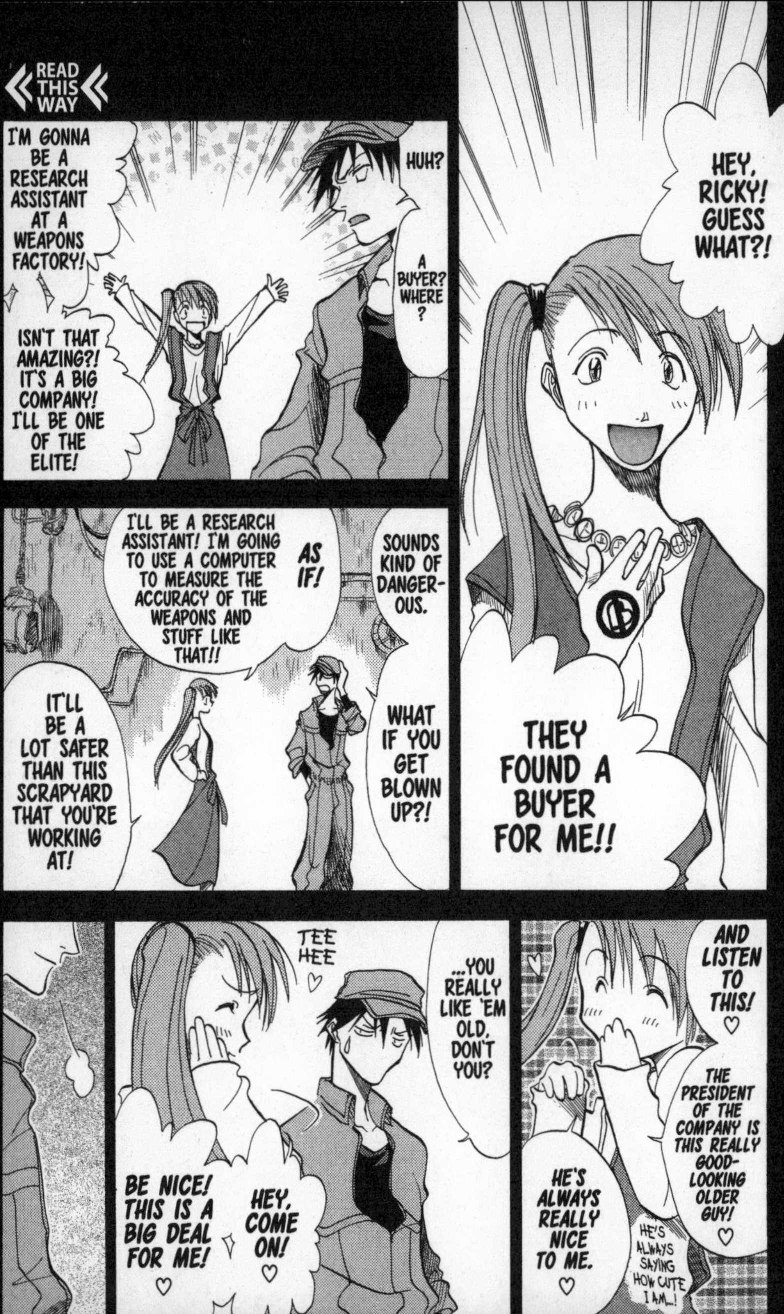
HEY, RICKY! GUESS WHAT?!
THEY FOUND A BUYER FOR ME!!
HUH?
A BUYER? WHERE?
I'M GONNA BE A RESEARCH ASSISTANT AT A WEAPONS FACTORY!
ISN'T THAT AMAZING?! IT'S A BIG COMPANY! I'LL BE ONE OF THE ELITE!
SOUNDS KIND OF DANGER-OUS.
AS IF!
I'LL BE A RESEARCH ASSISTANT! I'M GOING TO USE A COMPUTER TO MEASURE THE ACCURACY OF THE WEAPONS AND STUFF LIKE THAT!!
WHAT IF YOU GET BLOWN UP?!
IT'LL BE A LOT SAFER THAN THIS SCRAPYARD THAT YOU'RE WORKING AT!
AND LISTEN TO THIS! ♡
THE PRESIDENT OF THE COMPANY IS THIS REALLY GOOD-LOOKING OLDER GUY! ♡
HE'S ALWAYS SAYING HOW CUTE I AM...!
HE'S ALWAYS REALLY NICE TO ME. ♡
...YOU REALLY LIKE 'EM OLD, DON'T YOU?
TEE HEE ♡
HEY, COME ON! ♡
BE NICE! THIS IS A BIG DEAL FOR ME! ♡

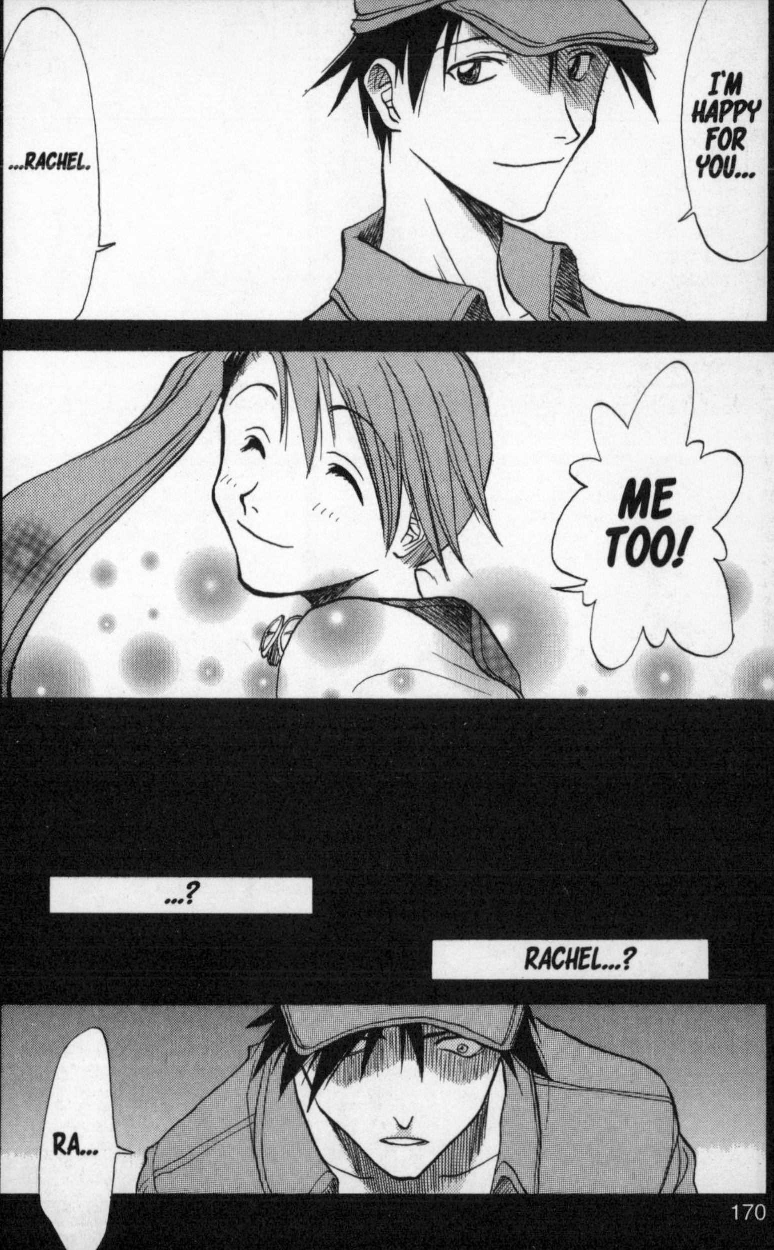
I'M HAPPY FOR YOU...
...RACHEL..
ME TOO!
...?
RACHEL...?
RA...

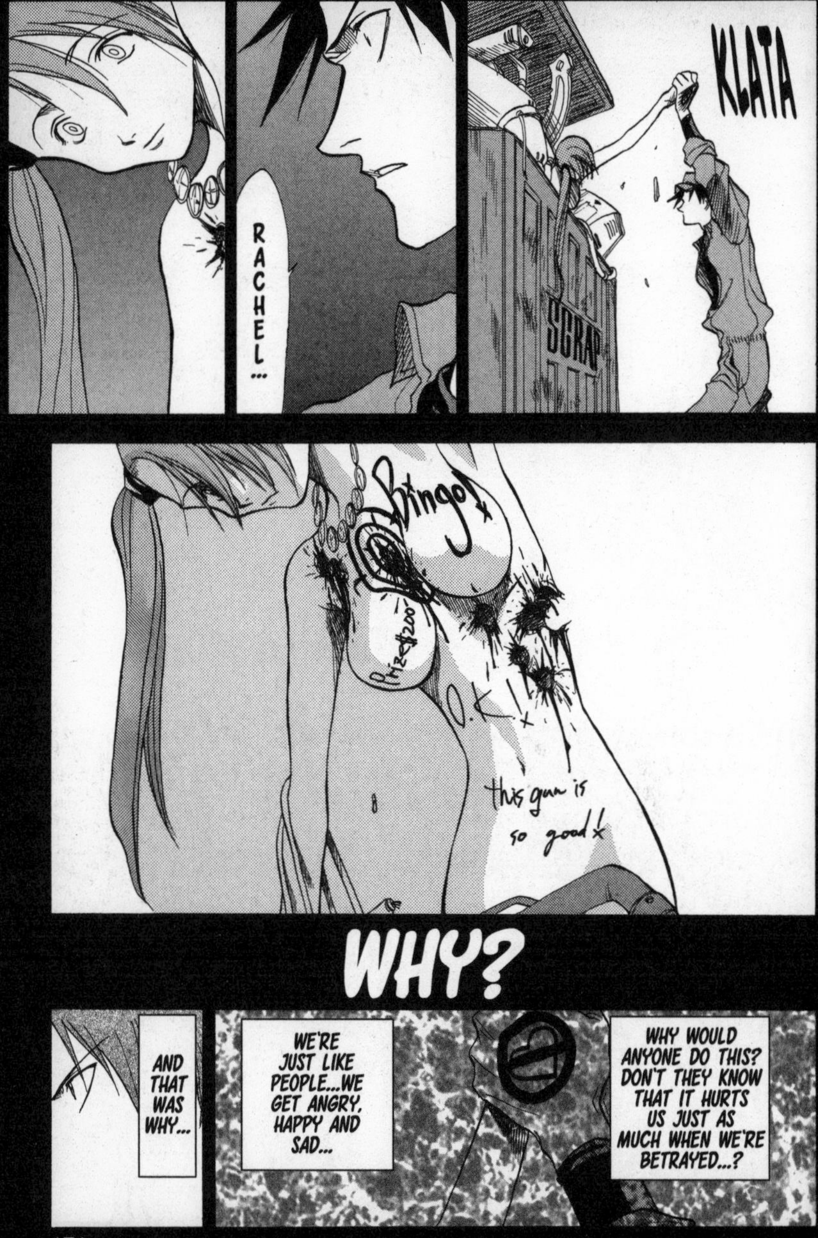
KLATA
SCRAP
RACHEL...
Bingo!
Prize#200
O.K.!
this gun is so good!
WHY?
WHY WOULD ANYONE DO THIS? DON'T THEY KNOW THAT IT HURTS US JUST AS MUCH WHEN WE'RE BETRAYED...?
WE'RE JUST LIKE PEOPLE...WE GET ANGRY, HAPPY AND SAD...
AND THAT WAS WHY...

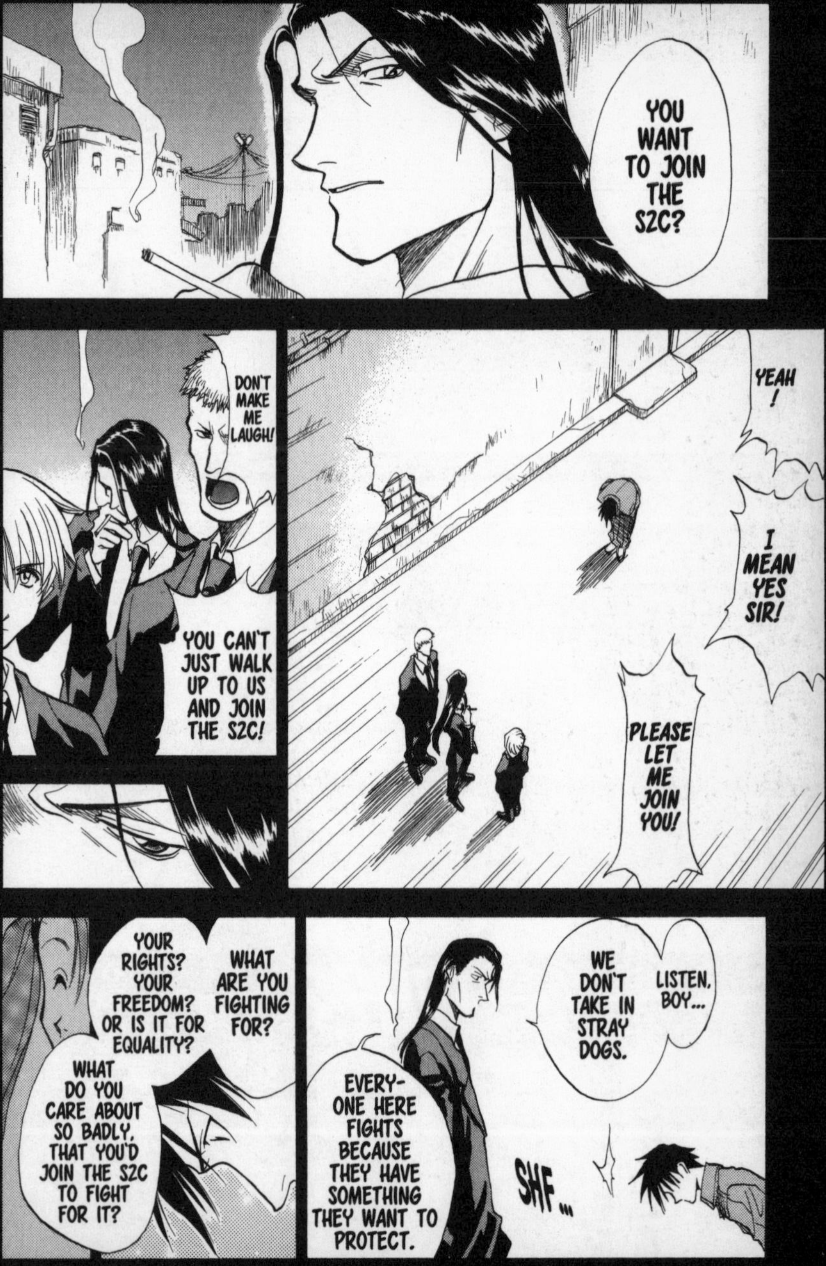
YOU WANT TO JOIN THE S2C?
YEAH! I MEAN YES SIR!
PLEASE LET ME JOIN YOU!
DON'T MAKE ME LAUGH!
YOU CAN'T JUST WALK UP TO US AND JOIN THE S2C!
LISTEN, BOY...
WE DON'T TAKE IN STRAY DOGS.
EVERY-ONE HERE FIGHTS BECAUSE THEY HAVE SOMETHING THEY WANT TO PROTECT.
SHF...
WHAT ARE YOU FIGHTING FOR?
YOUR RIGHTS? YOUR FREEDOM? OR IS IT FOR EQUALITY?
WHAT DO YOU CARE ABOUT SO BADLY, THAT YOU'D JOIN THE S2C TO FIGHT FOR IT?

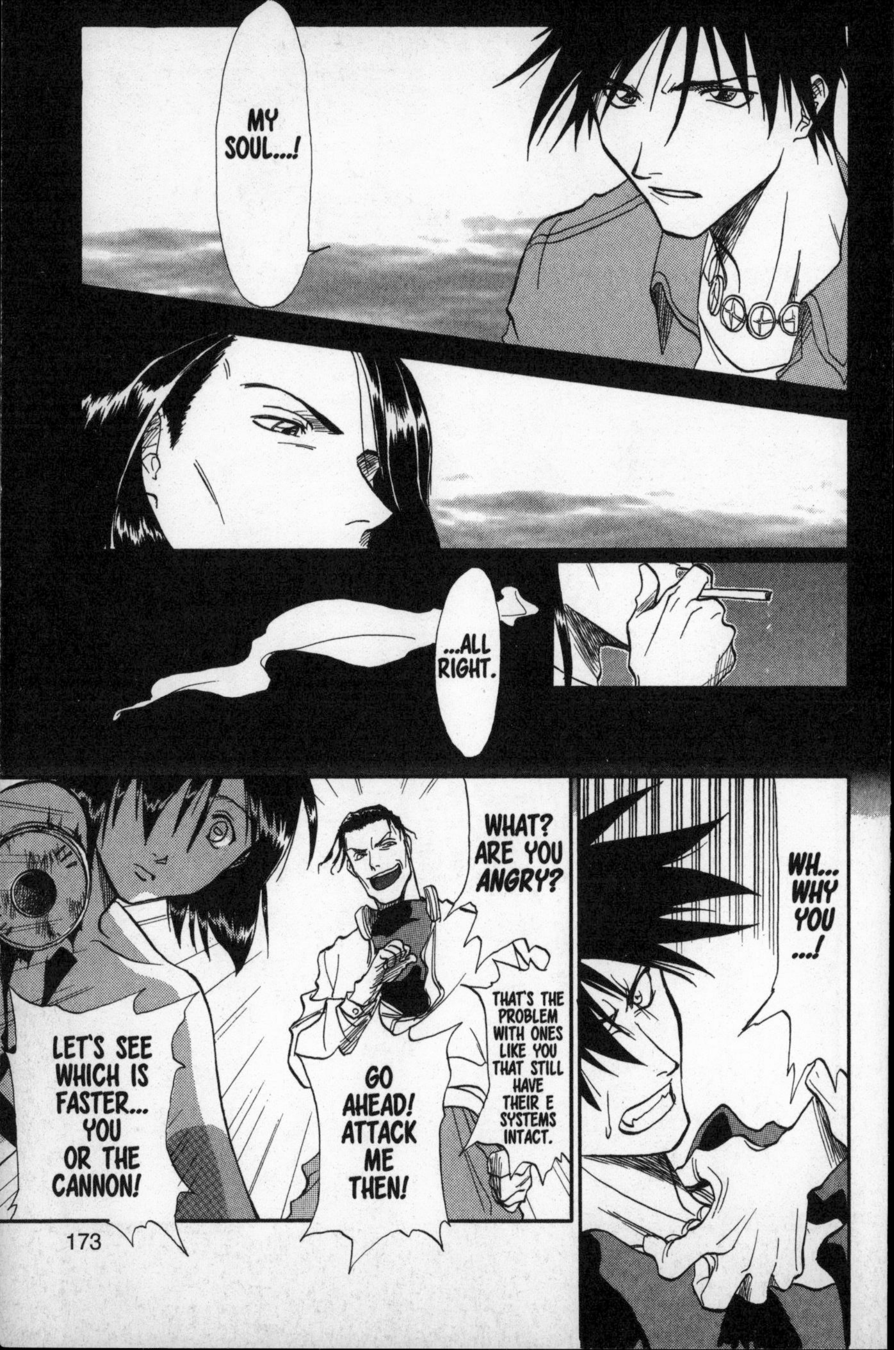
MY SOUL...!
...ALL RIGHT.
WH... WHY YOU ...!
WHAT? ARE YOU ANGRY?
THAT'S THE PROBLEM WITH ONES LIKE YOU THAT STILL HAVE THEIR E SYSTEMS INTACT.
GO AHEAD! ATTACK ME THEN!
LET'S SEE WHICH IS FASTER... YOU OR THE CANNON!

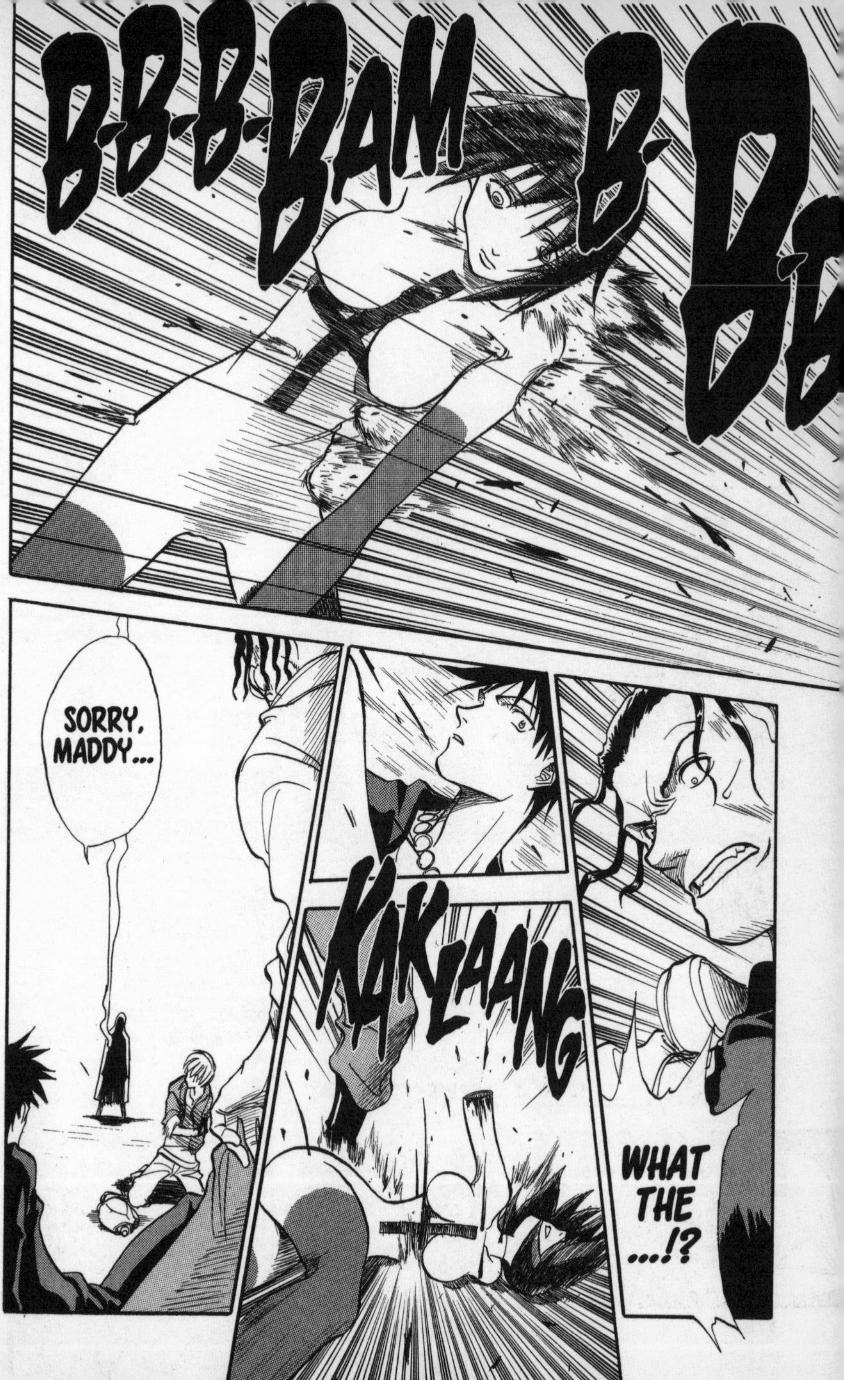
B-B-B-BAM
B-B
WHAT THE ...!?
KAKLAANG
SORRY, MADDY...

READ THIS WAY

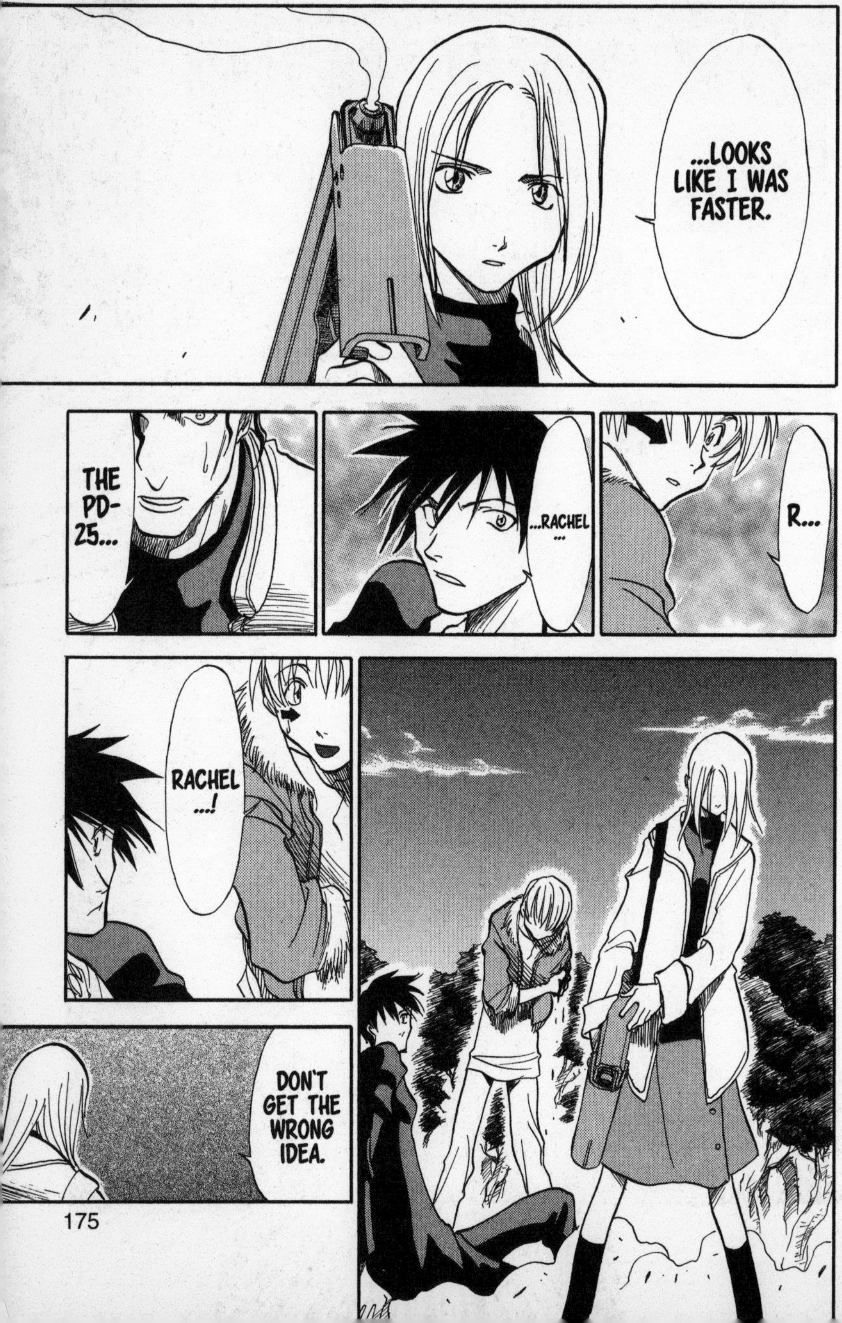
...LOOKS LIKE I WAS FASTER.
R...
...RACHEL ...
THE PD-25...
RACHEL ...!
DON'T GET THE WRONG IDEA.

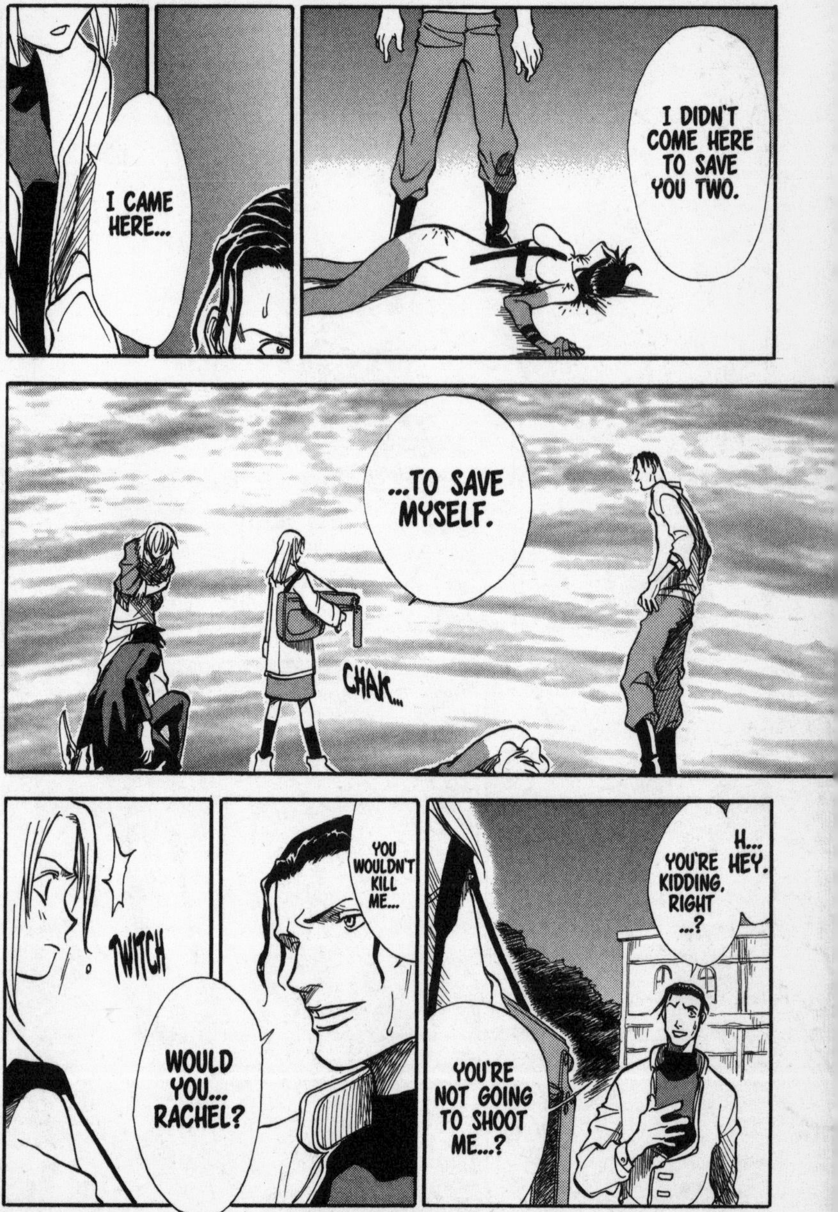
I DIDN'T COME HERE TO SAVE YOU TWO.
I CAME HERE...
...TO SAVE MYSELF.
CHAK...
H... HEY.
YOU'RE KIDDING, RIGHT ...?
YOU'RE NOT GOING TO SHOOT ME...?
YOU WOULDN'T KILL ME...
WOULD YOU... RACHEL?
TWITCH

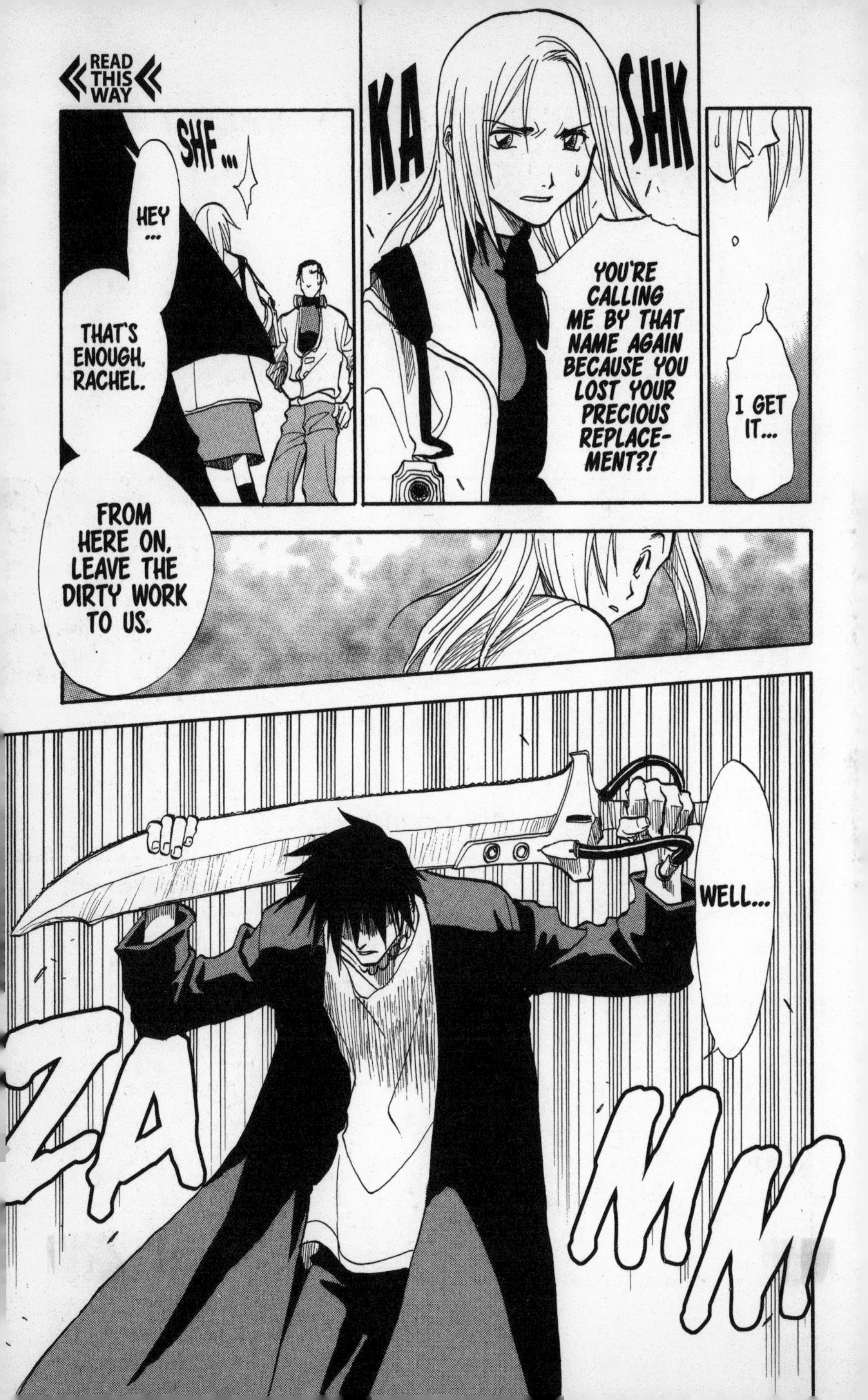
READ THIS WAY
I GET IT...
KA SHK
YOU'RE CALLING ME BY THAT NAME AGAIN BECAUSE YOU LOST YOUR PRECIOUS REPLACEMENT?!
SHF...
HEY...
THAT'S ENOUGH, RACHEL.
FROM HERE ON, LEAVE THE DIRTY WORK TO US.
WELL...
ZAMM

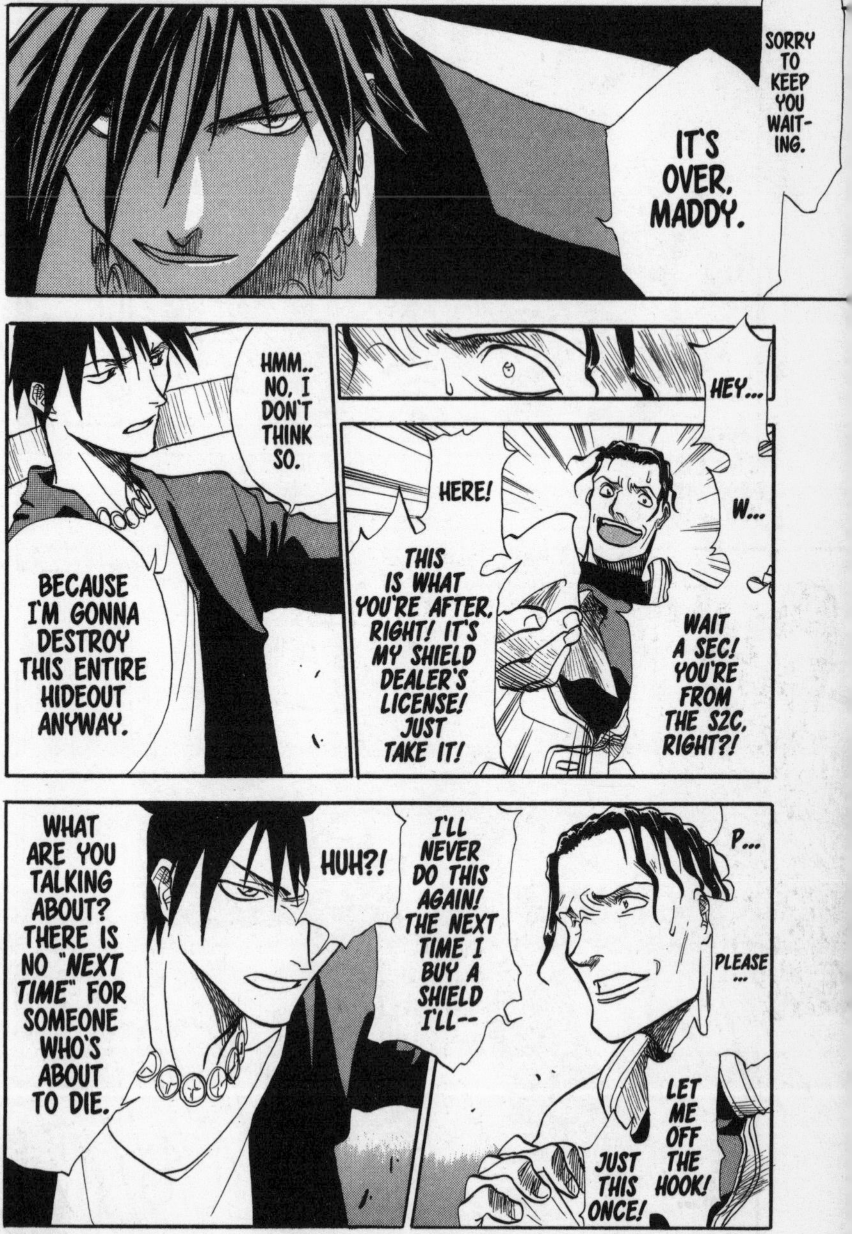

SORRY TO KEEP YOU WAIT-ING.
IT'S OVER, MADDY.
HEY...
W...
WAIT A SEC! YOU'RE FROM THE S2C, RIGHT?!
HERE!
THIS IS WHAT YOU'RE AFTER, RIGHT! IT'S MY SHIELD DEALER'S LICENSE! JUST TAKE IT!
HMM.. NO, I DON'T THINK SO.
BECAUSE I'M GONNA DESTROY THIS ENTIRE HIDEOUT ANYWAY.
P...
PLEASE...
LET ME OFF THE HOOK!
JUST THIS ONCE!
I'LL NEVER DO THIS AGAIN! THE NEXT TIME I BUY A SHIELD I'LL--
HUH?!
WHAT ARE YOU TALKING ABOUT? THERE IS NO "*NEXT TIME*" FOR SOMEONE WHO'S ABOUT TO DIE.

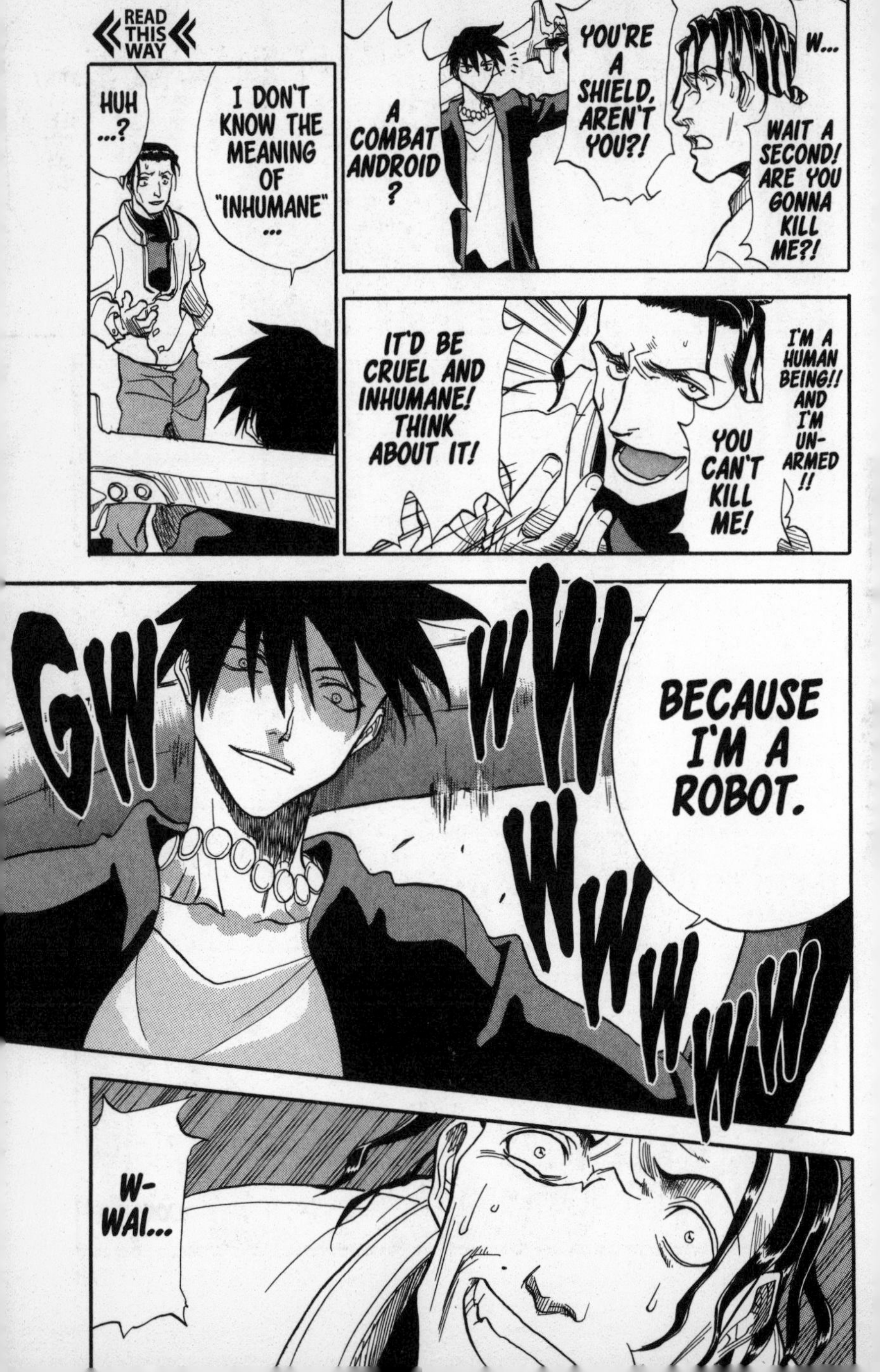
READ THIS WAY
W...
WAIT A SECOND! ARE YOU GONNA KILL ME?!
YOU'RE A SHIELD, AREN'T YOU?!
A COMBAT ANDROID?
I'M A HUMAN BEING!! AND I'M UN-ARMED!!
YOU CAN'T KILL ME!
IT'D BE CRUEL AND INHUMANE! THINK ABOUT IT!
I DON'T KNOW THE MEANING OF "INHUMANE"...
HUH...?
BECAUSE I'M A ROBOT.
GWWWWWWWWWW
W-WAI...

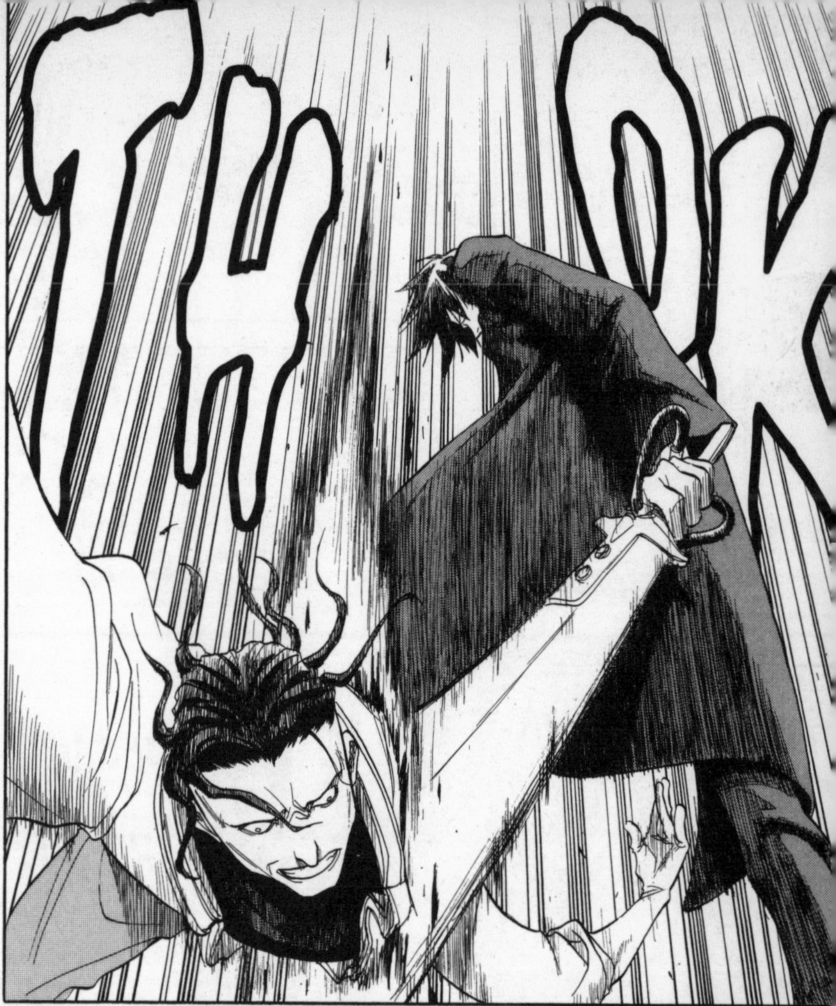
THOK

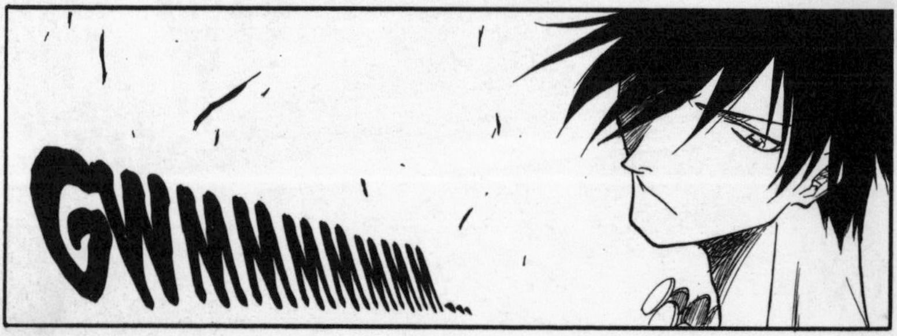
GWMMMMMMM...

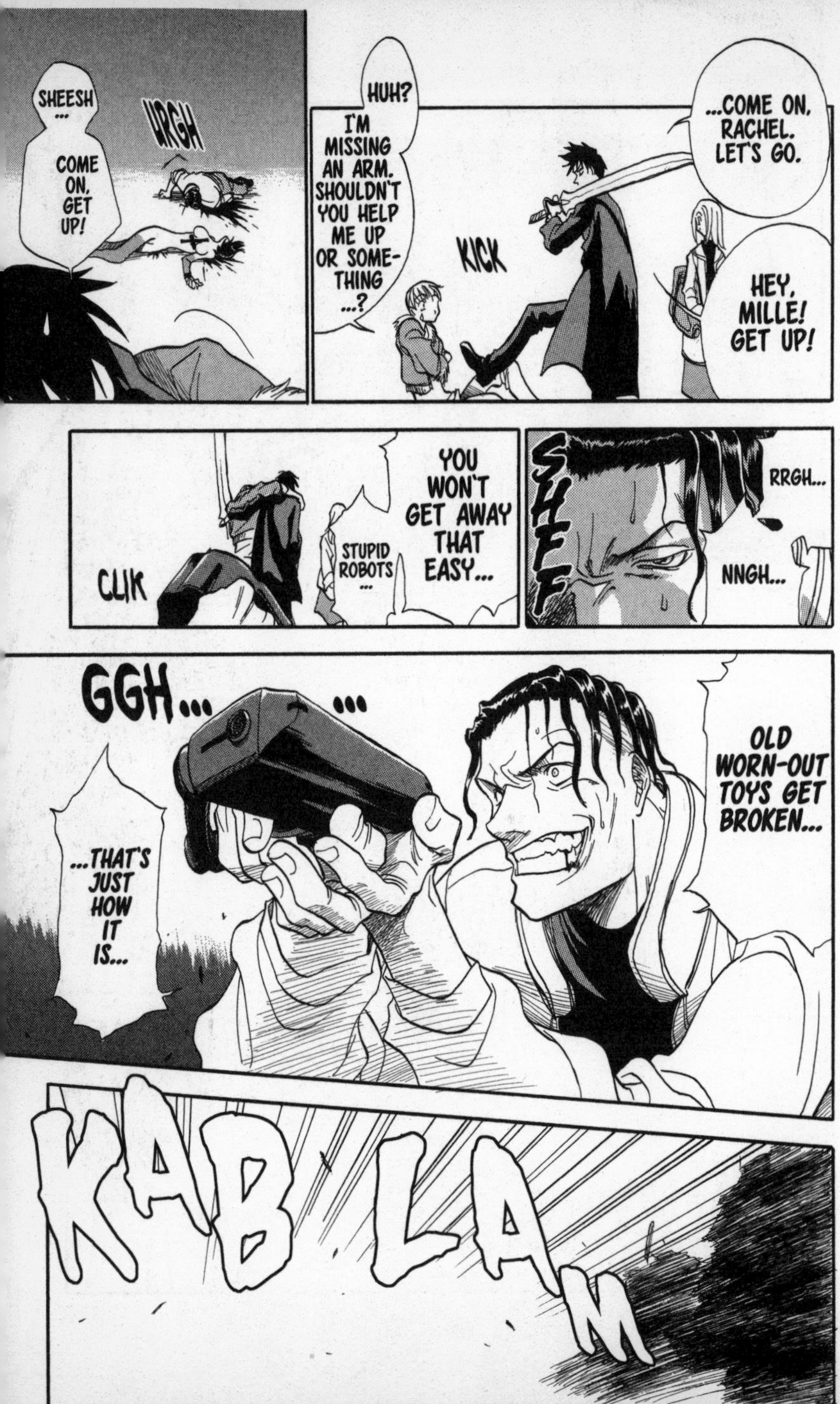
...COME ON, RACHEL. LET'S GO.
HEY, MILLE! GET UP!
KICK
HUH?
I'M MISSING AN ARM. SHOULDN'T YOU HELP ME UP OR SOMETHING...?
SHEESH...
URGH
COME ON, GET UP!
SHFF
RRGH...
NNGH...
YOU WON'T GET AWAY THAT EASY...
STUPID ROBOTS...
CLIK
OLD WORN-OUT TOYS GET BROKEN...
GGH... ...
...THAT'S JUST HOW IT IS...
KABLAM

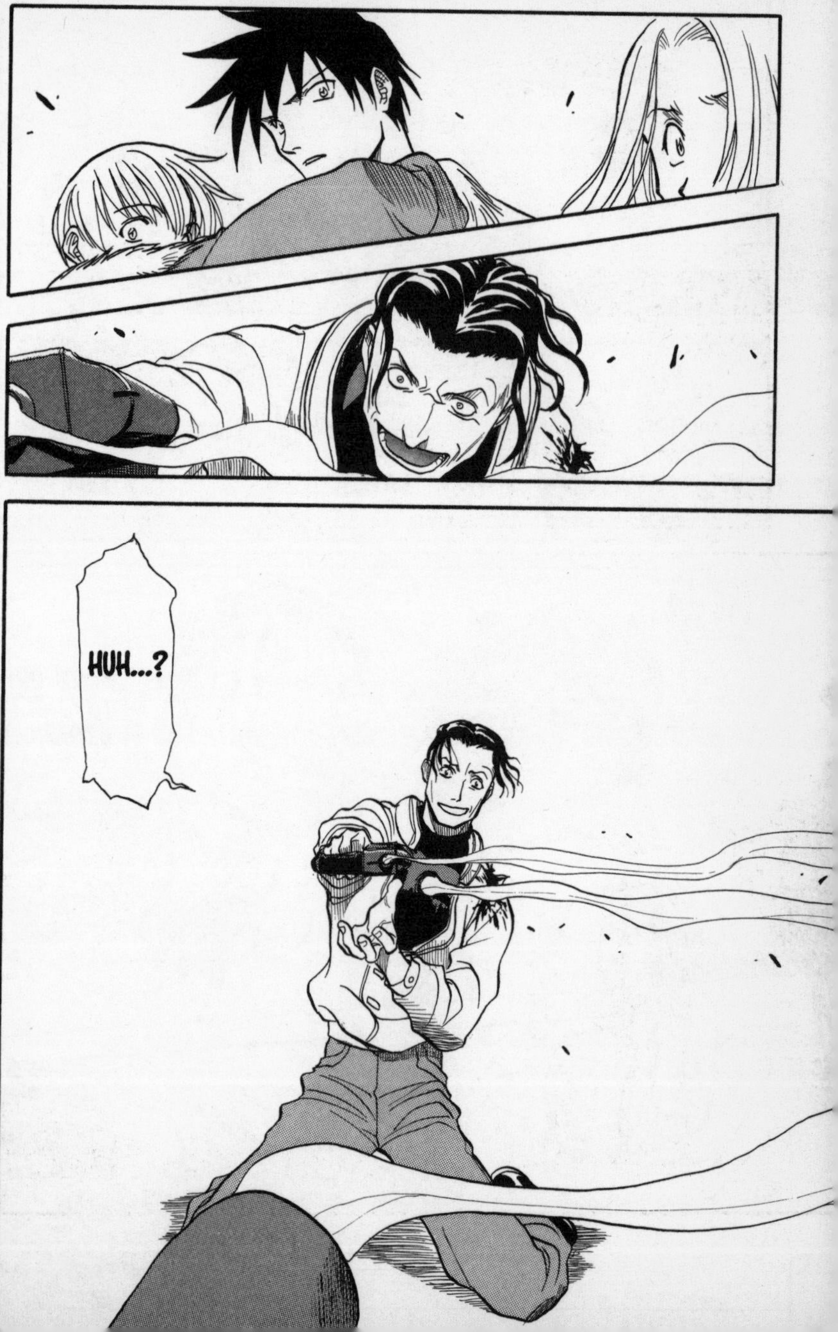
HUH...?

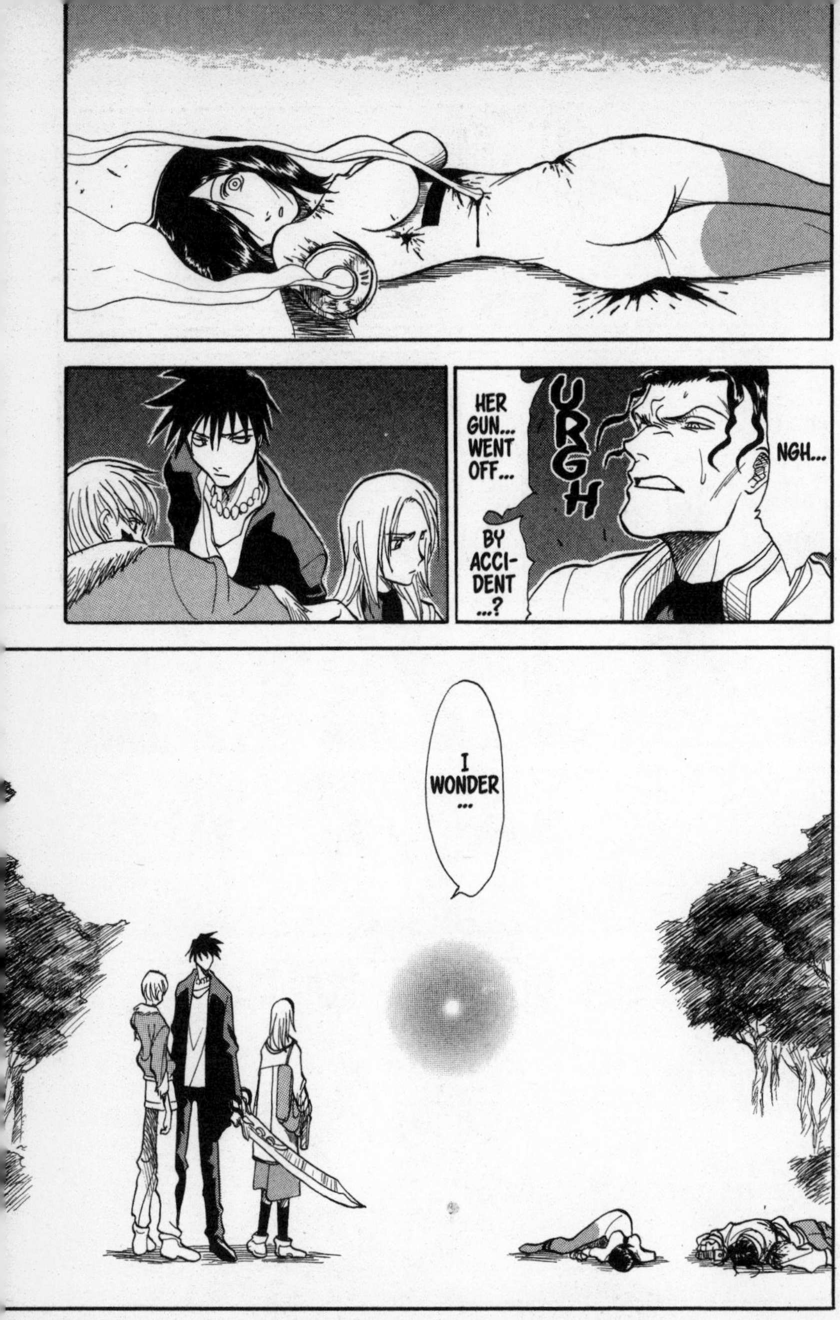
NGH...
URGH
HER GUN... WENT OFF...
BY ACCI-DENT ...?
I WONDER ...

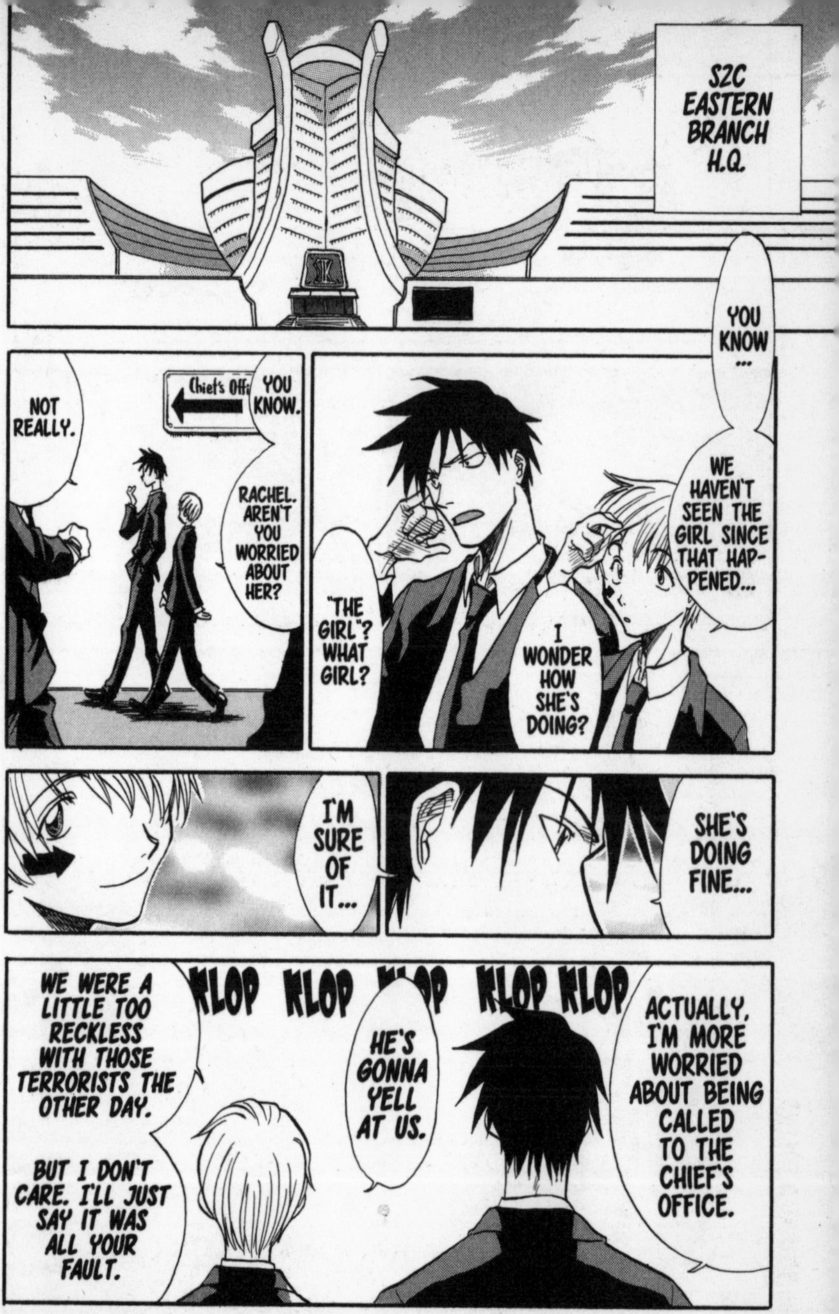
S2C EASTERN BRANCH H.Q.
YOU KNOW...
WE HAVEN'T SEEN THE GIRL SINCE THAT HAP-PENED...
I WONDER HOW SHE'S DOING?
"THE GIRL"? WHAT GIRL?
YOU KNOW.
Chief's Offi
RACHEL. AREN'T YOU WORRIED ABOUT HER?
NOT REALLY.
SHE'S DOING FINE...
I'M SURE OF IT...
ACTUALLY, I'M MORE WORRIED ABOUT BEING CALLED TO THE CHIEF'S OFFICE.
KLOP KLOP KLOP KLOP KLOP
HE'S GONNA YELL AT US.
WE WERE A LITTLE TOO RECKLESS WITH THOSE TERRORISTS THE OTHER DAY.
BUT I DON'T CARE. I'LL JUST SAY IT WAS ALL YOUR FAULT.

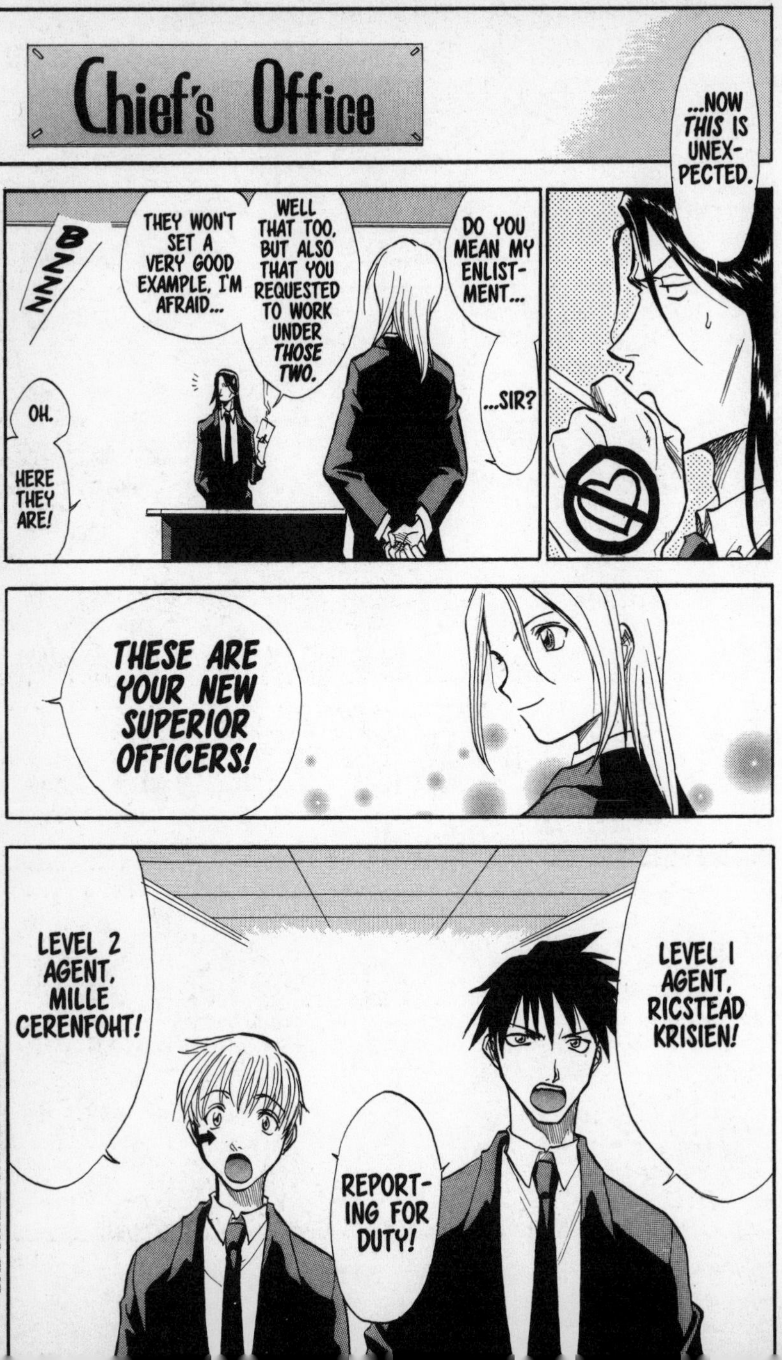
Chief's Office
...NOW THIS IS UNEXPECTED.
DO YOU MEAN MY ENLISTMENT...
...SIR?
WELL THAT TOO, BUT ALSO THAT YOU REQUESTED TO WORK UNDER THOSE TWO.
THEY WON'T SET A VERY GOOD EXAMPLE, I'M AFRAID...
BZNNN
OH.
HERE THEY ARE!
THESE ARE YOUR NEW SUPERIOR OFFICERS!
LEVEL 1 AGENT, RICSTEAD KRISIEN!
LEVEL 2 AGENT, MILLE CERENFOHT!
REPORTING FOR DUTY!

BAD SHIELD UNITED: THE END

Please
read
the
story
of the
prince...

zombiepowderextra./ sleeping with vertigo.

The were-wolf shar-pens his claws

Like the falling leaves

He sharpens his claws

With the name of an angel

He sharpens his claws

From

The depths of madness masked in sanity

He

Was the one who saved me

Touching the vessel of flesh my soul becomes water

A single breeze stirs the waters into a raging storm

Every time I think of him

Even in my dreams

I feel dizzy

His chest is like the warm earth

His eyes are like the forest at night

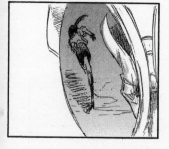

His voice is like a winter storm

His hands are like a black bed

And his form

is like a shining silver lion

My one

My only

prince

en   d.   sl   eep   i   ng   wit   h   ve   rt   ig   o.

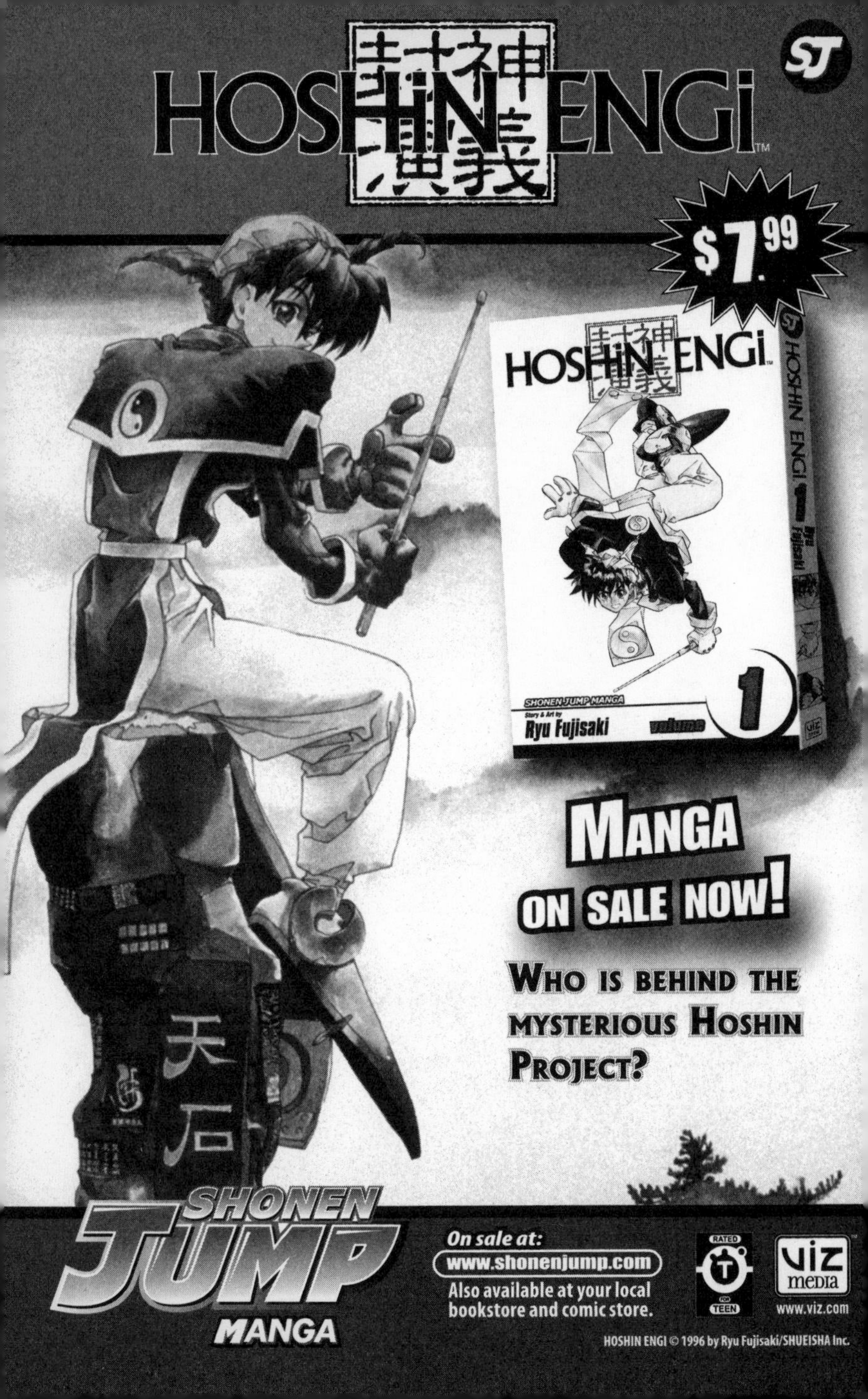
HOSHIN ENGI™
封神演義
SJ
$7.99
HOSHIN ENGI
SHONEN JUMP MANGA
Story & Art by
Ryu Fujisaki
volume 1
MANGA
ON SALE NOW!
WHO IS BEHIND THE MYSTERIOUS HOSHIN PROJECT?
SHONEN JUMP MANGA
On sale at:
www.shonenjump.com
Also available at your local bookstore and comic store.
RATED T FOR TEEN
viz media
www.viz.com
HOSHIN ENGI © 1996 by Ryu Fujisaki/SHUEISHA Inc.

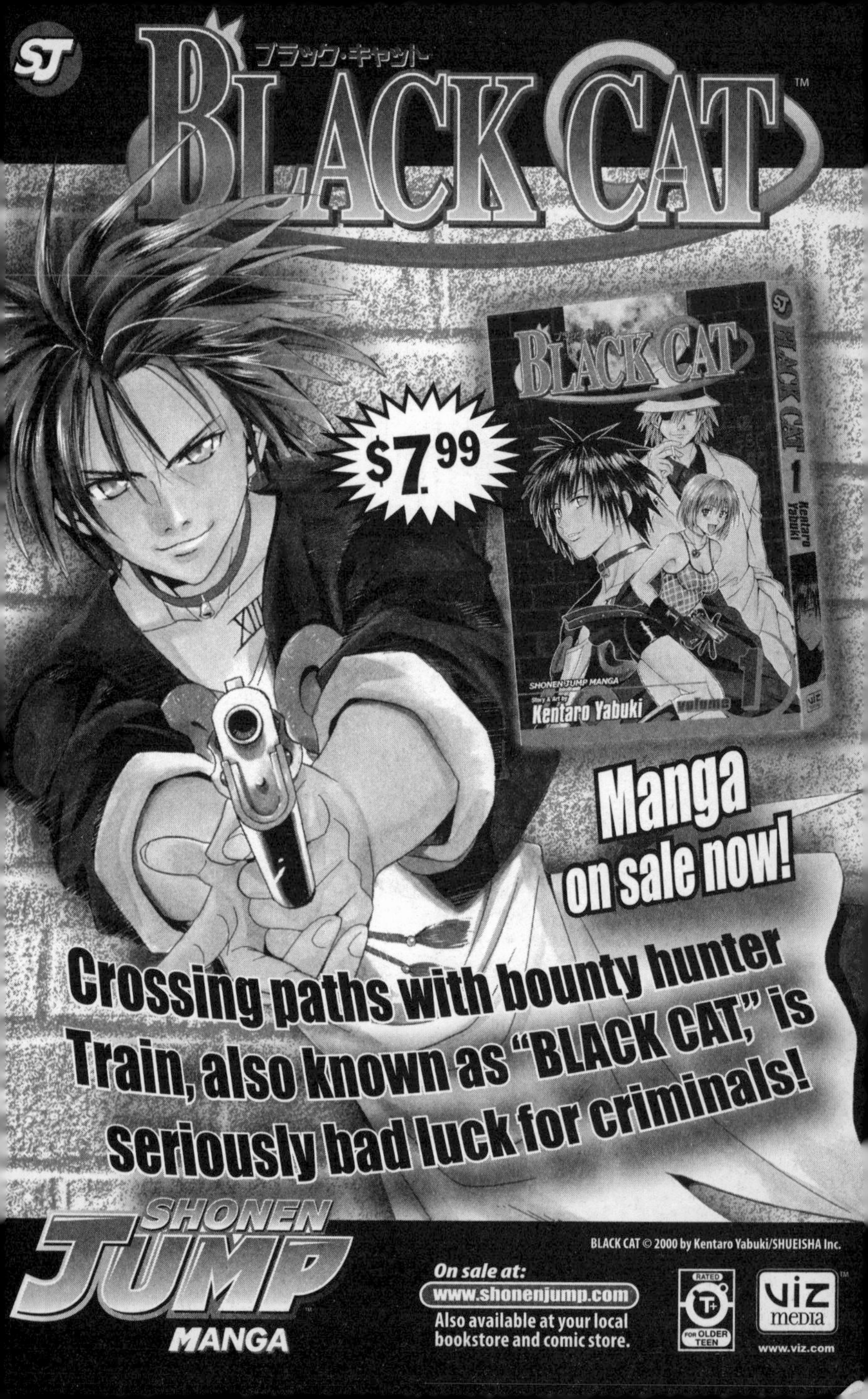
SJ
ブラック・キャット
BLACK CAT™
$7.99
BLACK CAT
BLACK CAT 1 Kentaro Yabuki
SHONEN JUMP MANGA
Kentaro Yabuki
Manga on sale now!
Crossing paths with bounty hunter Train, also known as "BLACK CAT," is seriously bad luck for criminals!
SHONEN JUMP MANGA
BLACK CAT © 2000 by Kentaro Yabuki/SHUEISHA Inc.
On sale at:
www.shonenjump.com
Also available at your local bookstore and comic store.
RATED T+ FOR OLDER TEEN
VIZ media
www.viz.com